ARCHITECT OF EUROPEAN UNITY

Robert Marjolin

ARCHITECT OF EUROPEAN UNITY

MEMOIRS 1911–1986

Translated by
William Hall

Foreword by Eric Roll

*Preface to the French edition
by Raymond Barre*

WEIDENFELD AND NICOLSON
LONDON

First published in France as *Le travail d'une vie*
© Éditions Robert Laffont, S.A., Paris, 1986

English translation © William Hall, 1989

Published in Great Britain by
George Weidenfeld & Nicolson Limited
91 Clapham High Street
London SW4 7TA

ISBN 0 297 79652 6

Printed in Great Britain by The Bath Press, Avon

Contents

v

Contents

Part Two

THE WAR

Part Three

THE RECONSTRUCTION OF FRANCE AND OF EUROPE

Contents

Part Four

THE COMMON MARKET

Part Five

BUSINESS

Contents

Foreword by Eric Roll

This is a remarkable book by an exceptional man – a man of both thought and action who here shows himself also to be an accomplished writer. The combination is rare; and when to it is added a subject of the highest interest and importance, the result is an outstanding literary work.

Robert Marjolin's life (1911–86) spans the most important events in the history of this century after the First World War: the inter-war period, which saw the rise of Fascism, the great depression, the rearmament of Germany and the approach of the horror of a new world war. Then, the war itself, the occupation of his country and so much of all continental Europe, the eventual triumph of the allies, the reconstruction of Europe and the revival of the world economy. By virtue of his innate talents as much as by a training in Philosophy and Economics combined with an early experience of Politics, Marjolin was an acute observer and this quality alone would have made any account by him of these great events a memorable one. But he was not merely a spectator: at an early age he became an active participant in these historic developments and soon played a leading part in shaping many of them.

In writing his memoirs, Marjolin has done much more than most authors of autobiographies. This is a moving and fascinating story of a man's life set down in classically simple language, sensitive, perspicacious and filled with its author's astute yet generous attitude to people and problems. This aspect of the book, especially evident in the early part, would alone make it an important document. The account of his rise from the most humble material origins (yet from a home filled with affection and the appreciation of lasting values) and of the struggle to acquire an education after leaving school at fourteen, leading to high academic achievement and position, would in itself make this a story of extraordinary interest. This is, however, only one feature of it.

Marjolin was from an early age a socialist (or social-democrat, as he says himself) and remained so for much of his life. His was, however, a socialism of a kind which fitted most uneasily – and later not at all – into the accepted party-political pattern. In the mid and late 1930s he worked with Léon Blum but he soon realized that the economic policies of the Popular Front Government were weakening the French economy to the point where they were in serious contradiction with a foreign policy of resistance to Fascism and preparedness for a war which seemed increasingly inevitable. An article by him of 1938 sets out clearly many of the inner contradictions of the policies of European socialism with which we have become all too familiar many decades later.

During the war, Marjolin played an important part in the Resistance, including a lengthy spell on behalf of the French government in exile in the United States. He already knew that country from an earlier stay as a Rockefeller Fellow at Yale and viewed it with great admiration and affection. It was during this period that he made many of the friends – particularly American and British – whom he was to meet and with whom he was to work in the next four decades in many important enterprises. It was also at this time that he formed a close partnership with Jean Monnet which was to continue after the war when Marjolin became Monnet's deputy in the 'Plan' and thus had a major part in the extraordinarily rapid and effective reconstruction of France. He then applied his newly-gained experience to the reconstruction of Europe through the Marshall Plan and later still to the movement for the unification of Europe through the Coal and Steel Community and the Common Market.

In every one of these developments, Marjolin played a most important part. He was one of the seminal members of the relatively small European team which worked with leading Americans in the realization of the Marshall Plan, later becoming the first Secretary-General of the *Organisation for European Economic Cooperation* (later *and Development*). He left that post to resume an earlier University career which did not, however, last long for he was soon re-absorbed into the heart of international economic negotiations: those for the Common Market. The signature of the Treaty of Rome opened a new career for him, that of Vice-President of the first European Commission, concerned with economic and financial matters – though also with much else, including the first British negotiations.

When he left the Commission in 1967 he hesitated between a return to the University, a political career and business. The first – on a full time basis – was clearly not going to satisfy him after the extremely active life he had just left. A political career seemed unattractive after a brief, unhappy, electoral experience some five years earlier and a certain disenchantment with the pattern of political parties and programmes. So, for the remaining years of his life, Marjolin found the satisfaction that comes from engaging in just that sort of activity that is of help to others while enabling one to utilize one's own special talents: as a non-executive director, or in some cases as adviser, to a number of the world's most important companies – Shell, IBM, Chase Manhattan, General Motors, Robeco, Amex Bank and many others.

Marjolin was as much at home in Britain and America as he was in his own country; and English was his second language. It is, therefore, highly appropriate that this book should now be available to the English-speaking public. This is an extraordinary story of one who from very low beginnings reached positions of great power and renown and it is here told by him without false pride or false modesty, with a keen critical spirit and an engaging candour about personalities, yet always with understanding and generosity. It is told, above all, with a simplicity and directness that presents to the reader almost as if he were meeting him face to face the intellect, the vivacity and the charm of its author.

Eric Roll

Preface to the French edition by Raymond Barre

Nothing can better describe or summarize the life of Robert Marjolin than the few concluding notes to his Memoirs that his death prevented him from writing up:

'*Je suis parti de très bas; je suis monté très haut (ou assez haut) par un effort de volonté.*' [I started very low; I climbed very high (or fairly high) by an effort of will.]

The child of a very modest family, of straitened circumstances completely lacking in any security, he was to become Secretary-General of the OEEC and Vice-President of the Commission of the European Economic Community.

Educated at elementary school, he interrupted his studies at the age of fourteen to earn his living as an apprentice in an orthopaedic workshop. By sheer hard work he obtained the diploma of the *Ecole pratique des hautes études* giving him the equivalent of the *baccalauréat*; he acquired a degree in philosophy; he won a scholarship to the Rockefeller Institute; he turned his attention to the study of law and economics, passing with flying colours the *agrégation de sciences économiques*; he then became a lecturer at the Paris *Faculté de Droit et de Sciences Economiques* (Law and Economics), a member of *L'Institut*, and a doctor *honoris causa* of the University of Harvard.

After working for five years as a clerk for a broker on the Paris Bourse he became, after a brilliant career of national and international public service, a member of the Board of Directors of the prestigious group Royal Dutch Shell.

Success of this order is obtained not only from hard work but also from a great intellectual capacity, a lively curiosity and an unquestionable sense for human relationships. Robert Marjolin gave constant proof of these capacities but above all he showed remarkable independence of mind.

He joined the Socialist Party and the *Jeunesses Socialistes* in 1929 as a result of 'natural destination' but also under the influence of leading academics and socialist intellectuals such as Georges Bourgin, Célestin Bouglé and Elie Halévy. In 1934, Léon Blum appointed him economics editor of *Le Populaire* and when the Popular Front Government was formed in 1936 called upon him to be *chargé de mission* to the President of the Council and Secretary-General of the Government. Disagreeing with the Government's economic and social policy, Robert Marjolin resigned to write for the weekly *L'Europe Nouvelle*, advocating a different policy for France. He strongly criticized the legislation introducing the 40-hour week and from 1937 onward, conscious of the peril to democracy from the rise of Nazism and Fascism, he emphasized that 'the absolute priority was national defence and preparation for war'.

Secretary-General of the OEEC since 1947, after six fruitful years spent in assisting the reconstruction of Western Europe, he became increasingly aware of 'the futility of this form of international action, at least in the present circumstances'. Despite having no prospect of another position, he decided to leave his post to return to university at Nancy, where he taught political economy.

Similarly, after eight years with the Commission of the Common Market, where he played a major role in implementing the Treaty of Rome, he decided in 1967 to leave Brussels in the belief that the dynamic phase was essentially at an end: he was anxious to turn to something else. For Robert Marjolin, independence of mind accompanied a profound disregard for power, money and honours.

But this indifference did not prevent him from holding deeply felt convictions and a total commitment to those ideas in which he believed. Since the 1930s, his actions had been inspired by the idea of the necessity for the economic and social modernization of France. Between 1936 and 1940, he had observed his country's rapid economic decline with sadness and deep concern. In March 1938 he wrote in *L'Europe Nouvelle*:

'It may be anxiously wondered what will happen tomorrow to France if, on the one hand, through class feeling and hatred of communism part of the French bourgeoisie persists in its pro-German and pro-Italian sentiments, and if, on the other, the working class refuses to see that its present economic and social action is in direct contradiction with the foreign policy it would like to see practised.'

In London he reflected during the war years on the reconstruction of France as 'a young technocrat smitten with ideas of growth, rigour and power through effort,' conscious of the fact that 'France would have to fit into an international framework and accept a division of labour with the other great powers' and favouring, because of predictable shortages, the adoption of an economic plan. He envisaged also an eventual unification of Western Europe centred around France and Great Britain. At the end of the war he dreamed of 'a political and military Europe whose first and foremost function would be to ensure its own defence'.

In this way he prepared for the three great projects which, starting in 1945, were to occupy his life: the plan for the modernization and equipment of France, the Marshall Plan and the Common Market. The postwar years were, for Robert Marjolin, compensation for the 'intellectual and moral breakdown' which marked the world and France between the two world wars. It was the time when he took part in 'a great undertaking, which was to result in the resurrection of France, in a veritable rebirth of the nation'. This period also saw the rebirth of Western Europe thanks to the massive economic aid from the United States, which allowed the nations of Europe to wipe out the effects on production of both the Second World War and the Great Depression, as well as eliminate the enormous payments deficit vis-à-vis the United States.

Convinced that the salvation of Europe depended on the acceptance of competition and the creation of a European Customs Union, Robert Marjolin devoted his energies from 1956 onwards to the question of Europe, that is to say 'the matter of France, her economy and her necessary rebirth in the framework of a unified Europe'. This he pushed with great clearsightedness and plenty of pragmatism. Sceptical of federalist ideas, he thought that 'the nation-state was not on the way out and that one could not expect the emergence of a European state in the foreseeable future'. The institutional dispute between the integral maintenance of national sovereignties and their dismantlement always seemed to him 'rather pointless' and he looked for a middle path. 'Because the term "United States of Europe" creates illusions in minds that are ignorant of history, I have always refused to use it', he would write. Vice-President of the Common Market Commission, he had no sympathy with those 'who wanted to inflate the importance of the Commission and present it, by juggling with protocol, as a government in embryo; the reality, in the shape of the powers conferred on it by the treaty, was enough for me'. His idea of independence for the Commission rested entirely on 'its role as a mediator'. Finally, at the time of the institutional crisis of 1965 which led to the famous 'Luxembourg Compromise', he worked to prevent the breakup of the Community and to prevent pragmatism from carrying the day. On the ever-recurring question of the unanimous or the majority vote, Robert Marjolin sensibly remarked: 'How could one imagine that an issue affecting the fundamental interests of one or more member states could be settled in defiance of the opinion of those states?' He recounts how in 1978, when charged by the European Council to report on the reform of Community institutions, he found that 'none of the nine governments of the Community, not one, wanted the re-establishment of the majority vote for settling a question considered, even by just one government, to be of major importance, and there were only a few of them who simply asked that the unanimity rule should not be abused'. This lesson in wisdom from one of the great architects of European reconstruction should still be kept in mind today.

Robert Marjolin showed the same ability and the same independent spirit when he entered private business at the highest level, that is when he joined the Board of Directors of Royal Dutch. His activities in this major company, and in other international industrial and financial companies, gave him an inside view of the workings of big corporations which play a major role in the international economy and in particular gave him specialist knowledge of the oil industry. His analysis of that industry before the first oil crisis in 1973 will dissipate many false ideas on the policy of the large oil companies, especially with respect to the size and use of their profits. His observations on the present oil economy emphasize the new role of these companies as well as their extraordinary ability to adapt.

A success such as that of Robert Marjolin, especially when not favoured at the outset by the advantages of social position or fortune, owes a great deal to the men he met during his years of study or at the beginning of his professional life, the kind of men who are able to recognize ability in people and give them their chance. Robert Marjolin never failed to pay tribute to 'a series of men who helped [him] in a totally disinterested way, wanting to make life easier for this young man from nowhere'. Georges Bourgin, Deputy Director of the

National Archives, a historian who was active in the popular universities and in the consumer cooperatives, guided him from 1930 onwards while he was preparing for the diploma of the *Ecole pratique des hautes études*. Célestin Bouglé, principal of the *Ecole normale supérieure*, a respected academic in the tradition of the Third Republic, secured his appointment as librarian of the school's *centre de documentation sociale*. Charles Rist, an economist with considerable national and international influence, a *grand bourgeois* with an open and generous spirit, found paid work for the young socialist at the *Institut de recherches économiques et sociales*, which he founded in 1937. Emanuel Monick, *Inspecteur des Finances*, financial attaché in London, and future Governor of the Bank of France after the Liberation, asked Robert Marjolin in August 1940 to accompany him to Morocco as his *chef de cabinet*, thus enabling him to make an active contribution to the negotiations with the United States for the shipment of vital supplies to North Africa, and then in March 1941 facilitated his plan to rejoin General de Gaulle in London via Martinique and Washington. Early in 1944 Jean Monnet appointed him Head of the French Supply Mission to the United States under his direct authority. In early 1945 Monnet appointed him Director of External Economic Relations in Paris before recalling him in Autumn 1945 to become deputy commissioner general for the modernization and equipment plan, thus paving the way for the 'European career' in 1947.

Furthermore, how could he not have benefited during the 1930s from the intellectual influence of Elie Halévy, who instructed him in the history of socialism, and from the constant exchanges with intellects as remarkable as Raymond Aron, Eric Weil, Alexandre Kojève and Olivier Wormser, who shared with him the fear of Hitlerism and who deplored the weakness of the western democracies and the absence of international cooperation?

Although many brilliant personalities appear in his Memoirs, the most moving passages are those which concern his own family; his parents and sister who gave him a 'happy childhood', his wife, Dottie, whom he met in Washington during the war, who brought him so much and whose death in 1971 affected him profoundly: 'My inner life has lost substance.'

What Robert Marjolin wanted in his adolescence was to 'stand out from the crowd, to be somebody'. This will to be somebody took the form of a passion for learning: 'This was the way the impecunious young man I was then, without connections or backing, would succeed in making a name for himself.' He reached that goal by a life of work.

He was not attracted by money, of which he said that it had never made him do anything he would not have done anyway. He did not want power: his life was marked by periods away from the public eye, showing that he had no desire to be continually in the limelight. He always served ardently the causes he stood for and, with them, France and Europe.

In July 1955, after leaving the OEEC, Robert Marjolin published in *Paris-Presse l'Intransigeant* a series of articles on 'The opportunities for France in the Europe of tomorrow.' The title given to the biography introducing the author could not have been more apt: 'He chose life.' Is not this the best way of ensuring the success of a life?

Raymond Barre

Acknowledgements

The publication of this English translation of the memoirs of Robert Marjolin has been made possible by the support of four of the international companies with whom Robert Marjolin worked as an adviser or director in the 1970s and the 1980s: American Express Company, General Motors Corporation, IBM Corporation and The Royal Dutch/Shell Group of Companies.

Readers may wish to note that an annual international economics essay competition is run in memory of Robert Marjolin, by *The AMEX Bank Review*, the monthly publication of American Express Bank. Robert Marjolin was Editorial Adviser to the *Review* from 1975 until 1986.

The Translator

William Hall, a British national now resident in France, worked in the Translation Service of the Organisation for Economic Cooperation and Development (OECD) in Paris for twenty-two years, specializing in the field of economics. He received his degree in Modern Languages from the University of Cambridge.

Part One

FROM THE ORIGINS OF MY FAMILY TO WORLD WAR TWO

1

CHILDHOOD

I know little about the origins of my family. My parents' *livret de famille*[1] records that my father was legally recognized only by his mother (Joséphine Clémentine Marjolin) and that my mother was the daughter of parents unnamed. All I have in the way of information is a recollection of remarks made by my parents in my presence when I was a child, and a very hazy recollection at that. My paternal grandfather's name was Chareau. He worked for a tradesman as book-keeper and odd-job man. He had two sisters whom I never knew and who, I was told, worked in the post office. He, my grandmother and their children lived somewhere in the 15th arrondissement of Paris in a big building overrun with rats. They were still alive in 1914 or 1915, having by then moved into an old people's home called *Les Petits Ménages* in the suburb of Issy-les-Moulineaux.

I also heard, but am unable to verify, that my great grandparents on my father's side were two blind persons who had met at the famed Quinze-Vingts eye hospital off the Place de la Bastille; he was a musician and even conductor of an all-blind orchestra. On my mother's side, I know that my grandmother came from the Loir-et-Cher department, from Romorantin to be precise, where a few distant cousins still live. Her name was Vacher and she was a streetsweeper back in the days when they used reed brooms. Family lore has it that she died of a strangulated hernia that came upon her while she was out sweeping. She and the man she cohabited with lived in a place, now vanished, called *La Cité Creuse* off the Rue des Belles Feuilles in the

3

16th arrondissement. As for my maternal grandfather, all I know is that he came from Lorraine, was a carter, a very big man of Herculean strength and drank heavily. One day he upped and left for his native Lorraine and that was the last anyone heard of him.

What I know of my grandparents, on both sides, recalls Zola's world, a world in which it was quite usual for couples not to marry or recognize their children officially. My father and mother took a giant step forward in getting married at the town hall, starting a proper home and recognizing their children, as well as giving them a normal basic education. The symbol as well as the most tangible expression of this improvement in social status was our accommodation; in renting it my parents realized their most cherished ambition. Not that it was sumptuous; by today's standards it was extremely modest. Two rooms and kitchen, plus a minute bedroom capable of holding only a single bed in which my sister slept. My parents had their room and I slept in the dining room. A bathroom or shower was a luxury we did not even dream of. For lighting we used oil lamps. It was at the kitchen table, by the light of one of those lamps, that I used to do my homework. The gas came later – when I cannot remember – then electricity. This little flat, situated at 2 Rue de la Grotte (today Rue Firmin-Gillot), has been in the family since 1908 or 1909. I was born there and my sister lived in it until 1982.

My father had only gone part of the way through primary school and had received no vocational training in today's sense of the term. At eighteen he enlisted in the marines and spent the years from 1894 to 1898 serving in Tongking. He married my mother in 1900. In turn carpenter, decorator and travelling salesman, he was a serious, upright man, entirely devoted to his family, who never indulged in any expense he considered superfluous. He went to the café only on Sundays, and then not every Sunday, accompanied by other members of the family. He was very skilled with his hands and excelled at doing all the repairs around the house, making furniture and crafting all kinds of toys for our Christmases. A very good draughtsman and a talented painter in his spare time, when he reached the age of seventy my wife gave him a box of oil paints (till then he had done only water colours) and he painted a series of pictures I still possess of townscapes at Neuilly (where we were living at the time) and Vaugirard, including the Eglise de Vaugirard where I made my first communion. They still move me deeply when I look at them. It was a great joy to my father when one of his paintings – of the Eglise de Vaugirard, in fact – was accepted for the *Salon des Indépendants*[2] in the early 1950s; my wife had taken it upon herself to send in the picture without saying anything to him for fear he might be disappointed if it were rejected.

My mother, at the time of her marriage, was a laundress, an occupation she gave up shortly after in order to give her whole time to her children. She went back to work later on as a cleaning woman, first when my father fell seriously ill, and then again when I went back to my studies. She was a very kind woman who adored animals and I remember how she used to feed about half a dozen stray cats that had taken up residence in the local food market.

My sister Marcelle was my elder by ten years and a second mother to me. Hers was a rather sad existence. Working continuously as a seamstress until the age of sixty-five when she had to retire, she never married, had no man in her life, no children. She lived with my parents until they died, and then alone with a cat she doted on. My wife, until her death, looked after her a lot. Afterwards, I tried to take over. Today Marcelle, aged eighty-five, is forced by illness to live in a home for the elderly.[3]

We were not rich. The money that came into the home was provided by my father, whose earnings were modest and often undependable, my mother when she cleaned house for others, my sister, who entered a *maison de couture* as an apprentice at the age of twelve, and myself when, on leaving school at fourteen, I went out to work. Our finances were tight, but I never wanted for anything. What we all suffered from, at certain times at any rate, was an utter lack of security. When my father lost his job because business was bad, there was no unemployment benefit; when he was ill, there was no Social Security. For my parents the future was bleak: no prospect of a pension, retirement would come when they could no longer work. Then either their children would take care of them, or it would be the poorhouse.

But let it not be thought that our life was an unhappy one; uneasy, yes, but with its joys too.

My mother loved to cook and have people around for a meal, particularly her sister's family. My uncle, my aunt and their six children lived in a two-room flat in the 17th arrondissement, with no running water or WC; the lavatories were on the other side of the inner courtyard separating their building from the one opposite and served both. Their two rooms had no windows, only fanlights. In spite of this poverty, the lunches *en famille* were joyous affairs. We would sit down to table at noon and rise at four or five in the afternoon. Then we would go out for an aperitif and a game of billiards. We sat down to dinner, all appetite gone, at half-past seven or eight o'clock.

Another source of entertainment and pleasure was the families living in the same building with whom we were on friendly terms. No one, naturally, had a car or a house in the country. There was no television, no radio (except in the last couple of years before World War Two) to tell us of the world outside. We never ate out, never went away on a trip. I don't think my parents ever took a holiday. But we were always seeing our neighbours. We did little jobs and ran errands for one another whenever necessary; we baby-sat for one another; we spent the big festive occasions like New Year's Eve together. Those who have never had the experience of these neighbourhood communities will find it hard to picture what life was like in those days.

This, then, was the setting in which I spent a happy childhood. Shortly after the start of World War One I came down with an ailment which the doctors wrongly diagnosed as Pott's disease. I was strapped to a plank and remained immobile for several months. I recovered as unexpectedly as I had fallen ill and nobody ever discovered what had been wrong with me.

My father was drafted into the auxiliary service of the army in 1914 when I was three. My earliest memory, the first picture I have in my mind's eye, is of my father leaving to join up. At that time we were in the Sarthe department, staying with Madame Damange, the old woman who had been my sister's nurse. It was through Mère Damange, as we used to call her, that close links were forged between my family and a number of farming families in the Sarthe, links which time has loosened a great deal but which still exist today; I never found out how my parents came to know her. I can still see my father crossing the garden to get to the railway line which he would follow until he reached the halt where he was to board the local train. In 1918 when the Germans began to bombard Paris with Big Bertha, my parents sent me to the Sarthe to stay for a few months in the care of another kindly old soul, Madame Fontaine. This was my first visit to Rouperroux-le-Coquet, a village close to the town of Bonnétable. Subsequently I was to spend all my school holidays there.

For most of the duration of the Great War I lived in Paris. My recollections of that time are few, though I do remember the march-past of July 14, 1919 which I watched with my father from a window on the Rue de Rivoli: those little clusters of eight or ten men around a tattered flag, each constituting all that remained of a regiment. Yet it would be true to say that my whole childhood was steeped in the reality and remembrance of this appalling slaughter. For years we continued to talk in our family about Verdun and Chemin-des-Dames, and about those we knew who had been killed. Someone at the time, I no longer remember who, perhaps my schoolteacher or Dr Moreau the family doctor, said that the Germans would never accept the Versailles Treaty and that there would be war again in 1938. Obviously he was not far off the mark. But perhaps my memory is playing me tricks and the story is really an invention in the light of hindsight.

So back to Paris and the Easter of 1918. I entered the *Communale* of the Rue Saint-Lambert, the local primary school where I was to remain until 1924. I learned very quickly to read and write and during those years I was always top or near the top of my class, eager to learn and well regarded by my teachers.

Much has been said about the primary schoolteachers of France's Third Republic; they are depicted as republicans, Jacobins, men of the left, fervently patriotic, regarding their job as an apostolic vocation, dedicated to their charges, sparing neither time nor effort to ensure that they learned and rose as high as they possibly could. That description admirably fits the teachers I had at Saint-Lambert during the six years or so I was there. One of them, in particular, had a profound influence on me, perhaps because I had him as my teacher for two years running, my last two at the school; both of us had moved up to the next class at the same time. His name was Marcel Prat. I remember him as being very quick off the mark and a bit short-tempered, but most of all I remember the passion with which he taught history; among other things I am indebted to him for a solid grounding in that subject which has been very useful to me in life. He lent me books to read at home and treated me affectionately but never indulgently. Later, after I left school, I continued to see him. We corresponded until his death ten or fifteen years ago.

I still look back with some emotion on those years I spent at Saint-Lambert. I benefited fully from the education which the primary school had to offer, and an excellent education it was too. Much of what I know I learned there; in addition to French history, I gained a sound and all but ineffaceable knowledge of spelling, French, arithmetic and mental arithmetic. School over and my homework done, I would play in the street with boys of my age, at ball or other games; there were hardly any cars about in those times. Saturdays or Sundays I would go to the local cinema with my parents and my sister; on Thursdays I went with my mother.

What used we to talk about in the family, with my uncle, aunt, cousins and the friends in our building when we got together on

Sundays or holidays? About what had just happened or was happening to the people we knew; about everyday life, events recounted in the newspaper, never or almost never on general topics. No one read books; there weren't any at home and no one ever went to the municipal library. Many did not vote; my father and a few of the neighbours voted socialist, then communist a little later on. We still talked about the Dreyfus case[4] and the name that cropped up most frequently in the conversations was Jaurès. We were vaguely antimilitarist and we were anticlerical.

My summer holidays I spent on a farm in the Sarthe, in the village I mentioned earlier. For two months I would live the life of peasant friends, the Tessins, accompanying them to the fields and helping them a little with their work, going with them from farm to farm to do the threshing, eating their simple food; the lack of comfort was utter but there was a *joie de vivre* about it all I sometimes wish I could experience again. Perhaps I am idealizing a little. The Sarthe represents the only provincial roots I have ever had. Even then they are very tenuous. To be honest, I have never wanted anything more solid. I am essentially a man of the towns and cities; I like the asphalt, the big buildings, the anonymity.

Between my parents and my sister, who doted on me, and my teachers who treated me kindly and encouraged me to work and learn as if that were the only thing in the world that counted, and with long weeks of school holidays I always looked forward to eagerly and enjoyed to the hilt, I can say I had a happy childhood perfectly in tune with my home and school surroundings. I had no desire to get out; moreover I did not know what 'getting out' might have meant since we had no contact whatever with circles above our own. The people we knew were as poor as or poorer than ourselves, workmen or petty clerks. I used to hear the bourgeois referred to but for me 'bourgeois' was a totally abstract notion; I did not know any. My father would sometimes complain bitterly of not having any 'connections'. He thought that having connections was the key to success; lacking them doomed one, if not to wretched poverty, at least to mediocrity. Perhaps he was not entirely wrong.

I almost forgot to speak about the local church, the Eglise de Vaugirard, which constituted an important part of my life. Catechism on Thursdays and mass on Sundays were more than formalities for me, especially by the time I was twelve or thirteen. I still remember the customary retreat before my first communion. I was not completely overcome or even impassioned. I felt a gentle emotion which the anticlericalism of my father and some of my teachers did not affect. Also a certain taste for the mystery of it all, an attraction to an irrational hereafter, probably corresponding to a sort of superstition widely held in our milieu. I remember often having candles burned before the image of St Antony of Padua whom my mother regarded as her patron saint. This rather vague hankering after religion grew in me until I was fifteen or sixteen and then disappeared, although leaving some traces.

My life was spent almost entirely between the family home, the school in the Rue Saint-Lambert and my church in the Rue Gerbert. For people of our sort, Paris was made up of a seemingly infinite number of villages. Vaugirard was our village with the Rue de Vaugirard, as far as the metro station of the same name, its high street. To all intents and purposes we never left it from one year's end to the next, except perhaps two or three times a year to go to the Rue de la Félicité in the Batignolles district to visit my mother's sister, my uncle and my cousins. And that was a real expedition. We had to take the metro to Saint-Lazare, change there, go down never-ending corridors to catch a train bound for Porte Champerret and get off at Malesherbes. Then we had to walk for quite a while before we reached the Rue de la Félicité. My mother, who very early on suffered from leg trouble, dreaded these trips. One of the biggest treats I was able to give her, when I started to earn a little money, was to take her home occasionally in a taxi. It made her feel a bit proud too: ordinary folk never took taxis.

I now come to my last year at school, or perhaps I should say the last year of my first scholastic experience. At thirteen I sat the competitive examination for entrance to the Jean-Baptiste-Say upper primary school and got in fairly low down the list. The year I spent there was a great turning point in my life, which was to have many. I embarked on this new phase without any specific goal. I found myself suddenly transplanted from the school in the Rue Saint-Lambert, so full of friendship among pupils and between pupils and teachers, to a vast impersonal establishment where I knew no one and no one knew me. Nothing out of the ordinary, one might say. But in my case the experience was complicated by a grave crisis in the family.

One day in late 1924 or early 1925 my father collapsed in the street with a perforation of the stomach caused by an ulcer he did not know he had. He was taken unconscious to the Hôpital de Beaujon where half or two-thirds of his stomach was removed. He had to remain in hospital for several weeks followed by a long period of convalescence. In those days, as I have said, there was no Social Security. His employers, who I believe were the *Magasin de la Place Clichy* store, dismissed him there and then: no work, no pay. My parents had no savings; if I remember correctly there was just 220 francs in notes in the drawer of the sideboard. In order to be excused the hospital fees my mother had to have her name put on the commune's list of destitute persons. She went out to work again, housecleaning; what she earned plus my sister's meagre wage (seamstresses were particularly badly paid) constituted the family's sole resources.

And there was I, almost fourteen, still at school! School and the acquisition of knowledge, which up to then had been the hub of my existence, suddenly appeared unimportant in my family's present predicament. I was also very anxious to emulate my classmates of the *Communale*, most of whom had become apprenticed at the age of twelve or thirteen, and gain my independence quickly. At that time I asked myself no questions about the more distant future. The questions would come later, when I had become sufficiently mature to answer them.

I finished the school year as best I could, with very middling results. During the summer of 1925, which I spent as usual at Rouperroux, I reached a final decision of which I informed my parents in September: I would not go back to school, I would go out to work. My mother was very distressed, she was hoping for a brighter future for me; she would have liked to see me get out of what one might call the working class or proletariat and become, say, a minor civil servant, sure of his employment and of a pension for his old age. My father was uncertain; his illness had affected him greatly. But the decision had been made and in September or October of 1925 I became an apprentice in an orthopaedic workshop in the Rue de Cadiz, a couple of hundred yards from our home. The son of neighbours with whom we were very close had recommended me.

That was the first break, the first departure in my life. Several others were to occur later. I do not think one can ever know oneself through introspection; only by contemplating one's life can one learn what one is. As far as I am concerned, I seem to have an irresistible penchant for sudden changes, or at any rate what appear to be such, as many have been preceded by long solitary meditation. Each time my life, from one minute to the next, has changed out of all recognition. I have never regretted any of these breaks.

So ended a childhood which, except for the last few months, had been serene and happy. The time of doubts, unanswerable questions and mounting frustration was about to begin.

2

ADOLESCENCE

My efforts to learn a craft soon revealed an exceptional clumsiness that is proverbial in the family even today. First they tried to teach me the rudiments of metalworking like filing down to a perfectly flat surface or making simple parts to be fitted to artificial arms or legs. The results were atrocious; the piece of iron was filed down to almost nothing by the time I managed to get a flat surface; most of the parts I made were unusable. Finally they decided to have me make casts; this was a simple job that consisted in putting liquid plaster into moulds with the shape of a torso or a limb, letting the plaster dry and then breaking the mould. I managed this reasonably well but finished the day covered with plaster from head to foot. My mother had terrible difficulty getting my overalls clean but she never complained. Needless to say, my standing with the other workmen (there were five or six of them) was not very high. My existence was made bearable by the fact that the workshop was run by a foreman who liked to discuss history and literature with me. He was a monarchist who belonged to *Action Française*[1], drank heavily and lived in a world of philosophy. He stood up for me when the other workers jeered. 'You can talk', he would tell them, 'when you know as much as Marjolin' – though, heaven knows, my knowledge did not amount to much at the time!

In spite of this support my situation was untenable; I realized clearly that I would never manage to acquire a manual skill and that I had to look for something else. My former teacher, Marcel Prat, whom I went to see several times when school got out, would have liked me to go back to Jean-Baptiste-Say. But that was out of the question; I was sticking firmly to the decision I had made the previous summer. Besides, my family's present situation would have made it difficult. I asked Monsieur Prat if it would be possible for me to get some occupational training in one of the fields I had done well in at upper primary school, such as chemistry. He told me, and I remember his answer very distinctly, that all I could hope for in that direction was to end up as a junior assistant in a laboratory.

The Bourse

It was then that my father remembered an old army mate, whose name I have forgotten, who had made good on the Paris stock exchange as a *remisier*, a half-commission man who acted as an intermediary between a group of clients and the stockbrokers. I was taken to see him one day at lunchtime in a café in the Rue Louis-le-Grand where he was usually to be found at that hour. He was a plump, florid man, always eager to be of help. Later, at the time of the big monetary speculations, he acted imprudently with some clients' money and spent some time in prison. Maybe ten years later he came to see me when I was at the Institute of Economic and Social Research in the Rue Michelet and asked me if I could get him a job as an usher in a ministry; all I could do for him was to give him a little money. But in 1925–6 he had a lot of connections on the stock exchange. Within a few days he found me a job as a ledger clerk with a *coulissier*, Paillard Frères et Lacroix, brokers not on the official list who dealt in unlisted securities only. I was assigned to the *caisse des titres*, the office where the security certificates were kept. This was at the beginning of 1926 and I spent five years with the firm.

I am trying to see myself again, to imagine what I could have been like at the age of fifteen. I can only arrive at an approximation by transposing to that distant past and to a radically different setting the fundamental traits I now discern in my character and behaviour, adjusting them of course to allow for the fact that a whole lifetime has passed and that events and my reaction to events, my action too, have enabled me to gain some measure of self-awareness. An adolescent who had suddenly shot up in height, when perhaps only two years earlier, at school, he had been small and fat (*la boule* to his schoolmates). Sensitive, or perhaps just thin-skinned, to a degree that sometimes bordered on the pathological. Extremely maladroit, as I have already said, practising no sport and not wanting to, even taking no exercise except for long walks that enabled him to daydream, in short with no confidence in his body and its potentialities; wanting above all to be liked by the people with whom he was in contact, but discovering with every move towards them how very different he was from the others in his milieu; suffering in consequence from a deep feeling of insecurity that made him a constant prey to self-doubt and paralyzed him in any projects he might conceive. The attribute to compensate for these weaknesses, a certain force of intellect that enabled him a few years later to be recognized as an equal by people he himself esteemed or admired, was only in embryo at the time of which I am speaking and he was unaware of it.

Those five years I spent at the Bourse saw a slow maturing that led me into enterprises I would never have imagined possible. My memories of the time are imprecise, vague, confused, but I think I can divide this period rather arbitrarily into three phases. For a year or so I was an office clerk trying to be a model employee. Day after day I copied out the brokers' transactions into huge metal-bound ledgers; I totted up endless columns by hand. Fortunately I was very good at figures, mental arithmetic included. Relations with my fellow employees and my superior, who was in charge of the office, were good without being friendly. On the other hand, the chief clerk, a certain Monsieur Martin, did not take to me at all. He was an inflexible, narrow-minded man who was to commit suicide later on because his daughter had made a match not to his liking. His entire career had been with Paillard Frères et Lacroix, starting at the bottom of the ladder and working up to a position of authority. I recall being taken to task by him at least twice, the first time because I was apparently handling the precious metal bindings a bit too roughly, the second, and on that occasion I admit I was very much to blame, because I had inadvertently consigned to the dustbin several thousand francs worth of coupons that had just been clipped from securities on deposit.

Anyway, I soon began to want a change of scene. An opening eventually presented itself in the active part of the business, *au comptant* [spot transactions] as they used to say then and probably still do today. My application was accepted and I found myself promoted to the rank of *grouillot*, a runner. This was the start of the second phase, the change occurring at the end of 1926 or early in 1927. For those who might not know, *grouillots* were young men whose job it was to take, or rather run with, the purchase and sale orders to the *commis* [traders], also known as *teneurs de carnet*, who operated in the different divisions of the Bourse. In prewar days, the centre from which the orders for each *coulissier* emanated was a few boxes usually hanging from a pillar inside the Bourse building, whilst the different groups of operations were transacted outside under the peristyle. Back in the office our job was to go through the transactions and record them. Since I was for a while the youngest or at any rate the latest arrival, I had to stay until everything was over and then take the *pochette* to somewhere in the Rue Feydeau; the *pochette* was a big portfolio containing the forms on which the purchase and sale operations were recorded. A good part of the night was spent at the place in the Rue Feydeau collating the forms originating from the different *coulissiers*.

I have no recollections, even vague ones, of the years 1926–7 except that the foreign exchange market was very turbulent and speculators often gave me what then seemed handsome gratuities when things went their way. A little later I was promoted to *commis* and given a *carnet* in which to enter all the operations I was entrusted with. No longer did I have to chase up and down the steps of the Bourse, I was responsible myself, or to someone senior, for the execution of orders relating to a group of securities. I was assigned, I forget in what order, to over-the-counter stocks, bonds and a division that dealt in certain secondary securities, such as Mossamédes (mines in Angola, I seem to remember). I had the right to speculate a little myself on behalf of the firm and kept half of any profits I made. Another source of income, when I was in over-the-counter transactions, was the 'under-the-counter' commission that some of the more dubious bank representatives slipped to the trader who brought them purchase orders.

Thus until 1929, say, I led a comparatively relaxed and carefree existence. Though not a 'whiz kid', I was doing quite well in my new occupation. I had become friendly with a trader some ten years older than I, by the name of Raleau; I would keep his accounts straight for him in return for which he would take me out each month to a copious dinner at Wepler in the Place Clichy, usually with one of his mistresses in tow. For a time I felt part of the stockbroker set, where conversation generally turned on money, cars and women. Afternoons or evenings, when work was over, we would go and play belote at the Vaudeville, a brasserie in the Place de la Bourse. I was a past master of that game and recall having a few big wins, but also being 'cleaned out' by a group of Corsicans who played a somewhat less than orthodox game.

A few former colleagues I have seen again recently remember me as a studious young man always with a book in his pocket to read during the slack periods of the day. It is probably true, but these memories relate more to the second half of 1929 and more certainly to 1930. From 1925, when I left school, to some point in 1929 I probably read nothing except newspapers, though during that period, I don't know exactly when, I took a few English lessons. The fact remains that the intellectual interests that were later to take hold of me so completely had not yet emerged. But this was to be a brief interlude in my life. Even before the stock market crash came to alter my existence radically almost overnight, a change had occurred in me that I would place somewhat arbitrarily in the second half of 1929 when I was just about eighteen. This was the start of the third phase of my time at the Bourse.

A vague and almost indefinable restlessness had taken hold of me, or perhaps I should say had resurfaced since it probably had never been dispelled. A fire was smouldering beneath the embers. Truth to tell, I did not know exactly what I wanted. A void had suddenly opened up within me. The Bourse, the games of belote at the Vaudeville, the occasional family festivities no longer sufficed. I remained attached to my family in some respects, but at the same time I was drawing away. I was looking for something else.

Money did not attract me; I was earning more than I had ever hoped. In fact, throughout my life money has never made me do what I would not have done anyway. It comes later, a bit like pleasure for Aristotle, as something which complements the act but which one could do without if need be, at least up to a point; something one is glad to have but not an end in itself. By this I do not mean that I despise money; in fact, I like to feel comfortable within the extent of my budget. But the latter can be reduced at will, or rather I am careful not to take on financial commitments that would restrict my freedom of action. Not until I was thirty-five, when I was married and my daughter Elise had been born, did I feel I had to amass a little money to ensure my family's security. At eighteen my ambitions did not lie in that direction.

Nor was I hungry for power, either the kind that can be bought with money or the power that can be obtained through political activity, even though I was for a while an enthusiastic member of a political party. The rest of my life has demonstrated this. At the same time I had not yet reached the point where I wanted to do something, create something; that would come later. When I look back on my adolescence I see that what I wanted in a confused way was to stand out from the crowd, to be somebody, to be recognized as someone who, whatever his level of endeavour, possessed a certain uniqueness. Very quickly this desire for singularity took the form of a hunger for knowledge. This was the way the impecunious young man I was then, without connections or backing, would succeed in making a name for himself. But I am looking too far ahead.

It was at that time, 1929 probably, that I joined the SFIO[2], the forerunner of France's present socialist party. I no longer know exactly how it happened. I remember a man, Maurice Delépine, a lawyer, who had something of a role in the party then. Of noble presence, his face framed by a luxuriant pepper-and-salt beard, expressing himself with great eloquence, he was kindness itself and only too happy to help people. Some time later, he did me a great service which I shall speak of further on, but I am not sure it was he who got me to join the SFIO. I probably met him after I had joined.

It was inevitable that once having decided to engage in political activity I should join the socialists or the communists; those two parties were then, as they are today, the natural destination of people of my social background. Why did I not enter political life through the communist party? Actually, I tried to. I joined a cell that operated in the vicinity of the Bourse; I attended a few meetings and then gave up, shocked by the total lack of objectivity, the impossibility for the militant of retaining freedom of mind and expression. If I remember rightly, the talk was only of blows struck and blows received. But what I wanted was not to listen to detailed and often picturesque accounts of brawls with the different youth movements of the day, be they *Camelots du Roi, Jeunesses Patriotes* or even *Jeunesses Socialistes*[3], but to be among people who would discuss the issues I was beginning to be aware of. So I joined the socialist party and found what I was looking for, at least for a while.

My activity as a young socialist completely changed my way of life. I no longer spent my spare time playing belote at the Vaudeville, I was an active militant in the *Quinzième Section*[4] and in the *Jeunesses Socialistes*. To be truthful, I didn't much care for sticking up posters and distributing pamphlets; I liked to listen and, soon, to speak. We spoke a great deal and very freely in the socialist party then, as I suppose they do today. I realized later that the discussions among militants in which I was a passionate voice represented for me a kind of intellectual awakening. That is why, even when I became estranged from the party because of profound differences of view, I retained a great sense of gratitude toward it for having given me the opportunity to start thinking.

In these frequent debates I was able to pit myself against boys my own age who had completed their secondary education and many of whom were at university. I felt inferior to them because they had the *bac*[5] and I hadn't. Yet at the same time I began to sense within me talents that were still lying fallow. Little by little a certain strength emerged, until the day came when I could, without too much fear, measure that strength against the men I admired most. Without too much fear, but always with a certain unease, for even in the fifty or so years that have elapsed since then I have never acquired self-assurance, that aura of calm strength and confidence that many people carry with them.

It was at that time that I began to be interested in economic, financial and monetary questions; almost certainly because I was living in the stock exchange environment, but also because the professedly Marxist socialists attached particular importance to those questions. But this interest was far from exclusive. I soon realized how crippling such a specialization could be, at my age at any rate, and that before all else I had to make a general survey of human knowledge. This is why, when I resumed my studies, I did not begin with economics but with philosophy. What I present here as the outcome of reasoning was at the time largely instinctive. It is likely too that I was partly influenced in the choice of what I would study by associates I admired and have now forgotten.

Very quickly the question arose of how I was to fill the huge gaps I was conscious of in my knowledge. Getting the *bac* would have been the simple solution. But I did not know how to go about it and the thought of the exam terrified me. I took a few Latin lessons but did not persevere, not at that time. I preferred to go direct to university. But how, without the *bac*?

My higher education begins

It was then, in 1929 or early in 1930, that Maurice Delépine recommended me to Georges Bourgin. He was the first in a series of men who helped me in a totally disinterested way, wanting to make life easier for this young man from nowhere whose all-consuming desire to learn touched them, men of learning, in some inner fibre of their being. A former Dreyfusard, a man of the left, excellent historian, active in the *universités populaires*[6], connected with the consumer cooperative

17

movement, Georges Bourgin, who when I met him was deputy director of the National Archives, belonged to that group of generous,
rationalist humanists who believed, perhaps not entirely wholeheartedly, that science would solve the world's problems. When I think of
him, after all these years, I always feel a certain emotion. If on occasion
I doubt that man is capable of being truly good, the memory of
Georges Bourgin suffices to dispel that doubt and make me optimistic
about the future of mankind.

I learned from him, or possibly from some other source, that the
diploma of the *Ecole Pratique des Hautes Etudes* at the Sorbonne was
recognized as an equivalent of the *bac* and I resolved to get it at all
costs. The undertaking was not so much unreasonable as it was crazy,
since this diploma is normally awarded to those who, having completed their secondary and higher education, write a thesis that represents an original contribution to a particular science. Anyway,
Georges Bourgin made available to me, at the National Archives, a
collection of documents that had never been consulted. They concerned the famines and agrarian turmoils that had disrupted certain
regions of France after the fall of Napoleon and had persisted until
1818. Every evening, when my work at the Bourse was over, I made
my way to the Rue des Francs-Bourgeois and the archives to peruse the
reports of regional prefects and sub-prefects, police reports and other
documents of the period housed in cardboard boxes brought to me by
an archives employee.

Thus I spent several months, maybe a year, leading a double life so
to speak, days in the office of the *coulissier* and in the Bourse, evenings
at the archives until they closed. Afterwards I often went to socialist
meetings that lasted late into the night. These were either section
meetings, in which we discussed business internal to the party, or
public meetings, where we often fell foul of the communists. The latter
were determined to be the party of the left and not to allow the
socialists any kind of public appearance. The result was violent clashes
in which matters were settled with fists or with chairs. Eventually we
managed to reestablish ourselves.

By now I felt completely detached from my stock exchange activities
and from the environment in which I had lived all these years. So 1930
went by, with me hoping I would get round the obstacle of the *bac* and
be able to start at the Sorbonne on the philosophy studies that already
held me in thrall.

This situation lasted until January 1931, when Paillard, Frères et
Lacroix gave me notice. Business was bad and they were making staff

cuts; besides which, I had not been particularly discreet about my socialist activities and these were hardly to the liking of ultrareactionary employers. Although my dismissal cut off all sources of income (there was no unemployment benefit then), my first reaction was one of profound joy at being finally free to pursue my studies as intended. I had a little money put by and while it lasted there was no point in worrying about what would happen next.

3

THE SORBONNE

January 1931 was the major turning point in my life, a complete break with the past, a desperate attempt to get back into harness where my formal education was concerned, to pick up where I had left off at the age of fourteen. By now I was almost twenty.

In practical terms, the pattern of my life changed almost overnight. I did not embark on this new period of my existence with the calm of a student who has spent six or seven years at a *lycée* reading the classics, learning the rudiments of philosophy and whose curiosity has inevitably lost some of its edge. I knew nothing and I was frenziedly eager to learn; for me nothing existed except knowledge. Corneille and Racine were as fresh, as new as a flower that has just bloomed. This produced a state of violent tension in which I was to live for several years. So I entered into a headlong race that often left me breathless. I did not manage to slow the pace until much later in life. For the time being I felt myself driven by a powerful force whose nature I had not yet analysed. Only sheer physical exhaustion caused me to interrupt my work.

My normal schedule was as follows: I got up at 6 or 6.30 a.m. and worked at home until 8.30. Then I went to the Sorbonne, where I attended one or two lectures during the day. The rest of the time I spent in the Sorbonne library, which closed at 6 p.m. I then went to the Sainte-Geneviève library where I read and took notes until 10 p.m. Often I walked home in order to unwind; all the way from the Latin

20

Quarter to the Porte de Versailles, this nocturnal journey took me three-quarters of an hour to an hour. Back home my mother had dinner waiting for me. I forgot to mention that I usually lunched off a sandwich at Capoulade, the café on the corner of the Rue Soufflot and the Boulevard Saint-Michel.

That was my regular timetable. I also had to put in a few hours' work each week at the National Archives to finish going through the documentary material that was to help me write my thesis for the diploma of the *Ecole Pratique des Hautes Etudes*, as well as one evening a week at the Lycée Charlemagne where I took Latin lessons, provided free by the *Association Philotechnique*[1], from Mlle Ducaffy, an old lady who was kindness and dedication personified.

Sunday mornings I spent at the Hôpital Saint-Anne[2] doing a practical course in pathological psychology (psychology then forming part of the philosophy degree) conducted by Georges Dumas, a doctor, philosopher and psychologist whose *Traité de Psychologie* was an authoritative work at the time and was republished after the war.

Philosophy

When I undertook to resume my studies, philosophy seemed unquestionably to be the only discipline worth channelling my energies into. Why did I think that way? Probably because of my socialist party activities in 1929 and 1930. The kinship between politics and philosophy was for me self-evident. Or more accurately, I was certain it was impossible to think politics and find answers to the many questions confronting the citizen without a solid grounding in philosophy.

I think that is why at the beginning of 1931 I decided to devote myself to philosophy studies. At that time the *licence d'enseignement de philosophie*, representing a first university degree, was divided into four parts each carrying a certificate: morals and sociology, psychology, logic and metaphysics, history of philosophy. A person without the *bac* could take three of these, but for the fourth, which carried the degree, it was necessary to have the *bac* or its equivalent. Courageously or recklessly, depending on the point of view, I decided to take two certificates, morals and sociology and psychology, in June 1931. I had about five months in which to prepare. I spent those months in a frenzy of work. I built my sociology studies around Durkheim, of whom most of the Sorbonne professors had been students and disciples, notably Bouglé and Fauconnet. For psychology I was guided by a man who proved to be a good friend, Ignace Meyer-

21

son, nephew of the philosopher Emile Meyerson. A slim, small man, crackling with intelligence, he loved to guide young people who impressed him with their will to work. At the time I knew him he was specializing in experimental psychology. I lost sight of him when I gave up philosophy, but I know that his intellectual authority never ceased to grow during the half-century that followed; I learned from the newspaper that he had died at an advanced age in 1985. Of the books I read or rather devoured then, I remember Durkheim's *Les Formes Elémentaires de la Vie Religieuse* and *Le Socialisme*, Bergson's *Matière et Mémoire* and *L'Evolution Créatrice* and *Le Langage et la Pensée* by Henri Delacroix.

The weeks and then the months passed and suddenly the exams were upon me. I was filled with fear, or perhaps terror would be the better word; I had never taken an exam other than the certificate of primary education. I was so strung up that I was unable to sleep the night before the ordeal, a condition that was to repeat itself throughout the rest of my life. The written paper in morals and sociology was on incest (among primitive peoples, it should be understood) and in psychology on intelligence, a subject which Henri Delacroix had chosen for his course of lectures in 1930–1. My results for the written papers were good in morals and sociology and only fair in psychology where I just attained the average, and that thanks to Ignace Meyerson who had liked a paper I had read in his course the previous winter on the psychology of Hippolyte Taine.

Then came the *viva voce*, which in a sense was to determine the rest of my existence. The psychology and pathological psychology orals went off without any problem. Georges Dumas even gave me an excellent rating: apparently I knew, if not a lot, at least more than the other candidates about schizophrenia. Of the test on morals I remember nothing. That left sociology. In the examination room were the two examiners, Fauconnet and Bouglé. Fauconnet was reputed to be easy, he would ask you what books you had read and then question you about one of them. Bouglé, on the other hand, it was said, plied you with difficult questions to gauge the extent of your knowledge. So all the students hurried to get in line for Fauconnet.

As it was nearly six in the evening, the hour at which everything was supposed to be over, the usher cut the Fauconnet line in two and pushed seven or eight candidates, of whom I was one, towards the rostrum where Bouglé was. I started to feel panicky, I recall, at this sudden change of prospect. The student Bouglé questioned before me floundered miserably, confusing totem and taboo. When my turn came, Bouglé asked me to say something about socialism. I had read Durkheim avidly and, having by then been a socialist party member for maybe two years, I had done a little thinking on the subject. I answered him without any hesitations, basing myself essentially on Durkheim's arguments but allowing myself a few critical reflections. Bouglé listened attentively. 'Good', he said. 'In which *lycée* did you do your philosophy?' When I told him I had never been to a *lycée* and had been doing university studies in philosophy for less than six months, he was apparently surprised. He gave me an excellent mark, 18 or 19 out of 20, and told me to come and see him the following morning at the *Ecole Normale Supérieure*[3], of which he was the deputy principal. Needless to say, I kept the appointment. When he saw me, he beckoned me over and pointed to a pile of books on his desk. 'That', he said, 'is your vacation reading'. Then he held out a piece of paper. 'And this is a one-month study grant for you to go to England. You will compile for me a bibliography on the consumer cooperative movement in England'.

Thus began a long relationship that was to end only with Bouglé's death in 1940. What can I say about him? His life had so many different facets that it was almost impossible to grasp: scholar, teacher, journalist, a man deeply interested in things political and who would have liked to be in politics, he was chairman, vice-chairman or member of a considerable number of associations. Most importantly, he was a great academic who embodied the noblest aspects of the great values of the Third Republic. A Dreyfusard, friend of Jaurès and of many political men with socialist or radical-socialist sympathies, he was moved by profound democratic sentiments and ardent rationalist convictions. He liked to encourage and help young men in whom he saw or thought he saw promise. He was above all a kind, generous and disinterested man.

At the time he took me under his wing he was mostly occupied with the *Ecole Normale Supérieure*, of which he was shortly to become the principal. There he had set up the *Centre de Documentation Sociale*, which was at once a library, a meeting point for students of the school and young intellectuals who were interested in economic and social questions, and the scene of evening lectures given by one or other of his protégés on a subject he knew well. For a time I was librarian at the Centre and there I got to know men who were to become some of my best friends: Raymond Aron, Georges Friedmann, Raymond Polin and Jean Stoetzel.

But to go back to my first meeting with Bouglé, I came out of his

23

office that morning in June or July 1931 overjoyed. Only a few months after leaving the Bourse there I was with half of my philosophy degree already gained, my work for the diploma of the *Ecole Pratique des Hautes Etudes* was going well and one of the great university professors had singled me out. Innocent that I was, I had the impression of already knowing so many things!

In London, in July 1931, I lodged at the French Institute's hostel and went every day to the British Museum to compile my bibliography. I remember little of this first stay in England, except that I met two other French students, one studying philosophy like me (his name was Mougin, I think), the other medicine. We got on well together, though there was a lot of admiration on my part (they had the *bac*) and a little condescension on theirs.

On my return to Paris I handed in my bibliography. I think it was that year that I stayed for the first time in the Bouglé family home at the seaside resort of Le Val-André. Bouglé was very nice to my father, who was seeing me off at the station. 'Your son is a worker,' he said to him in substance, 'he will go far.' My father was ecstatic. At Le Val-André, I met the whole family: Madame Bouglé and her four daughters. I believe that one or possibly two of them were already married at the time. I went fishing several times with the master of the house on his small boat, regularly experiencing a ghastly feeling of seasickness I was too nervous to mention. It must have been noticed, though, for the fishing trips ceased. So the summer of 1931 went by. Back in Paris I put the finishing touches to my thesis for the diploma of the *Ecole Pratique des Hautes Etudes*. It was handwritten; I had not been able to afford to have it typed. My sister, I remember, numbered the pages. I handed it in at the end of 1931 or the beginning of 1932.

I had decided to attempt only the third part of the philosophy degree in June 1932, the logic and metaphysics certificate. The fourth, history of philosophy, was much more difficult than the other three and I did not feel my general knowledge of philosophy was sufficient yet for me to tackle it. So I went back to the Sorbonne. At home the situation was the same as during the previous months. My mother was still doing housecleaning for other people. As for me, I did a few small jobs and helped Georges Gurvitch, a French sociologist of Russian extraction, to correct the French text of one of his first works. My command of my own language was far from perfect at that time and today I have the feeling that my help to him was strictly limited. I also gave French lessons to a German girl; before each lesson, I had to teach myself what I was going to teach her.

It was during that academic year of 1931–2 that I discovered Kant. His work left a deep imprint on me. I read the *Critique of Pure Reason* with the excited feeling that I was discovering the truth and wondering how that truth could have eluded me for so long. I had the conviction then, which I have retained ever since and have tried to impart to my children, that Kant is the culminating point of all the philosophy that went before him and contains the seeds of all the philosophy to come after him. In June 1932 I was lucky enough to have as an examination question 'The Forms of Sensibility in Kant'. I turned in a good paper. In the oral, Léon Brunschvicg asked me what I thought of monism. I think I answered that it represented the only tenable philosophical attitude, given that the mind of man perceives reality only through the forms of his sensibility and the categories of his understanding. I was resolutely idealistic in the Kantian sense of the term. I obtained the certificate of logic and metaphysics, passing with distinction.

Besides Kant, I read a great deal of Plato and Descartes at that time but rather neglected Aristotle and Leibnitz, although they were on the list of set reading. I also read Renouvier, Hamelin and Rauh, thus acquiring something of a background in philosophy. Hegel I was not to discover until much later. But the most important event of the 1931–2 year, and possibly of my life, occurred at the end of 1931, in December I think.

I am invited to America

One evening we were having dinner in the kitchen, my father, mother, sister and myself, when the doorbell rang. It was a telegram for me, which read: 'Would you like to spend a year in America? If so, come and see me tomorrow. Bouglé.' I was completely taken aback. Suddenly, for the first time, I thought of America as an actual place within reach. My parents and sister were even more surprised than I; furthermore, my mother was disturbed by the idea of my going so far away and for so long. The mystery was cleared up the next day when I saw Bouglé. The Rockefeller Foundation had come up with a project for a series of seminars on 'The Impact of Culture on Personality' in 1932–3; the idea was to bring together, at Yale, students and teachers of different nationalities, each of whom would be in a sense the expression of the culture to which he belonged. Bouglé asked me if I was prepared to represent French culture.

The outrageousness of the idea struck me immediately. I, whose culture was embryonic, was being asked to represent French culture! I objected as much to Bouglé. He replied that I was too modest, that culture was not a sum of knowledge, that it expressed what was most spontaneous and genuine in the spirit of a nation and that I was particularly suitable for this mission because my spontaneity had not been impaired by a protracted secondary education; it was a unique opportunity for me to show what I was capable of. This last argument was probably the truest; that year in the United States would be a test of my abilities and Bouglé could see if he had placed his trust in someone worthwhile. I accepted.

In the months that followed I saw a number of persons attached to the Rockefeller Foundation including Kitteredge, the Foundation's representative in Paris – a rather starchy Britisher but basically very nice – and a young American professor who was to be one of the two US directors of the following year's seminar series. They endorsed Bouglé's choice and stood me English lessons at the Berlitz School.

I left for the United States in September 1932, but before telling of my American experience, I should like to say a few words about my activities in 1931 and the first seven or eight months of 1932, beginning with the training of my mind.

The thesis on which I had been working for the diploma of the *Ecole Pratique des Hautes Etudes* taught me what scientific work was. Up to then I had written hardly anything. I had to submit to the historian's discipline, the preoccupation with exact and complete references, the use of quotations that faithfully reflected the sense of a text taken as a whole, and so on. Above all, I began to learn how to write.

Reading the works of the great sociologists, psychologists and philosophers was a constant source of wonderment. Obviously I could only scratch the surface, but step by step I developed my own frame of reference, I learned to place one writer in relation to another, I prepared to go more deeply into this or that question that had struck me particularly. I think I can say that at this time learning was the only thing that counted in my life; I was in the throes of a kind of intellectual delirium. As for the distractions that young men of my age generally seek, they left me totally indifferent; in fact, it would be truer to say that I ignored their existence. I never went out for a drink; I had no friends, of either sex, apart from those whom philosophy or politics put my way. I realized later that this kind of life, which I was to live for several years, left deep imprints that are still present in me today. Work had become a kind of addiction I would experience until the end of my life. I had lost, or never acquired, the taste for simple pleasures. This has almost certainly had harmful consequences, for me and those closest to me. But perhaps I am putting the cart before the horse. Perhaps it is not the life habits I contracted then that are responsible for certain psychological traits I feel in me, but rather it is those selfsame traits, in existence prior to my new life, that led or even obliged me to choose it.

My relations with my family, while still affectionate, became more and more distant. I remember one evening at home with my parents when I explained my intentions for the future. My father and mother, as I have said, suffered from a very strong feeling of material insecurity. It was not therefore surprising that security, even in a humble job, should represent deliverance from an anxiety they often experienced. Security meant a steady wage and a small pension at the end of one's working life. They hoped to see me enter a branch of the civil service, which would give me precisely what they lacked; my father urged me to take the exam for recruits to the clerical service of the Paris police headquarters. When I told them I wanted to be a teacher in a lower secondary school in the provinces (at the time I did not dare think about the *agrégation*[4] which would have qualified me to teach in a *lycée*), they were dismayed. Secondary and higher education was a world they did not know; they saw me getting bogged down in indefinitely protracted studies. The end of the road was for them as obscure as the road itself. The discussion went on late into the night. I stuck to my guns. They loved me very much and my father finally told me to do what I thought was right and that he and my mother would help me to the very best of their ability.

4

THE CONSUMER COOPERATIVE MOVEMENT AND *RÉVOLUTION CONSTRUCTIVE*

I have already spoken about my joining the socialist party and *Jeunesses Socialistes* in 1929. When I started at the Sorbonne in 1931 I joined the socialist student movement. We had an office in the Rue de Lanneau on the Montagne Sainte-Geneviève. I spent a little time there each day, often between two lectures, and attended the meetings, which I think were weekly. My two best friends at the time were Modiano and Kokoczynski. I lost sight of them long ago. Those days also saw the start of a friendship with Pierre Dreyfus that was to remain untarnished throughout a lifetime in which our paths crossed often.

I was on the left or the extreme left edge of the party, my allegiance alternating between two men, Pivert and Zyromski. Marceau Pivert, a primary schoolteacher, was the guiding light of the *Quinzième Section*, more of an anarchist than a Socialist-Marxist; during the Spanish civil war he actively supported the Trotskyist *Partido Obrero de Unificacion Marxista*. Zyromski, more moderate in his thinking but also something of a firebrand, headed the *Bataille Socialiste*

28

movement; after the war he turned up in the senate on the communist benches. I was a young activist who acted without thinking very much, or rather whose thinking lay elsewhere. At no time was I tempted to join the socialist right wing, led at the time by a rather colourless militant, Pierre Renaudel, later to be expelled from the party for being rather too ardent a proponent of representation in the government. Nor was I to be attracted in 1933 by the neosocialists under the leadership of Déat, Montagnon and Marquet, whose fascist sympathies seemed dangerous to me.

I have said why I became a socialist; it was my natural destination. Outside the social class to which I belonged my sole connections, and only from 1929 on, were with young middle-class intellectuals who were socialist or communist, often as a reaction against their families. Add to that, if you like, a certain youthful generosity that was as yet untempered by reasoning and experience. But that is not the whole explanation inasmuch as it does not allow for all the thinking I had been doing in an attempt to justify my political commitment objectively.

The era of which I am now speaking, broadly the years from 1930 to 1932, was one of great mental turmoil. The Great Depression had suddenly materialized in the United States in 1929 and swiftly spread to Europe; prices were falling and unemployment soaring, larger and larger segments of production capacity were lying idle. The plight of the people was made even worse by the fact that there was no social security system at all and, in many countries, no system of unemployment benefit. Economists of every stripe, even the most reputed, were cudgelling their brains for an explanation. In a period of general deflation governments were seeking safety in pushing deflation still further and exporting their countries' unemployment by means of high tariffs and competitive devaluations. Political stability was threatened in many countries and notably in Germany, where Nazism was progressing dangerously and was soon to cut down the feeble defences erected in its path and overrun the nation.

It was not preposterous, especially for inexperienced youngsters with only a smattering of economics, to question the economic system itself. Had not Marx predicted seventy or eighty years earlier the final crisis of capitalism? We did not make ourselves read *Das Kapital* closely to ascertain whether the conditions he foresaw had come about. Along with capitalism itself, a number of us – although I personally did not go so far, at least not usually – were ready to throw parliamentary democracy, or what we used then to call 'formal democracy', overboard in favour of another democratic system that would extend to the means of production and exchange and their management. We did not really know what we wanted, but we were not the only ones groping in the dark.

Let there be no mistake: we were at the same time thoroughly antifascist and antinazi. The great tradition of French socialism, in which liberty was the supreme value, a tradition which once had been embodied in Jaurès, was very much alive within us. We had the example of Mussolini who had destroyed the labour movement in Italy, something which Hitler was soon to do in Germany. If I did not succumb to antiparliamentarism, it is because I soon realized it led to fascism.

To add to the contradictions that beset our thinking, and again in conformity with traditional socialist ideals, we were internationalists and pacifists. We had not yet understood that the only way to combat fascism and Hitlerism was to rearm and prepare to wage war. Even Léon Blum experienced at that time the same difficulty in convincing himself that universal disarmament was a utopian idea to which dictators would never subscribe, those men who wanted to redraw the map of Europe. I have probably said enough to describe my mental dilemmas when I was twenty years old. It was to take me another three or four years to arrive at a more realistic conception of things.

At that time there occurred two episodes in my life as a militant that warrant more than a cursory mention: my entry into the consumer cooperative movement and my association with a group of young socialist intellectuals known as *Révolution Constructive*.

I forget exactly who introduced me to certain leaders of the co-operative movement, notably Marcel Brot. I knew them before Bouglé had noticed me, so it was probably Georges Bourgin, himself a cooperator, who did. The movement was not, at that time, just a grouping of shops but a social philosophy whose declared aim was to conquer the future. My personal papers include a yellowed copy of the journal *Le Coopérateur de France* dated September 12, 1931 and containing the text of a speech I made at Nancy during a visit to the 'Cooperators of Lorraine' in the summer of 1931, before an audience composed of other students and a few local and national officials of the cooperative movement. The article is entitled 'The Forces of the Future, speech by M. R. Marjolin, student of the *Ecole Normale Supérieure*.' I had been styled student of the ENS without being consulted and I was very embarrassed when the article came out; I was afraid I would be held responsible for this factual error and that it would be thought I had appropriated the designation out of vanity. Even Georges Bourgin was a little anxious. But no one seemed to notice. That was the first time I saw my by-line in a newspaper and I was very proud.

Reading the speech again, I find it quite a fair piece of rhetoric inspired by vague and generous sentiments. Using as my argument the grave economic problems from which western world was suffering at that time, the simultaneous existence of superabundance, unemployment and poverty, I cited the cooperative movement as an endeavour to create a new society from which this paradox would be banished. The cooperative movement would restore to society its unity and substitute new moral criteria for those that had failed. Profit was the villain of the piece and the whole point of the movement was that it had eliminated profit as the central aim of its activity; through it, democracy would be extended to the economic sphere: production, exchange, consumption. The mainsprings of economic life, I said, had to be redirected toward the end purpose of any product: consumption. The day producers produced no longer to make a profit but to satisfy a specific demand there would be no more cyclical crises of over-production. In a great burst of oratory, I added that with the cooperative movement 'instead of the fight for survival and natural selection, instead of the brutal emergence of a personality deformed by struggle, we are witnessing a far more imposing and comforting spectacle in which mankind is being ushered into an era of boundless prosperity, the collective result of the efforts of all, the product of the labour of each and every one.'

I used these themes again in another speech I made in Strasbourg on September 20, 1932, just before leaving for America, at the 19th National Congress of the National Federation of Consumer Cooperative Societies. Speaking on behalf of the young cooperators, I referred to the ideal the cooperative movement proposed to achieve: man's total freedom, the emancipation of the individual freed from all the material, moral and intellectual chains that bind him.

Truth to tell, on those occasions I was more Fourierist or Proudhonian than Marxist. Bouglé had got me into a circle known as *Les Amis de Proudhon* that met every month for lunch somewhere in the Boulevard Arago. It was through them that Proudhon's complete works were published. We sought to bring about deep-reaching social changes through persuasion and in a general spirit of reconciliation.

The cooperative movement and friendships I had struck up with socialist students led me to *Révolution Constructive*, probably following a congress of socialist students that was held at Toulouse in April 1931. It was a group of intellectuals, mostly former students of the *Ecole Normale Supérieure* – history or philosophy teachers, active members of the socialist party – brought together by common sympathies or points of view. The group's most active members, those who acted as its leaders in a way, were Georges Lefranc, Pierre Boivin and Maurice Deixonne. All the members except me were men of between twenty-five and thirty; I was easily the youngest. I still have a touching recollection of the kindness with which these new friends treated me and the esteem in which they held me. Pierre Boivin was to die shortly afterwards of cancer that was diagnosed too late. I do not know what became of Maurice Deixonne. As for Georges Lefranc, he devoted himself after the war to the history of the socialist party and published a number of authoritative works. Our first objective was to write a book that would be a sort of manifesto. The result was, naturally enough, *Révolution Constructive* which came out on 1932. Among my old papers I found an article by Georges Lefranc which he sent me in 1963 and which recounts the history of the group[1].

For young men acting in an era of darkness and confusion we showed a certain realism. We had all been marked by the war (or in my case by the memory of the war passed on to me by my family and older friends during the ten or fifteen years that followed it). The treaties that concluded it had settled nothing, they had not restored a stable balance in Europe and war was threatening again. The Great Depression had added its trail of misery and unanswered questions to the dangers that again were compromising peace. In such a dramatic situation the socialist party seemed to us tragically unequal to the tasks that awaited it; rent by internecine struggles, cut off from the trade union and cooperative movements, engrossed in its electoral work and parliamentary life, might it not prove incapable of bringing socialism about if it came to power?

At the same time we had realized that a general process of socialization was under way and that, imperceptibly but surely, the old Napoleonic state was changing. But we did not intend to let it go at that. Human effort, we said, can accelerate the socialist advance, provided it is employed judiciously: 'The real fight for the new society has to be fought not so much in Parliament as in the trade unions, the cooperatives and the municipalities. The socialist party, for its part, must do more to put structures and minds in readiness[2].'

Révolution Constructive, the book, also contained a number of purple passages that caused us to be thought of as incurable romantics in some circles. The man who probably understood us best was Georges Bourgin. In *Le Coopérateur de France* of April 6, 1933 he wrote:

A very curious and sometimes very beautiful book... these adolescents have seen the collapse of a world, have conceived immense hopes and are now traversed by immense misgivings too... Their pages, replete with facts and amplified by footnotes, make a useful contribution to the history of human evolution since the Great War[3].

When I think back on this episode of my life more than fifty years after the event, the chief criticism I would like to make about us is that we left completely unclear what we understood by 'socialism.' For some of us it meant a revolution, a complete break with the capitalist system; for others, among whom I am inclined to count myself, socialist action in the cooperatives and trade unions notably, but without overlooking government, was supposed to bring about rapid social progress, to accelerate the movement of things. What I was led to write and do in the few years that followed my time with *Révolution Constructive* shows that my interpretation of what I was thinking then is probably correct.

For a very brief time, three months maybe, I belonged to a group of 'pacifists', I remember. There I met a well-known freemason and a priest who was secretary, I believe, to the Archbishop of Paris. That experience put me off 'pacifism' for good. It seemed to me that no sane being ever desires war, he does what he can to avoid it; but there are some situations in which it is the lesser of two evils. We lived through that kind of situation in the thirties. The pacifism of a great part of the political class during those years, combined with the inanity of governments' policies, whether right-wing or left-wing, helped to bring on the disaster of 1940. I feel the same way today about the pacifism that is developing in some western countries and whose advocates seem unaware that the only effect of their talk is not to avert war but to weaken the democratic world in the presence of Soviet tyranny. Those people confirm my belief that stupidity plays a significant role in history.

When I endeavour to recall what I was thinking in those years from 1931 to 1933, which include my year's stay in the United States, I have the impression of a young man taking his first steps in the political and social field, adopting a succession of different formulas and rejecting them one after the other, though in most cases retaining something. I have just said what I thought of pacifism. Cooperation, which tempted me for a while, I eventually found sterile in relation to the great problems of the time. As to trade unionism, I found myself even at that time in fear of its excesses. Perfectly legitimate when it sets out to defend the interests of the workers, especially the most disadvantaged, it is liable, when it ignores the interests of society as a whole, to become a kind of corporatism serving the best organized labour groups, to the detriment of the nation and very often to that of the majority of the workers themselves. That left political socialism, of which I shall speak at length later on.

I left for the United States at the end of September 1932. In 1933—4, after my return, I again had contacts with my friends of *Révolution Constructive*. I even belonged, briefly I seem to remember, to a group we set up within the socialist party. But my ties with the group gradually loosened. After my American experience my mind was elsewhere.

5

I DISCOVER AMERICA

My first visit to the United States lasted a year and most of it was spent at the Graduate School of Yale, in the university's library and at the seminars held several times a week to study the impact of culture on personality. There were thirteen of us students and young teachers from Europe and Asia. I was the youngest, the oldest being a Lithuanian who was supposed to represent the Jewish culture of eastern Europe. Our director of studies, an American professor named Edward Sapir, was nearing fifty and a highly respected name in university circles. A German Jew, he had emigrated to Canada very young. After studying Latin and ancient Greek, he had turned to the Indian languages and cultures of North America. His influence in the field of linguistics has been considerable. When I met him, his chief interest was psychoanalysis. He directed our work with great skill and much kindness and consideration. He was particularly nice to me, perhaps because I was the youngest member of the group. I often went to dinner at his place where we talked for hours on topics I have forgotten.

Apart from the discussions between students and teachers on problems of psychology and sociology, we talked with personalities from other universities and sometimes from other environments. The discussions took place in the relaxed atmosphere typical of American universities, where differences in status are not made apparent. Among those I remember coming to Yale were Harold Lasswell the sociologist and psychoanalyst; Malinowski the Polish-born anthropologist and ethnologist, already famous when he came to speak to us; Henry Stack Sullivan, a rather heterodox psychoanalyst whom I was to see again once or twice after my return to France; Frank Knight, an economist who made a major contribution to the theory of risk and profit; and there were many others.

My best friends in the group were a Pole whose name I have forgotten and the Italian Leo Ferrero, son of the well-known historian Guglielmo Ferrero and Gina Lombroso, who was the daughter of the great criminologist Cesare Lombroso. Leo Ferrero, who must have been about thirty when I met him, had begun to make a name for himself in Paris by publishing a series of essays. My two friends were to die tragically at the end of our year in America, in separate car accidents. Outside the group I fraternized with young American socialists (there were a few of them). I still see one of them from time to time: Myer Cohen, who made a career for himself in the United Nations. One of my best friends was a young Chinese, Chia-I-Cheng, whom I lost sight of a long time ago.

At the end of that academic year the Rockefeller Foundation offered me a second year in the United States. I declined the offer, being in a hurry to get back to France to prepare for the philosophy *agrégation*. The Foundation then financed two field trips I made in North America in July–August, one in Louisiana where I lived for a few weeks among the Acadians, the other in French Canada.

What effect did my stay in America have on me? First and foremost it was a release. Less than two years earlier I had been a stock exchange clerk in Paris, enclosed in a tight little world with no horizons. And suddenly I found myself in a kingdom of great teachers for whom I felt a real veneration and who treated me as an equal. Above all, I learned something new each day, I had a feeling of constant enrichment. The reader will doubtless think me naïve. It is true that I was or appeared to be; I am not sure I have changed much since.

At the Graduate School I had a simple but comfortable room with access to communal showers. I would eat at the university restaurant. I expressed myself in broken English, of such odd pronunciation that, right at the beginning, when I uttered a sentence or two in front of Edward Sapir he thought I was speaking German. I continued to work with the same passionate enthusiasm as before. Apart from the practical work and reading I did for the Yale seminars, I spent several hours a day studying Latin and Greek and the history of philosophy, for I was determined now to sit the *agrégation*.

I Discover America

The French intellectuals and America

But anthropology, sociology, psychoanalysis, philosophy, Latin and Greek did not take up all my time. I also endeavoured to discover America. Before leaving Europe I had done some reading. It was the time when Europeans, especially French intellectuals, generally treated America and Americans with a great deal of condescension: 'They have the material wealth, we have the culture.' This is the way their thinking generally went. What many Frenchmen felt on the subject was sketched in ludicrous caricature by Georges Duhamel in his *Scènes de la Vie Future*[1]. A few extracts from this book, fortunately long forgotten but having exerted some influence in the early thirties, are worth quoting if only because a certain primitive anti-American-ism continues to wreak havoc, more or less, in some French political and intellectual circles.

America is not, as one likes to say, a young country in every way. As regards material civilization, the American people are an older people than ours, a people which has aged suddenly, perhaps, and without really maturing, but which is now enacting many scenes of our future life.

The book reflects the anxiety which the French bourgeois and intellectuals felt up against the American phenomenon: the fear of seeing it jostle or even destroy the narrowly defined frame of reference in which their often cramped lives were lived. Hence the impression that a New York cinema made on Georges Duhamel: 'A luxury that calls to mind a great bourgeois brothel, an industrial luxury manufac-tured for soulless machines, for a crowd which the soul seems to desert too.' The soul is fair game for anyone, it would seem. Further on he says: 'I maintain that a people subjected to the regime of the American cinemas for half a century is headed for the ultimate in decadence.'

Against that I quite realize it will be argued that America has her big business, her big boats, her big buildings. I beg to differ. A building is put up at the rate of two or three storeys a week. It took Wagner twenty years to construct his Tetralogy, Littré a lifetime to compile his dictionary [...]. America has dedicated herself to perishable works. She puts up edifices, not monuments. Should she crumble tomorrow, we would seek in vain, among her ashes, the statuette of clay that suffices to render a Greek village immortal. Ruins of Chicago! I evoke you with horror, with ennui, prodigious pile of scrap iron, concrete and plaster, whose only beauty would be wild grasses and moss.

37

The entire book is in the same vein. Here is one last quotation: 'What is one to say about America, that prodigious tumefaction? She is no longer on the scale of the minds that created her. No man can now form an effectual and clear idea of her. God himself. . .' Bombast vying with stupidity. One is appalled.

When I left for the United States I was as yet unacquainted with the fantasizings of Georges Duhamel; on the other hand, I had read and studied the serious and carefully considered book that André Siegfried, professor at the *Collège de France*, published in 1927[2]. It is, of course, a far cry from the outrageousness of *Scènes de la Vie Future*. Even so, André Siegfried does not conceal his uneasiness. Has not the immense material success of the United States come about, is it not coming about at the expense of culture, individuality, freedom itself?

But this general affluence is possible only because production is concentrated on a small number of types, always the same, with which the public makes do. The price America is paying for undeniable progress is the sacrifice, through this uniformity, of no less than an aspect of civilization. There is advance on one side and retreat on the other: the practical advance, relative to the Old World, is immense; but the individual aspect, that of art and, basically, of refinement is sacrificed.

André Siegfried has some hard words to say about American higher education:

In the universities, the majority of students want to be taught ready-made truths, they ask of their teachers not so much to impart culture as to give them an instrument of success. Nothing more resembles the German discipline than this regimentation, susceptible of splendid material results, a marvellous tool of economic performance, but which causes the individual and solitary mind, often creative of art and wit, to rebel or to languish.

Freedom is threatened, if not already compromised:

The American milieu is coming to resemble a *de facto* collectivism, wanted by the elites and cheerfully accepted by the masses, which surreptitiously saps man's freedom and channels his action so closely that, in blissful unawareness, he signs his own abdication. . . In her eagerness to perfect an incomparable material success, is America not liable to extinguish that flame of individual freedom that Europe, childlike perhaps in its economic performance, had thought to be one of the essential treasures of civilized humanity?

This, then, was what was thought of America in the twenties by one of the most honest minds of that time, a man who had set out to study the economies and civilizations of the big western countries. As for me, I think I can say today that when I first made contact with the United States in 1932 I was a little wary, possibly for the reasons set out by André Siegfried but also because, as a young socialist, I could only regard with distrust the country in which capitalism had reached its furthest point of development.

My first experiences

These reservations soon vanished. At Yale University I found teachers quite the equal of those I knew in Europe. Discussions with them and with the American students I met were just as free, objective and disinterested as those I had had in Europe. Maybe the American masses were uneducated, but what about the European masses? To me the dividing line seemed to lie between the masses and the intellectual elite on either continent, rather than between the continents themselves. As for the connection between material affluence and freedom, I had a strong feeling, perhaps because I had spent my youth in poverty, that the former, far from threatening the latter, was if anything its prerequisite. One has to be comfortably off to be really free; an adequate income, it does not have to be astronomical, gives one the freedom to choose the sort of life one wants to lead. I could expatiate on the subject, but what I have just said probably describes well enough my reaction as a young man. The opposition of material wealth to culture, or freedom, struck me even at that time as an absurdity.

But perhaps my efforts then to form a balanced judgment were aided by circumstances. In 1932–3 America was certainly not the picture of capitalism triumphant. The country was in the throes of depression. In the twelve months I spent there I saw Roosevelt's election in November 1932, the financial crisis of early 1933, when all the banks temporarily closed their doors, and the setting-up of the New Deal institutions. I strove to understand.

I read everything I could get hold of concerning the history of the United States, the nation's formation and American culture. For the Yale seminars in which I was taking part our teachers had already assembled an impressive number of books which I devoured in a few months, including *The Rise of American Civilization* by Charles and Mary Beard. In addition, I made a thorough study of the US labour movement. I had arranged with Bouglé to submit a thesis on the subject in Paris in 1934, which was to get me my diploma of higher studies in philosophy. I must have read and examined at least a hundred books dealing with this aspect of American society. I was also an avid reader of books and periodicals on contemporary economic events. My lack of a proper grounding in economics hampered me and I did what I could to remedy that state of affairs; it was the cause of a number of errors of interpretation I committed at the time. I derive comfort from telling myself that the cardinal sin is not to make mistakes but to refuse to learn. I was to learn very quickly during my stay in America and in the years that followed.

I know roughly what I thought then, for in 1934–5, on my return to France, I published a number of books and articles that reveal how my ideas, not only on America but on the world in general, gradually took shape at that time. If I try to sum up those ideas, I cannot disguise the fact that, on the face of it at least, they were often contradictory. But the young, and even not so young, can live for a while in contradiction; it generates a tension that often spurs progress. That is what happened to me. Yet the different ideas I adopted then all had something in common: they reflected a profound admiration for the United States that has stayed with me throughout my life. This is an intrinsic part of my innermost thought and it will never disappear, of that I am certain.

First and foremost I admired the American nation, the way it was formed. That huge mixture of tens of millions of English, Scots, Irish, Germans, Poles, Italians, Swedes, etc., fleeing want, persecution and tyranny and giving birth to a nation, to a state, that would gradually come to occupy a central place in our western world; this was an epic that amazed me more than the wars that had bloodied Europe, than the Napoleonic wars for example. I admired those pioneers who, step by step, had conquered a continent. I forgot the slaughter of Indians and remembered only the toil and suffering of those who had really built America, the geographical entity and then the industrial giant. Their individualism, that of the farmer isolated in a hostile environment, seemed to me so different from the selfish, closed-in, sheltered individualism of the middle-class European. I was tremendously impressed by the extraordinary result of this titanic enterprise, the triumphant capitalism of the late 19th and early 20th centuries, and by the gigantic stride in productivity it represented. I think it was at that moment I learned that there is no solution to ecomonic problems without growth and that growth cannot come from bureaucratic manipulations, but only from the individual efforts of all, working in freedom that is as near complete as possible.

My mind, as I said, was not proof against certain contradictions. An admirer of American capitalism, I also had the utmost admiration for Roosevelt and his efforts to restart a machine that had stalled. Although an outside spectator, I was carried away by the torrent of hope and enthusiasm unleashed by the New Deal. More than anything, I was fascinated by an economic and social experiment on such a vast scale. The efforts of the Europeans seemed to me petty and of no historical importance. The young socialist I was then would have liked Roosevelt to be on the same path as himself; I tried to interpret what he did in a socialist light. It was ridiculous, I soon realized that; but not before I had written a number of things I would not write today. The truth is that I was then, as I was often to be subsequently, intellectually and emotionally torn between a desire for social justice and equality and a deep aspiration towards an efficient and productive society. It could be that this kind of tension is the key to my personality.

Anyway, at the time I believed that the Great Depression was the essential crisis of capitalism that Marx had predicted. I could not really see, and no one had any more than a vague idea on the subject, how the prosperity of the twenties could be brought back. I thought that the economy had to change its nature, that it could not remain based on profit. To give some idea of what I was thinking then, here is a brief extract from a brochure on the Roosevelt experiments (*Les Expériences Roosevelt*) which I wrote at the end of 1933 or early in 1934, just after my return from the United States:

In less than ten years, America has had the unique privilege and the heavy burden of placing before the astonished world two creeds of material life based on different and often conflicting principles. One land has seen, in rapid and dramatic succession, two social experiments of such magnitude that they could not, by virtue of their consequences and the example they have set, leave the other peoples of the world indifferent. In the very country where capitalism reached its furthest point of development, where economic freedom seemed to have brought about a durable order and lasting prosperity, theories are being developed and events are rapidly accumulating that one likes to think are at variance with that same capitalism and economic freedom[3].

What I had failed sufficiently to discern, behind the outward appearance of a radical change, almost a revolution, was the element of permanency, of durable validity, in the American economic and political regime which was to reassert itself powerfully once the circumstances had changed. It was not Roosevelt's ambition to transform American society or the American economy, but to get them out of a state of temporary paralysis; which does not mean, of course, that his action did not have deep-reaching and durable effects, only that these did not represent a break with traditional American philosophy and ways of life. I have to say that my vision was coloured at the time by the fact that I was unconsciously seeking, at least at the beginning of this period, to transpose to America what I knew or thought I knew of Europe and to predict an evolution that would make the latter a prefiguration of the former, at any rate in the social context. The notion was only half true.

Another factor that influenced me a great deal was my study of the US labour movement, which I mentioned earlier, As the reader knows, I was already in profound sympathy with European trade unionism, and I extended that sympathy without any trouble to American unionism. Even today I think a powerful labour movement is essential to a smoothly functioning society, provided that its opposite number is organized management prepared to resist excessive demands and that government does not systematically tip the scales one way or the other.

The early years of the Roosevelt era saw a rapid development of the American labour movement, not so much craft unionism with its corporatist leanings, which had hitherto been the dominant form of labour organization in the United States and relied on a membership consisting almost entirely of skilled workers, as industrial unionism, still in its infancy, which set out to organize entire industries like steel and automobiles including their semi-skilled labour. This new type of unionism sought and obtained the support of government, initially at any rate, at a time when relations between the Roosevelt Administration and business interests were extremely strained. Relations between the unions and the government became less friendly, at times even hostile, when the crisis, or at least the worst of it, had been surmounted and Roosevelt tried to get on a normal footing with industry and banking.

What fascinated me in this study of American unionism was the kind of unconscious transformation a labour movement of European origin (many immigrants had brought over with them the fight-for-rights traditions they had absorbed in Europe) must have gone through to adapt to a completely different kind of industrial society. The subject was one, I felt, that warranted special thought. The outcome was a thesis I presented on my return to France. Bouglé had it printed by Presses Universitaires de France. It was titled *L'Evolution du syndicalisme aux Etats-Unis* [The development of trade unionism in the United States] and had a certain success due to the subject's novelty for the French reader.

In 1936 or 1937 my old mentor Georges Bourgin, the man who had done so much for me when I was eighteen, reviewed it in *Le Coopérateur de France*. Modesty prevents me from quoting from what he wrote. Let me simply say that he spoke affectionately of the tranquil assurance with which I was scaling the ladder of university initiation and of the calm and serenity with which I was building the edifice of my ideas, beliefs and wishes. Friendship can mislead. Never have I felt the 'tranquil assurance', the 'serenity' that Georges Bourgin attributed to me. My inner life of those years, and of the years to follow, has left me with a memory of turmoils that time alone, and often very long periods of time, could calm, of profound upheavals whose effects I was to have great difficulty in erasing. What is true is that those years were the most peaceful or, perhaps more accurately, the least externally agitated I have known, with an apparently stable framework in the shape of the university and clearly defined ambitions within my capabilities.

6

THE THIRTIES: FRIENDSHIPS AND INFLUENCES

I was twenty in 1931, twenty-eight when war broke out. This period of my life has left me with the memory of multifarious and all-consuming activities. Endless studies, all of them fascinating, took me to success in the economics *agrégation*. A total political commitment, up against a changing reality to which I reacted feverishly, led me first of all to pin my hopes on the formation of the first government of the *Front Populaire*, then at government headquarters to be a dissenting voice against what I considered to be the fundamental errors of the socialist experiment, and finally to break provisionally with the social-ist party.

By the end of the thirties I had only two things on my mind, France's economic and political decay and the advance of the German peril. I devoted most my spare time to active militancy with the aim of changing a course whose inevitable outcome I saw only too clearly.

What for me is perhaps the most important aspect of those years is that in study, deliberation and action my thought was taking shape. I was gradually building the storehouse of ideas, reactions and convic-tions that would stay with me for the rest of my life. If I try to identify the thread that guided me throughout this period, I have to say, self-important though it may sound, that it was the search for truth. Like everybody else, of course, I was carried away at times by unreasoning bursts of enthusiasm that distorted my perception of the world, but the illusion did not last long. An uneasy, then unhappy conscience would

44

oblige me to go back, often to square one, and reexamine completely the situation in which I stood in my action or my thinking.

My studies

Back in France in September 1933 after a year in America, I had made up my mind to take the philosophy *agrégation*. I was no longer so sure that philosophy was the only mental activity that mattered, but it still had such a hold over me that I did not seriously consider the possibility of changing my intellectual destination.

During the 1933–4 academic year I completed my qualifications to take the *agrégation:* the last part of my *licence* degree, my postgraduate diploma in philosophy, plus the diploma of the Institute of Ethnology. I worked on my Latin and Greek and attended the *agrégation* lectures at the Sorbonne. Bouglé employed me as librarian at the *Centre de Documentation Sociale*. It was in late 1933 or early 1934 that he introduced me to Charles Rist who had just set up the *Institut de Recherches Economiques et Sociales* (ISRES) in the Rue Michelet. He took me on as his economics editor.

When I met him, Rist was a big name. Aged sixty, he had behind him a long career in the university, at the Bank of France and in the world of business. This was the first time in my life that I had the opportunity to be near a man whose opponents, together with others a little short on judgment, said that he embodied capitalism, both national and international. And yet I, the young socialist, understandably over-awed, never had any difficulty in my relations with Charles Rist. More than that, reciprocal feelings of trust and even affection developed over the years. The explanation is simple. Charles Rist was a man of extreme generosity of heart and mind. Before becoming, in the eyes of economists and politicians, the exponent of economic liberalism, he had in his youth and his prime ardently championed the Dreyfusard cause, the *universités populaires* and Saint-Simonism. If reason urged him sometimes towards conservative positions, instinct more frequently inclined him to the left. His journal of the war and the occupation is a savage indictment of the Vichyite bourgeoisie, and in particular of certain business circles he knew well: 'I really think', he wrote, 'that the true characteristic of the French bourgeoisie is stupidity[1].' But above all, and this was more important than his personal preferences in economics and politics, he belonged to that generation

45

of academics, and intellectuals in general, who worshipped truth to the exclusion of almost everything else. Thus in the years following World War One he did not hesitate to become the champion of Keynes's ideas on the question of reparations, when almost the entirety of so-called enlightened opinion was frankly hostile to them. During the five or so years I worked with him I often happened to express in his presence ideas that were diametrically opposed to the theories he held dear. Not once did he utter the slightest word of reproach, never were our relations affected in any way.

Once I entered ISRES my financial difficulties were at an end. I forget what the pay was, but it was much more than enough to satisfy my wants, which were small. I had my meals at my parents' home, having rented for myself a small two-room flat in the Rue Thureau-Dangin in the 15th arrondissement. I could even give my mother a substantial sum each month, which was much appreciated as my father had been obliged at some point during these years to cease work because of deafness and general fatigue.

It was probably in 1934, during the summer or in the latter part of the year, that I decided to give up philosophy and try for the *agrégation* in political economy, the switch being an after-effect of my US experience. The Great Depression and its profound repercussions on politics and society, the Roosevelt experiments, France's all too evident decline and many other phenomena had convinced me that a knowledge of economics was essential to an understanding of the world and enlightened political action in consequence.

I made this decision fully aware of what I was letting myself in for. Since the philosophy and economics degrees were not recognized as equivalent in status, I had to start my studies from scratch like any *bac* holder just out of the *lycée*. Moreover, it was not possible in France to read economics without reading law at the same time. And in the law-economics coupling, law had the greater weight in the courses for the *licence* and the doctorate (except for the thesis). What it added up to was a three-year course for the *licence* and three *diplômes d'études supérieures* (of which one in civil law and one in law history and Roman law), a minimum of five years in all, without counting the doctorate thesis. I began this cycle in 1934–5 and finished it in 1939 with the completion of my thesis, which I was unable to defend before being called up.

Throughout those years I worked full time at ISRES in a relationship of trust and friendship with Charles Rist, whose chief collaborator I had become. I divided my time between the activities of the Institute as such and the writing of my thesis. In particular I was in charge, under Rist's supervision, of the Institute's main publication *L'Activité Economique* to which I frequently contributed articles on subjects close to the one I had chosen for my thesis. I often went to London to meet British economists of the London School of Economics, with which Rist's institute had a collaborative arrangement. I recall that my English friends used to meet on Wednesday evenings at the Reform Club in Pall Mall. Whenever I was in London I attended those meetings where we would discuss at length the economic and political issues of the day.

The purpose of my thesis was to analyse long-range economic movements and determine their causes. The idea had been given to me by Charles Rist and initially I developed certain themes he himself had investigated, essentially the correlation, which appeared to be close, between the general price level and precious metals output. But the statistical correlation was not enough for me; I sought an explanation. French economic literature on this subject, as on many others, was very scant indeed and I set out to explore the writings of the British, Scandinavian and Austrian economists[2]. The knowledge I derived from them was a discovery that enriched my thinking lastingly and made an economist of me; it led me to Keynes, directly or by roundabout ways. Finally, despite the objections of my thesis director, Gaëtan Pirou, who would have liked me to take a more empirical approach, I wrote a thesis in three parts, *Théorie, Histoire, Méthode*, and entitled it *Prix, Monnaie et Production: Essai sur les mouvements économiques de longue durée* [Prices, money and output: essay on long-run economic movements].

I shall say no more about the content of this work, which I have hardly opened since 1945. Today the scientific validity of some of the ideas I maintained in it seems arguable. Published by Presses Universitaires de France, the book had some success with young economists on account of its analysis of Anglo-Saxon doctrines as yet unknown or little known in France. The faculty awarded me a thesis prize. But I am getting too far ahead. In June 1939 I took the last of my doctorate exams. I was already attending the *agrégation* lectures given by Gaëtan Pirou and François Perroux, whose complex and profound thinking I admired. My thesis was finished and I was preparing to defend it when war broke out.

I was as happy as could be, living modestly but with all my desires satisfied. I was already a name among French economists; I had my own weekly spot on the radio; requests for articles poured in. There were no clouds on the horizon. Having taken my doctorate I would sit the next economics *agrégation*. I had a good chance of succeeding, if not at the first at least at the second attempt. Then I would go and teach for a few years out of Paris while continuing my own education. Already I had taken up mathematics.

At this point I feel I should say something more about the Marxist temptation to which, like nearly all the other young intellectuals of my generation, I was exposed during the thirties. Confronted with a crisis that was taking on the proportions of a world cataclysm, how could one fail to be intrigued by a theory that seemed to have foreseen everything, while the economists were vainly seeking a plausible explanation? I had read *The Communist Manifesto* with a certain fascination, as well as Karl Marx's historical writings, including *The Class Struggles in France* and *The Eighteenth Brumaire of Louis Bonaparte*. For a while, historical materialism seemed to me to account for the course of history as I knew it. Then I got down to a serious study of *Das Kapital*.

This is not the place for a critique of Marxism. I shall tell briefly how it affected me and why I turned away from it. I think my stay in America was more influential here than all the reading I did. The United States in 1932–3 was a picture of desolation, but despite the plunge in output and the relentless rise in unemployment one could not help feeling the power of this industrial giant and acquiring the conviction that relatively little was needed to put it back on its feet.

A modicum of experience and some knowledge of history were enough to cast doubt on the theory of an inevitable decline of capitalism due to a falling rate of profit. Even though the crisis of the thirties was of unprecedented gravity, the capitalist world had gone through situations in the past that appeared extremely serious to witnesses at the time and had emerged with its system augmented in vitality. How could one regard as irreversible and leading up to a complete economic and social transformation an experience that was no more than two or three years old, when the United States, to speak of only that country, had previously known long decades of unprecedented prosperity? A moment's thought and the idea that the world's working classes were condemned to 'increasing misery' stood revealed as having absolutely no foundation in history.

With Roosevelt's arrival in office I became progressively convinced that even though the capitalist system was imperfect, vulnerable and unstable, it could be made to work better. The events of the thirties, the revival in the British and American economies that occurred then, and especially the long period of continuing rapid growth that followed the end of World War Two, finally persuaded me there was nothing intrinsic in the capitalist system that doomed it to disappear. That men could destroy it through their ignorance, their errors and their folly was another matter; to me this seemed possible, if not probable.

Friendships and influences

My friends fell into two groups of different generations: there were those who had already produced a body of work and those who were getting started. Among those I can call my mentors were men of whom I have spoken already, Georges Bourgin, Célestin Bouglé, Charles Rist. But the man of that generation who influenced me most intellectually was Elie Halévy.

He is a little forgotten now, but I am certain that one day he will be seen to have played a very important part in the formation of modern thought. His best-known book is *L'Histoire du Peuple anglais au XIXe siècle*, which remains a classic for English and French specialists. One should also mention *La Formation du radicalisme philosophique*, the first of his major works. But what interested me the most by far, when I used to see him during the thirties, was his reflections on socialism, a subject that was to fascinate him throughout his life. He made it the theme of one of his lecture courses at the *Ecole Libre des Sciences Politiques*[3].

Halévy had little sympathy with Marxism, which he saw as more of an ideology than a scientific theory, but he was very attracted before the 1914–18 war to pre-Marxian French socialism, especially to Saint-Simonism of which one of the principles was 'solidarism', the idea of solidarity among the different social categories as opposed to class warfare. One might almost say that at that time he was a social democrat, although the originality of his mind defied any classification. His vision of things darkened after the war when the Communists had seized power in Russia. He did not equate communism with fascism, but at a time when so many people of the left remained blind he quickly understood that communism was a form of tyranny.

His reflections led him to think that there was an internal contradiction in socialism. On the one hand socialism appeared as a generous movement whose origins went back to the French Revolution, which professed an ardent desire for the progress of liberty and sought to push democracy to its furthest point by overthrowing the last remaining bastion, the power of money. On the other, once victorious as it was in Russia, it took the shape of an omnipotent bureaucracy that imprisoned the citizen in a system depriving him of virtually all power of decision and any possibility of personal initiative. Everything was nationalized; the life of the individual, both public and private, was at the mercy of faceless functionaries. What stood clearly revealed in Soviet socialism was present in embryo, Halévy thought, in the programmes of the West European socialists: they were all organization, nationalization, equalization. Furthermore, however internationalist in its phraseology, socialism is set on a path down which it slides irresistibly into nationalism. This tendency, often invisible when it is in opposition, becomes apparent when it gains power and seeks to introduce programmes incompatible with the international environment; it then tries to isolate itself from external influences by means of exchange controls, protectionist measures, and so on.

In 1936 I personally sensed the contradiction of which Elie Halévy spoke. Though I did not subscribe wholly to this view of things, it did influence me strongly at the time of the *Front Populaire* and later, after the war, when I took up again with the socialist party, which I had left in 1937. After long experience of the socialists I would add today that, confronted with the consequences of their economic policy and compelled to choose between isolation in an autarkic-type nationalism and relinquishment of that policy, they invariably opt for the latter and beat a hasty retreat. It is probably because the vast majority of them are more attached to political freedom than to uncertain economic theories. This attachment became stronger in the post-war period when socialism in western Europe underwent a profound change. Expressions like 'revolution' and 'dictatorship of the proletariat' no longer represented something definable, assuming they ever did; they took on the nature of magic incantations uttered in order to summon the faithful. Some countries' socialist parties have never used them or, like the German socialist party, have explicitly given them up. Socialist parties have become Social Democratic parties. When political circumstances have brought them to power, in Britain, France, Germany and elsewhere, they have not, after an initial period of indecision, behaved very differently from the so-called bourgeois parties.

I had my first conversation with Elie Halévy probably in 1934. It was

Bouglé, I think, who introduced me to him. I recall that he talked to me in one of our early conversations about an article I had published in the *Revue d'histoire moderne* under the title *Troubles provoqués en France par la disette de 1816–1817* [Troubles caused in France by the dearth of 1816–1817]. This was a résumé of certain parts of the thesis I had written for the diploma of the *Ecole Pratique des Hautes Etudes*. I soon became an intimate of the Halévy home. As of 1936, if not continuously at least over long periods, I spent nearly all my Sundays there, drawn as much by Elie Halévy's force of intellect, by his ever alert critical faculties that would not allow him to settle automatically for established truths, as by his kindness and that of his wife Florence to the very young man I then was. Thanks to him I discovered a body of political literature of which I was unaware, notably Montesquieu and Tocqueville. I took his death in 1937 as a great personal loss. After the war my ties of friendship with Florence Halévy became still closer. I introduced to her my young wife whom I had just married in the United States. Florence guided her first steps in France and often came to see us at Neuilly, where we were living at the time. Her death in 1956 affected both of us the same way as that of a dearly loved parent.

It was in the thirties that by one of life's hazards I found myself part of a small group of people slightly older than I but in fact contemporaries, who became my mentors for a time. I shall speak first of Raymond Aron whom I got to know in 1934 or 1935 and who captivated me instantly with the brilliance of his intelligence and the power of his analytical mind. We went through a rough patch to begin with, but after that we became close friends. In the three or four years that preceded the war we saw each other nearly every day. We were united in our hatred of Hitlerism and fascism, in our indignation and dismay over the absurd economic policies of the French governments, whether right- or left-wing, in our feeling of solidarity with the Spanish republicans. In a word, our moral and intellectual universes, our systems of values were the same, not only as a whole but even in detail.

In 1935 Aron introduced me to Eric Weil, a German philosopher who had chosen to leave his country and was leading a hand-to-mouth existence in the suburb of Clamart, with his wife Anne and his sister-in-law Catherine. Weil gave me German lessons for two years. As Aron has said somewhere, he had an encyclopaedic knowledge, not only of philosophy but of almost everything. I learned an enormous amount from him. We used to have interminable discussions. At first he had no trouble gaining the upper hand, but little by little I learned to hold my own. I remember one of these verbal contests that took place, on the eve of war, at Argentière in the valley of Chamonix, where we were both spending a few weeks' holiday. The discussion went on far into the night. I no longer remember what it was about, but each of us was as fiercely determined as the other. Never toying with ideas, a man of complete intellectual integrity, Eric Weil produced a large body of philosophical work the significance of which I find hard to under-stand, having given up philosophy myself more than forty years ago. But philosopher friends tell me it counts in the history of ideas.

It was through Eric Weil, I think, that I got to know Alexandre Kojève. I do not recollect having seen him before the autumn of 1938 when I first attended the seminar on Hegelian phenomenology he was conducting at the *Ecole Pratique des Hautes Etudes* in the Sorbonne. The meetings took place on Friday evenings. There I found not only Weil and Aron, but also the psychoanalyst Jacques Lacan, a Jesuit, Père Fessard, and a few others. A very young woman, Denyse Mosseri, who came from Egypt, was a regular participant; she was to become a very great friend whom I have gone on seeing throughout my life and for whom I have always had much affection. First of all Kojève would speak, displaying great rhetorical skill that reflected precision and rigour of thought; then there would be a discussion in which the Catholic and pagan interpretations of Hegel frequently clashed. When the session was over, we would go and have a drink in the Place de la Sorbonne followed by dinner in Les Halles at a restaurant called Benjamin, which disappeared during the war or just after. I generally went home by metro with Kojève. My journey would end at Porte de Versailles, while Kojève would go on by bus to Vanves where he lived. We often stopped off *en route* at Gare Montparnasse to eat chocolates in a little shop we had discovered somehow or other; at Porte de Versailles we had a last beer before going our separate ways; and all the while we talked of philosophy, the world, the coming war and many other things.

I saw Kojève again in 1945 when I was Director of External Economic Relations in the Ministry of the National Economy. He came to see me one day and explained that he wanted to get into the civil service. I had him appointed *chargé de mission*[4] in the ministry, where he was to stay until his death in 1968. Valued counsellor of Olivier Wormser, Bernard Clappier and many others, he enjoyed considerable authority there.

Every human being has several facets, displaying one or another of them depending on whom he is with or the situation of the moment.

Kojève had many more than the other people I have known. He could be the perfect French civil servant during the day and then go home in the evening and create a colossal corpus which I am told plays a very great role in contemporary philosophical discussion. Conversing in his own circle of friends he was a man of very great independence of mind, paradoxical, at times cynical; at the international meetings in which he took part he became the fierce defender of the French government's positions. To this day I do not know who he was really. For a time he used to say he was Stalin's conscience, but I always took that statement to be part of the game he liked to play.

When I try to recall the immediate prewar scene the three names my mind latches on to among my contemporaries are Raymond Aron, Eric Weil and Alexandre Kojève. To them I owe a great part of what I think, of what I am. In spite of our disagreements we were fundamentally as one in the way we felt about the world around us and the course that events were taking. Given that war was inevitable, the thing was to win it and put an end to the monstrosity that went by the name of Hitlerism.

It was also at that time that I met Olivier Wormser. A friendship formed that was to last until his death. Our relationship over nearly fifty years can be likened to a long dialogue in which I was able to appreciate his keen and constructive intelligence, his sharp critical mind, his amused but never resigned scepticism that sometimes checked me when I was tempted to take extreme stands. I was to encounter him, at the different stages of my life, in the succession of eminent posts he held, from the economic and financial directorship at the Foreign Affairs Ministry to the governorship of the Bank of France, not forgetting the Moscow and Bonn embassies.

The war was to disperse this group of friends. It completely changed my own existence. But before I speak of that time when the fate of the free world hung in the balance, I have to go back a few years and say something about my political and journalistic activities during the period from 1933 to 1939, which I conducted alongside my work as student and researcher.

Political and journalistic activities

On my return from the United States in September 1933 I resumed my socialist party activities and began to militate again in the *Quinzième*

Section and in the socialist student movement. I renewed contact with my friends in *Révolution Constructive*. I also attended meetings of socialist intellectuals held each month at the home of Henri Lévy-Bruhl in the Boulevard Raspail where I regularly encountered, among others, the sociologist and ethnologist Marcel Mauss, for whom I felt much respect and admiration.

As far as I remember, the internal politics of the socialist party, the infighting, the coalitions that were formed and unformed in order to dominate the party, did not interest me much. That was why I ceased now to play any important part in the activities of *Révolution Constructive*, which had become deeply involved in this continual struggle. But I was still a socialist and said so. How did I think at that time? I have no reason to believe that, until 1934 at any rate, my thinking was anything other than conventional socialist thinking. I was a little better acquainted with world affairs than the average socialist militant or intellectual, but we were cast from the same mould. It was my experience of America that set me apart, broadening my horizon and enabling me to compare political and economic developments on either side of the Atlantic. But I did not draw from my first contact with the United States all the conclusions that a better trained and less biassed mind would have drawn and that I would reach a little later.

The best testimony to what I was saying and writing then is the brochure, mentioned earlier, entitled *Les Expériences Roosevelt*, which I wrote for the Lévy-Bruhl circle. This small work represented, apart from its information content which was all but unique in France at the time, an affort to interpret contemporary developments in the United States in terms of European socialism, with which, to be honest, they had little to do.

What is rather extraordinary is that this youthful work was to be of great importance in my life. One day, it must have been in 1934 or early 1935, I got a letter from Léon Blum, whom I did not know but greatly admired from afar, telling me that he had happened to read the opuscule and thought it very good. He asked me to drop in on him at the offices of *Le Populaire*[5]. I lost no time in doing so. I found a simple, charming, quietly intelligent man who put me instantly at my ease. I have forgotten exactly what the conversation was about, but the upshot (on that occasion or on another very shortly after) was that Léon Blum asked me to take charge of the economics column of *Le Populaire*; this would run to one page weekly, plus feature articles from time to time. The editor of the newspaper Oscar Rosenfeld, who later on was never to forgive me for my dissidence at the time of the *Front*

Populaire government, turned out to be as friendly as Léon Blum; this marked the beginning of a collaboration which was to last two or three years and which took me to the paper's offices several times a week.

The situation in which I then found myself may seem paradoxical: I was working simultaneously for *Le Populaire* and for ISRES. I was the collaborator of both Léon Blum and Charles Rist, the socialist leader and the champion of economic liberalism. Neither of them saw anything untoward in this. I enjoyed very great freedom at *Le Populaire* and, as I have already said, Charles Rist, a former Dreyfusard and impelled by violently antifascist convictions, leaned instinctively to the left. In any case, I reconciled my different activities without difficulty. I remember that Bouglé, to whom I had spoken of Léon Blum's offer, congratulated me warmly and urged me to accept, slapping me affectionately on the shoulder in the characteristic way he had. So from 1934 to 1936 I was a young socialist with liberalist leanings, whose conviction had not yet been put to the acid test of his political party's arrival in government.

Yet there was plenty to exercise my mind in those troubled years, with the consolidation of Hitler's power in Germany, the agitation of the leagues and the formation of fascist movements in France, the growing admiration of an ever larger segment of the French bourgeoisie for dictatorial governments that knew how to 'keep order' in their countries, the development of a left-wing pacifist movement that was partly responsible for France's utter failure to react to the Hitlerian peril, and the emergence within the socialist party itself of a fascist-inspired movement, neosocialism. I knew a lot of people belonging to very different circles who tried to draw me towards this or that group in order to effect this or that amalgam of the most discordant sympathies. I attended meetings that brought together people of the left and of the right, sometimes even the extreme right, with the avowed aim of overcoming apparent antagonisms and establishing real unity of the country. It did not take me long to discover that, consciously or unconsciously, these groups were moving towards a French-style fascism. Antiparliamentarianism, drawing strength from the Stavisky scandal and its aftermath, was one of their favourite themes. After a few of these meetings I withdrew into the socialist party where I felt spiritually at ease. My doubts about the party's goals and policy on the economic front, as well as in foreign affairs and defence, had not yet crystallized to the point of being a serious embarrassment.

Concerning these groups of people of every stripe who claimed to be seeking solutions that transcended the limits of parties, I shall simply say a word about the one that was to produce what was called *Le Plan du 9 juillet*, the title deriving from the fact that its drafting was completed on July 9, 1934. The mastermind of this endeavour was Jules Romains who was perhaps seeking characters for his *Hommes de bonne volonté* and who wrote a foreword to the plan. In it he paid tribute to the young people assembled under the plan's auspices and belonging to the following movements and organizations: trade unionism, SFIO socialism, neosocialists, young radicals, agrarian party, *Croix de Feu, Jeunesses Patriotes, Jeune République*[6]. The result was pitiful: a jumble of generalities displaying ignorance of the real problems – the Depression and the Hitler menace – accompanied by appeals to public spiritedness and virtue. Pre-Pétainism, as it were. After attending a few meetings, I parted company with the group and refused to sign the manifesto.

Léon Blum

During those years from 1934 to 1936 Léon Blum exerted a strong influence on me. For him I felt the admiration that the great man of the French left was bound to inspire in the young socialist I was then. I was also mightily impressed by his vast knowledge of literature; when I met him at the *Populaire* offices we began by talking about the economic and political situation in France, then I listened in surprise as he discussed Stendhal, of whose work he was a connoisseur, Goethe and other literary figures. It seems to me now that he had a special regard and affection for me. I remember his telephoning me one Sunday morning in 1935 at my parents' home, where I happened to be at the time, to ask what I thought of the decree-laws which Pierre-Etienne Flandin, then President of the Council[7], had just issued and which aimed to organize French industry along corporatist lines. It made a big impression on my father and mother that the leader of the socialist party should ask their son his opinion on an important matter of state.

Nevertheless I broke with him in 1937, as I shall recount later, because of a profound disagreement on his economic and foreign policies. My feelings had prompted me to attack the socialists bitterly in the press and I knew this had affected him. I am not sorry that I expressed my disagreement, but perhaps I should have done so with more discretion and tact. I was carried away by youthful ardour and knew nothing of moderation as yet. Later I was to regret my rough behaviour then, for Léon Blum was a kind and generous man, a man of distinction one might say. We came together again after the war and I went fairly often on Sunday mornings out to Jouy-en-Josas where he lived, but the spell was spoken and I was never again to experience the feeling of trust that existed between us in 1934–6.

During those years Léon Blum expressed several times a week in the columns of *Le Populaire* his conception of socialist doctrine in relation to events of the day, building up a certain orthodoxy that was to be accepted by the great majority of the party's militants, but opposed by minorities to the left or the right of the movment. The opposition from the left, led by men like Zyromski and Marceau Pivert, was comparatively moderate and not insensitive to the prestige and authority of Léon Blum. The opposition from the right led by Marcel Déat, after Renaudel had left the scene, was to become more and more radical and drift to positions increasingly removed from democratic socialism. As for Léon Blum, he was in the great tradition of French socialism, of which he shared the humanism, the generosity, the tolerance and also the contradictions. He was the worthy successor of Jaurès, a Marxist in moderation and a great admirer of the French Revolution, the excesses of which he did not know about or preferred to ignore, seeing in it only justice and liberty. The transition from parliamentary democracy to democratic socialism was never clear in his mind, I thought. One might say, as Saint Thomas did of grace and freedom, that he had the impression of holding both ends of the chain, democracy and socialism, without the least idea of how they would come together one day, what the intermediate links would be that would permit the junction of the two great principles. In this he was no different from the other socialists I have known.

He waged a relentless fight for both democracy and socialism. In 1920 at the Congress of Tours, the assertion of democracy as the supreme value had finally resulted in a split with the socialists identifying themselves with the October Revolution and in the formation of the SFIO. The socialist party had remained a party in which freedom prevailed, where militants were free to hold opinions different from those of the majority and to go on voicing their opposition within the party even after a decision had been taken. The decisions themselves were the outcome of a democratic process that left nothing to be desired.

In the fight for democracy, the socialists were first and foremost republicans who made common cause with other republicans on their right when democracy seemed endangered, as in 1934–6 with the agitation of the leagues. The fight for socialism was something else.

What was socialism then in the minds of the left-wing militants? Something complex that combined traces of pre-Marxian French socialist ideas with the Marxist tradition itself, according to which true freedom, as opposed to 'formal freedom', necessitated collective appropriation of the means of production and exchange. The myth of revolution sprang up in socialist doctrine, since nothing short of revolution would permit this transformation of society. Revolution required the conquest of power by the proletariat, which the socialists were inclined to extend to all workers, by contrast with orthodox Marxism which confined it to manual workers. The democratic socialism of the thirties also maintained that to ensure the transition a dictatorship of the proletariat would be necessary over a certain period, carefully left unspecified. Revolution, conquest of power, dictatorship of the proletariat, the party commented endlessly on those terms, while taking care not to clarify them for fear of alienating the moderates that formed the bulk of the socialist voters.

If I linger over this reminder of what socialism used to be in those days the reason is that it represented the intellectual environment in which part of my thinking was steeped, until the break took place in 1936–7. Another part of my thinking consisted in an economic philosophy I was forming for myself at Charles Rist's institute and which leaned increasingly towards a kind of economic liberalism. I am still somewhat astonished today that I was able to live for two or three years in two completely separate worlds. Yet when I think about it, the explanation seems relatively simple. Paradoxical as it may sound, the socialists of those days had almost no knowledge of economics. The party had never had any hand in public affairs; it was sufficient to subscribe nominally to certain quasi-theological notions in order to remain within bounds. Léon Blum himself was not really interested in economic matters and prepared to rely on his collaborators, of whom I was one. I never felt any constraint. Things would change in 1936 after the victory of the *Front Populaire*.

Up to that time one of Blum's chief concerns was to preserve socialist purity, to see that it was not adulterated by alliances with non-socialist parties. Discussions within the party were essentially concerned with the question of 'participation', that is to say the socialists' participation in governments that were predominantly bourgeois. That question had come into prominence after the parliamentry election of 1924, and then that of 1932, which had returned left-wing majorities built around the radical party. It was then that Blum was able to give free rein to his dialectics, establishing in 1926 a distinction between the *conquest* and the *exercise* of power. The conquest of power was the act by which the party would take over political power in conditions that would enable the system of property ownership to be changed. But there was liable to be a long wait for this, with the danger that the workers might become disheartened and lose their confidence in the party. This was where the 'exercise of power' came in. It represented a halfway house between outright opposition and unbridled opportunism. 'The exercise of power was to correspond to a governmental experiment conducted by the socialists that would require the party to take on its responsibilities for a specific mission in a regime that was still capitalistic, but in conditions of clarity. Léon Blum could thus condemn ministerial participation that was not based on an adequate position of relative strength[8].' It was to be May 1936 before the balance of power seemed right to Léon Blum and to the party leadership in general. Moreover one cannot see how at that time the socialists could have refused to form the government. The issues had become too serious for it to be possible to get away with exercises in dialectics, however subtle. The threat from Germany, the rise of fascism, or rather of fascist thinking, at home, the deepening economic crisis in France, by comparison with other developed countries like the United States and Britian where things were looking up, demanded that the socialists assume the responsibilities that devolved upon the biggest party of the French left. The need for a compromise among the different left-wing movements was becoming evident, even to those socialists who most feared the idea of discrediting themselves with 'bourgeois parties'.

A final word about the socialist stance on a specific point: nationalization. Though it may seem curious today, the socialism of the twenties and thirties was little concerned with what was later to become one of the party's essential demands, if not its chief rallying call. The reason for this was the socialists' attitude towards the state, which stemmed from one of the fundamental Marxist theories. Until the system of property ownership had changed, the state would necessarily be the expression of the law and order of the bourgeoisie. It would be useless to wait for concessions which the struggling workers had been unable to wrench from private capitalism. A few nationalizations were not going to change anything. But pressure for nationalization was too strong within the labour movement for Léon Blum to be able to ignore it completely. So he embarked on one of those subtle dialectical exercises in which he excelled. I forget exactly when but probably in the thirties, he proposed a distinction between 'nationalizations' and 'socializations'. 'Socializations' could not come about until the working class had taken over power and set about changing society. Meanwhile, in the different phases of the 'exercise of power ', nationalizations could do some good by stimulating the economy and alleviating the plight of the worst off. But in no way would they alter the capitalist nature of ownership. State capitalism versus private capitalism was perhaps not quite 'six of one and half a dozen of the other', but only the naïve could think that nationalization would change anything fundamental in the system's operation.

Until 1936 I was in broad agreement with Léon Blum's options. In particular, I kept clear of two countermovements that might have appealed to the moderate I was, neosocialism and *planisme*, the latter being the movement of those who favoured economic planning.

Neosocialism, which as its name suggests aimed to renew traditional socialism, was the early thirties version of what used to be called 'revisionism', a movement that set out to revise Marxist theories. No, the state was not in every instance the political expression of capitalism; it reflected a balance of power. By joining forces with the middle classes, the working class could tip the balance in its favour and wrest from the state decisions that would lastingly change the manner in which the economy functioned. Win over the middle classes and use the state to benefit them and the working class, these were the watchwords of the socialist right wing until 1933. In effect they amounted to a stance in favour of 'participation'.

In 1933 things changed. Marcel Déat took over the leadership of revisionism, which was rechristened neosocialism. Its sorry history is well known. When I met Déat in 1933 he seemed destined for the heights. Graduate of the *Ecole Normale*, an excellent speaker, endowed with a fertile mind always in motion, his personality contrasted sharply with the mediocrity of most of the socialist leaders. For quality of the written and spoken word he could be compared with Léon Blum. His rivalry with the latter, for both doctrinal and personal reasons, was to become one of the causes of his downfall. The contrast between the upper middle class Jew and the brilliant intellectual from the lower middle class could not have been more marked. One could elaborate on this theme indefinitely.

Marcel Déat was fascinated by the growing ascendancy of the Italian and German systems of fascist nationalism. He knew nothing of the Anglo-Saxon world, to which (especially England) Léon Blum inclined almost instinctively. 1933 was the year in which Hitler established his power in Germany. The contagious effect on a part of public opinion in the neighbouring countries was beginning to make itself felt. In contradistinction to the traditional internationalism of the socialist parties, the neosocialists were being drawn towards the assertion of national reality as an essential phenomenon of modern times. This reality would be embodied by a strong state. By means of this state, which was no longer the bourgeois state of the Marxists but a state dominated by the working class and the middle classes, it would have be possible to construct an intermediate economy, which would have ceased to be a capitalist economy even if it were not yet a socialist economy. The neosocialists split away in the autumn of 1933, taking with them a few members of parliament and a minority of militants. They would have little influence until the war. After the defeat of 1940 they entered ignominiously, under Marcel Déat's leadership, into a close collaboration with the Germans. Déat's new party, *Rassemblement National Populaire*, would openly wish for Germany's victory.

Even in the days when the neosocialists were ostensibly no more than socialist moderates, I was never drawn to them. I can see two complementary reasons for this. First, I was viscerally antifascist and antinazi. Already in 1933 when Léon Blum, after hearing Marcel Déat, stood up in the Socialist Congress and exclaimed 'I am horrified', I was in complete agreement with him. The neosocialists' attraction to fascist regimes was obvious to me. Second, when I broke with the orthodox socialists a few years later, I quickly shifted to liberal stances. The idea of moving first to the neosocialists never occured to me.

Another movement, which emerged on the left in 1934, was less far removed from my thinking at the time; I refer to *planisme*. It should be remembered that the crisis years of 1933–6 saw the greatest intellectual confusion in France and in other countries. No one could understand the origin and causes of the depression that was devastating the world. As soon as a new explanation turned up it tended to become a fashion. Minds famished for certainty seized on it for a while. Such was the case in 1934 with *planisme*, a doctrine that Henri de Man had got the Belgian socialists to adopt in 1933. Conceived as a reaction against traditional Marxism, rejecting both class warfare and collective appropriation of the means of production and exchange, at least in the latter's extreme form of total socialization, it advocated the creation of a mixed economy with a public and a private sector. In the months that followed their adoption by the Belgian socialist party the theories of Henri de Man won a number of adepts in France. My friends of *Révolution Constructive* took them on board, as did a group of intellectuals from the *Ecole Polytechnique*. More seriously, the CGT[9] became a convert to *planisme* for a time and even produced an economic plan in 1934. I remember attending a number of meetings on the subject. I was even taken with the idea of a plan myself for a while, but soon gave it up as I did not see how the plan would help us over the crisis.

Perhaps I owe the reader a word of explanation here as to why the idea of an economic plan, which I rejected in 1934, compelled my acceptance after the war. The answer is that, like many 'isms', *planisme* is an equivocal notion. During the war and the years that followed, its sense became perfectly clear. The idea was to allocate scarce resources – labour, raw materials, foreign exchange, plant and equipment – among the uses that appeared the most important. For this it was necessary to draw up an order of priorities. And one could do so without being *dirigiste*, i.e. an interventionist on principle and all the more necessarily a socialist; for a liberalist, the plan was needed only if allocation of the means of production through the play of market forces proved impossible. By contrast, prewar *planisme* was an ideological construct. It aimed to replace the market forces at a time when these could still function and would have yielded the results sought (economic expansion, reduction of employment) if only the necessary conditions had been met. And I was beginning to sense what those conditions were. My American experience had taught me that in certain circumstances government has to prime the economy by injecting purchasing power through a budget deficit that may attain considerable proportions. My frequent trips to England and my regular conversations with British economists, notably those from the London School of Economics, had made me understand that sterling's devaluation in 1931 was having the expected effects and that the first requisite for getting France's economy started again was to bring the exchange rate down to a level that would make French exports competitive on world markets.

It was with those ideas in mind that I embarked on the *Front Populaire* experience in the spring of 1936.

7

LE FRONT POPULAIRE

In May 1936 Jules Moch, who had just been appointed Secretary of the Cabinet, asked me to come and see him and offered me a post as *chargé de mission* to Léon Blum and himself. At that time I was doing my military service as a meteorologist and was stationed at Mont Valérien[1]. Moch requested and easily obtained my secondment to Matignon[2]; it was understood that my collaboration with Charles Rist would continue.

My disagreement with Léon Blum

For the first time in my life I was faced with a difficult choice: to remain loyal to politicians who trusted me, in full awareness of the errors they were committing, or to voice my dissent and possibly be obliged to break with the socialist party.

I decided first of all to speak my mind to Léon Blum and Jules Moch but otherwise keep secret my growing differences of view with the *Front Populaire* government regarding its economic and foreign policies. Where foreign policy was concerned, I was violently and emotionally opposed to nonintervention in Spain which I considered, rightly as events turned out, a fool's game. Even today I fail to understand how the western democracies could have let the Germans and Italians openly support Franco and not come to the aid of the Spanish Republic. I remember a conversation I had with Raymond Aron in July or August 1936 at Le Val-André, where Bouglé had invited me to spend some time. We had high hopes that aid would be sent to Madrid, we were following events from day to day. Those hopes were soon to be dashed. In fairness to Léon Blum, the radicals, who were in his government, would probably not have agreed to overt intervention. In the socialist party itself there was a strong pacifist current. Finally the British, from whom Léon Blum did not want to become estranged, were embarked on the suicidal policy that was to lead to Munich and the war.

Now the economic considerations. I took up my duties at Matignon convinced that the deflationary policy applied during the crisis by different governments, particularly the Laval government in 1935, could only aggravate the situation. I was not hostile to austerity measures but these, I felt, had to be accompanied by a franc devaluation to bring French prices into line with world prices. The Gold Bloc, I thought, was an absurdity. How could the franc maintain its pre-Depression gold parity when sterling had been devalued in 1931 and the dollar in 1933? In March or April 1935 I had written enthusiastically about the Belgian franc's devaluation in the columns of *Le Populaire*, earning myself a spate of indignant letters from socialist militants accusing me of wanting to save capitalism. So I was expecting the socialist government to devalue the franc soon after coming to power and, for a while at least, to practise a policy of wage restraint. Imagine my disappointment when I found Léon Blum and his ministers as steadfast as preceding governments in their refusal to touch the exchange rate!

In August 1936 I published in the weekly *L'Europe Nouvelle* an article on the government's economic policy. I was *chargé de mission* at Matignon and as such required to exercise a measure of restraint. In that article, nevertheless, I did not conceal the fact that I was hoping for a franc devaluation. Recalling that the government had declared its intention to act within the established framework of the capitalist regime and that the supreme law of the capitalist economy was profit and its mainspring the expectation of profit, I wondered why France did not follow the successful example of many other countries and try to redress her economy by way of devaluing the currency. Devaluation had become even more necessary and more urgent owing to the recent wage and payroll tax increases which, at 18–20 per cent of total wage costs, had further aggravated the situation in the business sector, especially on the export front where production cost differentials between France and most of the other industrial countries had widened again.

The government, as we know, finally brought itself to devalue the franc at the end of September 1936 but the devaluation did not have the effects expected, possibly because it was too small, essentially because it was carried out in the context of a general economic policy that tended to restrain production. In May 1937, one month before the fall of the first Léon Blum government, I wrote in L'Europe Nouvelle that there had been no real upturn in the economy and that unemployment would remain high if there were no change in policy.

The few articles I published then, from June 1936 to June 1937, are but a pale reflection of what I was saying at Matignon and of the memos I wrote to Léon Blum and Jules Moch. Unfortunately I kept no copies of those memos nor any records of meetings. I do remember, however, that meetings took place several times a week in Moch's office and that I was frequently cast in the role of the opponent. At the outset, I behaved like an economist with liberalist leanings; I was for a big devaluation, coupled with austerity measures, and against the introduction of exchange controls, an idea that was favoured by most of my socialist friends. To me it seemed absurd to erect monetary barriers at the frontier, the problem being at least as much to bring capital back into France as to prevent it from getting out. But very soon, probably in the last months of 1936, it became clear to me that the cardinal error of the Front Populaire government was the legislation on the forty-hour week. This is what I stressed in May 1938 in an article published in the English review Economica – here I am indebted to Raymond Barre for reminding me of it – in which I analysed the events of the two preceding years and tried to determine the reasons for the failure of the Front Populaire government's economic policy.

Whatever the government's initial miscalculations, the situation could certainly have been quickly redressed had it not been for the introduction of a statutory workweek of 40 hours by virtue of legislation passed by parliament in June 1936, under popular pressure, and phased into effect between the end of 1936 and May 1937. By the latter date the whole of French industry was subject to this law; employers were formally prohibited from asking their employees to work more than forty hours a week. The restriction was absolute. Overtime was prohibited, except in cases of force majeure. The intention was excellent, as it nearly always is in political programmes, but

the result was counterproductive. The government's aim was to eliminate unemployment in order to improve the workers' living standards.
In the event, the measure choked off the economic growth that had
started after the devaluation in 1936.

The fact is that France at that time did not have an unemployment
problem comparable with that of the United States, Britain or Germany. The population census of March 1936 showed that only 4 per
cent of the labour force was unemployed. The maximum workweek
was cut from forty-eight to forty hours, i.e. by 17 per cent, and the
average workweek by 10 per cent. Unemployment and short-time
working vanished almost overnight, at least in the key industries.
Thus, paradoxically on the face of it, the French economy in the early
part of 1937 found itself in a state of full employment. With real
output levels not much above their Depression low point, all the
labour resources of the country were being utilized, with no possibility
of expansion other than that contingent on a problematic increase in
productivity. A survey made at the time shows that during the first half
of 1937 a large number of industries were unable to fill their orders. In
the *Economica* article I wrote:

We can now explain without difficulty what happened in the spring of 1937.
The devaluation in September 1936 set the stage for an expansion of the
economy, which began with a rapid pickup in production of investment
goods. In the ordinary way this should have been followed by an increase in
consumer goods output, with the stimulus of the purchasing power distributed by the investment goods industries. But the reduction of work hours
caused an artificial scarcity of labour in those industries and consequently cut
short the recovery[3].

In the October 16, 1937 issue of *L'Europe Nouvelle* I expressed my
astonishment that this legislation, when at the bill stage, had not
encountered any serious objections founded on the need to increase
output rapidly, and stressed the error a reduction of work hours
represented for a country desirous of raising the living standards of its
population and obliged to make a rearmament effort disproportionate
to the strength of its economy. Truth to tell, there were many who
believed in the absurd myth that output could be increased *ad libitum*
without much additional effort. This was the theory of plenty, the
childishness of which I vehemently denounced.

Since the fall of Léon Blum's first government in June 1937 I had
been able to express myself freely in public. At the request of Camille
Chautemps, the new President of the Council whom I met no more

than once or twice, I had stayed on at Matignon. I left in March 1938 when Blum's second cabinet was formed. In the meantime I had broken completely with my socialist friends. Each week in *L'Europe Nouvelle* I wrote articles in which I criticized, sometimes violently, the economic policies of the *Front Populaire*.

L'Europe Nouvelle

L'Europe Nouvelle, to which I contributed regularly in those fateful years, was a weekly run by Madeleine Le Verrier. Its editor Pertinax (his real name was André Géraud) had come from *L'Echo de Paris*[4]. *L'Europe Nouvelle* was a forum for people of all political backgrounds, left and right. Their common denominator was antifascism, anti-Hitlerism, the conviction that war was coming, that in view of Hitlerian imperialism it was inevitable. We therefore had to get ready and, since we had fallen way behind, make a gigantic effort. Everything, economic and social policy included, had to come second to the preparations for war. I said as much in an article published in March 1938, from which I now propose to quote fairly extensively since it well sums up my thinking at the time.

Today, I think, there is not one Frenchman who fails to see, disregards or underestimates the dangers that threaten our country, not only in its modes of life but in its very existence as a great nation and an autonomous political community. There is not one who can close his eyes to possibilities of aggression which the events of these past weeks have invested with a tangibility unknown till now[5]. The will to defend, as Frenchmen, the political sovereignty of France is joined, among those who are hostile to totalitarian ideologies, by the will to stem the advance of those ideologies in the world.

It is quite simply a matter of whether the commitment to national defence will be sufficiently widespread and sufficiently binding to secure an endeavour to bring about, whatever sacrifices are needed, the internal conditions, financial and economic, that will ensure the effectiveness of this national defence.

The fact is that the French economy is organized according to a system known as capitalist. The essence of the system is that it is left to individuals, to enterprises as the economists say, to employers in the simple vernacular, to satisfy social needs. The greater or lesser satisfaction of those needs, the economic power of France, the stability of its public finance, all this depends on the result of these individual activities.

It is not a question here of a moral judgment on capitalism. I am not saying that this regime is right, that it is the best conceivable regime, or even that it is the only regime possible. What I believe to be essential in the present situation is precisely the possibility for men whose value judgments are fundamentally different of agreeing on the minimum requirements of national defence and resistance to Hitlerian and fascist expansion ...

First, the capitalist regime is based on the activity of the private entrepreneur, second, no one can think at present of changing that regime; it would seem that the conclusion is self-evident and that unanimous or near-unanimous agreement can be reached on the conditions that will enable the present system to function acceptably.

The young man I was then had come a long way in two or three years. I was still a socialist, or rather a social democrat, but the approaching war was causing me to draw in my horns. For me the absolute priority was national defence and preparation for war. The social issues which for several years had claimed the entire attention of the French were no longer priorities. We had to create the conditions for optimal functioning of the economic system that was ours. Above all we had to work. But it did not seem to me that these prerequisites had been met.

Indeed, if the essence of capitalism is the private activity of the employer, that activity can be exercised only if it is allowed sufficient room for manoeuvre ...

In economic life there are opportunities that come only once. Who does not know that if in the years 1936–7 French industry could not meet demand at home and abroad, it was largely because it was unable not only to deliver promptly but to set terms of delivery? Who does not see that if the rationalization and mechanization now essential to the French economy is to be carried out, this will necessitate a displacement of manpower that will have to be effected as rapidly as possible? Who does not see that the expansion of French economic activity is liable to be hampered by collective agreements that are too stringent or by welfare legislation that is too punctilious?

More importantly, economic expansion in a capitalist regime requires that opportunities for profit exist for the entrepreneur, for the individual who initiates an operation. Here again the issue is not one of justice, of saying that profit opportunities should be commensurate with the risks incurred by the entrepreneur. All that matters is to create the conditions for a rapid development of the economy. And this presupposes the possibility of making large profits.

Moreover the workers have to realize that no welfare legislation, however egalitarian, will bring them the sum of material advantages they would obtain from a return to economic prosperity.

Yet the fact is that French capitalism is completely paralysed, that partly because of its own tendencies, partly because of the new social policy, a large segment of French business has lost all spirit of initiative and all desire for expansion.

In the past two years, despite the very best of intentions, one of the results of the economic and social laws introduced has been to place the French entrepreneur in an increasingly difficult situation. Every one of the measures passed has had the effect of restraining his freedom of action and initiative a little bit more. As if this were not enough, the conditions of their enforcement and trade union practices have if anything further restricted the sphere of free activity which the law had spared.

And so I arrive at a conclusion:

France's economy is in rapid decline ... This economic and financial enfeeblement is as serious for national defence as a shortage of guns, aircraft or ships. Think how much weight a decision of France could carry now in Europe if she had been able to achieve the economic recovery accomplished by countries like England, Belgium, Sweden, etc.

It may be anxiously wondered what will happen tomorrow to France if, on the one hand, through class feeling and hatred of communism part of the French bourgeoisie persists in its pro-German and pro-Italian sentiments, and if, on the other, the working class refuses to see that its present economic and social action is in direct contradiction with the foreign policy it would like to see practised[6].

For me the most manifest example of this collective abdication was, yet again, the shortening of work hours. I came back to this point almost every week. In April 1938 I wrote that no economic expansion of any breadth was possible unless the law on the forty-hour week were abolished. My envisaged lengthening of hours would be accompanied, when circumstances permitted, by massive imports of foreign labour. I concluded that France's work capacity was not sufficient for her to be able to withstand the threats of foreign aggression[7].

Daladier

1936, with Léon Blum, was the year of the *Front Populaire* with its misunderstanding of realities and its noble illusions. 1937, with Camille Chautemps, saw a watered-down *Front Populaire* policy that did nothing to repair the consequences of the previous term of management. 1938, after a short-lived second Blum government, was to be the year of Edouard Daladier.

We were filled with hope again, my friends at *L'Europe Nouvelle* and I. At long last the economy was going to be put back on the rails, the law on the forty-hour week abolished and the competitiveness of French industry restored. Disillusionment was not long in coming. When the new government published its programme we had to face the painful fact that it was just a vague outline, with no more than an indirect approach by implication to the life-and-death problems France needed to resolve. I wondered why the new government had not declared forthwith what sacrifices it intended to ask of the different social categories, why it had not unveiled the general recovery plan it intended to apply[8].

A week later I reached the conclusion that there was no overall plan and that the government was slowly constructing its programme as circumstances and chance dictated. More serious, it seemed clear that this programme in no way answered the demands of the situation in which France found herself. True, we were promised that enforcement of the forty-hour week would be relaxed but why, I wondered, not tell the country that there could be no recovery unless the law itself were abolished[9]?

On May 14, 1938 I expressed my approval of the franc devaluation the government had just carried out and welcomed the resultant capital backflow. But the crux of the problem lay elsewhere. I began to despair of a real recovery and discerned, as the foreign situation continued to worsen, the possibility, if not the probability, of military defeat.

It is absolutely essential to increase the work capacity of industry in order to convince the French that their country is not doomed to languish eternally in a wretched situation, with an output too low to meet the demands represented by the population's living standards and the nation's defence.

In this issue of *L'Europe Nouvelle* the reader will find a passage quoted from *L'Activité Economique*[10] which shows that any expansion of France's production and trade will soon be blocked by a shortage of labour unless the law on the forty-hour week is repealed beforehand. *To return to its 1929 level French output would have to increase by 50 per cent. Yet the total elimination of unemployment and short-time working – an absurdly optimistic hypothesis – would enable output to rise by only 7.5 per cent. Could any figure be more eloquent?*

The forty-hour week has to be abolished because it constitutes an intolerable handicap to the future development of production, because France is not a country whose ambition has to be confined to a 5 or 10 per cent increase in its economic power, because no policy of national recovery – liberalist or authoritarian – can succeed unless the country's work capacity has first been augmented.

I went on to point out that there was not a single skilled metalworker who was unemployed:

Our shortage of skilled workers is such that we could see economic activity contract quite a bit more without that category of labour being affected.

Let us go further. Not only are there specific skill categories that could work more than forty hours, there are entire industries that are unable to keep pace with demand. The coal industry was one of these not long ago and probably soon will be again, after the new devaluation. Above all it is the case with the armaments industries.

Referring to an article in *La Dépêche de Toulouse*[11] in which General Armengaud had described the lamentable situation in the French aircraft industry, I wrote:

We are turning out fewer than 50 aircraft per month, whilst England is producing 200, Italy 250 and Germany 350. Far be it from me to blame this tragedy solely on shorter hours. *But is it conceivable that a people threatened in its very existence as a great nation, seeing the disproportion between its air force and those of its adversaries grow daily, is it conceivable that this people should deliberately limit ... yesterday to forty hours, today to forty-five hours, the working week in its aircraft factories? Is this not plain suicide? Will there not come a prophet to cry to the French people and its shepherds that they are marching straight to military defeat?*

I then entreated the parties of the left and the trade unions to alter their attitude:

The political parties and trade unions have a big part to play in the French nation's recovery. They can be its life force, since the bourgeoisie seems to have lost awareness of its mission, while its most extreme fringe does not recoil from a policy that verges on treason. Do those parties and unions not then understand that if they behave simply like one faction among the other factions, defending interests that are doubtless respectable but still no more than particular interests, the recovery will be achieved without them and against them (today I would add: 'or will not be achieved at all')? *If there is a great lesson to be drawn from the ascendancy of the fascist and national*

71

socialist parties, it is that the workers' cause is lost wherever, in periods of crisis, they leave to others the task of representing the nation's interests[12].

I was haunted by the idea of France's economic decay and I strove to define, first in my mind, then in my writing, the conditions for recovery. Thus at the end of May 1938 I set out, in an article entitled *Impuissance de l'Etat* [The powerlessness of government], what I thought should be the key elements of a grand French economic and financial policy:

(1) To increase immediately, not by 5 or 10 per cent but by 100 or 200 per cent, the output of the factories working for national defence, factories for which the problem of orders does not arise, which can always sell as many aircraft, tanks and guns as they can turn out;
(2) To increase the work capacity of French industry as a whole;
(3) To reduce as far as possible, or at least not widen, the huge budget deficit in order to spare the country further currency depreciations, bring back the capital that has been exported and induce a lowering of interest rates;
(4) To stimulate the revival of private investment, since it is still from private entrepreneurs that a general economic recovery will stem.

When the government decided to embark on a policy of major public works schemes to reduce unemployment, I was astounded:

But there is no unemployment problem in France, there is no spare manpower, there is no idle production capacity. An absurd law has reduced that capacity to its lowest level since the last war ... The slightest upturn would encounter a shortage of labour.

The problem is not to reduce the labour reserve but to increase it immediately, to repeal this national treason in the shape of the law on the forty-hour week.

The view is held that there is a finite quantity of hours of work possible, a kind of 'substratum of work.' If an employer makes his employees work more than forty hours a week he is acting detrimentally to their interests, since if they work more today there is a kind of natural law that will make them work less tomorrow. So they need to be protected from redundancy. Understandably, in the circumstances, precautions are taken against the 'stealers' of labour, against the manufacturers who want more than their forty hours and who therefore have to obtain special authorization from the Ministry of Labour.

All this is impossibly demagogic ... Longer hours are today in France a question of national safety, independent of whatever political stance may have been taken, independent of whatever plan may have been devised to redress the economy. Abolish this pernicious law and everything is possible. Retain it and France is lost.

I ended the article with some thoughts on France's decline:

It is truly sad when one sees how the might of France has declined during the past seven or eight years! Our economy is stagnating at its lowest level for a quarter-century. We no longer have an air force, tomorrow even our army will see its relative strength decrease, for who can believe that we can maintain a strong army when our economy is going downhill? It is our industrial weakness that provides the strongest argument for the proponents of an external policy of submission to Germany and Italy. Most of our allies have turned away from us. If England remains loyal, it is because we are indispensable to her. But what despondency in England or America in the hearts of our faithful friends there, what contempt elsewhere! I counsel all those who want to base our foreign policy on the union of democracies and who nonetheless must own to a share of responsibility for the economic and financial policy devised in France during the past two years to take a trip across the Channel or the Atlantic. A few bitter comments await them[13].

On June 23, 1938 Goering, commissioner of Germany's four-year plan, issued a decree instituting for the Germans a 'duty to serve.' With the exception of children, mothers and old people, all Germans were required by the state to leave their work or recreation and perform whatever task had been assigned them. This measure was tantamount to the introduction of a system of compulsory labour and I seized the opportunity a few days later to return to the question of statutory hours:

This general policy of industrial manpower creation (without rural–urban migration) is the inevitable consequence of Germany's will to increase her armaments and attain the highest possible degree of economic self-sufficiency. This dual requirement is apparent again in the magnitude of the effort demanded of the workers. Whoever travels through Germany cannot fail to be impressed by the strain to which the population is subjected. The workdays are long, ten, twelve hours, sometimes more. The intensity of work is greater than anything experienced in the other industrial countries.

It would be easy, I added, to hold labour conscription up to ridicule and equally easy to stress its obnoxiousness. But that would be missing the point:

The struggle between free man and the man that is being created in the totalitarian countries will not be terminated by a decree of divine providence

73

ruling which of the two is worthy to survive. It is in the competitive markets and on the battlefields that the issue will be decided.

Just visualize for a moment a people 75 million strong, toiling to the limit of their powers to forge instruments of domination, doing everything humanly possible to win a war. Then look at the France of 1938 and what does one see? On the one hand, a bourgeoisie bereft of any national sense, ready to relinquish freedom, not even into the hands of a French dictator, but into those of foreign dictators. On the other, a working class that is told daily that the less a nation works, the greater it is and the more worthy to figure among the benefactors of humanity.

Then I stressed what I thought was the fundamental problem:

How is one to prevent the balance of economic power between France and her potential enemies from shifting in such a way that she is doomed to decline to the status of a second- or third-rate power whose independence is constantly threatened?

I concluded as follows:

There is a great national policy to be introduced, of which the main constituents would be a plan to rehabilitate government finance over several years, repeal of the law on the forty-hour week, large-scale imports of manpower, measures to increase the French population, liberalization of foreign trade, and so on. Is the government prepared to try it[14]?

The summer of 1938 went by slowly. Anxiety was mounting in all those who had understood what was at stake and were not resigned to political and soon military defeat. The days of reckoning were drawing nearer. My friends at *L'Europe Nouvelle* and I were vainly seeking the politician who would be able to take France's destiny in hand and work for her salvation. Without any real conviction we latched on to Edouard Daladier for a time. At the end of August I acclaimed a speech he had just made, in which he said that while the international situation continued to be so delicate it ought to be possible to work more than forty hours per week, and up to forty-eight hours in firms working for national defence. I wrote this:

For the first time since the introduction of the statutory forty-hour week a head of government has dared to put the need to produce above the law. Without pointless formalities or interminable discussions, any business that needs it must now be allowed not forty hours per week but the hours necessary to its activity.

The sole fact of having stated loud and clear that a country threatened, as

France is, by military aggression should place the demands of production and national defence above its immediate comfort, this single act of courage will earn M. Daladier the gratitude of all patriots.

And I appealed to the socialists and the communists to support this effort:

Either the extreme left will understand that resistance to Hitlerism and fascism requires on its part conversion to a rational economic and financial policy, or France is destined to slide ever more rapidly down the path that has led to economic ruin, social anarchy and military defeat[15].

It was the very man on whom I had just conferred the seal of lucidity and courage who one month later was to sign the Munich agreements.

8

FROM MUNICH TO THE WAR

Despair, humiliation, shame, these were the feelings that took hold of me when the Munich agreements became known. I remember rushing out of a cinema where they were screening a newsreel that showed Daladier and Chamberlain signing those agreements with Hitler and Mussolini. I was so deeply affected that the sight was unbearable.

In the next issue of *L'Europe Nouvelle* I published an article of no great interest about the full powers which the National Assembly had just granted Daladier. But it was the same issue's leader, written by Pertinax with the approval of the entire editorial staff, that best expressed the depth of our distress. Here are a few extracts:

We are witnessing the collapse of French policy, a collapse arguably without parallel in our country's history. It would not be a paradox to say that the 1914–18 war will have been lost after the event if the German floodwater that has burst the dikes is not contained quickly.

In the case that concerns us, it is fairly obvious that the smallest of threatening gestures from France on March 7, 1936 (when the German forces reoccupied the Rhineland) would probably have sufficed, without the need for a single blow to be struck, to preserve for another generation the foundations laid at the end of hostilities twenty years ago.

For France and England this late summer and autumn of 1938 marks the day of judgment, the tragic time of reckoning. When trouble came to

Czechoslovakia, a little country of seeming unimportance but a pivotal point of Pan-Germanism, they were appealed to but shirked the issue.

Our isolation is already perceptible. How can we envisage cooperation with England and Soviet Russia? Is it possible to rebuild a barrier, for now we can do no more than reckon in those terms? Can we arm ourselves to the same degree as the totalitarian states with their new resources? Only if we can will it be possible to seek, with Berlin and Rome, an arrangement that will leave us an undisputed status as a great power. If not, a war is almost certain ... Mr Chamberlain, confused by popular acclaim, spoke of the Munich 'miracle' and M. Daladier has said, before the deputies, that the Munich method would be used to overcome the other international problems. That is just empty talk. One could equally well say that the other problems can be resolved by acts of renunciation and withdrawal.

Where Soviet Russia is concerned, we are still in the dark about what resolutions she will make. The British government seems to be opening its eyes to what needs to be done to limit the disaster. But a terrible blow has been dealt to those who were advocating the closest possible union with France.

If no fundamental action to restore the balance is taken on our side, England will become discouraged and end by treating us as a second Czechoslovakia. We shall have to accept a readjustment of our symbolic status as a great power to our actual very inadequate strength. And let us not forget that we shall be threatened not only from without but also from within. Our institutions, our laws and our customs will have to fall into line with those of the dominant totalitarian states. We shall have to accept *Gleichshaltung*[1].

Pertinax could not foresee accurately what was going to happen, the military defeat of 1940 and its aftermath, but what prescience as to the final outcome!

During the year that followed I went on contributing articles to *L'Europe Nouvelle* nearly every week. I continued to attack the law on the forty-hour week and to advocate a more rational fiscal and monetary policy stance, but the emphasis had shifted. Now it was preparation for the approaching, inevitable war that had to take pride of place. And to avert disaster, the state had to be given increased powers or, at all events, use to the full those it already possessed.

For reasons of external policy that are perfectly clear, as I wrote back in June 1938, we cannot afford to be thinking today about making over our system of industrial relations, about replacing the present leadership by another.

It seemed to me that whatever the deficiencies of France's management class, and they were overwhelming, there could be no question, with war around the corner, of trying to replace it with another elite. The disintegration of management authority, which had begun in May–June 1936, had to be stopped for we were in no position to create a new social order. In the present dramatic circumstances it was for government to impose its own authority with the aim of serving not the immediate interests of the workers, nor those of employers, nor those of any particular social group, but the security and the greatness of the national community.

It is for the State to define the general interests of France and ensure that they are observed. The essential prerequisite of any policy of national rehabilitation is reestablishment of the power of the State[2].

The war draws nearer

In the interval between the Munich tragedy and the others that lay in store we had to try and pick up the pieces. With Daladier about to make a platform speech before the Radical Party Congress, I tried to identify once again, in the October 29, 1938 issue of *L'Europe Nouvelle*, the fundamental preconditions for France's economic rehabilitation. There was nothing particularly original in the article; I had been saying it all for a long time. The only new thing, perhaps, was the feeling of urgency, the feeling that the weeks and months were going by, that the time of reckoning was drawing near and still nothing had really been done to try and rescue France from her fate. There were some of us who felt that maybe it was already too late.

'Directed [*dirigiste*] economy', 'controlled economy', 'oriented economy', 'reflation', 'credit injection', and so on and so forth. We are by no means against all organization of the economy, but what is intolerable is that we are being offered words (and not even original ones at that) instead of solutions, or more precisely that clever dialectics are being used to try and evade the reality of a rehabilitation effort *that cannot be anything but arduous and painful.*

Whether one is for constraint or for freedom, there are a number of points on which it is possible to agree, provided that the sole aim of all is to save the country and restore its lost power.

What was needed, I said, was a plan with a target of something like a 50 per cent increase in production. And harping on the same old string: with the labour available no more than 10 per cent could be achieved, hence the need to do away with the forty-hour week.

'Free economy', 'planned economy', terms that more often than not are meaningless to those who employ them. France is not dying of the fact that her economy is not planned enough or free enough. She is wasting away because her people have lost the sense of effort, because her workers are not working any more, because her businessmen prefer incomes carefully tucked away from the risks of striving outward towards power and wealth, because her governments are living in an artificial atmosphere all but voided of the sense of reality and inebriating themselves with meaningless slogans without realizing that this regime is sinking, and taking France down with it.

One can read 'Munich' between the lines of this piece of profound pessimism and discouragement. Everything would change, for a while, with the arrival of Paul Reynaud at the Finance Ministry in autumn 1938. In the two years previous I had conceived a growing admiration for this man who was to prove, too briefly alas, to be the most intelligent politician the Third Republic produced.

On November 5 I wrote:

The situation has been completely transformed by the arrival of M. Paul Reynaud at Rue de Rivoli[3]. If France's recovery depended solely on the courage, intelligence and lucidity of one man, our minds would now be quite at rest. It would be true to say that no statesman has ever been more right, over a period of several years, than M. Paul Reynaud; it would be equally true to say that no one has ever been less heeded.

In 1934, when the French were still living with the memory of postwar inflation, M. Paul Reynaud was just about the only one to say that we would not pull out of the crisis unless we devalued the franc [...]. In 1935, when many minds were beginning to understand but for want of courage no politician of standing nor any party dared to go along with him, M. Paul Reynaud urged this indispensable devaluation as an alternative to the Laval government's deflation, which nearly cost him his seat in the Assembly. In 1936 and 1937 we found him severely criticizing the economic and financial experiments of the *Front Populaire*. From the outset he predicted their failure ... What distinguishes him from other politicians who have adopted the same attitude is the actual spirit in which he makes his criticisms. For him it is not a question of hitting back, of protecting more or less sordid interests from the popular groundswell, but simply of preparing France for her role in Europe.

If ever confidence in a man was justified, it is now. M. Paul Reynaud has thought right too persistently over the past four or five years for us not to be entitled to conclude that he is the French statesman best able to get our country out of its present mess.

In the following issue of *L'Europe Nouvelle* I tried to evaluate Paul Reynaud's chances of success. They were not inconsiderable: public opinion was moving away from the traditional parties and prepared to support the efforts of a new, independent, courageous man. Since 1930, I wrote, two series of governments had successively held power, their sole point in common being powerlessness. The radical and conservative governments prior to 1936 had sought to exorcise the evils afflicting our country with magic formulas that primitive witch doctors might envy: 'confidence', 'automatic establishment of equilibrium', 'power of nature', etc. The governments of the *Front Populaire* had rationalized the instinctive demands of the masses and justified them in the name of nebulous theories; the result, irrespective of the protagonists' intentions, had been a series of demagogic measures, of which the forty-hour week was the outstanding example. In the way Paul Reynaud set about the problems I saw a new spirit that disregarded all ideology:

It is no longer a question of whether France will be saved in conditions of justice or injustice, with liberalist or authoritarian solutions, but whether she will be saved at all. This climate is essentially propitious to the work of a team like that of M. Paul Reynaud, who is not attached to any political party and whose entire action is dictated by one consideration: 'the nation first.'

I had no illusions, moreover, about the difficulties of the task and the obstacles that had to be surmounted before one could speak of success. In the first place Paul Reynaud would need sufficient time. Would the congenital instability of the Third Republic allow him the number of years a real rehabilitation would take? In addition, management and labour would have to let him act without putting extra difficulties in the way, the people would have to devote their energies to saving the nation and forget partisan quarrels for a while; Frenchmen one and all would have to understand that their sole enemies were national socialism and fascism.

What strikes me today on rereading these lines, nearly half a century after writing them, is the naïveté with which I imagined that we still had enough time to pull the French economy around. I could see our defeat looming on the horizon but I did not realize how near it was. My failure to appreciate the military issues was largely instrumental in sustaining this illusion. But who in that autumn of 1938 would have suspected that eighteen months later the French army would have ceased to exist?

In the November 19, 1938 issue of *L'Europe Nouvelle* I commented on the decree-laws Paul Reynaud had just put through to try to correct the situation. On his arrival at the Finance Ministry he had found that the 1939 government borrowing requirement would amount to fifty-five billion francs in a government spending total of one hundred and thirty-seven billion. Reynaud's plan aimed to cut the 1940 budget deficit to thirty-six billion. But above all it virtually killed off the forty-hour week. No more absolute restriction on hours worked; the plan authorized overtime within the limits of a maximum workweek of forty-eight hours and a workday of nine hours, and provided for reasonable overtime rates (ten to twenty-five per cent). 'This simplification of overtime rules,' I wrote, 'these different measures ensure that henceforth an increase in production will not be stopped in its tracks by a labour shortage.' Needless to say, the plan was very badly received:

We are now witnessing an almost universal outcry against these new decree-laws. This is one more reason for me to say that, given France's present situation and all the economic and financial facts of the case, M. Paul Reynaud's plan, subject to some reservations concerning its technicalities, is the only one possible.

The parliamentarians in general feared for their reelection. M. Tixier-Vignancour spoke for them when he cried out at the Congress of the Democratic Alliance: 'Is it the intention with these decree-laws to have us annihilated at the polls?' The Right feared above all that it might be giving the Left a favourable platform for the 1940 elections. The Left was talking about 'preservation of hard-won reforms', 'social justice', 'equality of sacrifice'. The war veterans, reckoning they were being too hardly done by, stated that it was 'impossible to ask for any special sacrifice from war veterans and disabled ex-servicemen'. The language has a familiar ring.

In all this there is not even the slightest reference to France and the terrible plight of her economy and finance. One might well believe that the speech, at once so lucid and so moving, made by M. Paul Reynaud on Sunday evening has stirred no response, that the French are unaware of their country's rapid decline or have lost their public-spiritedness to the point of becoming indifferent to it. For my part, I prefer to believe that their real thinking is not represented by those who speak in their name.

I now championed Paul Reynaud's cause wholeheartedly, with a fire and fervour that might have been attributable to youth but which I could probably recapture today in similar circumstances. I was certain that his plan was a vital and inescapable necessity. I waxed indignant when I heard him criticized for lack of imagination. As if imagination were needed to understand that output could not be increased sufficiently without longer hours, or the budget deficit reduced without higher taxes or lower spending! On the left, too, Reynaud was criticized for trying to win the confidence of the capitalists, as if this were unworthy of a French minister. As if that confidence were not necessary in an economic system dominated by private enterprise, as if the contrary would not have been absurd! I could not but subscribe unreservedly to the Finance Minister's ideas at that time.

We are living in a capitalist regime. Some may regret this, but there is one fact on which we will all agree: just as one does not change horses in midstream, so France cannot afford to change her regime in today's Europe. The capitalist regime being what it is, for it to function its laws must be observed. Its laws are profit, individual risk, freedom of markets, the stimulus of competition ... No one has yet succeeded in making the capitalist system operate at a loss.

I went on to point out it was in the interest of the masses that the system function as well as possible, i.e. that the capitalists should make profits. I recalled that the times in the past when wages had risen fastest were also those when profits had been highest.

How can one not link the fate of France to the outcome of this experiment? If M. Paul Reynaud succeeds, there need be no limit to our hopes. A sound economic and financial base will allow France to speak again with the voice of authority in the concert of Europe. A revival in output would mean a concomitant increase in our military power; we are among those who today prefer guns to butter. How can the advocates of resistance to Germany not see that this has to go by way of a drastic correction of France's economy and finance?

If the opponents of M. Reynaud's venture succeed in bringing it down, then France will be precipitated into the greatest muddle she has ever known; she will be fair game for the worst that can happen.

In an article dated December 3, 1938 I went over what were to be the guiding principles of the new policy:

– France will not get back on her feet unless all the forces of production she possesses are utilized to the utmost and her work capacity expanded likewise.

– In a debt-pressed country like ours, where labour is in such short supply, where the slightest budget deficit is seen as heralding rampant inflation, the balancing of public expenditure and revenue must be an article of faith for any government.

– Export trade, although representing only a small share of total commerce, has always been the engine of economic activity; freedom of international trade is therefore vital to France and any measure taken in that direction is fully consistent with the overall plan for the country's recovery.

The lengthening of the workweek to forty-eight hours will not suffice to bring output up to its pre-crisis level. It will be necessary at last to introduce an intelligent and systematic policy of foreign manpower imports.

Abolition of import quotas and their replacement by a system of duties affording sufficient protection is the most effective contribution that France can make to the liberalization of international trade.

I stressed that Reynaud's opponents had produced no counterproposals that were not purely demagogic in character or went beyond generalities devoid of any real substance and in no way constituting a response to the issues of the moment. For Maurice Thorez[4] France's only economic problem was how to give work to the unemployed, for Léon Jouhaux[5] and the CGT it was necessary to create work. All of this, I wrote, completely misses the point. I followed the progress of the experiment day by day and at the end of December noted that it was beginning to produce results: short-term interest rates were moving down and long-term rates could be expected to do likewise, very substantial capital inflows were being recorded.

In 1939 my articles in *L'Europe Nouvelle* (or at any rate those I have preserved) became less frequent. This was probably because I was very busy writing my doctorate thesis and putting my affairs in order with the approach of a war I now considered not only inevitable but close. On February 25, 1939 I wrote, still in *L'Europe Nouvelle* and under the title 'La reprise économique et la crise politique internationale' [Economic recovery and the international political crisis], my last article inspired by a free-market philosophy.

The controversies surrounding Paul Reynaud's experiment have subsided; amid numerous difficulties ... it is pursuing its course and each day some piece of good news comes to confirm that we are on the right road. Doubtless the sum total of success to date does not constitute a decisive victory; but the achievements have been numerous and important enough to transform the economic and financial climate.

We are no longer exposed to a monetary crisis. Despite the threats of war, capital is flowing steadily into France.

A very marked economic upturn is under way. From nearly all industries, in the investment and consumer goods sectors alike, the news is good.

That France's economic activity is picking up there can now be no doubt. But the improvement is very slow. Why?

First we are suffering from an international economic depression which, while not very deep, still seriously limits the opportunities for recovery in France. But above all, it is difficult to envisage economic expansion on a large scale in the present international atmosphere. That is a commonplace, I grant, but worth stressing to show how threats of war inhibit any economic recovery.

Manufacturers do not decide to enlarge their production capacity, to buy equipment unless they have the prospect of being able to sell at a satisfactory price the goods produced with that new equipment during its life-span. But who can anticipate with any measure of certainty in a period like the one we are going through? The result is that, caught between an uncertain rate of profit and a high rate of interest, entrepreneurs prefer to wait until the horizon has cleared.

M. Paul Reynaud's policy since last November has augmented France's military strength. In the first place it has increased the quantity of goods produced; in the second, it has enriched our gold reserves in the event of war by some thirteen or fourteen billion.

The new policy was yielding the results expected. But it was essentially a free-market policy and therefore a peacetime one. Quite obviously, I added, the situation would be completely transformed if war broke out. 'Then there would be no two ways about it: exchange controls, mobilization of industry, military organization of the whole country would have to be the order of the day.'

The war economy

On March 15, 1939 the Germans occupied Prague and what remained of Czechoslovakia. War was imminent. I threw my economic liberalism overboard, or rather put it away until better times. On April 22 the government issued a new set of decree-laws. I then wrote an article entitled: *Vers une économie de guerre*[6] [Towards a war economy] in which I went along with the new legislation while stating it to be insufficient. To make it more impressive, the article was introduced by an editorial I had written myself:

The decree-laws of April 22, with their financial, economic and social measures, constitute a first necessary adjustment of the French community to this intermediate regime between peace and war. We must not allow ourselves to be overtaken by the worst events.

The decree-laws somewhat disrupt the legislation of 1936–37. But one of the faults of the governments of those years was to believe they were living in times of ease and to apply a social policy that went counter to the policy of resistance to the totalitarian states they had initiated. It is to be regretted today that the socialist party is loath to acknowledge that the division of society has to be completely bridged since other divisions threaten. Its leaders would be taking on a heavy responsibility if they were to incite and organize the secession of the workers at a time when for the sake of the nation's safety the greatest possible measure of national unanimity has to be established ... On the whole, the decree-laws represent the only possible solution to the problem posed, and it would be deplorable if class feeling were to stand in their way.

In the article itself I noted that the policy conducted by Paul Reynaud since November 1938 had yielded everything expected of it and more. Since November 1938 output had risen by 15 per cent, the average number of hours worked per week had lengthened from 39.2 to 40.3, the seasonal rise in unemployment had been much less pronounced than in the previous year. The currency was now firm; in less than six months we had earned back nearly twenty billion in gold. This justified the stance Reynaud had taken in November. 'Who was right, he or the advocates of exchange control,' I wrote, 'only time could tell. The experiment was conclusive. Capital has flowed back.'

The new decree-laws were not very ambitious. They aimed to distribute manpower more rationally, for example by providing for civil service staff cuts. They also set out to restrain consumption, notably by abolishing overtime pay up to the forty-fifth hour. To finance increased defence spending they provided for tax increases and capped the profits of firms working for national defence.

I justified the move towards a war economy in these terms:

Since November there has been a considerable change in the general stance of our economic and financial policy. The November plan was designed solely to permit the spontaneous development of a free economy. The necessary conditions were fulfilled for producers to take decisions to produce. The new plan, or rather the outline of it that can be discerned in the new decrees, is a plan for a war economy.

The problems have changed. It is no longer a question simply of producing, but of producing specific goods, even if this means preventing the production of certain goods judged in the present circumstances to be nonessential. It is no longer a question of eliminating unemployment, of lengthening the actual number of hours worked, or rather these problems are considered resolved in view of the impetus that defence orders are giving or will give the economy. What is needed is to use the manpower we have available in the most rational possible way. It is no longer a matter of stimulating consumption but of preventing it from expanding, so that the productive forces not yet tapped may be kept for the industries working directly to increase the military strength of France.

But in conclusion I had to own that the measures taken were not equal to the task.

The only problem now is whether these measures will suffice. One's immediate answer is no. As production expands in the war industries, while the peace industries are liable to see their activity reduced, transfers of manpower will be necessary and there is reason to think that these transfers will require authoritarian methods. Consumption will have to be further restrained. Taxes will have to be further increased. Such measures are essential if the French economy is to provide us with what we essentially ask of it: a powerful war machine.

On June 17, 1939 I published my last article in *L'Europe Nouvelle*, at any rate the last of those I have kept. I would be called up in September 1939. *L'Europe Nouvelle* ceased publication with France's defeat and did not reappear with the Liberation. In that last article I commented on the record of his first five months at the Finance Ministry that Paul Reynaud had just published. It was entirely positive. I am seen to be very Keynesian.

The solution to our financial problem depends essentially on the amount of slack in the economy. If there is a lot of slack, deficit financing (a planned deficit financed by borrowing) is justified. If, on the other hand, capacity is fully utilized, a balanced budget, or at least no increase in current expenditure, is necessary ... From the strictly economic standpoint, taxes are the only warranted means of financing government expenditure when the economy is close to full employment.

But this kind of economic analysis was of secondary importance to me then. I was obsessed by the approaching war and fearful that France had knuckled down too late to avoid defeat. We were coming to the point where it was going to be necessary to restrain consumption in order to let the rearmament effort develop fully. Addressing myself to the government, I advised it not to hesitate to take every measure needed for France to be ready to go to war.

Until now, apart from this rudimentary procedure that goes by the name of taxation, the central government has had no means of controlling consumption. It is possible that it will soon have to limit the possible expansion of certain industries not essential to national defence. This is usually something that is resorted to in the event of war, but is our present situation all that different from a state of war?

I then went on to the subject of exchange controls.

In any case, the question of exchange controls is not one of principle but one of expediency. Doctrinal considerations to one side, let the French government do everything needed to put France in fit condition for armed conflict. That is all we ask and that is something it has perfectly understood.

I was still labouring under some delusions.

In the five years leading up to the war I had criticized, sometimes violently, the economic policies of the radical and moderate governments, then of the *Front Populaire* governments, until I found in Paul

Reynaud the man my sense of reason was calling for. Was I right? Yes, I think so, when I was talking economics. But I understand now, as I sensed then, that there was more to it than economics. France's foreign policy and defence policy too were absurd, as devoid of a real national resolve as her economic policy. I did not have a very clear idea of these paramount issues at the time. Let us say, if you like, that the economic policy for which I was fighting and of which the essential theme was 'we have to work 45, 50 or 60 hours a week to ward off the danger of Hitler, or if war breaks out in order to win it', was intrinsic to any national defence as such.

September 1939 and it was war. My life, like that of so many millions, would be turned upside down. The plans I had made, the ambitions I had of becoming a university professor, of writing an economic work that would be a landmark of my time, all evaporated. To me the war was like a curtain coming down on the play I had been performing in for ten years. A new one was beginning in which I would play a different part, though I did not know yet what it would be. I cannot say that I gave the matter much thought. I would not go to meet my future, it would come to meet me.

Part Two

THE WAR

1

THE WAR (FIRST PHASE)
(1939–1940)

I greeted the call-up notices with immense relief. France and England, I now thought, would not repeat the infamy of Munich with Poland. I had no illusions about France's offensive strength. Entrenched behind the Maginot Line, having allowed the Siegfried Line to be set up, how could she go to Poland's aid? The Germano-Soviet pact of August 23 announced a further dismemberment of unhappy Poland. How could we taken on the Germans and the Russians at the same time? Yet anything was better than the dishonourable peace of 1936–9, which we had paid for with so many disavowals and the abandonment of our friends, the Spanish republicans, and our faithful ally Czechoslovakia. I knew nothing of the state of criminal unreadiness in which we were. I though we had a few months ahead of us and would use them to complete our defences and make ready to attack. Like most Frenchmen, I believed in the French army and its high command.

I have just looked at my old service registration card. It states that I was called up by way of public notice on August 26, 1939 and put on the strength of Air Company 26/102 the same day. In the train taking me to Dijon I dreamed of honour regained, of a France that had been able to get a grip on herself. For the first time in years I was glad to be French. I did not sleep that night.

At Dijon everything was complete confusion. It seemed I had arrived too early, so I had to spend two or three days just waiting.

Finally it turned out that my military file had been lost and I was assigned automatically to an air company as a sergeant of all-round competence and not as a meteorologist, which was my speciality. To make matters worse, I had absolutely no idea of what my new duties would be.

We spent a few days in Dijon, camping out in the factory where they used to make *La vache qui rit* processed cheese, and then left for our final destination, which was Couraloux in the Jura. I stayed there about two months, getting latrines dug and earth and stones moved to build the airfield that would be useful when some planes materialized. I was utterly incompetent and my total lack of manual dexterity was revealed at every turn. But the men under my orders were very good sports and did not try to take advantage of my inexperience, while the officers were forbearing. I got to know the local councillor-general, whose name was Toinet. He was a socialist and knew me by reputation. I spent all my evenings at his place. Even so I felt out of my element. I remember filling the spare moments one inevitably has in garrison life by reading Montaigne.

Finally, taking advantage of a leave to Paris, I called in at the Fort de Saint-Cyr (where the central command of military meteorology was headquartered) to report that I had 'gone astray'. A few days later I received a new assignment in charge of a meteorological detachment at Waldowisheim, near Saverne. I had under my orders two other noncommissioned officers (or maybe their rank was that of private, I can't remember) with whom I got on very well. Each day, using information sent from Paris and our own observations, we compiled several weather reports. These we forwarded to an air force headquarters located in the same village and in charge of an airfield and several squadrons. The squadrons existed only on paper, alas. I don't think there was ever more than one aircraft on the field and that was for the travels of the colonel and a few other officers.

Thus I spent the winter of 1939–40 in a little village of Alsace whose inhabitants spoke only German. For my part I was familiarizing myself increasingly with that language, spending my spare time reading German texts. Among other works I read the poems of Heine and both parts of *Faust*. I also read *Mein Kampf* for the first time. In it I found confirmation of all my fears. We were up against a megalomaniac conqueror and I suspected that we would be unable to resist him. I endeavoured to allay my anxieties by doing my completely pointless job as well as I possibly could. Several times I was approached from Paris. They kept asking me to go back and take up some kind of post at the Finance Ministry. I kept refusing, wanting to remain a modest part of France's army which I hoped would remain true to the tradition of 1914–18.

The weeks and the months passed and I was becoming prodigiously bored. When Jean Monnet, whom I did not know, asked me, through an old friend of mine Roger Truptil, to come and join him in London, I hesitated for a few days and then accepted. On May 10, 1940 I was appointed statistician to the Anglo-French Coordinating Committee and at the same time promoted to the rank of *sous-lieutenant*. A fateful day if ever there was one! In fact I had arrived in London earlier. Paris-London, that was my first ever trip by air. It also brought me to my first meeting with Jean Monnet.

The Committee had been in operation since November 1939. Its purpose was to pool the material resources and production potential of France and England. Jean Monnet had been appointed Chairman by joint decision of the French and British governments. His chief collaborator was René Pléven, a man of courage, common sense and reason, one of the first Frenchmen to join General de Gaulle in exile and who was to have a brilliant and productive political career in the postwar years. My role was a very humble one. In fact I have only a rather dim recollection of it. During the ten or fifteen days after my arrival I endeavoured to assemble a quantity of figures on the requirements of the allied armies and civilian populations. This laborious effort was soon to lose any point with the German offensive in the Ardennes, the headlong advance of the French and British troops to the north, the surrender of the Dutch troops, the German thrust into Sedan and the arrival of Guderian's panzer divisions at the sea. The Belgians then capitulated. The British and a large part of the French army found themselves enclosed in a pocket comprising northern France and southern Belgium.

Dunkirk

It was then that I carried out a military mission which could have been important in other circumstances but which turned out to be laughable. On the morning of May 25 Monnet sent for me and explained the problem. 'There is only one way,' he told me, 'to supply the British and French troops caught in the net and cut off from the rest of France, as well as the civilian populations in the area, and that is from England. I'm asking you to go to Dunkirk and see with Admiral Abrial (the

commander-in-chief at Dunkirk) how the thing can be organized.'
That was an order. I was a bit nervous as the assignment looked like
being no picnic, but happy at the same time to have my first opportunity since the outbreak of war to do something apparently useful. An
hour or two later I was getting ready to leave when Monnet came to
me and said: 'Forget what I told you. I like you and it's really too
dangerous.' I greatly appreciated this gesture of affection but did not
want to pass up the opportunity of proving to myself that I was
capable of braving physical danger. I pressed the point and Monnet
gave in.

He made an appointment for me with the British authorities who
were to arrange my transport. The last person I saw, I believe, was
General Ormsby-Gore who was in command of the Intelligence
Service or one of its branches. Jean Monnet and the British authorities
gave me all the letters I might need[1]. Since the arrangements had taken
longer than expected, the last of my contacts telephoned the station
and asked the people in charge there to hold the Dover train for me.
And so, nearly two hours after the train had been due to leave, I
ceremoniously entered the station escorted by two British officers.
They led me to a compartment which had been reserved for my sole
use and which they locked, presumably to protect me from attack or
some other impropriety. Once alone, I changed out of my civilian
clothes into my uniform of *sous-lieutenant* of the French Air Force.
When we got to Dover, during the night of May 25–6, I boarded the
trawler *Rob Roy*. We were hardly out of the harbour when we were
machine-gunned by German fighter planes. Fortunately part of the
deck had been converted into a steel-plated shelter. The crew and I
were able to take refuge there and I emerged unscathed from this first
ordeal.

When I arrived at Dunkirk I checked into a hotel whose name I have
forgotten and got in touch with Admiral Abrial who, after reading the
different letters of introduction I had been given and looking over my
orders, said kindly: 'You're very young for such a difficult assignment.
Still, I'll do everything I can to help.' I also saw other officers who were
to help me with my task, in particular Intendant Lobel the Refugees
Commissioner for the Nord and Pas-de-Calais departments. After
arranging to have lunch with him the next day at the Château-d'Eau, I
went back to my hotel for some much-needed rest.

At first light on the following day, May 27, the Germans set about
their destruction of Dunkirk. Every five or ten minutes brought a wave
of German planes over the town dropping their bombs. Thus I was

awakened at 4 or 5 a.m. by the most horrible noise. I looked out of my hotel window and saw that the town was already beginning to blaze. Dressing hurriedly, and leaving behind in my room a suitcase and some belongings I was never to see again, I went down to the basement where a makeshift shelter had been set up. Later in the morning I set out on a perilous journey to get to the Château-d'Eau. Dunkirk was burning and the German bombers, with apparently nothing to fear from French or British fighters or from ack-ack, continued to go about their work of destruction.

Each time a wave of bombers came along I dived into a shelter, emerging as soon as there was a lull and advancing another few hundred yards until the next alert. It was while I was between two shelters that a slightly ludicrous incident occurred, though it could have turned out badly for me. I suddenly found myself surrounded by four French soldiers under the command of a captain. The latter pointed to a man nearby in civilian clothes whom I had not noticed and said in an unpleasant tone of voice: 'This civilian says you have been seen in several shelters that have been hit. Your papers.' Fortunately I had been careful to keep on me all the letters I had been given in London. The captain read them and shook his head. 'These are in order, obviously, but how am I to know that the whole thing isn't a fabrication?' How was I to answer that one? Luckily an idea came that may have saved me from prolonged detention. 'I'm to have lunch at noon with Intendant Lobel at the Château-d'Eau.' I saw the captain's face light up in recognition. 'I know Intendant Lobel and he does lunch every day at the Château-d'Eau.' He turned to two of his soldiers. 'You two go with the lieutenant to the Château-d'Eau and stay with him until he has been recognized by Intendant Lobel.'

So we continued on our way across Dunkirk. If I remember rightly, the German bomb attacks had ceased but the town was burning. It was a gigantic inferno, walls and roofs came crashing down every other second with a horrendous din. The heat was intense, the light blinding, the air almost unbreathable. After we had advanced a few hundred yards in this furnace my two escorts stopped: '*Mon lieutenant,*' one of them said, 'we can see very well that you're genuine. If you don't mind, we'll leave you here. We'll say we went with you to the Château-d'Eau.' So I went on alone and found Lobel at the Château-d'Eau. That afternoon I saw Admiral Abrial again, who offered me the hospitality of his bunker but absolutely forbade me to try to go to Lille as I intended: 'You'll be killed or taken prisoner,' he said. 'All the roads have been cut off.'

I have found among my papers the report on my mission I wrote when I got back to London, for the information of Monnet, the British authorities and the French government[2]. Here are a few extracts:

During my stay in Dunkirk events moved so quickly that the details and even the essentials of the organization to be set up were called into question hourly. The military authorities' decision, at the time of my arrival, to turn back the Belgian refugees to their country of origin would have reduced the magnitude of the problem very appreciably. But other factors made that problem insoluble:

1. The German advance increasingly restricted the areas it might have been hoped to supply via Dunkirk. It was no longer possible to send on supply convoys to Lille and its surrounding area.

2. The heavy bombing raids to which Dunkirk was subjected during my stay, particularly that of May 27 which almost completely destroyed the town, caused a dispersal of the civilian population that made distribution of supplies among the latter very difficult.

3. As a result of the aerial bombardments I have just mentioned Dunkirk harbour has become practically unusable. In any case, the intensity of the bombing and strafing during my stay was such that unloading of cargoes was brought to a complete standstill. Most of the boats that were alongside sank.

On my arrival, in collaboration with the civilian and military authorities, I set up a first scheme for dealing with the refugees ... That scheme was overtaken by events before it could be put into operation.

I then set about devising a new scheme to meet the needs of the situation. Its essential features were the following: the pooling of all available supplies, with no differentiation of supplies by category of recipients, i.e. the armed forces, the resident civilian population and the refugees.

– distribution of those supplies, by the military authorities, among the different categories of consumers, in a manner consistent with the best interests of defence;

– distribution among the civilian population (resident and refugee) by Intendant Lobel of the supplies placed at his disposal by the military authorities.

Once again, the course of events prevented this new scheme from entering into operation.

On the evening of May 28 I reembarked on a submarine chaser that was involved in evacuating the British Expeditionary Force. I had lost the better part of my uniform, I forget in what circumstances, and had found somewhere or other an old French's soldier's cape that was too

long for me and a French helmet that was too big. I certainly looked
odd and was stopped and questioned by the British military police at
Dover Station. Fortunately I still had all my official papers with me
and everything turned out all right. Monnet and Pléven were very
relieved to see me again. A few days later I received the congratulations
of the British and French governments[3] and so the adventure ended.

During the first half of June I carried out a number of assignments
(two or three) that consisted in taking messages from the British
government to a French government that had left Paris and was
wandering somewhere on the roads of France. What I remember with
any clarity concerns only the last of these assignments. I had to get a
message through to Paul Reynaud from Churchill who was offering
France the support of Britain's air force if she refused a separate peace
with Germany. Flying over in a little two-seater plane, I landed at
Orléans where I learned that the French government was then at
Tours. I went there, by what means I no longer remember, and
appeared at the mansion that was now the official headquarters of the
government.

I did not get as far as seeing Reynaud himself. A colonel (Colonel de
Villelume), who was in command of his military household or a
member of it, intercepted Churchill's letter, read it and burst into
invective against the English: 'They've betrayed us and now they offer
us a few miserable planes!' During the few days I spent in Tours I was
able to gauge the intensity of the defeatist and anglophobic sentiments
that prevailed in the entourage of Paul Reynaud, in whom I had until
then placed my entire trust. I had to face the fact that there was
something rotten here. The head of government's brilliant intelligence
was not allied to the strength of convictions and willpower that would
have enabled him to face up to the terrible ordeals that were descend-
ing on France.

With the German troops drawing nearer, the government decided to
move to Bordeaux. That was my destination too. Olivier Moreau-
Néret, then the economic affairs secretary at the Finance Ministry,
offered to take me in his car. We drove all one night, taking secondary
roads and making wide detours to avoid the mass of refugees and
routed soldiers heading for the South of France. When we got to
Bordeaux I went back to London, I no longer remember how.

It now remains for me to tell of the last desperate expedition in
which I took part and which again took me from London to Bordeaux.
It took place on June 18, 1940 after the project of Anglo-French unity[4]
had come to nought as a result of Pétain's accession to power during

the night of June 16–17. The idea was to lift to North Africa, or possibly England, one or more French statesmen who there, out of reach of the enemy, would incarnate the legitimate French republic. Jean Monnet, René Pléven, Emmanuel Monick and I took off in a seaplane from a British port at daybreak on June 18. The aircraft could hold thirty passengers, that is to say us and the people at Bordeaux we could prevail upon to leave. In his *Pour Mémoire* Monick describes our state of mind at the time.

Marshal Pétain had announced that he was going to 'attempt to negotiate an armistice.' We had heard his announcement in London where we were residing. We thought that if the French government had taken such a decision it was in the conviction that within a month England would 'have her neck wrung like a chicken' by Germany. That was the actual expression being used in General Weygand's entourage. But on that score all four of us were convinced to the contrary. In our opinion, England was prepared to resist. With Churchill in the driver's seat there would be no weakening of policy. Britain's navy and fighter force were intact: they would do everything to secure the Channel. There was nothing to indicate that the war would not last a long time. In that case, America might be brought into it. The certainty of a final victory for Germany was in no way founded. It was our duty, we thought, to go to Bordeaux and set out our thoughts before the new French government in which each of us had some friends.

Jean Monnet in his *Memoirs* recounts that on that same June 18 Churchill drew up a very brief message offering the French government all the ships necessary to evacuate men and equipment (to North Africa)[6].

We put down at Biscarosse and from there we went to Bordeaux where the most extraordinary confusion reigned. Monick, Monnet and Pléven talked, together or separately, with some of the most important dignitaries of the Third Republic, Herriot, Jeanneney, Mandel and others. I, the young air force lieutenant, was present at a few of these talks as a witness. Not one of the men approached wanted to leave, some for personal reasons, most for loftier motives such as a refusal to leave French soil when the country was in such a tragic situation or the hope that the French government and parliament would be moving 'officially' to North Africa a few days later. Some thought there might still be something to be salvaged in France, others that it would be dishonourable to be the first to leave and shed all responsibilities. When evening came, feeling that we were liable to be arrested by Pétain's police, we decided to go back to London. By some miracle Pléven had found in the throng his wife and two daughters whom he had had to leave behind when he went to England; so they got on the plane along with a few other persons including one of my university friends, a young Jew whom I had met by chance in Bordeaux.

Looking back today on those far-off times, I do not know quite what to think of that enterprise. To hope to keep France in the war, to hope that men and equipment in significant quantities could be evacuated to North Africa, that the Bordeaux government would stop in its path towards abandonment and collaboration, all this seems utopian to me today. Pétain had taken his decision, the Germans were in France, wills had yielded, the story of France's occupation was already there to be read between the lines of the present. Would it have been possible to continue to wage war alongside Britain from North Africa, if a political personage of great stature had appeared there? Having spent a few months in Morocco in 1940–1, in circumstances I shall recount later on, I think I can say that there too the cause was hopeless. The Pétain government was ostensibly the legitimate government of France, the navy was utterly loyal to Darlan the new minister for merchant and military shipping; the North African proconsuls had neither the audacity nor the courage, nor even the necessary convictions, to secede formally, as General Noguès would show in December 1942. It should be added that the United States was not in the war and that Britain did not have the forces necessary for an effective intervention. If Herriot, Jeanneney or someone else, moved by us to Algeria, had tried to take power he would inevitably have failed. On the other hand, and although it is generally pointless and a waste of time to try and rewrite history, I think it can reasonably be said that if one of the eminent statesmen of the Third Republic had decided to get to London in those fateful days of June 1940, a French government in exile would certainly have formed around him. The British would have worked to make that happen.

Despondency

I have no clear recollection of the last days of June and the first days of July 1940, after my return to London. I was deeply depressed. The fact that the French army, in which I had placed so much hope, should have been annihilated without even really fighting led me to reappraise everything in which I had believed. The incompetence, the intrinsic weakness of successive French governments during the 1930s appeared to me with blinding clarity. True, I had been a severe critic of those governments from 1934 to 1939, but I had not said the half of what ought to have been said.

I must confess that for a while I began to despair of the future. I could not see any way out of the frightful situation we had got ourselves into. It was beyond me to visualize the kind of effort that might get us out. I allowed my talk to become tinged with hopeless pessimism. I remember saying one day to Raymond Aron, who had just arrived in London, these words which I now consider harsh: 'History gives victory to those who deserve it!' I spoke as if our defeat were past recall and Germany's triumph definitely established.

This state of mind persisted for two weeks perhaps or possibly a month. I shall shortly be telling what caused me to snap out of it. But before leaving this part of my story I should like to say that my sorrow, even in the light of the final outcome of events, was not unfounded. The fact remains that May–June 1940 marked the end of a phase of France's history and never again, in spite of the Resistance and the efforts of de Gaulle, would the country become what it had been before. I had been reared on the idea that France was a great military power, that she was in fact the arbiter of peace in Europe. Those illusions were dispelled in the space of a few days. I had seen, during my travels in France in May–June, what remained of that glorious army, a pitiful rabble of weaponless soldiers fleeing along the roads to unknown destinations.

Let there be no misunderstanding about the sense of these remarks. It was probably inevitable, even if events had taken a different course, that France would in time become a second-rate power. The same fate awaited Britain, even though she was to fight with the courage and tenacity of which we know. That America and Russia would one day become superpowers was already written into history. What was not was the way that this would come about. It was not foreordained that France would suffer the dreadful defeat of May 1940. If the Germans had been prevented from remilitarizing the Rhineland in 1936, if in 1936 or even earlier we had produced as many aircraft and tanks as we could, if we had listened to de Gaulle and set up armoured divisions, if we had followed a reasonable economic policy in the thirties, we might still have been beaten but we would have gone down fighting. We would not have witnessed the debacle of what was once a great army. There would not have been this blot on the history of France.

The high command's share of the blame is overwhelming, largely because of its imbecilic strategy in May 1940. France had virtually sealed her own fate after World War One with a purely defensive strategy that ignored her alliances and her essential interests. But however reprehensible such a military policy might be, it was vital to stick to it in the event of enemy attack. In the months that preceded the German offensive, or even well before, France could have fortified the Franco-Belgian border, assembled big tank units and in any case set up reserves that could have been dispatched to the points where the enemy had broken through. I am not a military expert and shall refrain from giving my opinion on whether the Ardennes could reasonably be considered impenetrable to a modern army; the Germans did not think so and history shows that they were right.

At all events, instead of the defensive strategy that reflected French military thinking of the interwar years, when the Germans attacked on May 10, 1940, France sent her army into the lowlands of Belgium and Holland, into mobile warfare for which nothing had prepared it, without air support and with its tanks dispersed in little clusters among a large number of infantry units. Behind, no reserves. When the Germans broke through at Sedan the disaster was total and irreparable. Purely defensive warfare might not have made it possible to avoid defeat, but the enemy would not have scored such a lightning triumph. France and England would have had time to think carefully about the future and set up outposts of resistance in their combined empire. Politically the situation would have been quite different.

Let it be added on this point that a German attack in 1940 was foreseeable and that the French government and chiefs of staff could not even plead surprise. Had Hitler not announced it himself? But that was taken as braggadocio. Yet surely it was clear that time was not on his side. The French and especially the British empires had immense resources that only the incompetence of prewar governments had prevented from being mobilized. The mighty American industrial machine had been set in motion and had begun to work for the Allies, to say nothing of the British and French military effort that was intensifying daily. Another year and German superiority would have been seriously dented. Another two and probably it would have vanished.

People whose opinions I respect told me after the war that the way things turned out was preferable after all to another bloodbath like the one France had known in 1914–18 and which would have claimed once again the greater part of her youth and prevented any future rebirth. I admit without hesitation that, at the stage events had reached by June 1940, the fighting in France had to end with the surrender of an army that had ceased to exist as an organized force. The choice did not lie between an armistice and continuation of the war in France, which might have pointlessly entailed considerable loss of human lives, but between an armistice and outright capitulation. It seems to me that the normal reaction of a country that had been defeated but whose will had not been broken would have been, after a surrender of the French army in France, to continue the war in the empire, with a government headquartered in Algiers and preserving the nation's alliances. 1940 is a date in the history of France which marks not only a military defeat without precedent but also, among the political elite with but few exceptions, a moral collapse of which I know no other example.

2

MOROCCO

Between late June and early July 1940, after our descent on Bordeaux, I found myself in London with time on my hands and a fundamental choice to make, one that was to influence the rest of my existence. Three possibilities were open to me: to join up with the Free French and General de Gaulle, which is what René Pléven did; to go to the United States with Jean Monnet, who was to play an important part in the Anglo-American war effort; or to return to France and see what could be done there. I discarded the idea of leaving for America, there was nothing for me to do there. I hesitated a long time before giving up, provisionally as events would show, the idea of joining the Free French. I had never seen General de Gaulle and knew hardly anything about him. On June 18 I was in Bordeaux and so missed his famous appeal to us to continue the war alongside our allies. Moreover, I mistrusted army men, a hangover from my socialist youth.

It was on the occasion of the Bordeaux visit that I had seen Emmanuel Monick again, having already met him in 1936–7 at the time of the *Front Populaire* government. With an outstanding record of service in the 1914–18 war, he was an *Inspecteur des Finances*[1] and later financial attaché in Washington, then London. After the 1939–45 war he would become Governor of the Bank of France, then President of the *Banque de Paris et des Pays-Bas* (PARIBAS). Seldom in my life have I seen so much intelligence and shrewdness combined with so much generosity and kindness. He was my elder by twenty years, but at no time in the close collaboration that formed between us did I feel this age difference. He had the art of putting people at their ease. At the same time he was extremely clear-sighted and I never once saw his judgment at fault. But let us get back to London and 1940. I saw Monick a good deal and finally came round to his point of view, which he expressed in these terms in *Pour Mémoire*:

For my part, sensing by some mysterious instinct that it should be possible to do battle in France itself and in the empire against the schemes of the enemy, provided that one were prepared to seize every opportunity and sometimes play the *franc-tireur*, I decided to go back to France and try my luck there. Robert Marjolin went with me[2].

Before going back to France, Monick went to see General de Gaulle and told him of his scruples: he had fought in the 1914–18 war but not in 1939–40.

Not having been exposed to the dangers of the war, the idea was abhorrent to me that I should be evading the dangers and suffering my country was now going to experience. I had every intention, moreover, of continuing to fight the good fight over there, the same as his over here, but on a different level and with different means.

The General listened to me courteously. He objected that I could no nothing in France. There I would be just one more prisoner. All my dreams of action in the home country were simply an illusion. It was at his side that I could have been useful! But he understood my scruples. He would not put any pressure on me. I left him with the assurance that if on experience I found that I was precluded from any action in France I would try to join him.

To be perfectly honest, there was another reason for my own decision to return to France: I believed that my parents, now elderly and in poor health, and my sister had left Paris when the Germans arrived. I wanted to see them again, reinstall them in their flat and give them a little money before deciding what I could do to carry on the fight.

With Monick I boarded a boat bound for Lisbon that was taking home the different French missions that had been in London at the time of the catastrophe. I got to Vichy in August. I shall not describe the Vichy of that time; others have done so before me and better than I could. Let me simply say that the mixture of despair among those who feared persecution, triumph among all those who had detested the Republic, blatant ambition on the part of those eager for office, all in an atmosphere of extreme disorder, made Vichy the most sinister place

I have ever seen. Fear and ignominy were everywhere. As far as I remember, the only people I had occasion to see there were ones who hated the new regime, like Robert Lacoste. At the same time I kept in close touch with Monick whose feelings, like mine, were unequivocal. But we were, at that juncture, in the greatest uncertainty as to what kind of action to undertake.

Everything changed suddenly when, during that same month of August, the post of Secretary-General to Morocco fell vacant and was offered to Monick. He did not hesitate for a moment, sensing that in North Africa the way would be clear for him to act for the good of France in a post where he could renew contact with numerous friends and allies in London and Washington. 'I accepted immediately,' he wrote, 'all the more eager to launch into action as a free man since I had feared I might be condemned to inaction as a prisoner[3]'. Monick made me the offer of going with him as his *chef de cabinet* [chief secretary] and I, in turn, accepted immediately. I asked him to allow me the few days I needed to make a flying visit to Paris for a brief reunion with my parents and sister who had returned home after a vain attempt to get to the Sarthe. Then I left with Monick, his wife and his two daughters. We embarked at Port-Vendres on the *Gouverneur Général Chanzy* and reached Rabat via Oran.

My stay in Morocco lasted from September 1940 to March 1941, approximately seven months that saw me engaged in intense activity and endless travelling as I worked with Monick in what had now become a total partnership of minds. I also felt a great admiration for him coupled with a strong underlying affection. This identity of views and our affection for each other were to last until his death a few years ago. The idea we had was simple: to forge very close links between North Africa and the United States that would facilitate a landing when America entered the war. For we did not doubt that when the opportunity arose President Roosevelt would seize it, and North Africa would almost certainly be the Americans' first objective. Our policy was as follows: to get the Americans to supply North Africa with essential foodstuffs and so make the Arab and French population kindly disposed towards them; to increase the number of US consuls and vice-consuls, ostensibly in order to supervise the movement of the goods America would be supplying but also to engage in some discreet information and propaganda. For this it was necessary to persuade the Americans, something that was to prove relatively easy, and to get the British to abandon the more extreme forms of blockade they were maintaining against North Africa, which was to prove more difficult. It was also necessary to convince the French authorities in North Africa to cooperate in this grand design and to get Vichy to turn a blind eye.

My part in all this was to be Monick's right-hand man and envoy. I shuttled to and fro between Rabat and Tangier, where I met American and British agents, Madrid, where my usual contact was the American diplomat Robert Murphy, Lisbon, where I spoke to the representative of Britain's Ministry of Economic Welfare, David Eccles, and Vichy, where I had established very close links with the American *chargé d'affaires* Freeman Matthews. There was some danger in all this. The Germans, the French navy in Casablanca and the Vichy secret services were keeping close watch on Monick and, by extension, on me. We succeeded for a while in throwing them off the scent and concealing the purpose of these dealings.

General Weygand had been appointed proconsul in North Africa in October 1940. He was of great help to us and I can only concur wholeheartedly with Monick's expressed opinion of him:

He had an inkling of my secret contacts with Washington (one of my best friends was on his staff). I did not mention them so as not to embarrass him, he did not question me so as not to have to forbid me. But he was able to intimate to me, by way of a particularly friendly attitude, that my secret action – provided it remained prudent – had his tacit support. For him an armistice was just a suspension of fighting that had no sense unless it were the prelude to a resumption of hostilities. He was working towards that end in his capacity; he was leaving me free to do so in mine[4] (...) Visiting the outermost confines of his territory, he explained to all that the armistice was only a truce. He forbade any contact with the enemy; in everything he did he was the opposite of Laval whom he accused of wallowing in defeat 'like a dog rolling on a turd'. In private he did not hide the fact that it would be necessary to take up arms again when the time came[5].

I went to see him myself several times in Algiers in the context of the negotiations I was conducting under the authority of Monick, but observing the same discretion as the latter. Weygand always treated me extremely kindly and without asking any embarrassing questions. I remember very clearly the last interview I had with him in Rabat in 1941. I had decided to go back to England, via the United States so as not to compromise Monick. I had already devised the smoke screen behind which I would shortly vanish. Monick told Weygand that I was about to leave for Washington and he asked me to come and see him. I told him I had been invited by the Rockefeller Foundation to spend some time in Washington and gave a detailed account of my projects. He listened patiently but not for an instant was he taken in. 'Well, all right,' he said, 'I can't stop you from doing what you want. And even if I could, I wouldn't. Everyone must be free to choose his own destiny. But I would like you to know before you go that things will not stay as they are. The time will soon come when we shall have to start fighting again. Then men like you will be needed in France. I hope that we shall see each other again.' I was deeply moved as I took leave of him.

Before my departure I did what I could to advance the negotiations with the Americans. To remove the British impediment Monick sent me to Lisbon, on the pretext of renewing a trade agreement between Morocco and Portugal, to talk with David Eccles. I encountered strong resistance from Eccles, so I asked Robert Murphy to come to my aid. His intervention was decisive: certain French boats, sailing with British permits, would be authorized to unload American merchandise in Casablanca. The Murphy-Weygand agreement was concluded in 1941 and served to raise the British blokade in part. It was therefore greeted with delight by the authorities in Algiers. But it was equally favourable to the United States in giving that country the chance to establish firmly its prestige and influence south of the Mediterranean. Additionally it authorized – for the supervision that would be required – the introduction of American consuls, the spearhead of the projected landing in North Africa[6].

Vichy, wanting no trouble in North Africa, did not object. The Germans, preoccupied with the offensive in Russia and fearing the possibility of dissidence south of the Mediterranean, did not veto the plan. But at their behest Monick was recalled to France on August 15, 1941. He left without regrets, having accomplished what he had set out to do.

I had left in March of the same year when the rumours of Monick's forthcoming recall began to take on substance. I decided then to go back to London. I unburdened myself to Monick who, though sorry that I would be leaving him, offered no objection. He even facilitated my plans by giving me written orders that I was to proceed to Martinique to inspect the harbour facilities at Fort-de-France, from where some of the American shipments to North Africa would be forwarded. I then had to go to Washington to report on my mission to the French ambassador. It was understood that there I would disappear and that my failure to return to Morocco would be explained by the Rockefeller Foundation's having awarded me a grant to continue my studies in the United States.

So I embarked that March in Casablanca on a banana boat, the *Belain d'Esnambuc*, bound for Fort-de-France. Monick, with his customary kindness, gave me some money to help pay my travel expenses. I had two travelling companions: the youngest son of André Istel, a great friend of Monick, and Olivier Wormser who, as a naval officer, had been demobilized at Dakar after the armistice and gone up to Rabat where Monick had taken him under his protection; like me, he intended to go to London and join up with the Free French.

We had an uneventful crossing that lasted about ten days. When we got to Fort-de-France the military authorities tried to put Olivier Wormser under house arrest at Morne Rouge on the slopes of Mount Pele, because he was a Jew. I approached Admiral Robert, who was in command in Martinique, and cited the authority of Monick, of whom, I said, Wormser was a great friend. Admiral Robert revoked the order and we were able to go on our way. The *Belain d'Esnambuc* had to put in for refuelling at the American island of Saint Thomas and we seized this opportunity to leave French territory. From Saint Thomas we made our way to Puerto Rico and from there to New York, where we separated. Wormser got to England by his own devices and young Istel enlisted in the Canadian army; he was to die tragically a little while after, from complications following minor surgery.

I went on to Washington where I saw Jean Monnet again; he got me passenger space on one of the bombers that the Americans were manufacturing for the British, and that was how I crossed the Atlantic. The trip was enlivened by two rather amusing incidents. When I arrived at the little airfield near New York from which the bomber was to take off, the American officer in charge sent for me and told me there would be two of us passengers in the bomber, myself and a German from Chicago whom the British were bringing over to London in order to obtain information. 'I don't know anything about him,' the officer said, 'except that he's a pilot and that he may try to take over the aircraft in flight. There's no weapon in his baggage, but he may have one on him. The radio operator, who'll be in a little cabin above where the two of you will be, has had orders to shoot at the slightest suspicious move. Try not to fall asleep.' What a night! I engaged in conversation with the poor German, who was innocent of the dire intentions credited to him, and went on talking so as not to fall asleep. I kept him awake all the way to Blackpool.

There it was something else again. I showed the British immigration officer the letters Jean Monnet had given me from himself and from others, including a letter of recommendation from Lord Halifax, then the United Kingdom ambassador to Washington. Everything was going swimmingly; a car had been laid on to take me to the station where I was to catch the London train. Then suddenly the immigration officer said to me: 'There's only one thing I haven't asked you. Just exactly what have to come to England for?' Proudly I replied: 'Why, I've come to join the Free French.' The officer's face clouded. 'Oh, that's a nuisance! I've had strict instructions to send all Frenchmen with that intention on to a camp, it's called the Patriotic School, where they screen you to try and find out if any enemy agents have slipped in among you. On the other hand, the letters you've shown me certify that you are quite above suspicion. Oh dear, how awkward!' He was obviously very embarrassed. Suddenly he had an idea. 'I'll tell you what. I'm going to ask to you forget that I've already asked you what your intentions are and that you answered. Go into the next room and then come straight back. I'll ask you the same question and you say you're in England on business. That way I'll be able to let you go. After that, you do what you want.' This is precisely what was done and I reached London the same day. It must have been May 1941.

3

LONDON–WASHINGTON
(1941–1944)

As soon as I got to London I joined the Free French. But I had to overcome one difficulty I had not bargained for. Having done in North Africa what I believed to be my duty, I thought the British would welcome me with open arms. I had forgotten that they were, at any rate as yet, hostile to the efforts made by Monick (and indirectly by Weygand) to provision North Africa from the United States. As someone closely associated with that enterprise, I was suspect.

I had an interview with Churchill's secretary, Major Morton, I forget at whose suggestion, his or mine. He questioned me at length about what was going on in Morocco; I answered him frankly and thought that the problem had been cleared up. But a few days later René Pléven, who was now de Gaulle's man in charge of external relations, sent for me and showed me a letter from Morton expressing astonishment that I had joined the Free French in view of my recent activities in Rabat. Pléven also showed me the reply he had sent in which he said that Morton's letter had to be the result of a misunderstanding and that I was a young patriot whom the Free French were happy to welcome among them. On that occasion Pléven gave me proof of a friendship that was never to fail. That was the end of the incident. No one took me to task any more for my action in North Africa, the whole point of which became clear with the Allied landing in November 1942.

The next thing was to determine what my activity in England would be and I found myself faced with the sort of situation all émigrés have known. General de Gaulle's authority was not yet firmly established, it was disputed by different groups of Frenchmen, all impelled by the same sincere desire to continue the war until the Liberation but having different views on how to go about it. In London at the time there were true-blue Gaullists; Frenchmen who had broken with the Vichy regime and had much the same stances as de Gaulle but denied his authority; persons of note who were working with the British but completely rejected what the Free French stood for; former diplomats and civil servants who had stayed behind in London but whose standpoint was not clearly defined; to say nothing of all the shadings in between. The polemic among them was sometimes ferocious.

La France Libre

For a few months I drifted before taking the path I would stick to. In London I had found Maurice Dejean, for many years head of the press service at the French embassy in Berlin, then in 1940 *chef de cabinet* of the Minister for Foreign Affairs. He had reached London by way of Morocco. De Gaulle had made him the political affairs director of Free France. I had met him a few months earlier at Rabat and we had become friendly. After the war he headed the political affairs directorate at the Ministry for Foreign Affairs, then for a while was French ambassador to Moscow. Dejean offered to make me head of the information service. I was wrong to accept; I was not cut out for the job. Information, especially in times of war, but also in peacetime when political passions run high and clash one with another, is nearly indistinguishable from propaganda. While recognizing that in the circumstances propaganda on our part was absolutely necessary to counter the German propaganda and that of Vichy, I felt ill at ease. I stayed about two months in my new job and then left because of an argument about respective prerogatives with Maurice Schumann, then the Free French spokesman at the BBC. Schumann, incidentally, was probably in the right.

I then tried to serve in the Free French air forces and took the tests to be an observer and take part in the bombing raids over Germany. I was turned down for being near-sighted. The Free French naval forces, then under the command of Admiral Muselier, took me and for a time I was attached to the admiral as an *aide-de-camp*; there were two of us performing this function, myself and Alain Savary. Meanwhile I had joined the team that published the magazine *La France Libre* and comprised André Labarthe, Raymond Aron, Staro and Martha Lecoutre. Raymond Aron was the moving spirit of the venture. He had managed to produce, and continued to do so throughout the war, a review that was of a very high intellectual standard. I can only agree entirely with the description he gives of it in *Le Spectateur engagé*:

Concerning our review, it was regarded throughout the world as the Gaullist magazine, the magazine of Free France *par excellence*. It had a quality that perhaps the General did not appreciate all that much: it was an analytical review rather than a propaganda paper. But which was more useful to the Free French cause? One propaganda paper among many ... or a review of a high intellectual standard[1]?

I worked regularly on the magazine for a few months and when I left it was with regret, so close was my understanding with the other members of the group, especially Raymond Aron. Apart from a few differences of detail, our convictions were identical concerning the need to continue the war and the rejection of everything that could come from Vichy. I, in particular, had completely separated and was keeping completely separate in my mind the efforts that a few men were making in North Africa to get it ready for the war and the policy of the Vichy government. If the latter had accepted the Weygand-Murphy agreements, or rather had not opposed them, it was because it could not do otherwise for fear of causing trouble on the other side of the Mediterranean.

Carlton Gardens

But however profound my intellectual sympathy with my friends of *La France Libre*, after a few months in their company I felt obliged to do some soul-searching and ask myself whether I was on the right path. Raymond Aron had one simple objective and one only: to make *La France Libre* the great magazine of the French Resistance the world over. He maintained great objectivity in his judgments of de Gaulle and the administration the latter had set up. I cannot say as much of Labarthe, who ran the magazine, and his ally, Admiral Muselier, who was in command of the Free French naval forces. Zealous and impassioned both of them, they seemed to be engaged in a sort of anti-

Gaullist crusade. I found it increasingly difficult to put up with their extreme language. Since I had a choice to make, I rapidly convinced myself that de Gaulle was, for France, for the empire and for the French abroad, the symbol of the Resistance and the only force capable of directing it and coordinating its action. I waited for the very first opportunity to join the staff at Carlton Gardens where de Gaulle and the French Committee of National Liberation had set up their headquarters.

That opportunity arrived late in 1941 when Hervé Alphand became the Committee's director of economic affairs. He asked me to work with him; I accepted immediately and moved to Carlton Gardens at the end of 1941 or the beginning of 1942. I was to stay there until September 1943. That year and a half of my life was a time of reflection and study, in which I endeavoured to visualize as clearly as possible what France ought to be and might be after the Liberation. Given my training, it was natural that I should interest myself particularly in the economic aspect of things. As will be seen later, I had more than one occasion after the war to turn to account the work I did then. I can truthfully say that the day I accepted Hervé Alphand's offer marked the start of a period of some twenty-five years devoted to the reconstruction of France and then the construction of Europe.

By that time of late 1941 or early 1942 I had settled all the qualms of conscience I had felt after the debacle of May–June 1940. I still felt from time to time a nagging sense of regret (or should I say remorse?) for having left London in June 1940, but I would soon shake off this feeling by telling myself that what I had done in Morocco with Monick had probably served the cause of France and her allies better than anything I could have done in England during the same period.

I would also ask myself sometimes whether the place of a thirty-year-old Frenchman was really in London, admittedly exposed to the odd bomb or two but escaping the infinitely greater perils he would have incurred on the battlefield or in the internal Resistance. I was a 'resistant' through my intellectual convictions and my joining General de Gaulle, but the peaceful life I was living in London was in no way comparable with that of the internal resistance, with that of the men in France who were waging a desperate struggle that could end at any moment in torture or death. My answer to that question was that I had voluntarily taken risks on several occasions and was prepared to do so again if asked to, but that since the men I was working for considered I could be of most use by paving the way for the future I had no sound reason for doing otherwise than they had indicated.

I had met General de Gaulle a few months before. When I arrived in London in May 1941, he was away. He sent for me in August or September when I was with Admiral Muselier. I found myself in the presence of a tall, thin man, very different from what this historic personage was to become, seeming to me to lack assurance, very nervy, chain-smoking and offering cigarettes to those with whom he was conversing. I no longer remember what we talked about. I just know he was very displeased that I had gone with Muselier. Relations between the two men were very bad indeed at that point. De Gaulle liked to end each conversation with a sentence that summed up the whole object of the exercise. This time it was: 'You won't be staying with Muselier.' I did not say a word and withdrew. Nothing happened. I left Muselier, later, of my own accord.

When I joined the staff at Carlton Gardens, the General had me come to his office several times in succession to talk about the matters I was dealing with. From time to time he asked me to lunch with him. I was surprised when sometime in 1942 or 1943, with no apparent reason, he asked me twice in the same week. Perhaps he was thinking of giving me an assignment and wanted to observe me more closely and at greater length. But nothing came of it and I was left to my conjectures. My admiration for the image grew with time, but our relations always remained just as impersonal. Yet I became convinced, as I saw his role in the war develop and aggrandize his place in the history of France, that I had chosen correctly and been right to place at his disposal the few talents with which nature and study had endowed me.

I spent most of my time working in a small office at Carlton Gardens or attending Interallied meetings Hervé Alphand asked me to go to. I studied the problems that would or we thought would face France and Europe after the Liberation, together with the problems of economic and monetary organization which the free world would have to resolve after the Germans' defeat. I have only a very hazy recollection of my life in London during those twenty or so months from the end of 1941 to September 1943.

I was a petty official or, if you like, an intellectual lost in the civil service. My role was very unobtrusive. This period was an extension of my prewar life, entirely taken up with study. I read an enormous amount, both during the day and in the evenings. In addition to my work for Hervé Alphand, I completed my initiation to Anglo-Saxon economic literature, notably with Ricardo and Alfred Marshall. I taught myself the rudiments of national accounting, then being developed in England and America. Without realizing it, I accumulated a mass of knowledge that was to prove very useful after the war. I had become a member of the Reform Club, an institution of liberal origin I knew well, having been frequently invited before the war. I spent most of my spare time there. I ate there and in the evening would withdraw into the library to read or write. Among the club's members were some very good English friends of mine, Lionel Robbins, George Schwartz, Frank Paish, Cyril Plant, and others. We would get together once a week to discuss current issues.

I remember one amusing incident that shows how well I had fitted into British society by then. It took place at the Reform Club. At the end of one evening I had spent in the library reading a book on history or economics I was getting up to go home to bed when an elderly man whom I had already noticed as one of the regulars of the club, where he spent most of his time ensconced in a deep armchair, came over and spoke to me. 'Young man,' he said benignly, 'I have been observing you for some time now. You are doing just what a fellow of your age ought to be doing. You are reading with great concentration, you are taking notes. Allow me to congratulate you.' I thanked him. He was surprised by my accent.'Oh! You're not English.' 'No,' I replied, 'I'm French, a Free Frenchman.' 'How odd,' he remarked, 'it never occurred to me that you might not be English.' And seeing my slightly indignant reaction, he added: 'You look so Reform Club.'

I made a short trip to the United States at that time (May–June 1943), accompanying Hervé Alphand to the United Nations Conference on Food and Agriculture at Hot Springs in Virginia. This was the first of the big international conferences that were held during the war. It would give rise to the Food and Agriculture Organization (F.A.O.). On that occasion I saw Denyse Harari again; she had been one of the participants, along with me, at Kojève's seminar before the war and had just got married in New York. Back in London I returned to the kind of life I had been leading before. (Previously I had shared a flat with Raymond Aron but now I had moved into a service flat near Kensington High Street.) An uneventful life from the strictly personal standpoint but punctuated by the great dates of the war: the German attack on Russia in June 1941; Pearl Harbor and America's entry into the war in December 1941; the Allied landing in North Africa in November 1942; the fall of Mussolini in July 1943. The world scene was changing before our eyes. When I had returned to London in May 1941 the outcome of the war was uncertain. In December of the same year, with Britain, Russia and America leagued together against

Germany, the latter's defeat along with that of her Italian and Japanese allies was no more than a matter of time.

I would not want to conclude this part of my story without mentioning the admiration which I conceived for the British people then and which has never left me. They showed, during that dramatic period of their history, qualities of courage, endurance and resistance to defeat that commanded the astonishment and respect of all those who, like me, lived the nation's life without really being a part of it. For a year or two Britain truly held the fate of the world in her hands. Had she faltered, we would probably be living today, or we would have lived for some time, in a German Europe.

Washington

De Gaulle had moved his headquarters to Algiers at the end of 1942. In 1943 Jean Monnet became a member of the French Committee of National Liberation. In the autumn of that year de Gaulle asked him to go to Washington and set up arrangements to supply France after the Liberation with foodstuffs, raw materials and capital goods. Monnet wired Alphand from Algiers to ask that I accompany him. I made a brief visit to Algiers to set up with Jean Monnet and a few other persons the assignment I had been given, the results of which would, in the event, determine the manner, the timing and the political atmosphere of France's reconstruction. We all thought the Liberation was now near. Monnet himself says in his *Memoirs* that his main task was 'to lay the foundations for Franco-American agreements to safeguard [France's] economic and financial future[2].'

We had been concerned with these problems since the summer, in a small informal group based, like so many others, on friendship and on attachment to a common ideal. The group included René Mayer, Robert Marjolin, and Hervé Alphand. Numerous memoranda produced at that time, in which everyone left the mark of his imagination, bear witness to an eager and sometimes prophetic concern for France's future and that of the new Europe[3].

I confess that I have no clear recollection of these conversations in Algiers, by contrast with those that were to take place in Washington a while later, more or less among the same people. My relations with Monnet at that time were not what they were to become subsequently. I was a young intellectual who had not yet seen action. I doubt whether

Monnet thought, in that autumn of 1943, that I would one day become one of his chief collaborators. Anyway, for several months he only gave me small jobs to do. One of them was to get in touch with the American philanthropic organizations to see what help they could bring to the French population when the time came. I went each weekend from Washington to New York to have lunch with old ladies who were living with the memory of the 1914–18 war, who were profoundly Francophile but whose means, however considerable, were not commensurate with the problem.

My ties with Jean Monnet grew closer at the beginning of 1944 when a scheme was hatched to replace him at the head of the Washington outfit. Monnet had gone to Algiers to maintain contact with the French Committee of National Liberation. In his absence a rumour was circulated by some French diplomats serving in Washington that he had fallen from grace and would not be coming back. It is not difficult to imagine the confusion that reigned for a while in the team he had set up. I took it upon myself to ask each one of them to go on with what he had to do and not worry about the rumours, and to consider that until we heard from him Jean Monnet was still the boss. The scheme evaporated in a few days and Monnet returned. From that moment our relations were transformed. Let us say, if you like, that he appreciated my loyalty. I also remember a visit by Alphand to Washington at that time. He knew me much better than Monnet did; we had worked together for more than eighteen months in London. He told him that I was too good for the minor jobs I had been given up till then. Anyway, the upshot was that I was promoted early in 1944 to head of the French Supply Mission to the United States, directly responsible to Jean Monnet.

Thus the milestones of a career often arise from comparative trifles. Those little fortuities at the beginning of 1944 brought me closer to Monnet and established relations of trust between us that were to last for more than thirty years. An optimist would say, perhaps, that if Monnet had not discovered me then, he would have at some later date. I am not so certain. Then again, if I had not been engaged in an interesting administrative career before the end of the war, I might have devoted my life to teaching and research and probably written a few books that would have made a name for me in another field. Be that as it may, from that point, and at least until the end of the war, I no longer had any choice. Having reached a certain level of responsibility, I was caught up in the system. No more time for personal reading; it was the office seven days a week, morning, afternoon and evening.

France was about to become a battleground again. Her economy had already been deeply disrupted by the Occupation. Several million French were prisoners in Germany. Stocks of food and raw materials were very low. Ports and railways had been seriously damaged by Allied bombing and would be even more so in the coming months. It was plain that the Allied merchant fleets would not suffice to transport the required men, military equipment and civilian supplies. One did not have to be clairvoyant to see that civilian supplies would be the first to be restricted. So it was necessary to make choices, establish priorities.

We endeavoured to draw up a list of France's requirements for the period immediately following the Allied landing in Europe. For this we used information sent to Algiers by the internal Resistance. We tried to visualize the complex arrangements that would have to be made to prevent life in France from being totally disrupted during the period of fighting and to get public services working again in the liberated areas. Monnet's chief partners in Washington were Hopkins, Stimson, McCloy and Dean Acheson. The American administration showed the greatest possible understanding in this matter. Monnet summed it up in these words:

To ensure that the French people's real needs in that still indefinite future were known and recognized was a task for men who were skilled both in economic forecasting and in negotiation. Alphand, [Marjolin,] Hirsch, and their experts performed it admirably. When the time came, the experience enabled them to take in hand without a hitch the revival of French industry after the war. Fearing that the battle to liberate France would be very destructive, and hoping that her three million prisoners and deportees would rapidly be brought home, we built up in the United States, North Africa, and Britain the large stocks that a country of France's size would need for six months – from coal to woollen blankets, from locomotives to footwear, from medical supplies to baby linen. As it turned out, our estimates were partly wrong: physical devastation was less catastrophic than we had imagined, and human suffering more cruel. But at least all due steps had been taken to limit our country's plight[4].

My most vivid recollection is of never-ending lists of food products, medicines, raw materials, capital goods and other items that we drew up day after day, constantly amending them and adding to them, in an attempt to grasp as fully as possible a virtually ungraspable reality, the needs of France after the Liberation. With the expulsion of the Germans during the summer of 1944, the situation changed:

We were no longer dealing with estimates, as in 1943: we were facing harsh and immediate realities. The great ports of Dunkirk, Saint-Nazaire, and La Rochelle were still in enemy hands; Nantes and Bordeaux were out of reach. What remained of our merchant fleet was requisitioned for war. We had fewer than three thousand locomotives. We had little coal, no steel, and no prospect of iron ore for months ahead (...)

Until the early days of December 1944 we spent most of our time re-examining with the French authorities the supply programme drawn up before the landings in France and therefore based in large measure on mere hypotheses. On the one hand, there had been less physical destruction than we had expected, and industrial capacity had remained at about 80% of its prewar level. The Germans had retreated so rapidly that they had been unable to carry off all our stocks. On the other hand, the paralysis of communications led to unforeseen shortages – with the result that some imported supplies proved less useful, while others, which were essential, could not be shipped to where they were needed[5].

In this gigantic task I had become Jean Monnet's chief collaborator in Washington. He designed, or we designed together, I executed. In a few months I had shed the skin of a young intellectual reflecting on France's future to become a senior civil servant, the second in command, in charge of organizing the huge flow of merchandise of all kinds that France would need to get back on her feet. A younger man, or an older one, come to that, would have been terrified by these responsibilities. I was thirty-three and I took them on without too many second thoughts. I probably made my share of mistakes, but no one ever took me to task. So I have to assume that I committed no heinous blunder.

I worked nonstop, leaving the office only to snatch a meal in a nearby restaurant. I was there that I met the young woman who was to become my wife. During those fifteen or so months in Washington I also made a few friends who, as I write these lines, still hold a very important place in my life. I am thinking in particular of Eric Roll and George Ball. I shall speak of these personal recollections further on.

Thoughts on economics and Europe

I have given a concise account of what I did, or tried to do, from the time of my return to London in May 1942 to the end of my stay in Washington in December 1944. Nearly four years elapsed between those two dates, four years of reflection and action. I find it hard to recall my state of mind then; so much time has passed during which I have changed without realizing it. But I intend to make an effort to recall what I was thinking in those days, for myself, for my children, for those who might be interested in the development of a mind which took the world as its object and which, even in its illusions, has always striven to be honest. Fortunately, since my recollections are not as clear as I would like, I, or rather some conscientious secretaries, have kept from that time a number of articles published in various magazines, together with a number of my memoranda to Hervé Alphand and Jean Monnet.

I had already become a Keynesian before the war on reading the *General Theory*. My economic beliefs were strengthened by the further reading I did in England and America and by the discussions I had with British and American economists. After the confusion that had reigned in economic thinking during the prewar years, we had finally arrived, or so I thought, at a number of certainties that would point the way to reconstruction and then rapid growth of our economies when the war was over. Within the space of a few years most of the problems had clarified and a body of doctrine had been formed; true, it was incomplete, but it did serve to answer the greater number of the questions that had baffled us so utterly in the thirties. The first material cause of this swift advance, chronologically, was the Great Depression of 1929–33 which shattered the optimism of classical economics. Then, more importantly, the preparations for the war and the war itself, by isolating countries from one another, had stripped down the mechanism of the international economy before our eyes and made it possible, without risk of external repercussions and unforeseeable reactions, to conduct real experiments on each national component. Necessity had done more in a few years than half a century of academic discussions. But if it took the depression and the war to arrive at an understanding of the mechanics of production and exchange, neither would have sufficed without the British scientific tradition that had persisted in an unbroken line from Adam Smith through Alfred Marshall to John Maynard Keynes and had furnished the essential conceptual tools with which to interpret economic experience[6].

My faith at that time in the science of economics may seem a little naïve today, after the disorders of the past fifteen years and with the present confusion in economic thinking. But I should like the reader to remember that this faith, which was then shared by nearly all economists, acted as a powerful spur when it came to organizing the war economy, reconstructing the European economies after the war and giving Europe a certain measure of unity. Even if one denies Keynesianism any theoretical value and consequently any permanent value (which I do not), one has to grant it a great pragmatic value, in the philosophical sense of the term. In other words, it worked.

I have just summed up the content of one of the articles I wrote at that time. In it I also set out what I thought should be the economic policy of the postwar years. For the first time perhaps, and in any case more forcefully and precisely than ever before, I stated my convictions as to the need for economic planning.

Even so I defined the conditions of state intervention in terms such that it could have its place in an economic regime founded essentially on free enterprise. My premise was the observation, taken direct from Keynes, that *laissez-faire* does not ensure full employment, either in the short or in the long term. And by *laissez-faire* I meant not only economic liberalism, i.e. a regime characterized by free competition and free trade, but any regime in which there is no rational central intervention, no government intervention guided by an overall plan. At the same time I refused to reject liberal capitalism:

Let me point out that this criticism of classical economics should not be equated with a criticism of the liberal capitalist regime itself. For whatever reason, the late 19th and early 20th centuries were the period in history that saw the greatest economic progress and the most rapid rise in the people's living standards.

I endorsed the doctrine of compensatory action by the state. If aggregate demand proved insufficient, government should intervene either through investment or investment encouragement, or through stimulation of consumption. Admittedly, I wrote, I was aware of the fact that before the war most producers were opposed to any form of state planning. But times had changed and we had learned a great deal. The most intelligent producers, even those most attached to a free-market economic system, would realize that without some measure of organization the system would inevitably break down and that it was infinitely better to make the vital sacrifices right away than to run the risk of violent upheavals in which private enterprise itself might well come to grief. Admittedly, the war economy methods would have to be abandoned when peace came. Price controls, exchange controls, restrictions on consumption, and so forth, would have to be phased out. But it was pointless, I said, to hope to turn the clock back and return to the prewar economic system. Government intervention had to be limited, but it was essential.

In normal times, when private investment is sufficient to keep economic activity, employment and national income at a high level, the state should refrain from disturbing the spontaneous workings of production and trade ... The economic function, the decision to produce or not to produce, rests in the hands of private enterprise.

It is in periods of crisis that the state has to intervene and add its own demand to private demand (individuals and enterprises) which is insufficient. The means of intervention that forward-looking producers prefer is investment support with resultant investment growth. That growth should be generated essentially by advantages granted to private industry. Substantial tax reliefs will ensure a return on investment where there had ceased to be one.

Government action should not replace action by producers. A shortfall in private investment, I went on, should be made good by public investment only for a brief period, after which the revival of private activity would make government intervention unnecessary. Nor was there any question of altering the country's politico-economic structure as a safeguard against slumps. Not only should the economic regime remain one based on private enterprise, but the general distribution of income and wealth should continue much the same.

I did not conceal my sympathy with this new body of doctrine, although I expressed certain reservations in the conclusion of the article:

It would remain to be seen whether the system is coherent, whether it really removes the dangers of prolonged depression and inflation, whether it answers all the requirements of modern society, including the political requirements. That it represents a renewal of capitalist thought and a vigorous effort to preserve the system of private enterprise, there can be no doubt[7].

I shall have occasion in the course of this book to cast a critical eye on the ideas I developed during the war. Why has fiscal policy ceased to all intents and purposes to be an effective means of maintaining economic equilibrium? Why is monetary policy directed solely at controlling inflation, to the exclusion of any other aim? How is it that the tremendous increase in public expenditure and tax and welfare charges over the past forty years has all but paralysed government action when it has been necessary to correct an endogenous or exogenous imbalance?

These questions will be posed in context later. For the time being, I shall simply say that the convictions I have set out above were those with which I tackled the problems of France's reconstruction. I could not but be strongly influenced by the environment in which I was operating, by the fact that in England and, to a lesser degree, in America I had firsthand examples of a war economy that had put to one side the rules of the free-market economy. My thinking was also coloured by the prospect of a period of reconstruction that would require methods analogous to those of the war economy. When I thought of France and her reconstruction, it was a France where shortage would be the rule that I had in mind.

In a memorandum of 1943 I set out a few general principles that I thought should guide French economic policy after the war. Any government of France would have to strive to ensure her existence as a great state. This meant rebuilding and developing her economic and military power; guaranteeing economic security to each Frenchman, especially the workers in industry and agriculture; maximizing the quantity of goods at the nation's disposal; distributing national income as fairly as possible with the aim of eliminating inequalities not due to differences in services rendered. The living standards of the workers in industry and agriculture depended on the productivity of the national economy, i.e. on its capital wealth. Rebuilding and developing the nation's capital stock was the best way to improve the lot of the masses. The working and peasant classes could not prosper in a state that was economically weak.

The foregoing propositions will strike many as trite, although some of them have still not been completely assimilated by a part of the political community and of public opinion. But coming after a long period of economic decline and a crushing military defeat, they took on the character of a manifesto, a manifesto written by a young technocrat smitten with ideas of growth, rigour and power through effort.

I had already realized that France would have to fit into an international framework and accept a division of labour with the other great powers. In my view, there were three prerequisites to be met here:

– sufficient international funds would have to be loaned to France at very low interest rates to rebuild her capital stock and raise the efficiency of the nation's plant to British and American levels;

– the other big countries should practise policies to safeguard the world against general economic crises;

– the countries supplying goods to France should accept hers at an exchange rate that would not imply a wastage of national labour.

It should be stressed, however, I wrote, that the establishment of an orderly international economic system is vital to the interests of France.

Then I developed the argument that since France had lost the demographic position that had ensured her supremacy in Europe for two centuries, she was duty bound, in order to avoid continuing decline, to stimulate the birthrate on a scale hitherto unknown, to practise an intelligent policy of immigration by attracting young workers who would be easily absorbed into the national population, to make the best use of the manpower available through a policy of vocational training designed to make France a nation of skilled workers and technicians, and to develop industry by means of general investment plans and inducements to rural manpower.

I asked that the allocation of scarce resources be effected by means of a national plan. Was I wrong? Wouldn't the economy of the immediate postwar period resemble very closely the war economy? 'The State will have to make itself responsible for the growth of France's capital stock and enforce the investment plans it has drawn up.' Then, returning to the socialist ideas of my youth, I subscribed before the event to the philosophy that was to inspire the nationalizations of 1945. 'Theoretically, control of the economy does not require extensive nationalizations, except for nationalization of the banks and insurance companies.' I suggested, however, that a number of basic industries like iron and steel, coal and chemicals should be nationalized so that the State would have directly under its authority an area 'in which it might vary investment as it saw fit and prevent big industry with its monopolizing tendency from exerting for its benefit, which was not that of the community, a dominating influence on the direction of the economy.'

This collection of views constitutes a phase of my thinking that I do not disown, even if some of those ideas seem today to have been overtaken by events. I did not foresee at that time the unprecedented prosperity Europe was to know during the twenty-five years that followed the war, and in a free-market economic system. I am not gifted with more imagination than other people. One of the traits of

124

man is that he finds it very difficult to conceive of a state of affairs much different from the one he is currently experiencing, at any rate for the near future.

However, in a article written in 1943 I gave way to an optimism which some of my friends found excessive at the time but which events were amply to justify. Starting from the premise that whatever assumptions might be made about the world's reorganization after the victory of the Allies they all presupposed the existence of a strong France, I posed the following question: would France find herself after the war in economic conditions that would enable her to reemerge as a great power? In reply, I ventured to predict that French industry would then experience more favourable conditions than in the past. One of the reasons, and probably the most important one, for its slow development in the 19th and early 20th centuries had been the lack of coal, but the time was drawing near when this deficiency would no longer be decisive. Hydropower would play a more important part. Furthermore, being able to 'offset its coal shortfall ... by the expansion of its refining capacity for imported crude oil', France would be able to develop a chemicals industry (producing plastics notably) and an important light metals industry. These new industries would not need the protection of high tariffs: they would simply be turning to account the native skills of France's manpower.

Now a word about what I thought then of a possible unification of Europe. My ideas on the subject at that time are contained in a note sent to Jean Monnet in 1944 and entitled 'The economic and political organization of western Europe'. By way of introduction I argued that preservation of the democratic regime and its adjustment to changed circumstances would be particularly difficult if western Europe remained segmented.

The obvious solution to the European problem, I said, the one that first came to mind, would be the creation of a region encompassing all the countries of the continent, a Europe from the Atlantic to the Urals, as it were. But the immediate difficulty here was the enormous imbalance in strength between Russia and the multitude of states in western Europe then. After the war Russia's power would be quite disproportionate to that of the other countries, victorious and vanquished. Not only would she have her initial mass, but she would continue to dominate the Balkans together with central and non-Russian eastern Europe and would occupy a large part of Germany. Of the three great armies that existed in continental Europe before the war, Russian,

German and French, only the Russian army would remain, considerably strengthened and superbly trained. As for the British army, admittedly backed by a very powerful navy and air force, its primary role would be defence of the British Isles. It should not be forgotten, I added, that Russia would be able to count on very active sympathies in all the countries of Europe, thanks to the work of communist parties that had undergone the test of clandestine action. On this point I concluded by saying that satisfactory relations between Russia and western Europe presupposed a regrouping of the latter's states.

Speculating on the pattern this regrouping might take, I ruled out right away the possibility of a Latin bloc that would bind France, Italy and Spain together. A Latin federation would be a predominantly agricultural state, with all the disadvantages this implied. Of the three countries that would be united under such an arrangement, France would be the most evolved politically and economically, but she herself would have to make a big effort at modernization. For this, she would have to seek models and influences not to the south but to the north. But I did retain something of this first idea. If France, I wrote, entered into a union with other north-west European states and formed with them a big industrial state, Italy and Spain would represent for that new state not only a source of manpower but a market for its products and an area whose economic development it could ensure.

I then turned to the notion of the coal and steel state which appealed to Jean Monnet at this time and which, with radical adjustments tantamount to a change of nature, may have been the origin of the European Coal and Steel Community. The idea was to group into a new political unit some of the countries or regions of continental western Europe that produced large quantities of coal and steel, notably Belgium, Holland and Luxembourg. Some people would have been quite happy to annex Lorraine to it. To me the idea did not seem realistic, at least not in the form suggested. What purpose would be achieved? The new state would naturally be unable to counterbalance the power of the Soviet Union and even that of a new Germany, risen from its own ashes. The objections were legion. Yet they vanished, I added, if one imagined that the coal and steel regions, instead of being merged into a separate state, formed part of a political bloc with Britain and France at its centre. '*It is our profound conviction that the key to any politico-economic reorganization in western Europe has to be sought in Franco-British relations*[8].'

It was therefore to Franco-British union that I devoted the main part of this report.

England will find herself after World War Two in the same position as France after World War One. In the camp of the victorious nations, having played a decisive role in the defeat of Germany, belonging provisionally to the group of great powers which will dictate the terms of peace, she will however no longer possess the strength that would enable her, in the long run, to deal with Russia and the United States as an equal.

It was Russia even then, with the war against Germany not yet over and the Allies seeming to be solidly united, that bothered me particularly. I concluded that it was necessary to unify western Europe.

Without imputing any sinister intentions to the Soviets, it is clear that Europe's future would be much more secure if Russia were confronted with another great power, of comparable strength, which would cause any attempt at sole domination to carry the risk of a prolonged war of uncertain outcome. But Britain is no longer able to take on Russia single-handed [...]. Everything would indicate that she is now resolved upon a close association with France. It may not be too difficult tomorrow to revive the occasion of June 1940[9] and make Britain understand that in the absence of political unity with France, the help the two countries give each other will not match the requirements of the European situation.

I did not rule out, in the event of a crisis, the possibility of American intervention in European affairs, but to me this seemed uncertain and definitely no substitute for a federation of western Europe around Britain and France.

A grandiose conception, I wrote, extremely difficult to implement, but representing the only hope of salvation for our western civilization in Europe. The first stage would be to form a federation comprising Britain, France, Benelux and Germany. I was greatly mistaken about the short-term possibilities. Yet I showed I was aware of the obstacles to be overcome when I stressed that the main difficulty would come from Britain's confused and often contradictory feelings about western Europe.

While appreciating the absolute need for a supranational government in this part of the continent, of which she herself would be a member, Britain feels with regard to France some anxiety due to the uncertainty clouding the future of our country. France has been beaten, her economy is in ruins, her recovery uncertain.

It was France that would have to make the first move, with the countries of the continent; Britain would not join the federation until later. Germany's future status was itself uncertain. It was therefore necessary to begin by attempting to unify France, Belgium and Holland. Later, perhaps, when the memories of the war had faded, Germany herself would join the federation.

Thus, my dream in those last days of the war was a political and military Europe whose first and foremost function would be to ensure its own defence. After the war, the economic aspect of things would partly overshadow this more classical aspect, which, however, is tending to reemerge today. How real, the embarrassing question goes, is a Europe that is unable to equip itself with conventional weapons that would enable it to repulse an enemy attack likewise carried out with conventional weapons?

Yet in 1944 I did not overlook the necessary economic unification of Europe, even if it was not then in the forefront of my concerns.

In the economic sphere, the unification of Europe would be marked by a progressive dismantlement of all barriers to the free circulation of goods, persons and capital, by a rational division of labour among the different regions, by a progressive equalization of living standards across the continent [though it will never be possible to achieve complete equalization ...]. The European economy as a whole would receive an extraordinarily powerful impetus from unification of the European market.

I have reproduced these few reflections in time of war, with their hesitations, soul-searchings and imperfections, to show the temerity with which some people, whether they were in the internal or in the external Resistance, tried to penetrate the secrets of a future that was still obscure.

4

DOTTIE

I met Dottie in Washington in February 1944. It was one evening at dinner time, in a restaurant called Corrigan at the corner of R Street and Connecticut Avenue. I had got into the habit of having my evening meal there at around 8 o'clock and then going back to the office and working until midnight. On that particular evening all the tables were taken. I called over a waiter who knew me well and told him that I had to dine in a hurry. After looking around the room, he said: 'There's no table free right now, but I can see a table for two where there's just one young lady. I'll go ask her if she'd mind sharing it with you.' The young woman, after looking at me, said she had no objection. And that is how we met. For many years Dottie would not tell her family how we became acquainted; when the subject was brought up, she would say vaguely that we had met at the home of friends.

She was twenty-two and had just finished her studies at Smith College, which was considered at the time to be one of the best university establishments for girls. She would have liked to study drawing and painting but her father, who was paying her way through college, had asked her to do economics and statistics, which seemed to him a better proposition than plastic arts. She had got her B.A. in these dull subjects and taken a job in the Office of Price Administration.

I gathered that she was not particularly keen on her work there. Her real interests were aesthetic: music, painting, sculpture. She would rediscover painting some years later when our children, Elise and

129

Robert, were old enough to start fending for themselves and Dottie could see they would no longer be requiring her constant attention.

She was from Charleston in West Virginia, where her mother still lives. Her family, although not wealthy, belonged to the town's upper set. She had had a difficult childhood; her parents did not get along and were divorced when she was twelve or thirteen. She had been brought up by her mother and was deeply attached to her.

I asked her to marry me a month or two after our first meeting. She said yes right away. Our relationship from the outset was built on a very simple foundation. We discovered each other step by step, without any unpleasant surprises. We accepted each other as we were, without any pretension or pretence. There was no crisis, no breakup, no reconciliation to leave a doubt hanging over the future.

I was thirty-two at the time and had had several affairs in my youth. The idea of marriage had occurred to me two or three times, but always in the midst of very stormy passages and as a means of finding a certain tranquillity. But there was always an enormous unknown: when the storms had subsided, what would life together consist of? With Dottie the question never arose: I loved her, she loved me, we wanted to live together. And our tastes were sufficiently similar for us to feel that the whole thing would be quite simple, once the material difficulties were out of the way.

When I thought back on it afterwards I realized that the decision had been, or ought to have been, much more difficult for her than for me. As far as I was concerned, the future was uncomplicated. I had met a young woman I adored. In a few months I would be going back to France with her to resume a life the war had interrupted momentarily; I would be back with my parents, my friends, my former habits. Dottie would enrich that life, give it a fullness it had never had, but I on my side would not have to make any painful efforts, leave behind people I loved, enter into a new existence whose unfamiliarity would make it that much more disturbing.

In asking Dottie to marry me, I was asking an enormous amount of her: to leave her family, especially her mother, to move four thousand miles to a country with whose language she was unacquainted and about which she knew next to nothing, to a Europe that was half destroyed, where a war was still on and where material life was still very difficult. And all that in order to follow a man whose future was uncertain, who earned only a small salary that allowed no indulgence or the occasional extravagance. Did Dottie have some second thoughts in the days that followed my proposal? If she did, I shall never know because she didn't tell me. I am inclined to think that the feeling we had for each other was too strong to be affected by considerations like those I have just mentioned.

In that spring of 1944 I went to Charleston to meet her parents and the other members of her family. They received me kindly but with slight astonishment. It was obvious they had never thought that their daughter, or niece, would fall in love with a European, and a Latin at that. I learned afterwards that they had asked Dottie to think it over. But seeing that her mind was firmly made up, they did not press the point.

The wedding took place on September 2, 1944 at Saint Margaret's church, very close to my office. We had chosen that one because it was conveniently located. It turned out to be an Episcopalian church, affiliated to the Anglican Church. Dottie was Presbyterian, I was nominally Catholic. One might say that we had met halfway, but it was pure chance.

We lived for a few months in Washington, in a small apartment we had rented in Riggs Place. Around the middle of December I left Washington for Paris where I had been appointed to the post of Director of External Economic Relations. I reached Paris on January 1, 1945 to be reunited with my parents whom I had not seen for four years. I arrived in the middle of their New Year's Day lunch. My mother burst into tears. She was already very ill and was to die of a seizure two weeks later. Dottie joined me at the end of January or early in February; she had travelled in convoy on a Norwegian boat and had had to sell her engagement ring to pay her fare to Paris.

That was the real beginning of our life together, which was to last until her death twenty-seven years later. It was cloudless, except for the last four years which were darkened by her illness. There were, of course, disagreements from time to time; more often than not they were over the children's education. I, who had been deprived of any secondary education, would have liked them to take full advantage of the schooling that was available to them, to learn eagerly everything I had been denied at their age, to have the life I regretted not having had myself. Dottie was more easygoing and more realistic; she understood that one cannot relive one's life through one's children; she tempered what was excessive in my ambitions and my demands. I sometimes feel that we complemented each other in that area too, as in so many others. The fact remains that Elise and Robert were successful students.

As for Dottie herself, she rapidly settled into her new life. She went about it with a will that enabled her to overcome all the obstacles. She quickly learned French and effortlessly filled the gaps in the education she had received in America. She had a lively intelligence that was only too eager to take in new knowledge and was enhanced by reading, which she loved, our travels throughout Europe from 1947 onwards, visits to museums, the people she met. She acquired a culture that many would have envied. She never tried to talk about things she did not know. During the long years we spent together I never once heard her say anything that might have been considered out of place. She preferred to admit that she didn't know.

As a result of my duties we knew a great many people. Her charm, simplicity and spontaneous interest in others made her loved by all. Around us, and very largely because of her, there formed a circle of European and American friends to whom we were very attached and who enriched our existence.

I never met anyone more discerning about people. Without any pretension, quite matter-of-factly, possibly without even realizing it herself, she had the art of dismissing appearances and seeing what the person we were discussing was really like deep down. I could always rely on her judgment in the relationships we were led to form with colleagues, associates and friends. One of the secrets of her appeal was her goodness of heart. I never heard her gossip about anybody or saw her take pleasure in unkind talk about people we knew. There was nothing base or petty in her.

I probably brought her something, given my age and long years of study. She brought me a great deal. Through her sensitivity and her aesthetic tastes she opened my mind to music and the plastic arts. Among my most treasured memories are several month-long stays we had in Salzburg during the festival, when we would go every evening to the opera or to a concert. There were also shorter stays in Bayreuth, Lucerne and other music festival resorts. For several years, in the late fifties and the early sixties, we spent August in Menton, going in the evening to the chamber music concerts given by different orchestras in front of the cathedral. Together we visited nearly all the museums of Europe, conscientiously marking our catalogues with one or more crosses to remind us exactly of what we had liked most. Thus from one year to the next we went through Italy, Spain, Egypt, Greece, Germany, Belgium, Holland and other countries too. Since Dottie has gone I still listen to classical music with pleasure, I still sometimes look at a picture with emotion, but the occasions have become rarer, I no longer seek them so hopefully. My inner life has lost substance.

5

EXTERNAL ECONOMIC
RELATIONS
(1945)

At the end of November or the beginning of December 1944 I received a telegram from Paris informing me that I had been appointed head of the D.R.E.E. (Directorate of External Economic Relations). I had not been consulted. I learned later that the decision had been taken by Pierre Mendès-France (then Minister of the National Economy) as the result of a deal with Jean Monnet. Mendès-France wanted to give me the Planning Directorate he had just set up in his ministry; Monnet wanted me to go on with procurement, this time in France while he would continue to take care of the Washington end. Monnet won. It is possible too that Monnet had an ulterior motive; he might have already had his eye on the Planning Directorate for himself, but with a different administrative shuffle. It didn't matter to me. I was happy to be in the French government service in a key post carrying great responsibilities. Glad also to be able to continue working with Monnet, even if now I would no longer be directly answerable to him.

In January I lived for a few days in a flat near the Gare Saint-Lazare railway station occupied by a couple formerly in Denyse Harari's service, Jeanne and Xavier, who were looking after everything she had left behind in Paris in 1940, paintings by famous artists, silverware and many precious things. It was quite impossible to find a flat in Paris then, with the war still on. Furthermore, I was absolutely without funds, having given my parents all I had. I should add here that my parents had been living till then on the money given to them by friends

133

like Monick, Florence Halévy and Roger Truptil and which I tried to repay once I was back in Paris.

I saw Monick as soon as I got back. Once again he gave me proof of his friendship. He lent me a small town house in the Rue des Belles Feuilles, owned by the Aga Khan, of which he was the tenant and which he had moved out of on being appointed Governor of the Bank of France. I moved in with Jeanne and Xavier, their son and a couple of friends, Andrée and Isia Levant; I had known Isia Levant in Washington and he had just been appointed deputy director of External Economic Relations. Dottie joined us shortly afterwards.

My memories of the first few months of 1945 are of intense activity in my office at the Finance Ministry in the Rue de Rivoli and on my constant trips to England and the US. I also remember the bitter cold, made worse by an almost total lack of heating. At the ministry I did my work wrapped in a blanket, with only a minute electric fire nearby that enabled me to warm my hands from time to time, when my fingers were too numb to allow me to write any more. At the house in the Rue des Belles Feuilles we had a primitive storage heater, obtained somehow or other, which gave off a very faint heat. Food was difficult to come by. I supplemented our meagre wartime rations by means of periodic forays into the Sarthe from which I would return in a car laden with butter, meat, sausage and other food products nowhere to be found in Paris, except on the black market at prices I could not afford. Dottie, who had never known any privations, endured the cold and other trials with a great deal of verve and courage. My frequent absences made her life even more difficult; she never complained.

As for my job, brought over specially from the United States as I had just been, I might have expected some difficulties with the top French civil servants on whom I had been landed. Nothing of the kind. I was very quickly on cordial terms with the incumbent deputy director of External Economic Relations, Jacques de Fouchier. The friendship of Guillaume Guindey, then deputy director of the Treasury before being made Director of External Finance the following year, was of great help to me. I shall be speaking of him again further on, in connection with the allocation of US aid after the war, in which he played a big part.

My work during that year of 1945 was coordinating the purchase abroad and shipment to France of the supplies of all kinds which the country needed. First it was necessary to determine the basic requirements, which had to be pared to the bone as the gold and foreign exchange reserves were very low. This was done at meetings in which all the ministries concerned participated, notably the spending ministries. Then came a discussion with Guillaume Guindey who held the purse strings and who gave the expenditure figure that could not be exceeded, given the current level of the reserves. Sometimes I would put friendly pressure on him to be a little more generous. When the final figure had been decided, we reviewed with the purchasing ministries the list of purchases authorized and the cuts required.

That was one part of my job. Another was to consider, with those in charge of the merchant navy, ports, railways and roads, the transport and distribution of the supplies purchased. I discussed this question in a previous chapter and shall not return to it except to say that, with the destruction of most of the ports and occupation of the others by the Germans, and the small quantity of shipping and rolling stock at our disposal, the problem was a veritable Chinese puzzle. On Sunday mornings in my new home at 59 Boulevard Beauséjour, loaned to us in a gesture of friendship by René Pléven's wife, Anne, and into which we had moved during 1945, I held a meeting of all the top transport officials. We reviewed the previous week's events and the prospects for the coming weeks. Sometimes the major difficulty was shipping, sometimes ports or locomotives. On occasion it was necessary to defer for quite a long time the arrival of highly useful goods to make way for others considered to be essential. I look back a little nostalgically on that work which went on all week, Sundays and public holidays included, and often during the nights too. The problems were technically difficult, the objective was simple.

Among the papers I have kept I can find no memo or article dating from 1945. The reason, I suppose, is simple: I just didn't have time to write. I do recall, however, a memorandum addressed to René Pléven, then Minister of Finance, in which I drew up an assessment of our essential requirements and our resources and proposed what I considered to be an optimum allocation of the latter.

So 1945 went by, as an extension of my 1944 activities in Washington. In 1946 my life took a different turn.

Some thoughts on World War Two

While, as Director of External Economic Relations, I was concentrating on the business of resupplying France and getting her economy moving again, the war ended with Germany's capitulation on May 8 and Japan's on September 2.

For five years I had followed the course of events with eager attention, playing the part in them which I have described in previous chapters. Now that we had come to the end of this long and tragic story, I could not help reflecting on its final outcome. Was the die cast from the outset? Could things have turned out differently? Could a German empire have been formed in Europe and lasted for several decades, with a concomitant Japanese empire in South-East Asia? These questions have had such significance in the lives of people of my generation that I trust I shall be excused for devoting a few pages here to the thoughts they prompted in me at the time or to which hindsight has led me.

Failure of the Anglo-American landing in Normandy was admittedly conceivable, but it would have postponed the eventual outcome by no more than a few months, and by one or two years at the outside. America's industrial might was such that her ability to increase her military potential was virtually limitless. From the bases set up in Britain and North Africa, the Americans would quickly have struck out again at the Continent. With two-thirds of the German army immobilized in the plains of Russia and Poland, an Anglo-American victory in the west would have come sooner or later.

The point in history at which the final outcome became certain was the end of 1941 with America's entry into the war and the Germans' failure to take Moscow. In other words, what made the outcome foreseeable, as in some Greek tragedy, was Germany's commitment to fight from that point on two fronts against two gigantic powers resolved to go to the bitter end.

How did the Germans get themselves into that situation, in spite of Hitler's concern, expressed repeatedly in *Mein Kampf*, to avoid this eventuality at any price, in spite of the efforts he made until the end of 1941 to avoid any incident that could have been construed by the Americans as provocation and have given Roosevelt the chance he was looking for to bring the United States into the war? After long reflection, aided by some reading, it seems clear to me that the turn taken by the war was due essentially to Japan's action in 1941. Japan could have made a temporary victory of the Axis a virtual certainty. The way she acted precipitated Germany's downfall and consequently her own.

First and foremost, Japan could have behaved the way she did during World War One, refraining from any new military initiative on a significant scale, not letting herself become involved more deeply in China, not invading southern Indochina in July 1941 and thus giving the United States the opportunity to embargo oil exports to her.

Would the United States have entered the war even if the Japanese had not attacked and destroyed part of the American fleet at Pearl Harbor? I think the answer has to be yes. A day would have come when the American people would have seen clearly, as Roosevelt had understood at the very outset, that the world's equilibrium had been disrupted and the scales tilted towards the Germans and the Japanese (even if the latter had provisionally stayed neutral) and that the United States would have to throw its weight into the balance to save what could be saved. But months and maybe years would have passed before the decision was made, Russia would have been beaten or neutralized and Germany would have consolidated her hold over Europe. Yet when I think about it, this hypothesis does not seem very realistic. It presupposes on Japan's part a self-control and long-term calculation that it is often useless to expect of a country that feels it can seize, unopposed, rich territories containing everything it lacks in the way of energy and raw materials.

On the other hand, the most elementary political wisdom should have told the Axis powers to complete the destruction of Soviet military power before provoking America's entry into the war. Japan could have attacked Russia during the second half of 1941 from the rear by invading eastern Siberia and at the very least immobilizing the Soviet armies of the Pacific. Moscow was saved only in the nick of time at the end of 1941. It is not possible to credit one single factor with putting a stop to the German advance into the Russian capital's suburbs at that moment, but the transfer westward then of some twenty Russian divisions, fresh, excellently equipped and accustomed to the Siberian cold, played a part that some historians consider decisive. This was also the feeling of Keitel, commander in chief of the German armed forces in 1941. The troops at Zhukov's disposal for the defence of Moscow were thus doubled.

If the Germans had taken Moscow and the Japanese had advanced into Siberia, would Russia have fallen or would she have sued for a peace for which Germany and Japan would have made her pay dearly? There can be no sure answer to that question. Let it simply be said that having to fight on two fronts, with no prospect as yet of an Allied second front in western Europe, Russia would have been unable to withstand the German advance and take the offensive as she did in 1942–3. Part of the Wehrmacht might have been transferred west when the threat of an Anglo-American landing began to take shape. In any event, the course of the war would have been different.

But the Russians knew, largely thanks to the Sorge network, that the

Japanese would not attack them. They had been informed that the Japanese were preparing for a sea war with the countries to the south; the Japanese army's new equipment was sufficient indication of this. The occupation of Indochina was part of the same strategy. From the autumn of 1941 onwards, Russia could therefore withdraw troops from her Far East front without worrying. But that was not the most serious blow that Japan dealt Germany and that was to bring both countries to the end of the road within a few months of each other. The attack on Pearl Harbor on December 7, 1941 unleashed the industrial and military might of the United States against the Axis. American public opinion, irresolute hitherto, wedded to a neutralism more than twenty years old, was instantly mobilized. The hesitations that might have remained on the question of who was the enemy, Japan only or all the Axis powers, were removed by Germany and Italy's initiative in declaring war on America.

How did Germany and Japan suddenly find themselves in the position of having mobilized the military might of America without having first crushed that of Russia? This question fascinated me and I was to find the answer in what is known of diplomatic relations between the two countries in 1941[1]. The Japanese seem to have been resolved to attack the United Sates regardless of what the Germans thought, but the attitude of the latter vacillated continually during the critical months. At the beginning of 1941 Hitler induced the Japanese to attack the British so as to immobilize their forces in the Far East to the maximum degree and divert America's attention to the Pacific. A little while later, the Germans were worried about Japan's neutrality towards Russia; they feared, rightly, that Russia would thus be able to move a great part of its Far East forces into Poland. So they tried to persuade the Japanese to attack Vladivostok. They were unsuccessful. For a few months, from June to October or November 1941, Berlin seems to have understood where Germany's interests lay and also those of her allies. From November, Hitler seems completely to have lost his reason. Fearing an arrangement between America and Japan, he urged the latter to take a hard line in the conversations to take place in Washington. It has to be said that these shifting pressures from the Germans did not affect the Japanese very much.

We know today that the decision to attack the Americans at Pearl Harbor came after a long period of hesitation and infighting in the Tokyo government. The navy represented the moderating influence and provided the best confirmation that, whatever the initial successes, the pattern of relative strengths did not favour Japan. The army, which was carried away by a sort of imperialistic frenzy, which wanted to seize forthwith the territories to the south, notably Indonesia with all its oil, and which was urging the government to neutralize the US Pacific fleet, carried the day after the French defeat of May–June 1940.

From that point, events followed their inexorable course. When on December 3, 1941, four days before Pearl Harbor, the Japanese government asked the other Axis powers to declare war on the United States immediately following the onset of hostilities, yet without specifying either when or how the first blow would be struck, Germany did not react. A few days later she declared war on America.

The thing that seems incredible at this distance in time is that despite the tripartite alliance signed on September 27, 1940 by Japan, Germany and Italy, there was apparently no prior consultation between Japan and Germany concerning their objectives in the war, or rather in the wars that were fought simultaneously in Europe, North Africa, the Pacific and elsewhere. Neither consultation nor even information before the event. When the German armies invaded Russia on June 22, 1941, Tokyo learned the news over the radio. Germany and Italy were not informed by Japan of the breakdown of the Washington talks in November of the same year until the Japanese fleet was already on its way to Pearl Harbor; they first learned of the Japanese attack on the same day the whole world did. There was no joint Germano-Japanese strategy but two absolutely separate plans of conquest, one in Europe, the other in the Pacific. It is difficult to avoid the conclusion that Japan was responsible for Germany's defeat. If Japan had attacked Russia during the summer of 1941, the Germans would probably have taken Moscow; if Japan had not attacked the US fleet at Pearl Harbor, America would not have entered the war, at least not in 1941.

The error committed by both Germany and Japan was to think that America did not have the power to fight a war on two fronts, one in North Africa and Europe, the other in the Pacific. The Germans did not try in November 1941 to dissuade the Japanese from their plan to make war on the United States, because they thought that America as a result would have to concentrate on operations in the Pacific and would not have the means to intervene on a large scale in Europe. The Japanese, for their part, attacked a country whose industrial and therefore military power was quite disproportionate to theirs, because they were convinced that Europe was much more important to the United States than the eastern Pacific. This is how conquerors often fall, as the result of an error or a series of miscalculations.

Part Three

THE RECONSTRUCTION
OF FRANCE
AND OF EUROPE

1

MEDITATION ON A NIGHTMARE

When Jean Monnet asked me in the autumn of 1945 to be the Deputy Commissioner General of the Plan of Modernization and Equipment (of France), my life entered a new phase that was to last more than twenty years. During that time, I first devoted my energies exclusively to the reconstruction of France and then, when it became clear that this task could not be accomplished unless the whole of western Europe were rebuilt at the same time, to the reconstruction of the latter. With circumstances on my side, I was able to move quite naturally from one post to another without ever having to ask for anything. Thus I had the rare privilege of being actively present from the inception of the French Plan in 1946 to the completion of the Marshall Plan, which can be placed somewhat arbitrarily in 1952, and, later, from the creation of the European Economic Community in 1956–7 to the moment, in 1967, when the Treaty of Rome had to all intents and purposes become fully operative.

What was the intrinsic aim of these different undertakings bound together by a fundamental link? Was it solely to rebuild Europe, to efface the scars left by five years of hostilities and, in many cases, military occupation, in short to return to the Europe of 1938, or even of 1929? No, my ambition and that of many men of my generation, European and American, went infinitely further. Our convictions had formed over the years in a long process of sorrowful and indignant meditation on the political and economic chaos that we saw as

143

characterizing the years from 1919 to 1939. Truth to tell, we found it hard, if not impossible, to understand how the men who had gone before us could have fallen into this long succession of errors, misjudgments and missed opportunities that punctuated the interwar period. The western world, and more particularly the United States, Britain and France, into whose hands the victory of 1918 had thrust the fate of the world for a time, could be likened, we thought – perhaps a little unfairly – to a drunken man without any sense of direction, any instinct of self-preservation, whose course was determined solely by the obstacles he encountered, with no idea of his final destination. As for Germany, she had thought she could take advantage of these errors and weaknesses and establish a Germanic empire in Europe, and possibly worldwide; the story of that endeavour is too well known for me to return to it. In point of fact, I was convinced that the period 1914–45 had an underlying continuity, that the First and Second World Wars were one and the same war, interrupted from 1919 to 1939 by a truce, itself marked by the Great Depression from 1929 onwards. A real nightmare.

What had to be attempted, therefore, was to pick up the thread of Europe's history from the point where it had broken in 1914 and, bridging more than thirty years, two world wars and the deepest, most devastating economic crisis the capitalist world had ever known, recreate a prosperous continent, whose peoples might enjoy all the benefits of modern technology. But we realized that this could not be achieved by copying the economic order prior to 1914. Too much time had passed, circumstances had changed too much, intellectual and moral attitudes had evolved too much for it to be possible to refer usefully to such a distant past, except for certain fundamental and very general values that needed to be maintained as a line of conduct. The problem was how to translate those values into contemporary terms so that they might be a useful guide in the action which had to be taken, in 1945 as opposed to 1914.

By studying the period from 1919 to 1939 we found many of the principles of action we were looking for. From our realization of the mistakes made in the interwar years and our reflection on the problems facing us at the end of World War Two there sprang a political and economic philosophy that was to give Europe, for twenty-five or thirty years, a prosperity it had never known, even in the most auspicious moments of its history, and was to transform its peoples' way of living.

Thus a knowledge of the essential economic and political events of the interwar period is of more than just historical value; it is a key element in the explanation of contemporary events. It is not my intention to retell the story of the interwar years, which is well known. On the other hand, I think it important to analyze briefly certain of the post-1918 policies followed by the ex-belligerents, where these policies are in striking contrast with those adopted after World War Two and where the comparison helps to explain the course of events after 1945.

Where I personally am concerned, as the reader will have seen, I lived the interwar period intensely. Or rather I should say that I really lived the second half of it, from 1930 to 1939. But the events of the twenties were close enough and their witnesses numerous enough for me to have been able in my youth to experience those years vicariously at least. Thus I built into the awareness I gained of the world in the thirties the happenings of European history during the ten years that followed World War One.

A victory lost

In 1919 Europe found itself up against the same sort of problems it was to experience a quarter-century later. This is what makes a comparative study of the two postwar periods so fascinating and enables one to appreciate the enormous intellectual strides made by Europe and also America in so short a space of time.

In 1919, as in 1945, although the scale of destruction in the first war had been much less extensive than it was to be in the second, Europe emerged from the conflict not only poorer but with an economy virtually paralyzed, unable even to form an idea of how to restart this infinitely complex machine that had been completely disrupted by the war. A contemporary who was soon to become famous wrote the following words a few months after the cessation of hostilities:

The war had so shaken this system as to endanger the life of Europe altogether. A great part of the Continent was sick and dying; its population was greatly in excess of the numbers for which a livelihood was available; its organization was destroyed, its transport system ruptured, and its food supplies terribly impaired[1].

Germany, although not having suffered the amount of destruction to be visited on her in World War Two, was in a state of total

145

prostration. It became evident one month after the armistice that 'we could have secured unconditional surrender if we had determined to get it[2].'

In 1919, as in 1945, labour productivity had slumped throughout continental Europe, the capital stock had shrunk drastically, export capacity was almost nil, Europe lacked the means to buy from the rest of the world the goods of all kinds it needed to be able to live and work. Britain and France had been forced by circumstances to liquidate a very large share of their investments abroad; as for Germany, her foreign assets had in effect been confiscated by the Treaty of Versailles. France, moreover, had lost all the holdings she had possessed in certain countries, notably in Russia where the chaos of revolution had taken hold. It was estimated that the income derived from her port-folio of assets throughout the world had been reduced by 1921 to about one-third of what it was in 1910–13.

But this great reduction in external assets was only part of the problem. To finance the war effort, Britain, France and the other Allies had had to borrow on a colossal scale, mainly from the United States. Their external debts far outweighed what remained of their foreign holdings. The United States had replaced Britain as the leading credi-tor vis-à-vis the rest of the world. Europe owed the US about $10 billion of 'political debts' and some $2–4 billion on private account[3]. In addition, the demands of the forthcoming period of reconstruction, understood not only as the repair of physical damage but as the reactivation of a European economy shattered by the war, meant that Europe's trade in goods and services would, on the most optimistic assumption, remain heavily in deficit for several years.

When the Versailles Treaty was signed and in the year or two that followed, the victorious European powers were firmly convinced that the repayment of war debts and the expenditure on reconstruction would be financed by Germany and the payment of reparations that had been imposed on her. When that conviction proved to be an illusion, it was clear that their sole recourse was the United States.

The situation was considerably aggravated by the fact that almost nobody in Europe was aware of the economic interdependence of the European powers, victors and vanquished. Anyone who had dared to say, in France especially, that the national interest, correctly under-stood, required that the German economy be reconstructed at the same time as the French economy, and that the return to a reasonable degree of prosperity in France and the rest of western Europe depended on Germany's economic recovery, would have been accused

146

of high treason. When Germany was unable to meet the payments demanded of her, France occupied the Ruhr early in 1923 and thus helped to paralyze German industrial activity, on which the payment of reparations depended. For thirteen years, from 1919 to 1932, the question of reparations made it impossible for normal relations to be established between Germany and the Allies, notably France. The absurdity of this whole affair is apparent in the different plans that were adopted at the time to set the amount of reparations owed by Germany and the schedule of payments. The last to date, the Young Plan of June 1929, reduced the German debt total but provided for payments until 1988!

In 1919, as in 1945, America was the triumphant nation in every sense; she was at the peak of her power; her economic, political and moral influence extended throughout the world.

The American armies were at the height of their numbers, discipline, and equipment. Europe was in complete dependence on the food supplies of the United States; and financially she was even more absolutely at their mercy. Europe not only owed the United States more than she could pay; but only a large measure of further assistance could save her from starvation and bankruptcy[4] ...

Europe, if she is to survive her troubles, will need so much magnanimity from America, that she must herself practise it. It is useless for the Allies, hot from stripping Germany and one another, to turn for help to the United States to put the States of Europe, including Germany, on their feet again[5].

These last words were prophetic and remained so for several decades. Unfortunately, they met with no response at the time. France, in the person of Clemenceau, insisted on a peace that was to keep Germany completely powerless for many years and prevent her economy from recovering from the disaster. The inconsequence that France displayed then was shared during the negotiation of the peace treaty by the other victorious European nations.

The future life of Europe was not their concern; its means of livelihood was not their anxiety. Their preoccupations, good and bad alike, related to frontiers and nationalities, to the balance of power, to imperial aggrandizements, to the future enfeeblement of a strong and dangerous enemy, to revenge, and to the shifting by the victors of their burdens on to the shoulders of the defeated[6] ...

To what a different future Europe might have looked forward if either Mr. Lloyd George or Mr. Wilson had apprehended that the most serious of the problems which claimed their attention were not political or territorial but financial and economic, and that the perils of the future lay not in frontiers or sovereignties but in food, coal and transport[7]!

There are a few exaggerations here, but basically what Keynes said was right.

Attitudes across the Atlantic were no more realistic than in Europe. After refusing to join the League of Nations, America withdrew into herself and for a while lost all interest in European affairs; she continued to demand payment of the war debts, at the same time refusing to allow these to be linked in any way with the German reparations.

With their adverse balance-of-payments situations, France, Britain and the other Allies could not discharge their debts to America unless Germany herself paid the debts imposed on her at the end of the war. But those debts were certainly beyond Germany's ability to pay, even allowing for the refusal of German public opinion to comply with what it regarded as the Diktat of Versailles. Keynes had seen the writing on the wall in 1919 when he maintained that the only possible solution was, on the one hand, for the United States to cancel the inter-Allied debt and, on the other, for a moderate figure to be set on the amount of reparations due from Germany.

What had to happen happened. In the early thirties the debtors defaulted one after another: the Germans never paid, for the most part, the reparations demanded of them; the European Allies never discharged their war debts to America. But the matter of reparations and war debts poisoned the air for many years, at a time when it would have been possible, perhaps, to reconstruct a European economy, and a Europe for that matter, capable of living in a state of peace and prosperity.

A crisis postponed

Given the situation I have just described, with Europe massively in debt to the United States and the US government's refusal to forgive that debt, let alone invest public money in Europe's economic recovery, the stage appeared to be set for an acute, deep and lasting crisis in Europe immediately after the war – a crisis exacerbated by the European Allies' determination to ignore Germany's needs and to subordinate their entire policy towards that country to the payment of an astronomical sum of reparations.

Yet for ten years things worked out differently. In the two years that followed the war, Europe and America experienced a surge in economic activity, powered in both cases by the strong growth of US exports to Europe and high government spending. The crisis which everyone had been expecting, but which had been delayed by this upturn, broke at the end of 1920; it was short and sharp, and by 1922 it looked as though order had been restored.

Indeed, for the next seven years the United States enjoyed an uninterrupted prosperity that was the admiration and envy of the rest of the world. The word 'miracle' was not yet in vogue or people would have been talking about the 'American miracle', or the 'American challenge'. Even at that time, specialists from Europe were going over to America singly or in groups to ascertain the causes of this extraordinary success. One spoke a great deal about mass production for the low-income groups. One marvelled at the wisdom of American producers who made do with small unit profits in order to expand their markets. American business was tops, both in America and in Europe.

In the Old World, it took several years, roughly until 1925, for the economy to regain some degree of equilibrium. Stabilization had been retarded by grave monetary troubles, which in Germany, for example, completely destroyed the currency. In France, it was not until the efforts of the Poincaré government that economic activity got back to normal. The Dawes Plan of 1925 proposed a solution to the problem of German reparations that soon proved illusory, but it did help to create the feeling during the last years of the decade that things were back in order.

By 1925 most of the difficulties of the reconstruction period seemed to have been resolved. A new political climate, which encompassed Franco-German relations, had been established that offered hope for a future of peace and cooperation. The monetary upheavals had subsided; the main European currencies, except for the franc, had stabilized and the major countries were back on the gold standard.

Between 1925 and 1929 industrial production worldwide increased by something like 25%. There was considerable progress in productivity and standards of living[8]. With 1913 as the base year (100), national income in real terms in 1928–9 was 109 in Germany, 113 in the United Kingdom, 124 in France and 166 in the United States.

As these figures show, the situation differed widely across countries. Britain had not managed to regain her former prosperity. An exporting country first and foremost, her trade had been particularly hard hit by the war. The nonsensical decision taken in 1925 to restore sterling to its prewar gold parity had exacerbated an already difficult situation and contributed to the relative decline of the British economy. The result was that unemployment in Britain, even during these few years of prosperity, remained high; at no point in the twenties did it fall below 9% of the labour force. Germany had to contend with the same problem; in the years following 1923 the unemployment rate fell below 7% only once, in 1925. In 1926 it was 18%; after declining steeply in 1926–7, it turned up again in 1928; in 1929, on the eve of the Great Depression and in an apparently thriving economy, it was still over 12%[9].

The fact remains that during the twenties, with ups and downs and an average performance that was generally poor by contrast with the United States, the European countries, victors and vanquished alike, did not experience the deep and lasting crisis that might normally have been expected in the wake of the war. And this despite the fact that they were heavily in debt to the United States and to each other and lacked the dollars to pay for their imports from overseas. The Americans provided limited sums for assistance operations, but after the end of the war US government aid to the Allies ceased completely.

Europe's enormous dollar requirements were covered by private American capital that crossed the Atlantic to take advantage of the higher interest rates then prevailing in Europe. Investment by US banks in Europe rose from less than $200 million in 1926 to over $1 billion in 1929[10]. This effectively masked the problems of the countries with war-ravaged economies. Much of this capital took the form of short-term investments that could be liquidated almost without notice. This financial dependence of Europe on private American capital was to prove disastrous once the economic climate changed in the United States. Germany's economic situation, in particular, which had looked desperate at the beginning of the twenties, picked up as a result of this huge inflow of US private capital. No one seemed to realize the precariousness of this rediscovered prosperity or the fact that the latter's continuance depended entirely on that of the capital inflows concerned.

During these postwar years Europe's fundamental situation was made worse by the growth of protectionism. Each country, when it experienced difficulties in certain sectors of its economy, resorted to this convenient device for eliminating or weakening foreign competition – even in the twenties, when the different European countries were getting their breath back after the headlong race of the war years. It has been estimated that European customs duties on finished products rose on average by 50% between 1913 and 1927.

As a result of this increased protectionism and of the profound structural changes that had taken place in the world economy, international trade grew only slightly, even during the years when the world had recovered some semblance of prosperity. From 1919 to 1928 it increased by no more than 8.5% and did not regain its 1913 level until 1924. Whereas world output of manufactures grew by 49% in real terms between 1913 and 1928–9, world trade in these products expanded by only 12%[11]. This progressive self-containment of the economies that formerly had been the most open prevented any progress towards a solution of the reparations problem. The only way that Germany might have met part of the sum demanded of her by the European Allies would have been to achieve a large current balance-of-payments surplus. But with her exports encountering ever higher tariff barriers, that means of discharging her obligations was ruled out.

An American economy in full boom, a European economy that seemed slowly to be getting back on its feet, that was the picture presented by the western world in 1929. Then came the whirlwind that in the years to follow was to sweep away structures which had appeared solid or at least in process of consolidation.

The Great Depression

In the reflections that my friends and I engaged in during the war and the period immediately following, we did think of the problems of reparations and war debts and of the huge movements of short-term capital that had marked the 1920s, but the question that literally obsessed us was the Great Depression, which began in 1929 and from which the world had not completely recovered ten years later when war broke out. It was an upheaval such as the capitalist world had never known and one that rocked it to its very foundations. Between 1929 and 1932 industrial output fell by more than 45% in the United States and by nearly 60% in Germany, with, for the latter country, the political consequences of which we know.

What had originated this terrible disaster? Were we going to experience something similar in the wake of World War Two, when arms production inevitably would decrease? What should we do then to make it less extensive and of shorter duration? For a long time after the cessation of hostilities the fear of a Great Depression was a demon we had difficulty in exorcising. As will be seen, it was not until the fifties that this nightmare went away, to reappear twenty years later with the economic troubles of the seventies.

I shall confine myself here to presenting some of the provisional conclusions we reached. First of all, it seemed quite clear to us that the crisis was purely American in origin, even if it was to spread swiftly to the rest of the world. But why this deep depression in the United States from 1929 to 1933, followed by a recovery that was still incomplete when war broke out? We did not know, and even today there is no wholly satisfactory, universally accepted explanation. As with the crisis of the seventies, one is forced to cite an accidental conjunction of several causal sequences. This great US boom of the twenties could not continue unchecked indefinitely. Inventories had built up to excessive levels that had to be reduced. Furthermore, fixed capital accumulation had been too rapid for a number of years to be able to continue at the same pace. Finally, during this time general prosperity of the economy as a whole had coincided with a building boom that came to an end just at the close of the decade. These factors, plus the state of the American farm sector at the end of the twenties, its serious financial overextension and consequently its extreme fragility, add up to a fairly credible explanation. Its somewhat cursory nature is common, incidentally, to all explanations in the social sciences. The impossibility of making real experiments, as in physical science, obliges one to make do with theories that more or less account for the facts.

An economic recession had started in the United States during the summer of 1929. No one at the time thought that it could be deep and lasting. The stock market crash that occurred in the autumn of the same year, and whose effects were to be felt for several years, was probably the trigger and as such partly responsible for the tragedy. Between the beginning of September and mid-November 1929, the New York share index plummeted from 542 to 224. By July 1932 it was no more than a tiny fraction of this last figure.

The crash is easier to explain than the depression itself. Given the excessive speculation in the years that preceded it, the day of reckoning had to come when share values ceased to bear any more than a remote relationship to the situation of American firms and their profit-making ability. At no time did the US authorities – either the Federal government or the Federal Reserve System – take the measures that would have curbed the rise and, by the same token, the ensuing fall.

Economists have an unfortunate habit of citing 'confidence', or lack of it, to account for movements for which they have no satisfactory explanation. In the present case, however, it seems justified to say that the stock market collapse in the years from 1929 to 1932 did something to aggravate and prolong the crisis by destroying for a time the confidence of the American public, especially the more affluent segments of it, in American financial institutions and American industry.

Finally, there was a problem at that time that was never to recur in later years: a steep and continuous fall in prices. Between 1929 and 1932 US wholesale prices plunged by more than 60%.

I shall return to the subject of the United States further on, and the factors that caused the depression to last so long and to be so protracted. But what interested us most at the time when we were reflecting on these questions was Europe. Given that we have no influence over the American economy, what could we do to ensure that if another crisis erupted in America it would not spread to Europe, at any rate with such tragic impact as in 1930–2? The prior question was why the American crisis of 1929 had caused the economic and financial collapse in Europe that did so much to bring Hitler to power and thus make World War Two inevitable.

Here the explanation was simple: it lay in the manner in which Europe – especially Germany – had financed its recovery during the twenties. It had done so by means of a huge inflow of private American capital, much of it sight or very short-term. At the time of the Wall Street crash and in the months that followed the Americans quickly repatriated the capital they had invested in Europe. Since the European central banks had in many cases invested this money borrowed at short term in medium- or long-term loans, the inevitable result of the American withdrawal was the collapse of a great part of the financial system in Austria and Germany.

I am not trying to say that Europe could have avoided the consequences of the American crisis. But when it broke, Europe was in a particularly vulnerable situation and the financial crisis aggravated the economic crisis. At least that is what we thought. Anyway, industrial production collapsed in Germany and by 1932 about six million people were out of work there.

Since this is not the place for a history of the Great Depression, I shall simply say what conclusions we drew from it as to the policy that ought to be followed after the end of World War Two. Even admitting that cyclical recessions are probably unavoidable, why was that of the thirties so deep and so prolonged?

Inevitably we looked to the United States, whose economic power

153

had been so great before the war and had even increased during it. We were greatly drawn to the New Deal, which after 1932 had constituted the free world's most significant effort to get out of the depression. We accepted its underlying principle that when economic activity is at a level lower than that which would ensure full employment of the labour available, and showing no signs of picking up sufficiently, it is for government to intervene and create the additional incomes needed to reduce involuntary unemployment and possibly eliminate it altogether. That is what Roosevelt had done, after a period of hesitation during which his intentions seemed uncertain. It was to such a policy that Keynes, in his *General Theory*[12], later gave theoretical justification.

At the same time we could not overlook the fact that the New Deal had been only a semi-success. The production index (1923–5 = 100) had fallen from 121 in 1929 to 64 in 1932. In the first nine months of 1937, before the United States was jolted by another recession, the index stood at 116, in other words still short of its 1929 level. At best it can be said that there was no advance for a period of eight years. At the peak of the recovery there were still 8 million unemployed in the United States, i.e. 15% of the labour force. We were asking ourselves two questions about the US situation at that time. What had brought about the upturn recorded between 1933 and 1937? And why had it not removed all traces of the crisis, leaving America in a state of semi-depression? It seemed to us beyond doubt that the uptrend in the economy during the four years following Roosevelt's arrival in office was due to the New Deal, and more precisely to the large budget deficits that had marked those years. Verification was provided by the 1937 crisis, which caused the American economy to lose much of the ground it had regained and which we blamed on the shift in fiscal policy to greater financial orthodoxy.

As to the incompleteness of the recovery, we attributed this to the fact that US investment had remained well below its pre-1929 levels. Whereas investment spending had fallen from an average of $18.5 billion a year during the period 1923–9 to $5–6 billion in 1933, it had climbed back to only $12–13 billion by 1937[13]. The recovery had been due mainly to the increase in consumption expenditure, with public investment providing a secondary stimulus. Private investment had picked up only slightly.

What was the reason for this shortfall in private investment? One can, of course, cite the business world's hostility to Roosevelt during the first years of the New Deal, even though the latter had probably prevented, after 1933, a complete collapse of the capitalist system in the United States. Once the worst of the crisis was over, American industrialists and bankers saw Roosevelt only as the man with the dangerous ideas, advocating a redistribution of income to the advantage of the poorest members of the population, favouring the labour unions and allowing them a privileged relationship with the government. Even if these reactions were excessive and partly unfounded, they did curb the recovery of private investment for a while. But an explanation of this sort seemed too cursory to me. Businessmen have never refused to make money, even if they dislike the people who are in power.

Of the numerous explanations given for the investment standstill, the most plausible seems to me to be the fact that prices having collapsed in 1929–33, as we have seen, profit margins had been completely eroded in almost all activities. Interest rates were admittedly very low in nominal terms, but as long as prices kept falling, real interest rates went on rising. They reached fantastic levels during the Great Depression. To attract borrowers they would have had to become negative, which was impossible without massive interest subsidies. When prices did stabilize, several years of strong output growth were necessary before new investment was warranted.

It was largely this American experience of the years from 1933 to 1939 which convinced the Europeans, in Britain and the United States during the war, in liberated Europe after 1944, that a high investment ratio was the fundamental requirement for the new European economy; that only large-scale investment, leading indirectly – but only indirectly and secondarily – to increased consumption, would establish growth on solid foundations, without which it was liable to be short-lived.

At the same time the idea took hold in our minds that full employment of the factors of production, and notably of labour, was only one of the aims that the economic policy of the future should pursue. Sustained and as rapid as possible 'growth' was the supreme objective, to which the others had to be subordinated. We had some excuse for not putting price stability at the forefront of our concerns. Had we not lived through an era when a continuing price fall had destroyed all possibility of a real economic recovery? Had not the Americans carried out in 1933 a monetary operation that proved ineffectual for America and ruinous for such economic stability as remained in the world, a dollar devaluation of which the aim was not to correct a balance-of-payments deficit, since one did not exist, but to make prices rise?

It was this prewar experience that essentially accounts for the fact that in the immediate postwar years we tended not to regard inflation as a very dangerous evil. Many of us were prepared to accept a certain amount of inflation in return for rapid growth. We were obliged to change our attitude when it became apparent that inflation could kill growth and lead to economic stagnation.

We learned two other major lessons from our experience of the Great Depression and, in general, of the economic events that marked the interwar years.

One of them concerned external monetary stability. The crisis had been exacerbated by the competitive currency devaluations carried out by a large number of countries during the thirties. We considered reasonable the sterling devaluation of 1931, which rectified the absurd revaluation of 1925 and brought Britain's prices into line with those of her competitors, resulting in a rapid and sustained upturn in that country's output. We thought unreasonable, on the other hand, and motivated by nebulous theoretical considerations that proved false, the dollar devaluation of 1933. Many of the currency adjustments that took place between 1933 and 1939 were simply a response to devaluations carried out by other countries in order to gain an edge over their trading partners.

The world monetary situation became so chaotic and so unstable that it was difficult to calculate equilibrium parities. The policy of a few European countries which, having formed the Gold Bloc, tried to maintain the pre-1929 parities, and which as a result suffered from the crisis longer than the others, seemed to us particularly devoid of common sense. It became quite clear to us that a new monetary order that would replace the pre-1914 gold standard system, an order that would ensure fixity of exchange rates but with the possibility of adjustments in case of proven necessity, would be needed in the postwar world.

The other lesson concerned trade policy. Protectionism, which had developed rapidly in all countries after World War One and which had first limited, then suddenly and steeply reduced, the volume of international trade, was, along with monetary disorder, the other great evil that had at all costs to be curbed if not eliminated.

Britain's imposition of a relatively high tariff in 1931 and the creation of the imperial preference had assumed great political importance in the eyes of the world, given that country's traditional attachment to free trade. But Britain was experiencing great balance-of-payments difficulties at that time and we could understand her trying to get out of them by the means at her disposal. Much more reprehensible, in our opinion, was the raising of American customs duties in 1930, the famous Smoot-Hawley tariff, which was in no way justified by the US payments position, since that was showing a large surplus, but was motivated solely by a wish to protect domestic economic activity. The aim was, in a sense, to export American unemployment. It was not achieved as a large number of countries decided to take a leaf out of America's book and raise their own customs duties or erect other trade barriers.

What we witnessed during the thirties was a veritable disintegration of the world economic, trading and monetary system, or rather what the 1914–18 war had left of it – as if gangrene had emerged in the most vulnerable parts of the system and gradually spread to the whole of it.

A world adrift

Among the lessons we drew from the events of the interwar years there was one that was more important than the others. A great part of the chaos that marked the twenties, and even more the thirties, was attributable, we thought, to the absence of any international cooperation. *Each country sought to resolve its difficulties as if it were the only country in the world.* There were, of course, some international contacts; occasionally one country would try to help another; but no government came near to appreciating the interdependence of all the partners in the world economy. The international implications of the decisions taken by each country were seldom weighed realistically. The possible 'boomerang effect', i.e. the consequences for a country of the decisions which other countries would inevitably take in reaction to its own, was seldom foreseen, and if foreseen it was ignored. There was no international forum in which the statesmen directly concerned could meet regularly and discuss their problems. The only organization that might have been able to do something was the League of Nations, but the United States was not a member. Even in the political sphere, where it ought to have played a major role, the League quickly lost all credit when it proved incapable of taking decisions or of enforcing those it did take.

Already serious in the twenties and early thirties, this lack of international cooperation became disastrous as of 1933, when Hitler came to power in Germany. Very rapidly the most perspicacious realized that war was inevitable. The world was divided into two, with those who were attached to the existing order on one side, and those who wanted to destroy it on the other. One might have thought that the western countries would close ranks and that the United States, Britain and France would cooperate intimately in the political, economic and military spheres so as to ensure a joint defence. As we know, nothing of the kind happened.

What the world lacked most, perhaps, in the years between the two wars was one great country that would have assumed the leadership of those that wanted to prevent the war or to win it; a great country with weight enough to be able in particular to contribute decisively to the restoration of some degree of economic, commercial and monetary order. In theory, Britain could have played this part in Europe; but she made no effort to do so, because of anachronistic traditions which required her to remain apart from the Continent and make no move towards it for fear of losing her role of arbiter among the great powers. France was not a first-rate economic power, although the French army was universally regarded as the most powerful in the world and, in a manner of speaking, as the world's peacekeeper. But in the economic sphere she had little influence; such as she had was all but destroyed during the thirties by a succession of disastrous economic policies. As for America, she could have been a recourse had she not retreated, after World War One, into a total isolationism that said little for her generosity or her political intelligence.

That world of the twenties and thirties, which men like Raymond Aron, Jean Fourastié, Alfred Sauvy and myself had experienced day after day, seemed to be the story of a complete intellectual and moral breakdown: all strength of will had vanished. We found it very hard to understand how most of the western statesmen could have been so blind, how they could have made so many mistakes or not known what decisions to take at any given moment in this sorry period.

2

THE PLAN
(1946–1948)

At the end of 1945 I found myself drawn into the first of the three great undertakings that were to occupy me for the rest of my life, namely the French Plan of Modernization and Equipment (the other two were to be, first, the Marshall Plan and, later, the Common Market).

The birth of the Plan

The causes of my involvement in the French Plan belonged both to the immediate present and to the more distant past. One of the immediate causes was a conversation Jean Monnet had with General de Gaulle in August 1946, in the course of which he explained to the General that France, if she was to become great again, had to modernize her economy, which had become archaic. 'They [France] need more production and greater productivity. Materially, the county needs to be transformed[1].' De Gaulle, who over the past year had realized how weak France's economy was, said that he was open to suggestions and asked Monnet to get a plan drawn up.

France had obtained from the Americans sufficient credits to see her through the winter. But, as Jean Monnet wrote:

It was urgently necessary to exploit this breathing-space; and that was why,

159

in November 1945, I came back to Paris and gathered together our faithful team. We made our headquarters in (. . .) rooms at the Hôtel Bristol. There, [I together with] Marjolin, Hirsch, Gaillard took counsel about how to modernize France. The old-fashioned décor of this requisitioned mansion, where we worked in bathrooms and the beds were covered with documents, astonished the visitors whom we asked to come and discuss the future[2].

On January 3, 1946 the Plan was established by a decree of which the first article stated: 'within six months a first overall Plan for the modernization and economic equipment of metropolitan and overseas France shall be drawn up.'

A few weeks earlier Monnet had asked me to leave the D.R.E.E. to become the Deputy Commissioner of the Plan and I had agreed immediately. At that time I had no clear idea of the way ahead as far as my own future was concerned. Would I remain in government service? Would I go back to being a professional economist, as a researcher or a teacher? Would I say yes to the enticing offers that had been made to me by private business? In point of fact, without admitting it to myself in so many words, I had decided in favour of government service, provided that people and events gave me the opportunities for really important work. I was not ambitious in the generally accepted sense of the word, and politics, which I could have entered easily with my past as a member of the Free French, did not tempt me. Money was no inducement; I didn't have much, but I felt instinctively that I would always have enough for the simple life I led, which satisfied me completely. In 1946 Dottie and I had found an extremely pleasant flat in Neuilly, where we were to remain for twelve years. Elise was born, while we were living on Boulevard Beauséjour; Robert was born when we had already moved out to Neuilly.

In the autumn of 1945, urged on by François Perroux, I had taken the *agrégation* in political economy. It was not my intention to teach, but I looked on the *agrégation* as a safety net in case my public service career happened to be interrupted.

The overall design

Before the war when I stated nearly every week in my articles for *L'Europe Nouvelle* that France's essential aim should be to redress her economy, I did not speak of a plan because one was not necessary; it would have been sufficient to practise a monetary policy similar to Britain's, and not to commit certain idiocies, like shortening the workweek to forty hours, for the French economy to get back on its feet. But during the three or four years I spent subsequently in London and Washington my thinking evolved. It was no longer a question of catching up with the other developed countries, it had become necessary to reconstruct a country partly destroyed by the war, to modernize its plant made obsolete by the depression crisis and enemy occupation, to invest on an unprecedented scale when the nation would be clamouring for rapid satisfaction of consumer wants. In short, a plan was needed that would give priority to investment in general, and more particularly to capital expenditure that would lead the economy's development and make it possible to attain, after an initial phase of relative austerity, a level of consumption the French had never known. In London in 1943, then in Washington in 1944, I had written memo after memo to Hervé Alphand and Jean Monnet respectively, stressing the need for an overall effort along the lines I have just indicated.

What share did I have in the Plan's design, one may ask. The question is pointless, for in the great affairs of this world it is seldom possible to identify the individual responsibilities and merits of the participants. A lot of people contributed. I tend to think, perhaps presumptuously, that my ideas as outlined above rhymed with those which Jean Monnet had formed in the United States from 1940 to 1942 while taking part in the American war effort, when the need to plan arms production, and consequently the entire economy, had become the overriding concern of the authorities in Washington.

Anyone who thought about the future of the French economy in 1945 could not but be profoundly disquieted. Was our country about to go through a deep crisis which would destroy the national unity that was reemerging? Once the crisis was over, would it revert to its second-rate status of the prewar years? Would it find within itself the necessary strength to make an enormous leap forward and join the ranks of the most developed industrial countries? Today, nearly forty years later, we know the answer to those questions, but at the time it was by no means obvious. For the country to emerge from the abyss into which it had been plunged by a history of backwardness in the movement towards industrialization, by a profound decline during the thirties, and then by the war and the Occupation, a number of conditions had to fulfilled, some material, some psychological.

161

It was necessary, first of all, for the country, or at least its front-rank politicians, senior civil servants, trade union leaders and the representatives of industry and agriculture, to gain awareness of the effort to be accomplished. Reconstruction, to begin with, for it must not be forgotten that the damage sustained by France in World War Two was more than double what she suffered in World War One; but most important, a renewal of the nation's capital stock, which had been destroyed, depleted or reduced to obsolescence: France had to develop rapidly her heavy and engineering industries, not only to meet the population's needs and underpin exports but also to be able, if need be, to mass-produce modern armaments and thus play her part as a great power in the system of collective security.

Thus, while ensuring a gradual improvement in the population's living standards, the effort had to focus essentially on investment and exports, so as rapidly to increase the country's production capacity and import possibilities. In other words, a large share of national income had to be saved, a much larger share than before the war. Investment and exports were for me the two essential priorities, although at the beginning of 1947, when France had almost nothing to export, I put the emphasis on investment. Understandably, therefore, I castigated the government's fiscal policy which was resulting in a large budget deficit, and consequently in excessive borrowing by the consumer state on the capital market that commensurately reduced the sums available for investment.

As can be imagined, the economic policy implied by the Plan was not to everyone's liking, although enlightened public opinion understood the need for it. I remember that at the beginning of 1947, a few weeks after the Plan's adoption by the government, I gave many lectures and wrote several articles to try and explain the logic of it and make a population that had just gone through five years of extreme privation, in the towns at least, understand that three or four more years of stringency and austerity were necessary to enable France to rebuild, or in many cases create, the foundations on which to establish a newfound prosperity.

The objection I encountered most frequently stemmed from the comparison that people were making between France and Belgium, where consumer goods were in relatively plentiful supply and where the consequences of the war seemed to have been erased as soon as the fighting was over. My reply was that the two situations were not comparable. Belgium had not fallen behind in economic development and investment as France had by 1939; in 1945 Belgian industry was relatively modern. Secondly, Belgium had emerged from the war comparatively unscathed; the general destruction there had been much less than in France. Finally, I added, I was not sure that, in spite of these favourable factors, Belgium had made the best possible choice in according so much importance to consumer goods.

The targets

The fact remains that we were aware, however imperative the need for a massive investment effort, that a slow but sure improvement in the living standards of a people that had suffered so much was necessary in order to avoid undue social tension that might endanger the undertaking as a whole.

Was the Plan 'inhuman'? In an article published around the middle of 1947 by the *Revue de Défense nationale*, I tried to answer that question.

One might think, to read certain comments, that the Plan is conforming to the cult of the machine and that, in order to create a gigantic industrial sector, it does not hesitate to crush the people beneath a mass of capital investment disproportionate to their strength. Or again, that in order to pave the way to a golden age for future generations it contemptuously dismisses the most basic needs of the present one.

I then gave some figures that illustrate what I was thinking at the time. By 1950 gross national output, I estimated, would be over 30% more than in 1938. Imports would be up slightly, while exports should be about double what they were in 1938.

The total value of the goods and services at the disposal of the population and of French enterprises will therefore increase to a lesser degree than output, the increase being in the region of 25%. The sum of capital goods that French enterprises will be able to acquire will be about 90% more than in 1938. Consumption should not only return to its prewar level, but even exceed it by 10 to 15%.

To put the investment effort into perspective, I added that for the period considered as a whole (1946–50), the share of national resources allocated to investment would amount to about 23–24%, against 19% in 1946, 16% in 1938 and 20% in 1929.

The division of labour in the team that Jean Monnet had gathered around him was effected without any difficulty. Monnet, whose deputy I was, relied on me for the overall design and general balance of the system we were trying to set up. Etienne Hirsch was responsible for the individual sectors of industry; it was his job to draw up a balance sheet of needs and resources for each of the major products on which the Plan's realization depended: coal, steel, cement, etc. Paul Delouvrier, who in the course of a brilliant career was notably to become chairman of the board of Electricité de France in 1969, was in charge of financial affairs. Jean Fourastié was the Plan's economic adviser. Alfred Sauvy, Félix Gaillard, Jacques Dumontier, and others, gave us valuable assistance.

Of course, Monnet did not accept my conclusions without our having discussed them at length and, in some cases, my having been talked into amending them. As is the way with all strong minds, he appreciated resistance, even if it sometimes irritated him. I remember, though I cannot place it exactly in time, a discussion that lasted a whole afternoon and was, I think, about the Plan's targets. The discussion had become what I am tempted to call a passage of arms between Monnet and myself, the other participants in the meeting having reached the end of their arguments. Late in the evening, when we were all exhausted, Monnet wound up the discussion with these words: 'Marjolin, the trouble with you is that you're an intellectual. All right, I give in, but I want you to know that if I do it is not because you have been so insistent, but because I convinced myself, in spite of your cussedness, that you were right.'

I mention this little incident because it illustrates the kind of relationship that had developed between Jean Monnet and me, the fighting spirit we showed, he and I, in our search for the truth, the great objectivity he was capable of demonstrating. Needless to say, the situation was frequently reversed; I, too, knew how to give in when his practical sense, which was nothing short of genius, enabled him to identify clearly the goal to be attained.

Early in 1946 I proposed the targets, in terms of national output, that were adopted by Jean Monnet: to reach the 1938 level by the end of 1948, to rise to the 1929 level in 1949, to exceed the 1929 level by 50% in 1950. These targets make sense only if one remembers the situation of the French economy before the war and the latter's destructive effects. Even if the few figures I am about to quote are not strictly comparable, they do represent orders of magnitude close to reality. In 1939 industrial output in France was 15 to 20% lower than in 1929, whereas in Germany it was more than 20% higher and in Britain more than 30%. In France the war had reduced national product by about 50%, whereas in Britain the latter had risen by about 15% and in the United States by over 70%. I do not remember whether the targets mentioned above were achieved on time or whether an extension was needed. Their only value here, like that of the figures mentioned in my article for the *Revue de Défense Nationale*, is to show the lines along which we were thinking then.

But now I must go back a little way to pick up the thread of our reasoning at the time. I had left off at the point where we were convinced that a gigantic production effort was needed to get the French economy out of the state of extreme weakness in which it found itself in 1945; it was vital too, in our opinion, to concentrate on investment, even if consumption had to be given short shrift for a time. But the reasoning did not stop there. It was also necessary to establish an order of priorities in the allocation of savings, to give preference to a limited number of industries that would act as pacesetters for the economy, even if other activities had to be sacrificed temporarily. Housing, in the event, was one of the latter.

As it turned out, this order of priorities was inescapable. However one might visualize France's future growth, it presupposed a much bigger output of coal, steel, electricity, cement; transport facilities would have to be reconstructed and modernized; greatly increased quantities of food products, which would rapidly be needed, could be provided only by mechanized farming, which would necessitate a stock of agricultural machinery bearing no comparison with that of prewar years.

A fundamental characteristic of the Plan, which earned it the name of 'Modernization Plan', was the seeking-out and application of the most modern methods for the purposes of reconstruction and development. French industry and agriculture in 1939 were antiquated, outmoded, had not assimilated the new technologies; the industry and agriculture that would emerge from the Plan would use the techniques of the British (immediately after the war Britain was seen by the French as a country that could serve as a model) and, above all, of the Americans. The action of Jean Monnet, who had spent much of his life in England and America, was decisive in this regard. In short, the aim was not just to expand production, by increasing investment and employment; the overriding objective, one might say, was to push productivity to its maximum.

External aid

The biggest problem we had to contend with during the five years that followed the war was the shortage of foreign exchange. France had little to export or, more exactly, it was essential for her to keep almost everything she produced for her own use and consumption. Furthermore, her import needs were immense as regards raw materials, food and capital goods. The supply of gold and foreign exchange she possessed when the war ended was used sparingly, but it was in any case insufficient to meet requirements. External assistance, from America, was essential to see France through those few years. It was generously given. Jean Monnet has summed up vividly the predicament in which France was placed:

There was a very real danger, indeed, that France might content herself with [getting by] behind a protectionist shield. This, after all, had been a national tradition. But I knew that the mere allusion to such a possibility would be enough to win support from the new, Resistance generation and to carry the day with General de Gaulle. He was following our work very closely. He could not falter on any course that meant greatness and independence for France, and I should have no difficulty in convincing him that this was the only way. But I made no secret of the fact that it would require foreign loans if we were to move quickly – and that to move slowly would be extremely dangerous. 'Without these loans,' I wrote, 'modernization would still be needed, but the conditions for achieving it would be different. It would necessarily take longer, and the French people would have to be asked to accept greater cuts in domestic consumption.' To tell the truth, we never seriously imagined adopting this second course, which not only would have delayed France's recovery, but would have distorted it, and would perhaps have led the country in a different direction altogether[3].

Indeed there was no hope of reestablishing durable current payments equilibrium before 1950. In the interval, given the level of our gold and exchange reserves and allowing for liquidation of French private assets abroad, a bridge of several billion dollars for the period 1946–50 was necessary.

During the years from 1944 to 1947, that is to say before the Marshall Plan, Jean Monnet played a decisive part in American lending to France thanks to all the friends he had made in the United States during the war and the confidence the Americans placed in him. In the second half of 1944 he had arranged for France's huge purchases from the United States to be effected on the lend-lease basis. In the early part of 1946, in the context of the negotiating assignment on which he was sent to the United States with Léon Blum, he obtained an agreement that tided France over for a while.

It wiped out what remained from Lend-Lease, and with it the very principle of 'war debts', which has so often poisoned the return to peace ... $300m were lent to us to purchase American surplus goods at low prices ... On May 28, 1946, the Chairman of the export-Import Bank told us that he was opening a new line of credit of $650m, intended for French purchases of capital goods and raw materials. At the same time, we were promised a loan of $5–600m from the International Bank for Reconstruction and Development. In addition, we were to receive 75 Liberty Ships on deferred-payment terms – a 50% increase in our merchant fleet. The total value of all this was about 1½ billion dollars[4].

This was a substantial amount of aid. It was insufficient, however, to cover the French deficit foreseen for the period of the Plan's execution; but it did buy us the time to wait for an American initiative on the grand scale, which was to come in the form of Marshall Aid.

The Plan's justification

Mention of the Plan immediately tempts one to ask whether a national plan was really necessary in order to resolve these problems. France was the only major country at that time to have introduced one. Germany, Italy and Japan had to contend with the same difficulties, but in those countries no plan was spoken of. Britain did not have an overall plan.

The first point that should be made in reply is that this is really a question of words. In the countries I have just mentioned the word 'plan' itself was not used, but in fact there was one. The military occupation authorities or the national governments of those countries had to resolve the same problems as France, and it was not possible, or even conceivable, in the state of extreme shortage that existed to rely solely on the play of market forces. An order of priorities had to be established and the public authority, whatever it might be, had to see that it was enforced. Lastly, production targets had to be coordinated and inter-industry relations harmonized. An overall scheme was therefore necessary. We shall see later on that when the Americans offered the former European belligerents, victors and vanquished alike, massive aid to help them get back on their feet, the condition they posed was that an overall programme be drawn up, namely the European Recovery Programme.

This first reply is not entirely satisfactory, however. Even if it is a fairly accurate reflection of the period from 1945 to 1950, the years of great shortage, it overlooks the intrinsic features and highly specific character of French planning that were to be so influential when times of plenty returned. That specificity can be defined in one sentence. On the one hand French planning took into account the preeminent role played by the state in the country's economic development, while on the other it sought to correct the excesses of this centralization by actively involving in the Plan all the vital forces of the nation, in the persons of representatives of industry, agriculture, the labour unions and government itself.

If, not only during the period of shortage but for a long time after, the state had not used all its authority in order to develop national production rapidly, by means of modernization, the country would probably not have been transformed so soon. The nature of the Frenchman is such that he needs to feel urged and supported by the state, to see the state give him the assurance that his individual efforts form part of an overall effort, and that if mishaps occur along the way it will intervene to get him out of difficulty. Or, to put it a little differently, even if there had been no Plan, given France's immediate postwar situation the state would in any case have performed its historical role of guide and impetus-giver, but there would have been a danger that the national effort would split up into an infinite number of partial efforts, making it impossible for anyone to gain an overall view and to act accordingly. It was this overall view that the Plan brought. At the same time it enabled the country's limited financial resources to be put to the best possible use, in accordance with the priorities which the planners had succeeded in establishing.

There can be no doubt that the state played a decisive role in the Plan's execution, and more particularly in the implementation of the six basic programmes for which imperative targets had been set.

The public sector was already very large at this time. In terms of non-farm employment, it accounted for roughly one-fourth of the French labour force. The share of capital investment directly or indirectly under the state's control was even larger. Transport, coal, electricity, gas, arms factories, aircraft corporations, most banks and insurance companies, and Renault, were nationalized. Almost the entire activity of the building and civil engineering industries was concerned either with transport, coal mines and public services or with reconstruction, over which the state could exercise tight control by way of war damage compensation. I calculated at the time that, in 1947, investment by the state (including reconstruction) represented nearly 80% of the investment scheduled for the economy as a whole. This proportion declined subsequently, but it remained very high.

Furthermore, the nationalized industries were at strategic points of the economy. Just by coordinating the nationalized activities, which was one of the primary aims of the Plan, the state could shape the course of the economy as a whole. But the state was also able to exert a powerful influence through the allocation of raw materials and credit, and through the grant of building permits.

Even then the state, comprising in fact an infinite number of administrative centres each having only a partial and often very limited view of things, had to act according to an overall plan, with objectives that were imperative for what was deemed essential and indicative for the rest. That is what we provided. But there was still a danger that the impetus given from above would dwindle away in a maze of bureaucracy and be virtually exhausted by the time it reached the level at which the decisions were to be carried out. This is apparently what still happens in the centrally planned economies, such as that of the Soviet Union. Another danger was that the country would not clearly appreciate the importance of this vast undertaking and become divided in the defence of the individual interests of the different social groups.

In order to avert these dangers the active forces of the nation were involved in the design of the Plan itself. On the *Conseil du Plan* [the overall planning board] and the various modernization committees set up for each major area of activity sat representatives of industry, agriculture, the trade unions and the main government service departments. Even though circumstances dictated that they should play an often decisive role in the construction of individual plans and of the overall plan, the decisions produced by this machinery had received acceptance beforehand. All concerned were pledged to take part in carrying them out. It would be true to say that in a country traditionally torn by rival factions, for the first time perhaps in its history, and for a period that was to be relatively brief, a consensus was established to restore life and strength to the nation's economy. The result was spectacular. An impetus was given that was to propel France to a state of prosperity she had never known.

Of course, after the first few years the character of the Plan changed. It was no longer a question of sharing out shortage and proceeding along paths well known in advance, but of choosing new paths suited to the coming changes in the structure and functioning of the world economy. The imperative content of the First Plan would diminish gradually in subsequent plans until it all but disappeared; a market economy would reemerge and free enterprise would be able to operate within the boundaries drawn by a bureaucracy whose invasive tendencies would continue to assert themselves. I do not intend to say more about what the Plan was to become later; but I would stress by way of conclusion that it was to remain a valuable instrument for bringing together the viewpoints of the different social groups and of the government and one which the state could use to maintain or introduce the maximum degree of harmony in the social life of the country.

Thus 1946 and the first half of 1947 went by. It was a difficult period, in which we had to face the fact that the consequences of France's decline during the thirties and those of the war could not be easily erased, that a sustained effort would be needed for many years, along with foreign aid exceeding anything that could have been imagined hitherto.

I had known and lived intensely the period from 1931 to 1939, when hope dwindled a little further each day, when the incompetence of France's leaders plunged the country into a seemingly bottomless abyss, when it became increasingly apparent that military defeat would be the probable outcome of so much folly and so much weakness. The postwar years, in spite of the countless obstacles that had to be overcome, provided an opportunity to get even with the past. The incompetents, or most of them, were no longer in office. I felt instinctively that we were on the right road, that the mistakes of the prewar years were being rectified, that the principles guiding us were sound. And in this great undertaking, which was to result in the resurrection of France, in a veritable rebirth of the nation, I had found my place, one in which I could sway the course of things in the direction I thought most promising. I had reached that place without having to fight for it, simply because I, along with others, conveyed ideas that represented hope.

Questions pending

The first French Plan suffered from two weaknesses of which I was aware, but which could not be remedied at the time it was devised and shaped. Being placed in a strictly national context, like all political or economic plans formulated in Europe at that time, it aimed first and foremost to rebuild and restart the French economy. The only occasion on which we were led to place it in an international context was when we examined the question of its financing. It became perfectly clear then that the Plan was just a blueprint, the outlines of an imaginary figure that could not become reality unless a great amount of external aid were injected into the construction. In the world's present state that aid could only be American. This gave rise to a number of questions which in 1946 we were incapable of answering. Would this American aid materialize? How much would it be? What conditions would France have to meet in order to obtain it?

These questions were obvious; others were less so and could be understood only by those who remembered the difficulties Europe had known between the two wars. Furthermore, they did not arise with the same immediacy as did rebuilding of the railways, roads, ports and factories or the reestablishment of commerce between rural and urban areas. I was perhaps more alive to them than many other people, owing to my international experience. The issue was easy to state, more difficult to grasp in its practical reality: 'France' was an abstract notion conceived in time of war; the true economic reality of normal times that would have to be reestablished one day, somehow or other, was a cohesive Europe.

Let me be quite clear on this point: for me, in those difficult times, when the real questions were how to supply the towns from day to day and to get industry going again, this was not a matter of more or less vague ideals, of long-range political or moral aspirations, but of something almost tangible. Europe was not only a geographical reality. Prior to 1939, and above all before the Great Depression, it was a complex system of economic and commercial relations; the states of which it was composed were, despite their antagonisms, closely interdependent, as was the case with the world as a whole. The fact remains, however, that solidarity was much closer between European countries that were geographical neighbours.

The question we were therefore led to ask ourselves, if not in 1946, at least in 1947, was the following: was France's economic recovery possible, was it conceivable, without simultaneous recoveries in Germany, Benelux and Italy? The answer was not clear-cut in every case. As regards Germany, many minds, and leading ones at that, found themselves back on the same slippery slope that had led to the interwar disasters. Conscious of the interdependence of the French and German economies, they put the problem in terms of the German economy's necessary dependence on its neighbours, the ones that Germany had invaded, pillaged and martyrized.

I shall return to this question later. For now, let me simply say that as of 1946 or the beginning of 1947 there was no doubt in my mind that reconstruction of the German economy was the *sine qua non* for the revival of France's economy and that of Europe as a whole.

Jean Monnet

The time has come for me to speak about Jean Monnet at slightly greater length than I have up till now, about his personality and about my relationship with him. As I said earlier, we met for the first time in London in May 1940 and again briefly in Washington in the spring of 1941. Our real partnership dates from autumn 1943, when Monnet asked me to assist him in purchasing the goods that France would need after her liberation. It continued during 1945 when we, Monnet in Washington, I in Paris, strove to ensure that France would be supplied with raw materials, food and capital goods. The Plan was the end point of our first experience of working together, one that was marked essentially by the war and the effort to erase its consequences.

Jean Monnet had one of the most inspiring personalities of anyone I ever met, one of the most complex too. To people who saw him but occasionally he might have seemed an uncomplicated man, never concerned at any moment of his life with more than a few ideas, and often only one, which he stubbornly persevered to bring to realization, never allowing himself to be distracted by other concerns; a practical mind that sought efficacy through concentration of effort on one objective at a time, or on a few closely interlinked objectives, such as to win the war first of all, then to reconstruct France and finally to unify Europe.

172

In this regard I learned a lot from him, though without succeeding, most of the time, in achieving the single-mindedness that seemed to characterize his thought. For ten years, until the war, and even further during my years in London, I had tried to become generally acquainted with human knowledge in the social sciences and I found it very difficult to disregard the complexity of things and set my sights on just one goal. But it did not take me long to understand that Monnet was right in that to succeed one absolutely had to simplify. I have often noticed that in a discussion, when one wants to get a point across to someone else, it is essential to hammer one simple, seemingly obvious idea and to forget about the complications that would inevitably arise in the other's mind if the way were not kept firmly barred.

But I would be overlooking another essential trait in the character of Jean Monnet if I were simply to describe him as a man of action with a particularly developed sense of the practical. He was also, I am tempted to say above all, a man of ideas. True, he was guided at each moment of his life by one overruling idea, but it was not a small idea: more often than not it was a vision of the world. The aim was not simply to change one particular aspect of reality, but to alter the whole of reality along the lines that Jean Monnet had chosen. The word 'ideologist' would fit him perfectly had it not been deformed by a usage bearing little relation to its true sense. Let us say that he was a man who believed in the power of ideas and in whom ideas indeed took on a very great force.

It was this exceptional ability to conceive original ideas, or ideas he was able to make appear original, combined with an extraordinary talent for putting them into practice, that largely explains the fascination that Jean Monnet held for a great number of people from the most varied of backgrounds. He had a force of conviction I have never encountered in any other human being. I would add that he knew how to combine, when necessary, the power of argument with a personal charm, graciousness and delicate tact that often disarmed those most predisposed against him.

But his powers of concentration, the sheer force of effort he put into whatever undertaking he was engaged in, his refusal to admit that things were perhaps less simple than he thought, these did not exclude a great flexibility, an extraordinary faculty of adjustment when he encountered a seemingly immovable obstacle. One might say that there were basically just two kinds of moments in his life: those when he would hammer away relentlessly to drive his argument home, and those when he laid down the hammer and opened his mind to counter-argument, to the suggestion that perhaps the way he had chosen was not the right one and that other possibilities existed. In one's dealings with him it was important to know which sentiment was uppermost in his mind at the time of talking to him, an exclusive determination to further his current project or a certain hesitation before the difficulties that had arisen.

My relations with him from 1944 until his death in 1979, a span of thirty-five years, were those of a friendship that never failed, even when we clashed over a particular idea or project. A magnanimous man in the truest sense, he never stooped to petty political considerations. I could not but feel a great respect for him. At the same time I must in all truth say that I was not one of his unconditional admirers, and there were many, who formed a worshipful congregation around him and for whom the word of the master at any time was a truth revealed.

I have said sufficient earlier on about all that I owed to him, and how in his company I came to appreciate the concrete aspect of ideas and the force of total commitment to just one, to recognize that I was never able completely to shed my fundamental personality, which had slowly formed as I studied economics, history, sociology, psychology. I shall recount later how much I was put off from the first by a simplistic notion like 'the United States of Europe'. I don't think I ever used that expression, even when it was convenient to do so. I knew that Jean Monnet was right and that one had to simplify if one wanted to get results, but I never went as far as he did in trying to boil down the issues. Perhaps I was wrong.

To conclude this short analysis of the character of Jean Monnet, I do not think I can do better than to quote Olivier Wormser, who was not one of his close associates and who did not share, at least in their extreme elements, his convictions on the subject of European unity. On Monnet's return from a trip to the United States, where he had done wonders in winning the Americans round to a deal in the interests of France, Wormser said to me: 'All things considered, I can't help thinking that France is very lucky to have a Jean Monnet.'

3

PRELUDES TO THE RECONSTRUCTION OF EUROPE

I was soon given the opportunity to use on a European scale the experience I had garnered in attempting to solve France's problems, and in this way to try and overcome the difficulties I had detected in national planning as such. I had the extraordinary good fortune, for a young man, to be present at the creation of the Marshall Plan and to be able to play a prominent part in that undertaking which, it can never be said enough, gave birth to the modern Europe we still know today as we approach the end of the 20th century. Despite the efforts of a small number of biased historians to belittle its importance or dispute its significance, nothing can hide the fact that it was *the most dazzling political and economic success in the history of the western world since 1914* and an extraordinarily powerful demonstration of human intelligence and its creative ability, in total contrast to the errors of judgment and displays of weak will that had marked the interwar years.

Having spent all of 1946 and the first months of 1947 engaged essentially in working on the French Plan, I was still at the Plan's headquarters in the Rue de Martignac when America and Europe began to understand that the path they had taken could not lead to the result which they were seeking; that a set of individual national efforts, whether they took the form of plans or any other form, could not bring about the reconstruction of a Europe that would be prosperous and, ultimately, independent of external aid.

175

I have already described the critical state that France was in at the end of the war. Nearly all the other countries of western Europe were experiencing equally grave problems. Italy was devastated, Holland greatly impoverished. Germany had been the theatre of military operations during the last months of the war; of all the European states she appeared to be the one whose situation was the most desperate. Time would show that, despite enormous destruction, she had perhaps suffered less than many others and that beneath the razed walls of her factories her industrial plant was comparatively intact. The fact remains, however, that she was irremediably divided and that her economy was to remain totally paralyzed for a time. Belgium had emerged with relatively little damage; she would give the impression, in these first two or three postwar years, of being an oasis of prosperity, but the weight of her economy on the continental scale was small.

That left Britain. Her prestige was immense. Had she not in 1940–41 taken on single-handed and with iron determination an enemy who was infinitely more powerful? Had she not been the base from which the Allied armies set out to reconquer Europe? Her economic power in those dark days of 1945–6 appeared immeasurably greater than that of the devastated countries of continental Europe. Was she not the centre of an immense empire, of which no one could know that it would disintegrate so rapidly? Was the sterling area not the biggest currency area in the world? It was not until 1946–7 that we were able to realize that behind that imposing façade, which conveyed the impression of enormous strength and potential, was an economy sapped by six years of war, total mobilization and progressive liquidation of foreign assets, six years in which there had been no renewal of the nation's capital stock. Gradually the world had to face the fact that, far from being able to help with the reconstruction of Europe, Britain herself would need a large amount of external aid in order to get back to normal.

American aid

We in the French planning circle had realized very quickly that the sole recourse was America. In 1945, 1946 and the first half of 1947 most of the European countries, one after the other, knocked at the door of the White House or of various international organizations to seek loans or grants which, without being able to pull them on to dry land, would at least keep their heads above water for a time. In these immediate postwar years the Americans had already given a lot of money to Europe, not to mention the considerable sums that the US armies of occupation were spending in Germany and Japan so as to nudge the economies of these recent enemies, for it was beginning to be understood that it was in the general interest to ensure their reconstruction.

American aid had taken different forms. There had been emergency relief through UNRRA (United Nations Relief and Rehabilitation Administration), which was also given to the Soviet Union and East Europe and which recalled the aid distributed by the Hoover mission after the end of World War One. But there was also bilateral aid, sometimes in very large amounts, extended to this or that European country. We have seen that it was loans of this kind that enabled France to muddle through for a while after the war and to set the Plan of Modernization and Equipment in motion.

All told, the sums given or lent by the Americans between 1945 and 1947 probably amounted to approximately $14 billion (roughly the equivalent of what would be disbursed between 1948 and 1952 under the Marshall Plan). But the large sums invested in these bilateral aid efforts seemed to lead nowhere and, far from improving, the situation was getting worse. US aid to Europe was like pouring water – in this case, domestic savings – into a sieve.

The event that was very influential at the time and put paid to the hopes formed immediately after the war's end was the failure of the operation launched in 1946 to restore sterling's convertibility into all other currencies, including the dollar. At that time the US made Britain a very big loan, $3,750 million, in return for a commitment from the British government to restore convertibility. Sterling did indeed become convertible again for a few months, but the resultant outflow of foreign exchange made it necessary for Britain to call the operation off and reintroduce exchange control.

This failure had a significance that went beyond Anglo-American relations. In 1946 and for a few months still in 1947 the United States had hoped to reestablish quickly a European economy whose currencies would be convertible into one another and into dollars, and whose trade would be freed from the impediments of all kinds by which it was then hamstrung and develop on a non-discriminatory basis. In this early part of 1947, as I worked in my office in the Rue de Martignac, I felt that the time for general convertibility and free trading on a world scale had not yet come, that something else – of which I could visualize no more than the rough outlines as yet – would have to be tried, failing which there was a great risk (I should really say a certainty) of an indefinitely protracted stagnation of the European economy, with the occasional shot in the arm from the United States to keep the patient going when his condition became critical.

In particular, the French Plan appeared to me to be stillborn, incapable of regenerating France's economy and of creating a modern industry and a modern farm sector without external aid, which should not be occasional but should be pledged for a period of several years. What made the Marshall Plan so original by comparison with US aid over the preceding years, what made it possible for France's plan, among many others, to be carried to completion, was precisely this guarantee of duration – I shall be coming back to this point later on.

In the spring of 1947 I made one or two trips to the United States which showed me that the Americans fully shared the concerns of the Europeans who had realized the gravity of the situation. After a swift but shortlived improvement during 1946, we suddenly had the feeling that we had reached a dead end. Moreover it was not only necessary to get out of the impasse but to do so in a way that would ensure rapid and continuing development of the European economy.

During the summer of 1947 the Committee of European Economic Cooperation, of which I shall be speaking later on, produced a report for the Americans, in the drafting of which I had participated. In that report we observed that after a rapid pickup during the two years following the end of the war, Europe was again about to enter a period of acute crisis that was liable to undo all that had been accomplished recently. The very severe winter of 1946–7, followed by a persistent drought, made it a certainty that the 1947 harvest would be a poor one. But that was not the main cause of the trouble. The most serious factor was the continuing outflow of gold and dollars which was threatening to exhaust Europe's reserves entirely. There was visibly no way to stem this drain other than an operation on a grand scale, i.e. massive American aid.

Throughout that summer of 1947 the situation worsened. On August 20 the United Kingdom was obliged to suspend sterling convertibility. On August 28 the French government announced the cessation of dollar imports, except for cereals, coal and a few other essential products. The other European countries had already taken or were about to take measures of the same kind.

The report's conclusions could not have been more pessimistic. We said in substance that if no steps were taken, the situation when stocks ran out would become catastrophic. If the steps taken were insufficient or came too late, there would not be the necessary impetus to get European recovery under way. The life of the peoples of Europe would be increasingly precarious and uncertain; owing to the lack of raw materials and fuel, industries that had slowed down would gradually cease activity; food supplies would decrease and begin to disappear from the market[1].

The Marshall Plan

It was in response to these fears, to prevent the situation from rapidly becoming tragic and to get Europe once and for all out of its difficulties and started on the road to sustainable growth, that the idea behind the Marshall Plan was born.

This was an entirely American initiative. The Europeans contributed to its emergence only very indirectly, by pointing out to the Americans the critical nature of the situation in Europe, which the Americans, incidentally, were quite capable of appreciating by themselves. Nevertheless I can imagine that our cries of distress helped to foster the idea in the United States that American aid to Europe should take a new form. Essentially the idea was to treat Europe as a unit and, more importantly, to ask the European countries to *behave as a unit* and take *together*, with American's help, the measures needed to ensure the recovery of the Continent as a whole.

For nearly forty years there has been much debate about the Americans' motives; yet these were clear. The Americans were alive not only to the physical hardships of the populations of Europe, but also to the danger of seeing the economic chaos on the Continent spread to the rest of the non-American world. Nor did the political dangers escape them. The Cold War had begun in 1946, if not earlier, and the USSR was certainly ready to take advantage of the disorders that might break out in western and southern Europe in order to extend its sphere of influence still further. Already, in March 1947, the Americans had had to take over from the British in Greece and Turkey; that was when the Truman doctrine had been formulated.

In addition, the Americans were aware of the danger to themselves. How could America remain prosperous, how could she maintain her economic equilibrium, avoid depression and unemployment, if Europe, South-East Asia, Latin America – the last two being regions from which Europe was accustomed to obtain a large share of its raw

179

materials and food supplies – and also Japan, where the US Occupation authorities were striving to overcome problems similar to those in Europe, in short if the whole world outside the United States were to sink into a state of poverty and languish helplessly for what would probably be many years?

No, the Americans did not act purely from disinterested motives. Altruism is not part of the political ethic. States can only afford to be generous when it is in the national interest to be so. What we were expecting from the Americans, and what they themselves were expecting from their government, was that the latter would behave intelligently by showing it understood that the free world's prosperity and its political equilibrium, no less, were indivisible; and that was something it understood perfectly. A run-through of the facts of the time will cast a great deal of light on the US government's behaviour then.

The USA was truly at the zenith of its power. It had saved Europe from Hitler's tyranny by means of a massive war effort. That effort had not impoverished the American nation, on the contrary it had generated an unprecedented economic expansion there. The Americans had an abundance of everything: raw materials, food, manufactures. Most of the world's gold supply was in Fort Knox. The US balance of payments showed a huge surplus year after year.

Europe, as I have already said, was on the brink of the precipice. Its lack of everything was about to become calamitous. Its peoples, who had lived on little but hope throughout the war, could not understand how, two or three years after the war, their situation could still be so wretched. The Soviet danger was beginning to loom. It seemed almost inevitable that the general shortage would lead to serious internal disorders.

The Marshall Plan was not so much a purely disinterested gesture as a supremely intelligent political move. The Americans undertook to save Europe a second time. Of course, they sought to impose their will, but their will was to put an end to Europe's plight and it coincided with Europe's interests. This explains why, on the one hand, no major economic decision could be taken in Europe without the agreement of the Americans and why, on the other, the latter never tried to make the Europeans behave in a manner contrary to their fundamental interests.

The history of the Marshall Plan is too well known for me to relate it at length. What I shall try to supply here is the testimony of one of the participants. Nevertheless, given that forty years have elapsed since the events in question, it might be useful to provide a few points of reference.

General Marshall, the then Secretary of State, observed in April 1947 that Europe's recovery was taking much longer than expected and that forces of disintegration were clearly emerging. A great public debate began in the United States, in the course of which the problems and possible solutions were discussed at length. Senator Arthur H. Vandenberg, leader of the Republican minority in the Senate Foreign Relations Committee and a long-standing isolationist, came to the realization that the United States could not isolate itself from the rest of the world, and throughout the preparatory period and that in which the decisions were taken he played a crucial role in Congress. The best minds of the US Administration and central civil service sought a formula applicable to Europe as a whole, notably Under-Secretary of State Dean Acheson, William Clayton the Under-Secretary of State for Economic Affairs and George Kennan, head of the State Department's Policy Planning Staff. Out of their deliberations and those of General Marshall himself came the speech that the latter made at Harvard on June 5, 1947, one of the great texts of world political history.

While there is no need to cite all the key points of that speech, its most essential passage should, I think, be recalled. After describing the critical situation of Europe, General Marshall concluded with these words:

It is already evident that, before the United States Government can proceed much further in its efforts to alleviate the situation and help start the European world on its way to recovery, there must be some agreement among the countries of Europe as to the requirements of the situation and the part those countries themselves will take in order to give proper effect to whatever action might be undertaken by this Government. It would be neither fitting nor efficacious for this Government to undertake to draw up unilaterally a program designed to place Europe on its feet economically. This is the business of the Europeans. The initiative, I think, must come from Europe. The role of this country should consist of friendly aid in the drafting of a European program and of later support of such a program so far as it may be practical for us to do so. The program should be a joint one, agreed to by a number, if not all, European nations.

These words were warmly received in Europe. We at the head-quarters of the French Plan immediately saw in them the possibility of making the Plan a reality. I, personally, saw in them the beginnings of an answer to a question I had been asking myself since 1945 or 1946:

181

how might French economic recovery be made part of an overall European economic recovery?

I discussed the matter at length with Jean Monnet. He went to see Georges Bidault, the Minister of Foreign Affairs. The latter, with British Foreign Secretary Ernest Bevin, initiated the action that was to end in the European Recovery Programme (ERP). France and Britain asked the USSR to join them in considering how such a programme might be developed. A tripartite conference was held in Paris from June 27 to July 3, 1947. From the outset the prospects were not favourable. Since the failure of the Fourth Session of the Foreign Ministers' Conference in Moscow in March 1947 the break between the two blocs had become virtually complete, and indeed Molotov took a totally negative position. The Russians were prepared to accept American aid, of course, but they refused its being tied to any condition, such as supervision of the use of funds or an assurance that Eastern Europe would progressively open up to trade with Western Europe. The result was the breakdown of the Paris Conference and the consequent refusal of all the Soviet-dominated countries to participate in the Marshall Plan.

Certain 'revisionist' historians, notably in the United States, have since maintained that, with the Marshall Plan, America deliberately cut Europe in two. This does not bear serious consideration. For one thing, Western Europe urgently needed American aid in 1947, and for a number of years. For another, the USSR, with its ideology and its regime, could not engage in an undertaking like the European Recovery Programme that aimed to reestablish the conditions for a smoothly functioning free-market capitalist system. It was just that the two regimes were totally incompatible.

The breakdown of the Paris Conference was greeted with a sigh of relief by many in Europe and in the United States, seeing how difficult, if not impossible, it would have been to get the US Congress to approve aid which would have gone in part to a country and its satellites that each day revealed a little more to be the determined adversaries of everything the West and its free-market system represented. Now it would be possible to get down to serious business.

The European Recovery Programme

Sixteen countries of western and southern Europe met in Paris on July 12, without any clear idea of what they were going to do. Germany had obviously not been invited; at this first stage she was not even represented by the Occupation authorities. The sixteen countries together formed the Committee of European Economic Cooperation (CEEC) and decided to draw up a programme for Europe's recovery. They gave themselves less than three months in which to do so, deciding that the programme should be ready by the end of September. Sir Oliver Franks (later Lord Franks) was elected Chairman of the Committee.

We were beginning to know and would rapidly learn what the United States expected of this undertaking. They wanted the programme to cover the four-year period from mid-1948 to mid-1952, at the end of which Europe should be able to do without American aid entirely. The programme should include individual country plans for output, imports and exports, to be supervised by American missions established locally. Production should be massively expanded and an increasing share of it devoted to exports. Monetary and financial stability should be gradually reestablished over the period of the programme. Customs barriers between European countries, at least as far as quotas were concerned, should be progressively lowered and intra-European cooperation developed to the full. Each country would be required to conclude a bilateral agreement with the United States that would be built into the joint programme. The idea of a permanent European organization was beginning to crystallize.

During the summer of 1947 the representatives of western and southern European countries who constituted the CEEC drew up a European recovery programme which was sent to Washington before the end of September. Germany's requirements, as formulated by the Occupation authorities, figured therein. This was the first sign of a reintegration of Germany into the concert of European nations.

Was the programme a spontaneous European creation or was it more or less dictated by the Americans? The answer is neither. During the weeks in which it was drawn up, the Europeans and the Americans were in constant, one might say daily, contact. The natural tendency of each European country was to ask that its own needs be given priority without taking into account those of the other countries. It was also understandable that each country's representatives, ministers or senior civil servants, should be obsessed with their own domestic political problems. Often they gave the impression of all having just one desire: to get the most, i.e. the most dollars, out of the United States. The role of the American representatives was to introduce a modicum of unity into this Tower of Babel. They made desperate efforts to see that the ERP did not amount to just a collection of national programmes or 'shopping lists' but to a real European programme that would ensure the European economy's 'viability', as one used to say then. They were only partially successful. But I can say that inasmuch as the Americans exerted any pressure while the programme was being drawn up, it tended in the latter direction. I tried to help them as much as I could, not with the intention of serving American interests, but because it seemed clear that the view which the USA was taking of the European situation coincided with the true interests of Europe, and consequently with those of France.

I should now say something about my personal activities during this period.

When the Paris Conference was convened, Hervé Alphand, then the economic and financial affairs director at the French Foreign Ministry, asked Jean Monnet to second me to him for a period of a few months as deputy head of the French delegation. I was, in a manner of speaking, the bearer of the French Plan, which I had helped to draw up in 1946–7 and which was going to represent the French component of the European Recovery Programme.

I discharged this national duty to the best of my ability, but I was progressively caught up in the machinery of this big European conference, to the point where I lost my national identity to some extent. Not only Hervé Alphand but the British and the Americans, with whom I had established excellent relations, as well as other delegations, asked me to serve as coordinator for the technical work that would go into the formulation of the ERP. I found myself the unofficial secretary general of the Conference, enjoying the confidence of all the delegations. As such I realized for the first time that it is by showing great objectivity in the treatment of international issues, without losing sight of the essential interests of one's own country, that one best serves the latter.

In particular, I found myself in charge of coordinating the reports that a set of technical committees had been instructed to draft, covering agriculture and food, energy, iron and steel, coke, land transport and shipping, wood, and manpower. I recall spending long days in the rooms of the Grand Palais, where the Conference had been installed, and in sweltering heat, trying to reconcile programmes of which almost all had been drawn up on differing premises or even by pure guesswork. Most of the governments represented did not have a national plan and some not even an overall picture of the national economy. Nevertheless, all of them submitted without demur to the rules the Conference had laid down and had their central civil services complete the enormous blank tables which were sent over from Paris and were to provide the basic data input for the ERP.

An amusing incident occurred in July or August 1947, when the Conference had adjourned precisely to allow the central civil services in the different capitals to get together the figures that would appear in these tables. I was in the Grand Palais with Eric Roll when we noticed the Greek delegate in his office with the tables spread out before him. Apparently deep in thought, he would enter a figure from time to time. Indignantly I called out to him: 'What are those tables doing here? They should have been in Athens for at least a week now. It's not for you to fill them in. You can't know the answers to those questions.' 'That's true,' he replied calmly and with a smile, 'I'm having to invent a lot, but do you think they know any more in Athens than I do?' Nonplussed, I retreated, and the Greek figures compiled in this way appeared in their due place in our overall tables.

Each technical report contained a four-year programme for the sector concerned, with forecasts for output, consumption and exports, and finally an estimate of import requirements. The conclusions of the technical reports were put together in a general report which I helped to draft. The knowledge and experience I had gained in the drafting of the French Plan were very useful to me, whilst my economic views automatically put me in tune with the British and American economists with whom I was working and who were all Keynesian.

It was no hardship for me to put into this new enterprise all the effort and enthusiasm of which I was capable. The first fundamental theme of the ERP was a drive for maximum production. And the young economists of the immediate postwar period, of whom I was one, had been raised essentially on the idea that a return to prewar stagnation had to be avoided at all costs; we belonged to the 'growth' generation. The fact that in the ERP the priority sectors were the same as in the French Plan was due less to my personal influence than to the fact that they were the obvious choice.

The second theme, establishment and maintenance of internal financial stability, was the response to the inflation being experienced by a number of countries, including Germany and, to a lesser degree, France. We had already observed, when drawing up and starting to implement the French Plan, that no economic calculation, no rational management of business, whether in a free-market economy or in a planned economy, was possible if the upward movement of prices exceeded a certain rate.

As to the programme's third theme, the development of economic cooperation among the participating countries, the years I had spent in London and Washington, in close contact with the British and representatives of the governments in exile, had prepared me for it. Like the US Congress and Administration, I thought that much of the solution to Europe's difficulties would come, if not from union, at least from a joint endeavour to carry out certain tasks of common interest, such as progressive dismantlement of customs barriers and the creation of a multilateral payments system.

Despite the violence of my feelings towards the Germans before and during the war, I had rapidly convinced myself after the hostilities ended that Europe could not recover unless Germany were rebuilt and became once again a great industrial country. Schemes like the Morgenthau plan, which sought to turn Germany into an agricultural nation, the granary of Europe as it were, seemed to me no better than diversions for the feebleminded. Nor did I believe in the dismemberment of western Germany, from which the Rhineland and the Ruhr, for example, would have been separated. That would have sown the seed for future wars. I was therefore quite ready to include the Germans in European cooperation and I did everything in my power, during the first few years of peace, to smooth the way for them.

The fourth theme of the ERP, namely a long-term solution to the problem posed by the balance-of-payments deficits of the participating countries with North America, was, in a sense, the key to the programme. I had already had experience of it when dealing with France's economic recovery. The French Plan could not come to fruition if France were unable to finance a large current payments deficit for a number of years. Without American aid the French Plan would exist only on paper. And the situation seemed to be similar in most of the other European countries.

This is the point at which to dispel a misunderstanding that has crept into subsequent discussion of this question of American aid. It has been maintained that the United States did France and the other European countries a favour by allowing them to dispose freely, for purposes of investment, of almost the entire national currency equivalent of the dollars they received. In point of fact, by stipulating that these counterpart funds be used for investment, the Americans were setting a limit on what had formerly been total freedom. The proceeds in domestic currency from imports of capital, in whatever form, are normally at the importer's disposal. This had been the case, in particular, with the financial assistance which America gave France prior to 1948. The reason why the Americans were now trying to introduce a restriction of this kind had to do with the inflationary implications of double use of American aid – for example, in dollars and in French francs – and the sheer scale of the Marshall Plan. There may be some doubt, moreover, as to the efficacy of this restriction, given the fungible nature of public funds. Although France was obliged to earmark for investment the counterpart of American aid, she could use for other purposes (current expenditure) the funds of French origin that otherwise would have been invested in fixed capital or inventories.

There was an obvious kinship between the plan the US Administration wanted to see adopted and the one to which the Europeans subscribed after a few weeks of discussions. Thence to conclude that there was an American 'diktat' was a transition that certain minds, particularly in America, did not hesitate to make. The truth of the matter is simpler. The ERP, in its essentials – an intensive production effort, return to internal financial stability, European cooperation, massive external aid – clearly suited the interests of Europe. In this affair the USA was not seeking to satisfy certain economic interests of its own[2]. What it wanted was the revival and consolidation, economic and political, of a democratic Europe.

The establishment of the European Recovery Programme was only the first step towards the ultimate goal, the provision of massive American aid to Europe that would be maintained until such time as the latter could do without it. The question of when this financial independence would be gained was to remain, moreover, a subject of doubt and controversy for several years.

It was necessary as well that the programme take a form that would give the US Administration the best chance of getting it through Congress. When the report was completed in September, I left for Florence with Dottie, determined to have with her my first holiday since the beginning of the war. I was recalled almost immediately. The Americans had asked that a European delegation go to Washington to help the Administration to prepare its file for submission to the Congress. Sir Oliver Franks headed the delegation. Hervé Alphand and other heads of national mission, plus a dozen or so technical experts, were also part of it. My job and that of a few other economists from various European countries was to coordinate all the documents that would be submitted.

It is not possible for me to recount in detail the discussions we had in Washington. Suffice it to say that a tacit complicity formed or, rather, confirmed itself between the Europeans and the representatives of the US Administration in the purpose of favourably impressing the Congress. For this to be the case, the situation in Europe had to appear critical (which was not difficult, since this was the truth) but not hopeless; it had to be shown that with large-scale American aid Europe would recover in a relatively short space of time, four years being the period on which the Americans were insisting. Obviously, the latter demonstration was difficult to make. Who could foresee what would happen over the years from 1948 to 1952? We went about it with a will, however, supplying Congress with all the figures it could want, and even more, describing a situation that would improve from year to year until the time, in 1952, when the umbilical cord could be cut. When I think back, forty years later, on our fine optimism then, I realize that this was purely and simply an act of faith, which the intelligence and energy of the Europeans and the Americans made a reality.

After our work had been concluded, President Truman sent on December 19 a message to Congress on the European Recovery Programme, thus opening a debate that would last for several months. On April 3 of the following year the President signed the Foreign Assistance Act of 1948.

The Administration had asked for aid to Europe of $17 billion for the period 1948–52, but the Congress finally decided to authorize only the appropriations necessary for the first year, 1948–9. It added to this decision, however, a declaration of intent whereby it undertook to authorize each year the appropriations deemed necessary for the programme's execution until June 1952. *At the same time it asked that a permanent European organization be set up to guide Europe on the road to recovery.*

Thus a new page was written in the history of Europe, which entered a period of rapid progress that was to transform the Continent completely.

The OEEC

The Americans had insisted on the establishment of a European organization to implement the ERP. The French and the British together decided that I and Eric Berthoud, a Foreign Office official, should be sent to the different capitals. Our essential assignment was to ask governments whether they would agree to set up a permanent organization. If I remember correctly, we made three trips: one to Rome and Berne, another to Belgium and Holland, the third to the Scandinavian countries. All the governments agreed to the idea of a European organization and to the constitution of a committee that would draw up its charter. I also talked at length on the subject with representatives of the US Administration who became excellent friends. I should like to mention first and foremost Henry Labouisse, whose intelligence and generosity of sentiment caused him to play a major role in the birth of the OEEC, and Miriam Camps, whom I shall be speaking of later in connection with the Common Market.

When the time came to define the instructions to be given to the committee required to lay down the rules of operation for the new organization, the British insisted on the latter's being an intergovernmental-type organization with a council of ministers that would take all decisions by unanimous vote. There would be a secretary-general, but he would not have any authority in his own right; his role would be to enforce the decisions taken by the council. The French, on the other hand, wanted to introduce a supranational element into the system – for example, by allowing the secretary-general to take certain decisions. The Americans went even further than the French and wanted the new organization to be able, in certain cases, to decide by majority vote. But they were inhibited by the fact that they did not want to give the impression of dictating to the Europeans.

The British won the day. All possibility of decision by majority vote was precluded. I cannot say that the unanimity rule seriously impeded the functioning of the organization in the years that followed. But the circumstances then were very different from what they were to become in a more recent era, at the time of the Common Market, for example. France and Britain carried particular weight in the decision-taking. Most important, in the event of conflict or the impossibility of taking a decision, the United States was generally in a position to act as umpire. It was America, after all, who was financing the reconstruction of Europe.

As to the Secretary-General's subordination to the Council, it never prevented me from taking the stances that seemed right to me and making the proposals I thought were necessary in the economic and political circumstances of the moment.

I was asked to chair the committee instructed to draw up the charter of the future organization. The government delegates were divided up into a number of sub-committees, the most important of which was presided over by Dag Hammarskjöld, the future Secretary-General of the United Nations. We worked fast. In less than a month the charter was ready and was signed by the governments of the participating countries on April 16, 1948. The Organisation for European Economic Cooperation (OEEC) began to form in that same month of April. I was appointed Secretary-General. I and my immediate collaborators set about constructing piece by piece a great international organization, which was for several years to be the forum for discussions concerning Europe's economic recovery.

To see Europe through until Congress authorized the aid he had requested, Truman sent Europe in December 1947 'interim aid' amounting to $597 million, the recipients of which were France, Italy and Austria. A further amount of $155 million was distributed in March 1948.

4

CREATION OF THE ORGANISATION FOR EUROPEAN ECONOMIC COOPERATION

When, in the spring of 1948, I was appointed Secretary-General of the Organisation for European Economic Cooperation (OEEC) by the governments of the sixteen member countries, it was the first time in my life that I found myself completely in charge. Up to then the decisions I took were covered, or supposedly so, by my superiors. Now I was out on my own. Admittedly, I could not take decisions without their first being approved by the Council. But a man with sixteen masters may well in effect have none. Someone a little skilful, who has understood where the true interests of his different mandators lie and who works towards the general interest, has a very good chance of getting them to subscribe to the policy that he is recommending.

Actually, things were not quite as simple as that. In principle the sixteen member countries were equal, but their respective weights were very different. When I put forward a proposal, I had to be sure of the agreement of the British and the French; I also had to be certain that the Americans were not opposed to it. For the small countries, the situation was different. More often than not they had no global view

191

of the problem at issue; on the other hand, they had their individual interests, to which they clung all the closer in that these were more narrowly defined and more concrete. What we had to do, in those first days of European cooperation, was to take initiatives consistent with the views of the big European countries and the United States, and at the same time see that these did not harm the interests of the small countries. All this demanded, in most cases, very lengthy preparations and endless private get-togethers, to explain to each one the real significance and most likely implications of the proposal concerned. It was a job that required infinite patience. Often, a slight adjustment of the text under discussion, which would not alter its sense but would sound better to the ears of those across the table, would be enough to get the decision through. I learned quite quickly this art of negotiation, for which my long stays in England and the United States had prepared me.

But the elation I felt when I was appointed to my new post had another cause. Not only was I happy to be in sole charge of an undertaking, but I had the feeling, subsequently corroborated by the successful outcome, that the OEEC, which was the fruit of the Marshall Plan, would enable Europe and the world to avoid the follies of the interwar years.

A little later, in the fifties, it became the thing to disparage international cooperation, and European cooperation in particular. What good was a system in which all decisions had to be taken on a unanimity basis, where each country, big or small, could veto any draft decision and block it, where Iceland and Luxembourg carried the same weight as Britain and France? At this point in time it can be said that the people who used those arguments were singularly lacking in a sense of history, and in plain common sense, for that matter. The OEEC, along with other international institutions, represented precisely what had been sadly lacking in Europe, and in the whole world, between the two world wars – or between the two phases of the same world war, if one prefers: namely, a dialogue between the great powers so as to ensure continuing peace and erase rapidly the scars left by the war and the Great Depression. This dialogue made it possible to maintain fundamental agreement on objectives and methods among the United States, France and Britain, who would be joined by Germany in the fifties.

The OEEC did not build this agreement from scratch. It already existed, but in a rather unspecific form; it was born of the war and of the awareness that the people in authority in the different countries had gained of the cardinal errors committed in the interwar years. But to be effective, this agreement had to take on a precise form that would respect the vital interests of the different countries and what remained of national ideologies in Europe and the United States; in other words, the agreement of principle had to be converted into a series of major political acts. This was the function of the OEEC and we shall see that it performed that function, if not perfectly, at least highly satisfactorily.

The team is formed

To return to our story, in those months of April–May 1948 I settled into my new post determined to make a contribution, however modest, to the reconstruction of Europe and, even further, to the creation of a new Europe.

First I had to choose my chief collaborators. For my second in command the British proposed Harry Lintott. We had a long talk and I immediately formed a very high regard for Harry. Educated at Cambridge, he had made a career for himself in the Board of Trade. In a sense, one could say that he was the perfect British civil servant. Always with a thorough knowledge of his brief, always even-tempered – outwardly, at any rate, for he could be a prey to high emotion – combining total loyalty to his colleagues with a strong individualism, allying a sober style of argument to great percipience, he was for me the perfect collaborator or, I should say, partner.

I had noticed Guido Colonna[1] during the Paris Conference. He presented a rare combination of qualities of mind and character that had made me want to have him at my side. He was a diplomat who came from a noble Italian family. Unlike Harry Lintott, he had never specialized in economic matters; but he made up for this shortcoming with a great intelligence which ensured that even in the company of seasoned experts he was never at a disadvantage. His natural nobility gave him a great authority. There was nothing petty in him. I turned to him in particular when difficult staff problems arose.

Lintott, Colonna and I formed a team in the truest sense of the word. There was no exclusive area of competence for any of us. Our offices were side by side and we saw one another several times a day. I can say that I never took a decision of any important without having discussed it at length with my two friends. Our dedication to the European cause

193

was boundless; it came before our national loyalties. Or, rather, we were convinced that the best way to serve our respective countries was to ensure that the great undertaking to which we were committed succeeded, even if a few secondary national interests had to be sacrificed along the way.

I immediately set about recruiting directors for the different sectors of the OEEC. I am not sure if I can remember all their names: they included Sacha Guéronik, Frank Figgures, Donald MacDougall, Guy de Carmois and, later, Milton Gilbert. With Harry Lintott and Guido Colonna, it was a splendid team, resolved to devote itself entirely to the task that awaited us.

The Secretariat General was mainly Anglo-French, but very soon it found itself working closely with the various European national delegations and with the Americans, and a kind of complicity developed between it and the latter respectively. While the Secretariat General strove to take as objective a view as possible of things, the national delegations themselves toned down or referred back for amendment the instructions they had received from their capitals whenever these contained demands that would have made general agreement impossible.

As to the Americans of the Economic Cooperation Administration (ECA), their major concern was to get the Europeans to come up with sound arguments that would favourably impress the Congress so that it would authorize the appropriations the ECA was requesting for Europe. The strongest argument was that the aid already given had been put to good use and that the recipient countries had made satisfactory progress toward the goals laid down in the European Recovery Programme.

There soon came to be a real climate of friendship, compounded of trust and respect for each other's point of view: a communion of minds established itself among the three groups (secretariat, European national delegations, representatives of the ECA). Nearly every day I would have a few people to lunch in the small dining room on the ground floor of the Château de la Muette, where we had finally found permanent premises after a spell at the Royal-Monceau Hotel, then at the Hôtel des Tabacs on the Quai Branly. Several times a month, along with Harry Lintott, Guido Colonna, Eric Roll, Guillaume Guindey, and other national delegates occasionally, I would have dinner with some of the Americans at Calvet, a well-known restaurant on the Boulevard Saint-Germain. These were brainstorming sessions in which each participant, without malice or ulterior motives, keenly attacked the other's position in order to reveal its flaws. Monsieur Calvet senior contributed to the animation by serving us some of his excellent *fine champagne* after the coffee.

The American services in Paris were run by Averell Harriman, with whom I had correct but rather distant relations. He would visibly have liked to be able to deal with a well-known politician, someone with all the prestige of a great career, instead of a young man (who looked like a youngster) of whom he had never heard before and who gave him the impression of a raw recruit in a command post. My relations with his successor, Milton Katz, were much more cordial.

Our conversations in Paris with the ECA officials were supplemented by frequent trips to Washington where we were able to meet members of Congress, who urged us keenly, sometimes excessively so, to make more rapid progress towards European integration. There we also saw Richard Bissell, whose great intellectual abilities and warmth of sentiment towards Europe contributed much to the success of our undertaking. I also had frequent meetings with the head of the ECA, Paul Hoffman, whose authority and prestige helped us greatly in this difficult task. I should also mention the name of Lincoln Gordon who, in various capacities, likewise played an important role.

France and Britain called the tune in the OEEC. In the national delegations I could count on the support of Hervé Alphand, who had been largely instrumental in my appointment, and Edmund Hall-Patch, head of the British delegation, a Catholic Scotsman who, within the compass of government instructions which he observed more or less scrupulously, always showed a high degree of objectivity and had thus gained great authority with the other national delegations. He chaired the Executive Committee for many years.

But here I must say a special word about an Englishman, Eric Roll, whom I had met in Washington during the war and whom I reencountered in Paris at this time. A man of exceptional intelligence with a perfect knowledge of economic theory (he was to write his *History of Economic Thought* a few years later), he was also a supreme practician who had already proved himself during the war years in Washington. In Paris he chaired the Programmes Committee, which was required to examine the different national programmes on the basis of which aid was being distributed. His keen mind enabled him quickly to spot the weak points in a programme under consideration and often to get it amended by the government which had presented it. We formed a close friendship that has lasted to this day.

Never in my experience, before and after the Marshall Plan, have I known an international team moved by such an intense desire to accomplish a joint endeavour, the success of which represented at that time a matter of life and death for Europe and for each member country, and to see that it succeeded in conditions such that each participant might derive equal benefit. We were convinced that the different European countries were indissolubly linked in their destinies. Later, the word 'cooperation' was somewhat corrupted. But at the time of the Marshall Plan and the OEEC, European cooperation proved to be the key to success, thanks undoubtedly to the circumstances, but also to the exceptional quality of the men who dedicated themselves to this common task.

The division of aid

It is not my intention here to write the history of the Marshall Plan and the OEEC. This has already been done several times, notably in the Anglo-Saxon countries. But I do wish to single out the most important episodes in the story and discuss briefly a number of questions that have been the subject of controversy over the past thirty years[2].

Our first task was to draw up a consolidated programme for all the member countries of the OEEC covering the period from July 1, 1948 to June 30, 1949. The Americans, applying increased pressure to make Europe behave as much as possible like a unit, declared that the responsibility of coordinating and integrating the individual country programmes should fall to the OEEC.

Each of these programmes ultimately represented a request for aid. Since their combined total considerably exceeded what the Americans were prepared to give, and almost certainly what was necessary, there arose the problem of the forthcoming division of aid. Who would do this? No one would have objected if the Americans had taken it upon themselves to do so. They were the ones who were supplying the money, so why shouldn't they be the ones to distribute it? I remember having lengthy discussions on this question in April–May 1948 with the US representatives in Paris, and notably with Harry Labouisse. I argued that Washington should leave it to the OEEC to allocate the aid. Nothing seemed to me better able to strengthen the nascent organization, and give it prestige and authority with national governments, than a right of intervention in the division of aid at a time when each country's economic recovery depended on the amount of dollars it received. In Washington itself, in the ECA and other government bodies, similar opinions were voiced.

The Americans hesitated for a few weeks, then in May they took their decision. Averell Harriman announced to the OEEC Council that the ECA would like the OEEC, in establishing the economic recovery programme for 1948–9, to indicate how, in its opinion, American aid should be apportioned among the different countries and the uses to which it should be put by each.

What the Americans were asking of us was a recommendation; they reserved the final decision for themselves, of course. Experience showed that they followed the European recommendations to the letter in 1948–9 and, with only a comparatively minor adjustment, in 1949–50. The Americans' essential motivation was to induce maximum unity among the European countries. A secondary consideration, but influential nonetheless, was their wish not to be involved in bilateral horse-trading with each of the European countries.

The European response was not immediately forthcoming. A number of countries, if not most, feared a public confrontation of their demands with those of the other members and felt that they would do better through a dialogue with Washington. The British, in particular, were counting on their 'special relationship' with America. It was one of the cases where, although without any decision-taking power, I succeeded, with the help of a number of members of the various national delegations, in pushing the decision in the direction I considered desirable for Europe. After lengthy discussions, the OEEC Council formally accepted the American proposal on July 16, 1948.

A group of high officials belonging to the national delegations, but who had been chosen by their peers to carry out leading assignments, was appointed to examine the national programmes and make proposals for the division of American aid for the year 1948–9. The group consisted of Guillaume Guindey, Chairman of the Balance of Payments Committee, Eric Roll, Chairman of the Programmes Committee, Dirk Spierenburg, Chairman of the Trade Committee, and Pietro Stoppani, Vice-Chairman of the Intra-European Payments Committee, who for health reasons soon had to be replaced by Giovanni Malagodi. As Secretary-General, I sat with the group, which my collaborators supplied with all the information they might need. When necessary, I formulated proposals designed to reconcile stances that were often very divergent.

During three weeks of intensive work we examined the programmes submitted by the different countries and questioned the civil servants who had compiled them. After this first operation the 'Four' and I withdrew to a small hotel at Lys-Chantilly, not far from Paris, to draw our final conclusions. There, over a period of a few days, the Four exercised all the intelligence and skill at their command. I endeavoured to play my role of mediator to the very best of my ability. My task was made easier by the friendship that bound me to each of them: they were not in the least put out by seeing someone who represented no one but himself call into question national positions laid down by imperative instructions from the different capitals. In his memoirs, Eric Roll excellently describes the qualities which the good negotiator must display and which were given free rein in this little provincial inn where we were playing with hundreds of millions of dollars. What was needed, he said, was 'patience, quiet persuasion, meticulous knowledge of one's brief with the consequent ability to answer the most unexpected questions, but also sarcasm, indignation, even carefully calculated loss of temper ...[3].'

The discussions lasted several days and, in spite of a few occasions on which voices were raised, we reached an agreement that Guillaume Guindey put before the Council. And who better than he? External Finance Director at the French Ministry of Finance, Chairman of the OEEC Balance of Payments Committee, he had played a big part in the discussions that had just taken place, always showing a great concern for moderation and objectivity. He enjoyed respect from all, not only for his perfect knowledge of monetary problems, but also for a scrupulous intellectual integrity. His keen mind enabled him to clarify every aspect of the issue under discussion and to propose what always amounted to each receiving his due. We were already friends when we came together again at the OEEC and that friendship has only become stronger with time.

Before a final decision could be taken, there was one last hurdle to be cleared: the allocation of intra-European drawing rights, which in the US aid share-out, which they had been part of, the Four had considered as already acquired. Thus they had eliminated from the programmes for imports from the United States, and therefore payable in dollars, those goods which the member countries could obtain in Europe. The result was a reduction of the dollar deficit, but also the emergence or widening of credit or debit balances in European currencies.

It was decided that each member state would negotiate with each of its European partners a bilateral agreement specifying, for the year

1948–9, the probable developments in trade between the two countries and the anticipated creditor or debtor position that would result. On the same principle that had proved its worth in the division of American aid, a group of five persons was appointed to assist the negotiators. It comprised high officials from Britain, France, Belgium, Norway and Greece. The idea was that creditor countries would 'give' debtor countries the balance that had been specified in the bilateral agreements. In return, the creditor countries in intra-European trade would receive dollar aid increased by the amount they had given to the debtor countries.

The matter was not settled easily. I still remember Frank Figgures, who was Trade and Payments Director at OEEC, and I working out a scheme of drawing rights distribution on a paper tablecloth in a little restaurant on the Left Bank. The agreement was finally concluded on October 16, 1948, thus sealing the first round of American aid. The main beneficiary in the distribution of drawing rights was France, the countries that contributed the most were Britain and Belgium. But the idea that the creditor countries in intra-European trade would receive additional dollar aid proved largely an illusion. US aid had been distributed on the basis of dollar deficits and was not adjusted after the conclusion of the payments agreement. The drawing rights therefore represented aid given by some European countries to others, a mini-Marshall Plan. There can be no doubt that the Americans had to prod the European creditors into behaving so generously.

The Four-Year Plan

The first division of US aid had made the Europeans euphoric. The Americans now wanted us to outline for them the prospect of a Europe that would quite soon be able to do without their assistance. At the outset of the work that culminated in the European Recovery Programme a time limit of four years had been set, a magic figure that rested on no measurable reality. It represented no more than a vague aspiration shared by the Americans and the Europeans; but there had to be a figure, preferably a very low one, to give Congress and the American people the feeling that Europe was not a bottomless receptacle. This, at least, was the conviction of the ECA. On July 25, 1948 Paul Hoffman, speaking before the OEEC Council, called for a plan of action of which the goal would be Europe's complete and definitive recovery at the latest by June 30, 1952, when American aid would cease.

And so the administrative machinery of member countries started up again in order to produce a four-year plan. It is clear that this undertaking fed on a great many illusions. In the first place, this was a plan for Europe, but Europe did not exist in the sense that there would have been a single economic policy, or at least coordinated economic policies. Britain, the Netherlands and the Scandinavian countries had national plans based on bureaucratic control of the economy that was as near complete as possible. Belgium was trying to attain the same objectives by free-market methods. France was in an intermediate position. As for Italy, then as now, it was difficult to say exactly what her economic policy was. Lastly, Germany was still under the rule of the military occupation authorities, whose ways were often mysterious. There was something of a paradox here: it was curious, to say the least, that the United States, whose philosophy was essentially liberalist, should seek to impose authoritarian planning on Europe. More particularly, and this is the fundamental point, no European country, even among those whose economic services possessed the most efficient and sophisticated statistical systems for that time, was capable of drawing up a four-year plan that was at most plausible (the situation has not changed much since). A little over a year after the terrible crisis of the winter of 1946–7 each country was still trying to find itself and, in a manner of speaking, navigating without instruments. Finally, it was a question of sovereign states, each contending with domestic problems radically different from those of the others and therefore basing their economic policies on different principles.

We tried nevertheless to give the Americans what they wanted. Few thought that the target of European payments equilibrium by 1952 was realistic. To most people Europe's dollar gap seemed likely to last for many years beyond that date. It was a very good example of the inability of men to conceive of a situation much different from the one in which they are at present. The four-year programmes that were written then led to the conclusion that Europe would still be running a deficit of $1 billion in 1952, but we added a reservation: it seemed more realistic to us to estimate that deficit at about $3 billion.

The plain truth is that the endeavour to establish a four-year plan failed. The OEEC, with the resigned agreement of the Americans, had to lower its sights and content itself with a plan of action, adopted in March 1949, which merely set out a number of principles designed to guide the economic policies of the member countries. The so-called plan consisted of the sort of clichés favoured by international organizations, and sometimes by national governments: financial and monetary stability in all the member countries, rapid export growth, reduction of non-essential imports payable in dollars, elimination of intra-European imbalances, etc.[4]

It was impossible for anyone relatively well informed and with a little insight not to realize that European planning, which both the Americans and the Europeans regarded as the key to success, was practically non-existent. It was never to see the light of day. What we did not realize sufficiently, if at all, was the immense vitality of which Europe was capable, provided that it were managed reasonably well and received the external aid it needed for a few years. In 1948–9 Europe had begun to pick up briskly, but the improvement had not yet been discerned in the leading member countries. In my mind, as in that of many others, the prevailing sentiment was one of unease and great uncertainty about the final outcome of the enterprise.

The Washington visit

Between 1948 and 1952 I made many trips to Washington to talk with my friends of the ECA and supply them with the ammunition of which they had such need in their ceaseless battle with Congress to get the necessary appropriations for Europe authorized. None of these visits was more important than the one from December 1948 to January 1949.

In Paris we had distributed nearly $5 billion in US aid and the Americans, in particular the Congress, wanted to know what use we were putting it to, what progress we were making, what the prospects were for a complete recovery of Europe. On the answers to those questions depended the authorization of a new round of appropriations for use in the year 1949–50.

In Washington I gave a press conference on December 31, 1948. Despite the fact that New Year's Eve is hardly the ideal date for discussions of a serious nature, it was very well attended and written up in most of the American and European newspapers. When I reread what I said on that occasion I am put in mind of a tightrope walker struggling to keep his balance. The reason is that I was having to deal with two contradictory requirements. On the one hand, I had to convince the Americans (read: Congress) that the aid they were giving was effective, that the Europeans were putting it to good use, that Europe was on the road to a recovery that would enable it to do without American aid. At the same time, I had to be careful not to go too far in this direction, for Congress would have been only too happy to believe that the Marshall Plan had already achieved its goal or would shortly; it had to be persuaded that several more years of substantial US aid were necessary.

With the Europeans, the problem was different. Within the different countries dangerous tensions still existed. In spite of the real progress made since 1945, they were in many cases even stronger than ever. For nearly ten years the Europeans had been living in the conditions of a war economy. Almost everywhere consumption levels were still lower than in 1938 and the peoples of Europe yearned for less restriction and more well-being, whilst their governments, spontaneously or under American pressure, strove to carry out very ambitious investment programmes and to stimulate exports with every means at their disposal. One did not have to be a genius to realize that, as soon as circumstances permitted, they would switch to less austere policies so as to remain in power and that they were only too ready to believe that those circumstances were already present or in the process of emerging. Another trap into which they were ever ready to fall was the belief that American aid could continue for many years on a large scale, which would enable them forthwith to satisfy the consumer wants of their populations. I therefore had to hit on the right mix of pessimism and optimism: pessimism for the present and the immediate future, optimism for the longer-term future. I am not sure I succeeded on that occasion.

Today, as we approach the end of the 20th century, what often remains in the minds of those who lived through the postwar period is the memory of Europe's renascent prosperity and of its prodigious economic expansion over twenty-five years. My testimony is designed, among other things, to dispel the belief that from the very outset we were possessed of a fine certitude, an indomitable faith in the future, an unshakeable optimism. On the contrary, what remains branded on my memory is the doubts, the dread of the morrow, the fear of failing, the concern with continually adjusting our action in the light of experience – and I can never say it enough – having the grievous reminders of the interwar years as a constant warning.

On this visit to Washington I was subjected, like all the other Europeans there with me, to an avalanche of questions, not all of them amiable, on why the Europeans were unable to unite. The Americans, who, a hundred and fifty years or so earlier, had found salvation in union, could not understand how Europe could remain divided, broken up, when it needed to combine all its forces in order to reestablish a normal life and stand up to the Soviet danger. The people we were talking to did not always see that it was impossible to apply to mid-20th century Europe solutions that had worked for late 18th century America.

It was to reply to this expectation that, during the same press conference, I made a remark that I was to repeat frequently, with variations, over the years and even the decades that followed:

We all want Europe to become unified, but we have to face facts: the essential responsibility for Europe's salvation still rests with national governments. The role of the Organization is that of European cooperation. It is paramount and consists in coordinating the efforts of individual countries and ensuring that these do not counteract one another; it consists in intensifying the impact of national efforts, not in replacing them.

That visit to Washington was the occasion of a somewhat bizarre dinner, on January 19, 1949, attended by members of the European mission and representatives of Congress. The American contingent included Senator Tom Connally and Congressman Sol Bloom, respectively chairmen of the Senate Foreign Relations Committee and of the Foreign Affairs Committee of the House of Representatives, and Senator Arthur H. Vandenberg, leader of the Republican minority on the Senate Foreign Relations Committee. The ECA was represented among others by Paul Hoffmann and Averell Harriman.

I noted on that occasion, perhaps for the first time, the terror that Congress inspired in the American high officials, even those who, in European terms, could be regarded as members of the government. They hardly dared open their mouths, much less contradict. Anyway, that evening it was as though they disappeared through a trapdoor. After a few words of introduction from Harriman, they left me on my own to defend the European programme and make known the efforts undertaken to ensure Europe's recovery.

The dialogue between the members of Congress and myself started out on a misunderstanding. For several months in Paris Harriman and his collaborators had insisted, despite our reservations, that the OEEC draw up a four-year programme (mentioned earlier) specifying the goal we hoped to reach by 1952. Naturally enough, I took this long-term programme as the point of departure for my statement. Imagine my surprise to find myself interrupted very sharply by Sol Bloom, seconded by Vandenberg, with the following words: 'All this stuff about a long-term programme is just a lot of hot air.' Then

Vandenberg added: 'Mr Marjolin, I give you five minutes to tell me what you are going to do during the year that is beginning. Forget about the rest.' I got out of it as best I could, quite well I was told later by some Americans who were at that memorable dinner. Paul Hoffman and Averell Harriman, who had more or less forced the long-term programme on us, did not say a word during the entire evening. The long-term programme was dead and buried as of that moment.

As I think back on that evening, a comic incident comes to mind. The discussion had gone on until a late hour. Sol Bloom had dozed off. He came to suddenly while Jean-Charles Snoy, chairman of the OEEC Council at the senior official level, was speaking. Without knowing what the latter had said, Bloom cut him off abruptly with more or less these words: 'You Frenchmen, you have the art of presenting things in a light that flatters you, but that's not always the true light!' Snoy was completely floored by this outburst. What could he say in reply? He was Belgian.

I should not like to end the story of that evening on a note of misunderstanding. Our American opposite numbers were in no way malicious. They completely supported the ideas of the Marshall Plan, but they knew they were up against a hesitant Congress which still included a fair number of isolationists and which felt somewhat sceptical about the Europeans' efforts at recovery. What Connally, Bloom, Vandenberg and the others wanted was arguments with which they could 'sell' American aid to Congress. That is why they put me on the spot that evening.

So we went into 1949, seeming to navigate in a fog, having the vague feeling that we were making progress, but unable to glimpse or even imagine journey's end. In fact, most of the European and American participants in this unprecedented undertaking, if not all, thought that the shortage of dollars, the dollar gap, was a state of affairs into which the world had settled for a very long period, ten years or more. America's technological superiority, which never ceased to increase, and her high rate of productivity growth seemed to indicate the indefinite continuance of a US balance of payments in heavy surplus.

The Americans, like the Europeans, for that matter, implicitly believed that Europe's reconstruction would be a very long haul. Germany, a formidable industrial power in the past, was rising only very slowly from her ruins; she was having to take in millions of displaced persons from East Europe, something that appeared to be a burden at the time. France was regarded as a lightweight industrial power: her entrepreneurs had the reputation of being uninterested in productivity growth and of preferring stout customs barriers; in addition, she was engaged in a war, in Indochina, that was draining a large share of her resources. Italy, with her high unemployment rate and the abject poverty prevailing in the Mezzogiorno, was not regarded as a power that counted. Only Britain found a little favour in the eyes of the Americans, but the weaknesses in her economic position and her continuing decline were becoming more obvious with each day.

5

THE TAKE-OFF

It is nearly always impossible to determine when a historical movement began or when it ended. So it is with the rebirth of Europe after the last world war. In this case, as in almost every other, it is useless to ask the contemporaries. They notice nothing until the moment when the process has been under way for a long time and the evidence suddenly stares them in the face: history is full of false starts that lead nowhere, of sudden stops that appear to be the end of a movement but are in fact only pauses, after which the advance resumes even more powerfully.

The people on the stock exchange are not the only ones to experience this. At the Château de la Muette we monitored trends from day to day, we always had our finger on the pulse of the economy, we compiled an impressive mass of statistics for those days (that achievement has been bettered since). But if anyone had asked me in 1948 or 1949 whether Europe's economic recovery had begun, whether the improvements discernible were the sign of a durable movement or transitory phenomena that might be followed by a relapse, I would have been quite incapable of answering on the strength of the information I possessed. I would nevertheless have replied 'yes, of course'. This assurance was not derived from the observed facts, but from the deep feeling that our interpretation of the situation was correct, that the action we were taking would inevitably, after some temporary setbacks and reverses, lead to the result we were seeking.

Later I realized that the upswing had begun back in 1945, once the Americans, instead of turning in upon themselves as they had done after 1918, understood that they had no choice and set about conveying to the world that they intended to assume all the responsibilities that their position of strength in every sector both required and permitted. This happened even before they were aware of it themselves, for they were moved by what may be called, for want of a better term, a historical instinct. They began tentatively, the situation being as new to them as it was to the rest of the world. Then in 1947, perhaps even a little earlier, their overall strategy began to take shape, first on particular points, then gradually incorporating all the elements that had to coalesce in order to make it fully effective.

The American government had to surmount internal conflicts of different kinds, their outcome being decisive for the success or failure of the strategy. In writing these lines I am thinking in particular of the struggle between the 'globalists' or 'universalists' and the 'Europeans', between those who thought it was necessary from the start to build an economic system that would encompass the whole world, including Europe, though in a somewhat incidental way, and those who were convinced that priority should be given to the reconstruction of Europe (and Japan) and that the stakes were high enough to warrant a few departures from universalist principles.

Never, I think, has a country played a more decisive role in world history than the United States did in the postwar years. First and foremost there was the nation's sheer power, then a disinterestedness born of the awareness of that power and of the extreme weakness of the rest of the non-Communist world; also the fear that the Soviet Union would take advantage of Europe's destitution to bring into its orbit the nations which the hostilities had not allowed it to occupy. If one adds to all this the feeling of having been partly responsible for the tragic events of the interwar period and the wish not only to avoid making the same fatal mistakes but to prevent them from being made, one has all the ingredients of America's economic and political philosophy after World War Two.

As to Europe, it was only too happy then to put its destiny into the hands of America, especially as what she was proposing to do would serve Europe's interests, not only as an act of generosity by a great victorious power whose hegemony no one in the West disputed, but also because the Americans intended to assemble around them a prosperous Atlantic world from which the most dangerous political tensions would have vanished.

1949

The year 1949 was a turning point in the history of postwar Europe. All the constituents of America's 'grand design' for Europe were finally in place: rapid expansion of output, along with the implementation of large-scale investment plans; maximum growth of European exports to the rest of the world; liberalization of trade between European countries, even though this liberalization, given the paucity of Europe's foreign exchange resources, had to be accompanied by temporary discrimination vis-à-vis the rest of the world, including the United States itself; reestablishment of a form of multilateral convertibility of European currencies to permit trade liberalization to develop without immediately encountering payments problems, which would inevitably have been the case with a bilateral payments system.

1949 is interesting for two other reasons. First, the free world experienced the first economic recession of the postwar period. Second, exchange parities were substantially adjusted, likewise for the first time since the war. These two events proved to be fraught with consequences and were largely instrumental in creating the European economy that we were to see develop during the next twenty-five years.

The recession, which began at the end of 1948 in the United States and then spread to the rest of the industrialized world, should, paradoxically enough, be regarded as a positive and beneficial development. To understand its significance, it is necessary to consider the state of mind prevailing at the time in western Europe and in the rest of the world. We were literally haunted by the memory of the Great Depression, terrified by the idea that a deep and lasting recession of that kind might occur again and ruin all our plans to reconstruct Europe. If truth be told, we were by no means confident that the depression of the thirties was really over. Admittedly, the world had not known any unemployment during the war; all the productive forces available had been marshalled in order to defeat the enemy, regardless of cost. But how could we forget that it was the war itself that caused the return of full employment in most countries? The Great Depression had not come to a natural end in a peace economy. Unemployment was still very high in the United States and elsewhere in 1939; Germany had reestablished a certain economic equilibrium in 1933–39 only by turning herself into a gigantic arsenal, an autarkic economy cut off from the rest of the world, save for imports of raw materials and food she could not do without. As for France, she was only just beginning to emerge from the crisis of late 1938, when Paul Reynaud in fact took charge of the country's affairs. Each time we detected a flutter in the world economy we were ready to think that the thirties were returning.

In the event, the 1948–9 recession astonished us by its brief duration and superficial impact. Between the fourth quarter of 1948 and the third quarter of 1949 US manufacturing output fell by only 10% and GNP by 5%. This short and relatively painless recession exorcised the demons of the past. Yes, the past was really dead; we were living in a new world; a bright future was possible provided we did what was necessary; the optimism we felt stirring again deep within us was not a delusion. The year 1949 can be said to be the starting point of a psychological progression which, setting out from the despair of the war years and the futureless context of the immediate postwar years, would generate the confidence of the fifties and the euphoria, sometimes inordinate, of the sixties.

The other important event of 1949, which marked the beginning of a return to the market economy, was the currency adjustments in the autumn of that year, notably sterling's devaluation by 30% against the dollar. Although carried out in the utmost disorder and without any prior consultation among Europeans, the adjustments did help to reestablish a certain monetary order and for many countries hastened the return to external payments equilibrium.

These monetary operations were the sign that times had changed. From the end of the war to 1948–9 the European countries had nothing to gain from a change of parity against the dollar or other currencies. They had virtually nothing to export, and in any case the volume of exports did not depend on the exchange rate but on the production capacity of the nation's industry. Similarly, the degree of satisfaction of domestic demand was largely linked to the volume of imports; there was no or only little competition between national industry and agriculture on the one hand, and imports on the other. In a world where there is a great shortage of everything, having an overvalued currency is a distinct advantage for a country; the terms of trade are in its favour. The 1949 devaluations showed that, if the days of plenty had not yet returned, at least goods were beginning to circulate again and that the different countries were trying, in the interests of the present and especially of the future, to establish advantageous competitive positions for themselves.

Output, trade, payments

Despite the American recession of 1949 the European Recovery Programme went off in a somewhat disorderly but on the whole satisfactory fashion. Industrial output of the OEEC countries, after growing by more than 9% from 1948 to 1949, increased by a further 6% from 1949 to 1950. The engine was turning over rapidly and it would have taken a lot to stop it. Agricultural output was also growing substantially, by over 9% from 1948–9 to 1949–50 and by 7% in the next crop year. In 1950 Europe's industrial output was more than 25% above its 1938 level. In the league table of big countries the United Kingdom, as only to be expected, was top with growth of 40%, followed by Italy (25%) and France (23%). Germany herself was quickly rising from the ruins, her industrial output amounting to 50% of its 1938 level in 1948, 72% in 1949 and 91% in 1950.

In each country a large share of the national effort was devoted to investment, i.e. to the future. In 1947 the ratio of capital formation to national product was over 20% in all countries, reaching 35% in the Netherlands and 48% in Norway. Nearly all the national investment plans provided for considerable capacity enlargement in such industries as coal, iron and steel, electricity, transport equipment and oil refining. Generally speaking, these were five- or four-year plans; they were similar in pattern to the Soviet plans and, like them, aimed at rapid capital accumulation. Consumption was consequently kept relatively low and did not return to prewar levels until the early fifties. Encouraged, and sometimes chivvied a little, by the Americans, who made it quite clear that the future of aid depended on the European effort and that the latter was measurable by the buoyancy of investment in particular, the team I headed at OEEC spared no effort to persuade national governments to let consumption rise only slowly and release the maximum amount of resources for investment and exports.

We were therefore satisfied by and large with the growth of output and the share of it that was going into investment. But was this really a European effort? I had to acknowledge that the overall result obtained represented the sum of individual countries' efforts, more or less uncoordinated, and not the outcome of a European programme such as might have been applied by a central government with the same powers, on a Continental scale, as those possessed by each national government. For the first time – I was to encounter the same problem some ten years later in the European Economic Community – it was clearly apparent that *there was no such thing as Europe*, at least in the sense of a European economy in which national policies were harmonized, investment coordinated and national plans, where these existed, merged into an overall plan.

As of this time I became permanently sceptical of the kind of high-sounding but essentially empty schemes that find particular favour with party politicians. How many times have I heard, over the years from 1947 to 1967 when I gave up my post with the Common Market, and later still in the press, on the radio or on television, moving pleas for unification, coordination, harmonization of economic policies, or of national programmes and investment plans! And all to no avail. At first I was distressed by what seemed to be a failure of intelligence or weakness of will, then I asked myself whether it really was for governments to decide, even in the national context and *a fortiori* in the European context, what investments were necessary or even desirable. I have witnessed too many major and sometimes disastrous errors committed in this area, with the best intentions in the world, by a central government which not only was ill-informed about the issues but prevented by their infinite complexity from ever becoming well-informed about them, to attach much importance to efforts at European planning or coordination of investment.

As for national economic policies, efforts to unify or harmonize them have, in my experience, always failed. Has that been due to a lack of understanding or will? I do not think so. Those policies are fashioned by national political and social realities that differ profoundly from one country to another. Pressure from outside to make them less divergent has never produced any result, except perhaps in the East European countries, whose governments, insofar as they are allowed to express themselves, finally have to accept their orders from Moscow. Fortunately we are not in that situation. And one would have to be very foolish, ignorant or determinedly partisan to spurn the truth and draw a parallel between Soviet domination of East Europe and the influence that the United States is capable of exerting in Western Europe. In the course of my experience, which now goes back over more than forty years, I have never seen the Americans try to impose on Europe forms of action which the latter considered contrary to its fundamental interests. The point in history at which they could have done so easily was the postwar period, when a prostrate Europe had virtually no means of withstanding the colossus across the Atlantic. They refrained, even when the true interest of Europe coincided with what the United States wanted. To take a more recent example, when

211

General de Gaulle decided in 1966 to pull France out of NATO, the Americans protested but deferred to his decision and did not try to take reprisals.

To come back to my subject, did the 'national character' of the economic recovery plans or programmes adopted after the war mean that the individual forms of action which derived therefrom developed quite unrelatedly, in a kind of intellectual chaos? The answer is no. Because, largely under American influence, a European market was created step by step, realities emerged which were independent of the will of governments and to which they finally had to submit. The omnipotence of states found its limits, notably in the need to maintain or restore external equilibrium when this was endangered or impaired.

A European market is created

And so I come to the essential part of America's plan for Europe, the creation of a European market, which, however imperfect, has exerted a moderating influence on national policies. Indeed one has to go back to the late forties or early fifties to find the origins of a European market in which goods, services, manpower and capital would one day circulate freely.

Somewhat paradoxically, it was in America that the idea of a united Europe was, if not born (one could show that it was born in many different places, notably in Europe itself as it struggled against Nazi Germany), at least expressed the most forcefully in the years that immediately followed the war. The Administration in Washington and especially Congress were entirely wedded to the cause of a unified Europe. I well remember being heckled by senators and congressmen during my many visits to the United States at that time with the same old question: 'Why don't you go ahead and unite?' I remember, too, that my answers, which were often embarrassed, were not considered very convincing. The fact is that, at national government level at any rate, the need for a Europe assembled around a common policy was much less clearly realized in Europe than on the other side of the Atlantic. By and large, Europe was thinking mainly about overcoming her immense material difficulties. She needed dollars; that was her primary and in many cases her only concern. It is certain, however, that during those years from 1947 to 1949 she could have gone much further in the direction desired by the Americans, had it not been for the stubborn resistance of the British to the idea of committing themselves irrevocably to the Continent.

Originally, America's ambitions went very far, as far as the creation of a European federation. The Americans were motivated first and foremost by a desire to see Europe stand on her own feet economically and politically, to live without American aid and possibly even without the presence of the American army. They imagined, somewhat naïvely, a western Europe that would be an extension, as it were, of the United States in the Old World, inspired by the same values, following the same policy as they, relieving them of a responsibility they had always felt to be very heavy, that of defending Europe against all external aggression.

Very quickly they realized that a European federation was not within the realm of possibility, at least for the time being. The Administration in Washington then fell back on the idea of a customs union. On October 31, 1949 Paul Hoffman, speaking before the OEEC Ministerial Council, ardently pleaded its case:

The substance of integration would be the formation of a single large market within which quantitative restrictions on the movement of goods, monetary barriers to the flow of payments and, eventually, all tariffs are permanently swept away.

This more modest idea of European integration in the form of a customs union might have become a reality as early as the beginning of the fifties, had the British not rejected it out of hand. It would take nearly ten years before the scheme was reborn among the Six and nearly twenty-five years before Britain found her place in it. France, Italy and Benelux would have accepted it unhesitatingly. In fact a project for a Franco-Italian customs union had already seen the light of day and negotiations had begun between the two countries to extend it to Benelux. The enterprise foundered because of Britain's refusal to join. The French were opposed to Germany's being a part of it, but were to reverse their attitude in 1950.

Why did the British back out like this at a crucial moment for the future of Europe? I made numerous trips to London to try to convince them to join the French at the head of a movement to unify Europe. My efforts were unavailing. The counterarguments used, notably that customs duties were not within the competence of the OEEC but of the GATT, fooled no one. The real reasons are set out excellently in a book published much later by Miriam Camps, *Britain and the European Community*. Moreover, the same reasons were to apply repeatedly during the twenty-five years that followed, until that day at the beginning of the seventies when the British decided, with no mental reservations, to join the European Community.

On the Continent the war had not only destroyed industrial plant, transport systems, and economic life generally but it had disrupted the whole process of economic life as well. Countries had been occupied, and governments had been discredited or had spent the war in exile ... The war had been different for the British and it had left them not with a sense of national failure and a feeling of national inadequacy but with a sense of national achievement and cohesion and an illusion of power. The emotional support for European unity, which was strong on the Continent, was almost entirely lacking in the United Kingdom. And the concept of a 'Third Force' which was attractive to many on the Continent found little support in the United Kingdom. This was largely because the very close wartime partnership with the United States carried over, for a time, into the postwar period, and the preservation of this 'special relationship' was a major object of British policy. But it was also partly because in the 1940s Britain was still the third world power, and the vast distance – in power terms – between the first two and the third had not been fully apprehended[1].

Having failed in their endeavour to unify Europe, first politically, then commercially, the Americans settled for a less ambitious objective: to develop commerce between European countries to the utmost, by liberalizing trade and 'multilateralizing' payments. Their motivation was essentially political, but they were also anxious to reduce dollar aid to Europe as soon as possible. What each European country found next door it would no longer have to import from the United States or from other overseas countries requiring payment in dollars. At the same time its productivity would increase all the faster if it could produce on a larger scale not only for itself but also for the countries to which it exported. A big expansion of intra-European trade would therefore mean a growth of exports in general, including exports to the United States.

Obviously, liberalization of trade and multilateralization of payments were closely linked or, more accurately, trade liberalization depended on a multilateralization of payments. As long as Europe continued to live with a system of bilateral payments, trade liberalization would be impossible or of little interest. If France, for example, derestricted her imports from Belgium with the result that the latter's trade surplus with France increased, for trade to be maintained Bel-

214

gium had to be able to draw on her credit with France in order to buy from other European countries with which she was in deficit. Hence the unremitting efforts, from 1947 to the beginning of the fifties, to get Europe out of the straitjacket of bilateral payments agreements. From the outset this endeavour seemed to me as important as American aid, or rather I had become convinced that it was the only way to ensure that this aid would be scaled down rapidly and one day cease to be necessary. I cooperated closely with the US representatives and never let up in my efforts to overcome the objections harboured by certain European countries, most notably Britain.

I shall not inflict on the reader the whole story of the series of payments agreements concluded in the framework of the OEEC between 1947 and 1950. If he wishes to inform himself more fully, he may refer to the book by my friend William Diebold[2], which is a classic in the field. Written shortly after the event, it traces faithfully and with great perception the various stages leading from the system that obtained at the end of the war, when all payments had to be balanced on a bilateral basis, to the European Payments Union of 1950, in which the only factor that counted was the aggregate position of each country vis-à-vis all the others. Suffice it for me to recall that the 1947 agreement provided for compensation (or clearing) of a member country's debit or credit balances only in very simple cases; it was of very limited significance in the effort to create a system of European payments.

The 1948 agreement introduced an entirely new principle. In response to pressure from the United States, it was agreed that dollar aid would be supplemented by a European aid which, on the strength of a balance-of-payments forecast, each European creditor country would extend to its debtors. More technically, the debtor country would receive drawing rights in the currencies of its creditors. This was an enactment of the principle stated by General Marshall in the spring of 1947, namely: 'Let Europe help herself and we will see what we can do for her.' It is true that, theoretically, the European creditor countries which granted drawing rights to their debtors under this system were entitled to additional dollar aid, termed 'conditional aid', but essentially this provision remained a dead letter.

The 1948 agreement represented a considerable advance on previous practices, but it still related to a system in which payments had to be balanced in each bilateral relationship. For example, France could import more goods from Belgium because of the drawing rights the latter had given her, but she could not use them to buy goods in

Germany or Britain. The 1949 agreement partly remedied this disadvantage. The drawing rights which a country received could be used up to 25% in a country or countries other than the one that had given them.

1950 saw the birth of the European Payments Union (EPU), which relegated bilateralism in European payments to the status of a museum piece. Henceforth the sole factor that counted was each country's aggregate balance with all the others. There was no longer a two-way relationship between debtor and creditor; debtors were debtors to the Union, creditors were creditors of the Union. Settlement was effected partly through credit granted automatically by the Union, partly through payment in gold or dollars. I shall not go into the technicalities of the system, on which we worked for many months. Let me simply say that it represented a degree of payments derestriction that Europe had not known since the beginning of the war, and in many cases since the early thirties.

It was not all plain sailing. In Europe, Britain was reluctant; she feared that the holders of sterling balances would use the European Payments Union as a means of converting them into gold or dollars. The Americans themselves were not unanimously in favour. A large group in the Administration considered that the time had come, or was drawing near, when general convertibility of currencies, including convertibility into dollars, could be restored. They feared that the creation of the European Payments Union would delay this eventuality, or even that the Europeans, locked into their own system, would lose sight of the ultimate goal of universal convertibility. Experience showed that they were wrong, but at the time one could understand, if not share, their misgivings.

The creation of the EPU opened the way to liberalization of trade. In the same summer of 1950 that saw the EPU come into being the OEEC adopted a code of trade liberalization. Its two principles were the progressive removal of quantitative restrictions in intra-European trade and observance of nondiscrimination in that trade. The combination of the EPU and liberalization of intra-European trade represented a gigantic step towards the goal of a system of free trade and payments – current payments, at least. It enabled rapid progress to be made in the direction sought, despite a number of mishaps along the way, due notably to the Korean war, which broke out in 1950, and to Germany's financial crisis in the early fifties. Since it is impossible for me to describe in detail the events of this era, I shall content myself with quoting from the book which an American professor has recently written about the Marshall Plan and which represents, to my knowledge, the best study to date of this great enterprise.

Essentially, liberalization was to proceed in stages, its progress being measured by the percentage of total intra-OEEC private trade that had been freed from quantitative restrictions at each stage. Although actual progress in reaching the liberalization targets, specified for each stage, varied from country to country, the overall OEEC record turned out to be quite impressive. By the end of 1950, barely three months after the commencement of EPU's operations, some 60 percent of intra-European trade on private account had been freed from quantitative restrictions on a nondiscriminatory basis. By April 1955, the overall percentage of liberalized trade reached 84 percent; and in January 1959, it stood at 89 percent. But the point to be emphasized is that these results could not, in all probability, have been achieved had it not been for the EPU's clearing and credit facilities. In fact, it can be argued that the OEEC countries, especially in the early 1950s, would have been neither able nor willing to contemplate, let alone undertake, the kind of trade liberalization envisioned by the ECA without the underlying support of the EPU payments mechanism[3].

On no other issue did the intelligence of American postwar policy reveal itself more impressively.

Not only were the Americans giving massive financial aid to their allies and ex-enemies, thus making possible or accelerating the economic recovery of the world's most developed region outside the US itself – one that could quite foreseeably end up as a formidable competitor for its benefactors – but they were even urging, sometimes to the point of hustling, the Europeans to unite and thus increase their economic and political strength.

More precisely, they got them willy-nilly to create a payments system, the European Payments Union, that restored interconvertibility of European currencies, though not dollar convertibility. Even beyond that, they virtually forced them to derestrict a large share of their imports from other European countries, while accepting that import restrictions should be maintained on the same products when these emanated from the United States.

This apparently absurd disinterestedness would bear fruit. In the 1950s it became possible for Europe's payments to the rest of the world to be financed increasingly without recourse to American aid, until came the day in 1958 when general convertibility, this time including the dollar, was restored. Discriminatory measures in respect of trade with the US were phased out and a unified system entered into

217

force governing the whole of international trade among the developed countries. The gamble the Americans had taken during the last years of the previous decade had paid off. History can boast so few examples of a long-term calculation, involving immediate and certain sacrifices in return for distant and uncertain advantages, which has been corroborated so clearly, that I feel justified in writing about this subject at some length.

It is difficult today to imagine the fervour with which the representatives of the different countries debated the apparently highly technical issues I have just mentioned. The fact is that beneath the abstruse language lay political realities of immense importance for the ministers and high officials taking part in the discussions. The most vital part of the payments debate took place offstage between the British and the Americans, with the latter trying to budge the former who were clinging, with a steadfastness and competence worthy of a better cause, to invariably very restrictive positions that in most cases signified no more than maintenance of the *status quo*. When the matter came up for discussion in the Payments Committee, the Executive Committee or the Council, we were frequently treated to sharp exchanges between the British, seconded by the Scandinavians, and the Belgians, discreetly supported by the Swiss. The Belgians, who had a very large trade surplus with the rest of Europe but an equally large deficit with the dollar area, wanted, of course, to be able to use their European surpluses with the maximum freedom. The ideal thing for them would have been to be able to convert their European claims into dollars.

I have kept among my papers a note I dictated in 1949 which is the record of a meeting that took place at the OEEC on July 1, 1949 at 1 a.m. and involved Stafford Cripps, Averell Harriman, Paul-Henri Spaak, Edmund Hall-Patch, Maurice Petsche and myself.

During the afternoon of June 30 we had witnessed a surprising turnaround of positions on the payments question. Up to then the British had been very distinctly in the minority in their opposition to any transferability of drawing rights. Only the Swedes and the Norwegians supported them. A glimmer of hope had emerged, however, on June 29 when Stafford Cripps declared that Britain was prepared to lose a certain amount in gold or in dollars, provided that the amount were limited. A general agreement was beginning to take shape on June 30, on the basis of 25% transferability of drawing rights, when Harriman came up with new ideas the details of which I do not remember but which were less favourable to transferability than those I have just mentioned and, most importantly, which required Belgium to make a larger contribution than the one envisaged hitherto.

Spaak, suddenly on his own and apparently very worked up, announced that he refused to go along and that he preferred to return immediately to Belgium and explain publicly the reasons for the breakdown. An acrimonious exchange followed between him and Cripps, while Harriman, whose proposals had started all the trouble, remained silent. Petsche, who was the French Finance Minister at the time, vainly proposed compromises. The meeting was on the point of disbanding, with the chairman proposing to announce the complete breakdown of the Organization's efforts to resolve the payments problem, when, true to my role of mediator, I begged the ministers not to go their separate ways without having made one last effort. And so the night session came about.

Harriman conceded that if it would facilitate agreement he was prepared to go back to the 75–25% solution (25% multilateral drawing rights, 75% bilateral). The best solution, Spaak replied cantankerously, would be for everyone to return to their respective capitals and let some time elapse before resuming the discussion; as for Belgium she was fully in a position to apply a different policy, to pull out of the payments system and grant credit on a bilateral basis, and on terms acceptable to the Belgian parliament, to the countries with which she wished to develop her trading relations. Meanwhile, he intended to give a public explanation of the disagreement.

Stafford Cripps then stated, with a touch of exaggeration, that failure in these circumstances would mean the end not only of European cooperation in the OEEC, but also in the Western European Union and the Atlantic Alliance. As for me, I asked how it would be possible to explain the breakdown. It could not be attributed to the last-minute American proposal, since Harriman had agreed to withdraw it; nor to a disagreement among the participating countries, since they all seemed to accept the 75–25% formula. We were no longer, for the time being at any rate, in the realm of rational argument.

Cripps then asked Spaak if he, Cripps, had done something wrong. 'Yes,' replied Spaak, 'you have placed me in an extremely difficult position; I have gone as far as I possibly can towards conciliation. I wrote to you on Saturday, as to a friend and a comrade (both of them were socialists), to ask if my latest proposals were acceptable to you. I have made ceaseless efforts during the past few days to bring our positions closer together, making numerous concessions. And just when we were almost in agreement, you walked out on me and accepted a last-minute proposal out of the blue which concerns a system radically different from the one we were discussing until then.'

To which Cripps replied that if he had offended Spaak by anything he had said he willingly took it back; very anxious and impatient to reach an agreement, he was ready, for his part, to accept the 75–25% formula without additional safeguards. After a little coaxing, Spaak agreed too. And so that memorable night ended.

The discerning reader will probably have gathered from the events I have just related that it was at the end of the forties that the Europe we know today began to take shape. Admittedly, the trade liberalization of the fifties was not yet the Common Market: it related only to quantitative restrictions and not to customs duties. Even in its own field it was far from perfect and lapses into protectionism were frequent. But without these first attempts gradually to create a European market it is unlikely that the Common Market would have seen the light of day.

More important still, payments between European countries had had to be multilateralized for free, nondiscriminatory trading, which is the essence of the Common Market, to become possible. By way of personal testimony, I can say that having played an active part in the drawing-up and then the execution of the European Recovery Programme, in the creation of the European Payments Union and the liberalization of trade during the fifties, and afterwards in the drafting and implementation of the Treaty of Rome, I always felt a very strong thread of continuity in my action. The European Economic Community was the direct descendant of the Marshall Plan; it was able to be set up the day the economies of Continental Europe were sufficiently consolidated to adapt without loss, or even with immense gain, to trade essentially freed of all restriction and protection, the day too that a few European countries decided to disregard the negativity of the British.

This close link between the OEEC and the Common Market has not always been accepted with equanimity by the partisans of the two organizations. The zealots of Little Europe, in particular, often refused to credit the larger European organization with any creative virtue. Because decisions there had to be taken unanimously, it was accused of impotence and sterility, with no appreciation or attempt at appreciation of the positive achievements to which it had given birth. To

Robert Marjolin's father, Ernest, and son,
Robert Jacques.

Maria Élise Vacher, Robert Marjolin's mother.

Robert Marjolin and, sitting opposite him, his wife, Dorothy Thayer Smith, in 1950.

MENTORS AND FRIENDS –
THREE GREAT PROFESSORS

(Top left) Célestin Bouglé.
(Left) Charles Rist.
(Top right) Elie Halévy.

At a rally of Young Socialists; Robert Marjolin is standing third from the left.

t Yale in 1932–33; Robert Marjolin is standing second from the left.

Robert Marjolin touring the USA in the 1930s.

With Dorothy in 1946.

En route to the United States with British representatives at the OEEC. From left to right: Robert Marjolin, Edmund Hall-Patch, Harry Lintott, Eric Roll.

op left) Visiting Turkey during the distribution of Marshall Aid. (Top right) With Emmanuel
önick, who presented him with the Légion d'honneur in February 1956.

bove left) With Olivier Wormsier, in March 1956. (Photo Marcel Fournes.) (Above right) With
an Monnet and Georges Bidault. (Foundation Jean Monnet, Lausanne.)

(Opposite top) The British negotiation team for UK entry to the EEC, 1961. From left to right: r Arthur Tandy, Edward Heath and Eric Roll. Harry Lintott behind Heath. (Above) The uropean Commission at the UK entry negotiations. From left to right: Sicco Mansholt, alter Hallstein, Robert Marjolin, Guiseppe Caron and Jean Rey.

(Opposite middle) The Commission of the European Community after its renewal in 1962. Front ow, from left to right: Guiseppe Caron, Walter Hallstein, Sicco Mansholt, Robert Marjolin. Back ow: Lambert Schaus, Lionello Levi Sandri, Hans von der Groeben, Jean Rey, Henri Rochereau. Photo Créations de presse–Marcelle Jamar.)

(Opposite below) With Maurice Couve de Murville and Edgard Pisain during a meeting of the Council of Ministers of the EEC at the end of 1963.

(Below) A meeting of the Committee of Action for Europe at Bonn in 1971. From left to right: Valter Scheele, Robert Marjolin, Jean Monnet, Walter Hallstein, Willy Brandt, Antoine Pinag. Denis Healey in left foreground. (Photo Presse und Informationsamt der Bundesregierung.)

The Secretary General of the OEEC speaks for Europe in Ju⎯ 1950.

With Raymond Barre and Jean⎯ Claude Paye, Secretary Genera⎯ of the OECD, at the presentation of his 'épée d'académicien', 1985. (Photo OECD Photolibrary/ Photothèque OCDE.)

Unless otherwise stated, the photographs come from the autho⎯ collection.

take but one example, the European Payments Union was a success of such historic importance that it alone should have sufficed to command recognition of the merits of the OEEC during the latter's lifetime.

The second and last division of American aid
The Snoy-Marjolin formula

I cannot conclude this chapter without speaking of the second division of US aid, for the 1949–50 round, which the OEEC worked out in 1949.

Back in Paris after my visit to Washington, I again took up the problem of US dollar allocation among member countries, a problem that exercised people's minds to the exclusion of any other, it seemed. On the face of it, the job was tedious and of limited significance. To the uninformed observer, it might have appeared unimportant whether we gave one or two hundred million dollars more or less to Germany, France or Britain. But the governments of those countries naturally did not see it that way: for them, the one hundred or two hundred million translated immediately into tons of coal or wheat, or into so many machine tools or locomotives. At OEEC the allocation of dollars was a powerful means of getting the different countries to pursue policies contributing to the general progress of Europe, or at least of deterring them from doing anything that might hamper the economic revival that was showing signs of getting under way.

It was a ticklish business. Countries' individual aid requests totalled $4,700 million. Using an aggregated approach, which was certainly a little arbitrary, we got this figure down to $4,350 million. But we were still well over the mark: we knew that the US Congress was not prepared to authorize more than $3,800 million. Moreover, the Americans had informed us of their intention to hold back a sum of $150 million for unspecified purposes, to encourage trade liberalization in Europe, they said. Finally, the experience of the previous year had shown that it would not be possible for many countries to agree to proposals for the allocation of direct US aid without first knowing the amount of drawing rights they would be getting or giving.

Thus the problem was already very difficult. It suddenly assumed dramatic proportions when the American economy went into a recession, a moderate recession admittedly, but no one at the time could tell how it would develop. Along with Jean-Charles Snoy, I sounded a warning on August 27, 1949. We noted that a sudden change had taken place in world trade conditions at the beginning of 1949. In the space of a few months Europe's exports to the United States had fallen by about 30%. For some European countries the fall was as steep as 40, 50 or even 60%. Exports from the rest of the world to the United States, including those of the overseas territories of member countries and of the non-member sterling area countries, were also down. We estimated the dollar loss for the OEEC countries between the end of 1948 and the summer of 1949 at between five hundred and six hundred million on a 12-month basis.

The crisis was not affecting all the European countries equally. It was largely sparing continental Europe, which by this time had started to become a distinct economic bloc. Germany's recovery, which was now under way and gathering speed in impressive fashion, was beginning to generate an overall revival in the countries with whose economies she had particularly close ties: Benelux, the Scandinavian countries and Austria. France herself found in the German economy's expansion a counterbalance to the difficulties she was having with her overseas sales; she was, one might say, in an intermediate position, between the countries whose economic activity was closely linked to German growth and Britain. Not until a few years later would she take her increasingly important place in the continental bloc and participate to the same degree as the northern countries in the rise of intra-European trade. Britain, on the other hand, was bearing the full brunt of the downturn in the US economy; her exports were destined in large part for the Empire, whose buying potential was seriously reduced by the fall in sales of food and raw materials to the United States. With their back to the wall, the British asked for a large increase in their dollar allocation.

Not surprisingly, in the circumstances, the traditional procedure, whereby such a matter was referred by the Programmes Committee up to the Council for decision, failed and in mid-August 1949 the Organization found itself in an impasse and obliged to seek an original formula in order to get out of it. The Council, in desperation, then asked Jean-Charles Snoy, its chairman, and myself to come up with a proposal. We worked for a week on the basis of documents prepared by the services of the Secretariat General. Our ideas ran along much the same lines and we had no difficulty in reaching agreement. We then drew up our proposal, incorporating in it a distribution of intra-European drawing rights. We were compelled by the difficulty of the

222

situation to include in that distribution the $150 million which the Americans wanted to hold in reserve.

I still have the text, dated August 27, 1949, which we put before the Council when it met on August 31 to give its verdict. The chairman –I think it was Hall-Patch – asked the national delegations to state their opinions in turn, starting from his right and working round the table.

And what a clamour of protest there was. One after another, the delegates denounced the injustice being done to their countries. To hear them, one would think that Snoy and I had violated all the universally accepted criteria of justice, equity and even good sense. As I remember, not one of them even gave us the benefit of extenuating circumstances. After the last speaker had finished, the chairman allowed himself a few seconds' thought before commenting on the situation in these terms: 'Gentlemen, it appears that we are unanimous in our sentiments concerning the proposal that has just been put before us by Mr Jean-Charles Snoy and the Secretary-General. It seems, therefore, that the only way open to us is to accept it.' Then he asked the delegates to give their opinions a second time. I have kept some handwritten notes on this second series of statements. The general tenor of the reactions was: 'Yes, if everyone agrees and if the figures are not changed in any way; provided, too, that the Americans give up the idea of keeping back $150 million.' A few delegates also expressed the wish that the Americans be told of the specific situation of their respective countries.

So this affair between Europeans was settled, but Averell Harriman was furious that we had touched the reserve of $150 million. He made this plain when, after the meeting I have just described, I went with Harry Lintott to inform him of the result. His reaction was that this probably meant the end of US aid to Europe.

Fortunately that was far from being the case, but the Americans rebuilt the $150 million reserve through a pro rata reduction of aid to the different countries. After 1949 there was no further exercise in apportioning American aid. The Council decided that the Snoy-Marjolin formula had permanent validity and that it would be used henceforth to allocate Marshall funds.

6

EUROPE REBORN

The new Europe took shape slowly in the years that immediately followed the war. From 1945 to 1949 progress had been rapid but had not been perceived as such; the day of hope had dawned, but the European peoples still felt that they were fighting an endless uphill battle against extreme difficulties. The Korean war, which broke out in the spring of 1950, confused the issue temporarily. It brought about the rearmament of a Europe that had almost completely disarmed after the end of the war in 1945, in particular the rearmament of Germany, and a large increase in defence spending that posed a threat to European payments equilibrium, which had nearly been achieved by 1950. Another of its effects was to create a new or, rather, greatly enlarged source of dollars: US military spending in Europe. Henceforth American aid to Europe would essentially take the form of military aid.

An appraisal of the Marshall Plan record

The Marshall Plan consisted essentially in vast-scale American aid to Europe. Its success depended entirely on the use the Europeans made of that aid. Driven by a will to renew, as well as by strong pressure from the Americans, they were able to put it to good use – that is, they concentrated their efforts on investment and exports, with only limited satisfaction of consumer wants, just enough to prevent social tensions from reaching the breaking point or, at any rate, from causing an acute crisis.

At OEEC we acted rather like sheep dogs: we rounded up the flock when it showed signs of dispersing; we exerted discreet but, in most cases, effective pressure when one or more member countries began to weaken under domestic strain in the form of the population's demands for a more rapid improvement in living standards. Our best argument was the threat, disguised to a greater or lesser degree, of a reduction in external aid. We were certain that the Americans would back us in all circumstances; sometimes they anticipated us by taking up the matter themselves in the capitals of the countries concerned.

Despite the fact that this work occasionally entailed some unpleasantness, I had no qualms of conscience. I was convinced that the stringency which thus had to be maintained five years after the war's end was essential to a revival of Europe and to a subsequent rapid and durable rise in the living standards of the European peoples. In short, it was not a question of sacrificing one generation to the following generations, but of getting the present generation to make do with a slow improvement in its living standards against the promise that, after a few years' effort, the reward would come and probably exceed all expectations.

The Marshall Plan (it is convenient thus to designate American aid and the European effort it sustained) was carried out in its essentials. Some of the targets were exceeded, as in the case of production and exports. Others were approached sufficiently close – and this applies particularly to the external deficit in spite of the heavy new outgoings necessitated by the rearmament effort – for us to feel convinced that the European economy was 'viable' (as one used to say then), if not without American aid, at least with aid that could be scaled down rapidly without unfortunate consequences. As regards the other goals, notably internal financial stability and the development of European cooperation that would survive the Marshall Plan, the results were less convincing, but experience showed that a solid groundwork had been laid for subsequent efforts.

I trust that I shall be forgiven if I now quote some figures that illustrate the magnitude of the success achieved. As regards production, the targets we had set in 1947–8 had largely been reached well before the date fixed by the Americans for the end of their aid to Europe. The European Recovery Programme had specified for 1952 a

30% increase in industrial output and a 15% increase in agricultural output over the 1938 levels. For these goals to be achieved, we calculated that hourly labour productivity would have to rise by 15% between 1948 and 1952.

By the end of 1951 the industrial output target had been exceeded and we were very close to the goal for farm output. Productivity growth was especially impressive: it amounted to 27% for the period 1948–52, well above the figure we had considered imperative in 1948[1].

The investment effort had been massive; in many cases it would remain so after the end of the Marshall Plan. Between 1948 and 1951 gross investment in western Europe grew by more than 30%, an average of over 9% a year. The local currency counterpart of American aid contributed greatly in many countries: out of a total of $7.6 billion worth of counterpart funds released by the ECA during the four-year period, nearly $5 billion had been earmarked for investment[2].

1950 is an important reference point. It was the second year of a two-year period in which the Marshall Plan was implemented in relatively normal conditions, before the Korean War temporarily changed the general picture of the world economy. In a little less than two years, during which the United States had supplied Europe with $9 billion of aid ($5 billion in 1948, $4 billion in 1949), European output had increased by some $30 billion. Britain was able to have US aid discontinued as of January 1, 1951. France's industrial output in 1950 was 20% more in volume than in 1938, whilst agricultural output was back to approximately its prewar level. In one year, 1950, Germany had expanded its industrial output by roughly 27%. In the OEEC countries taken as a whole, industrial output in the second half of 1950 was 25% above the 1938 level[3].

Thus, much more quickly than anyone had hoped, Europe succeeded with American aid in erasing, where production was concerned, not only the effects of the war but those of the Great Depression of the thirties. But this did not mean that Europe's big problem of that time was completely resolved: it was still necessary to eliminate rapidly the financial deficit with the dollar area, either by reducing imports or by increasing exports. It was this problem which, now that the European economy was moving again, occupied our every moment. For many years, even when it had already been resolved or was in the process of being resolved, we remain convinced that it was still as serious as ever. By way of example, one of my former

British collaborators at OEEC wrote a book in the mid-fifties on the dollar gap in which he stated that it was of a 'structural' nature – i.e. insoluble, in the short term at any rate – and there to stay for a long time.

Yet even by the end of the forties things were straightening out. A vigorous intra-European trade had begun to develop; the former belligerents were finding in one another's countries and, to a small extent, in those of the former neutrals an increasing share of what, at the end of the war, they had been obliged to import from North America or from other countries requiring payment in dollars. This intra-European trade more than doubled between the beginning of 1948 and the end of 1950, by which time it was about 50% greater in volume than in 1938. The strong upturn in the German economy, following the monetary reform carried out by the US occupation authorities in 1948, was one of the most important factors in this rapid expansion of trade in Europe. At the same time, helped by the 1949 devaluations, European exports to the rest of the world developed very strongly. In the last quarter of 1950 they were nearly 50% more in volume than in 1938.

The combined effect of falling imports and rising exports was to make Europe's trade deficit with the United States and Canada narrow rapidly. From $6.1 billion in 1947 it fell to $4.5 billion in 1948, $3.8 billion in 1949 and $1.75 billion in 1950. If overseas territories' exports and invisible earnings are included, the improvement is seen to be even more spectacular. Europe's dollar deficit, which had reached a staggering $8.5 billion in 1947, shrank to $5 billion in 1949 and to about $1 billion in 1950. American economic aid was being scaled down at the same time. Declining from some $5 billion in 1948 to about $4 billion in 1949, it would have been $2.7 billion in 1950 and probably less than $2 billion in 1951, the last year of the Marshall Plan, had the Korean war not altered the situation completely, with military aid essentially taking the place of economic aid[4].

I do not intend to go into the details of the changes which the Korean war wrought in the pattern of US aid in the years following its outbreak. Let me simply say that had it not been for this unforeseen upheaval, the Marshall Plan would in all likelihood have ended in the middle of 1952 with a record of total success as regards production, investment, exports and, generally, Europe's ability to do without American aid. Rearmament clouded the issue for a while, but the impetus, strong and durable, had been imparted. Europe would soon be able to stand on its own feet, even if US defence spending in Europe

227

was to represent for a time a big plus item in the balance of payments of most of the OEEC countries.

It was on internal financial stability that the Korean war had the most pernicious effects. By mid-1950 the European countries, by dint of great efforts, were coming close to relative stability when the hostilities in the Far East, and the rearmament they entailed, caused a steep rise in raw material and food prices that worked through to the general price level in all countries. In September 1950 I went on record as saying that, owing to the change in the international economic situation, inflation had become the most serious economic problem facing the European countries. After a price flare-up in the year or two that followed the outbreak of the Korean war, things calmed down in most countries, but a number of them, including France, did not reach a situation of equilibrium until the end of the fifties.

In numerous articles and speeches, in the OEEC and elsewhere, I expressed at that time the state of mind of many young men who were wholly committed to the gigantic task of reestablishing Europe, after the disasters of the war and the prewar period, as an area of prosperity that would have no cause to be envious of America. A state of mind at once simplistic and realistic. Simplistic because it tended to reduce human ambition to a set of objectives: namely to produce more and more, to invest more in order to produce still more, to modernize in order to give an additional boost to productivity. America hypnotized us, her material success was our ideal; we had almost no other aim but to bridge the gap between European industry and American industry. But at the same time I still believe that we were profoundly realistic. The proof is that for more than twenty years afterwards, Europe (at least, Continental Europe) faithfully followed the credo I expressed then, ultimately to arrive at the goal I had implicitly defined. Let us say, to put things into perspective, that even if economic expansion is not the be-all and end-all in this world, for Europe in 1950 it was a phase of her history that she had to traverse before she could seriously consider other fundamental issues.

Quite recently, many generous minds have been wondering why this gigantic leap forward by Europe after the last war could not be duplicated elsewhere. For example, there has been airy talk about 'a Marshall Plan for the Third World'. To think in these terms is to forget what made Europe's situation in 1945 unique. Despite large-scale destruction, the greater part of Europe's industrial plant was intact; the economic infrastructure needed extensive repairs, but in the main it had survived; the land continued to be farmed, even if yields were low at first. An inflow of capital representing only a fraction of what would have been necessary to rebuild the prewar economic machine from scratch was sufficient to repair it, seriously damaged, it is true, but extant. Much more to the point and in fact the most important element, an educated and highly skilled work force could not wait to get back into harness; it was able to get the equipment that had survived working again and manufacture new machinery to replace what had been destroyed or had become obsolete. These few considerations explain how it was possible, in a very short space of time and at comparatively little cost, to bring into being a modern industrial system that would rapidly become a competitor for America herself. The problems of the developing countries are clearly of a very different nature and require other forms of action.

The reasons for Europe's rebirth

Why was the European economy reborn so quickly in the years that immediately followed World War Two? How was it that its revival did not stop when performance had returned to prewar levels but became instead, in the fifties and sixties, a powerful movement of expansion that was to carry Europe to heights of prosperity she had never known before? What caused this enormous contrast with the years from 1919 to 1939?

The difference between the two postwar periods can largely be explained by the way in which the same problems were treated in those eras respectively. Whereas from 1919 to the beginning of the thirties the question of war debts and reparations had poisoned relations between Europe and America on the one hand, and between France and Germany on the other, in 1945–6 the difficulty concerning Europe's debts to America disappeared in a flash when the United States to all intents and purposes expunged its lend-lease claims. Where reparations from Germany were concerned, all that was done was to dismantle a few factories there and ship them west, then the matter was forgotten. One might say that John Maynard Keynes's 1919 vision of a durable return to peace became a reality twenty-five years later. As for reconstruction, in the twenties this had been financed by very large flows of American private capital, which in many cases could be repatriated without notice or at very short term and indeed was in 1930–1, whereas the second time around it was financed by American official aid, consisting mostly of outright grants.

The truth of the matter is that the contrast, in every respect, between

229

the two postwar periods was essentially the result of US policy: whereas in 1919, after having contributed decisively to Germany's defeat, the United States withdrew into an isolationism that was to last, despite a few deviations, until 1941; after 1945 the Americans assumed all the responsibilities of a great victorious power whose intervention had once again, but this time one might say once and for all, put paid to German imperialism and also Japanese imperialism. The Americans decided to establish in the part of the world under their control peace as they conceived it, a *Pax Americana* which, of course, reflected the balance of power at that time, but which also derived from a fervent idealism well known to all those who worked with them just after the war.

This policy did not come about in the United States without dissent, hesitation, introspection, lengthy debates in Congress. But the opposition remained weak. One might be tempted to say that the Americans did not have any choice, but this would be untrue. They could have decided once more to go home and leave Europe to its sad fate. But this was an era of statesmen, Roosevelt, Truman, Acheson and others, who understood that such a decision would have disastrous consequences, a general breakdown of Europe into which the United States itself would inevitably be drawn.

The Soviet threat, the fear that the USSR would establish its hegemony over the whole of Europe, was a major factor in the decisions taken by Washington in the postwar years, even more so in the comparative ease with which those decisions were accepted by Congress and public opinion. Dean Acheson, who succeeded General Marshall as US Secretary of State, stressed this in his memoirs when speaking of American aid to Europe:

If General Marshall believed, which I am sure he did not, that the American people would be moved to so great an effort as he contemplated by as Platonic a purpose as combating 'hunger, poverty, desperation and chaos', he was mistaken. But he was wholly right in stating this as the American *governmental* purpose. I have probably made as many speeches and answered as many questions about the Marshall Plan as any man alive, except possibly Paul Hoffman, and what citizens and the representatives in Congress alike always wanted to learn in the last analysis was how Marshall aid operated to block the extension of Soviet power and the acceptance [by Europe] of Communist economic and political organization and alignment[5].

Acheson was perfectly right in establishing a distinction between the government and public opinion. The government was resolved in any case to act decisively in Europe, to enable it to recover from the trials it had undergone during the previous twenty-five years. If Russia had behaved with more restraint after the war, if she had not been Stalinist Russia, if she had not been equated by the American citizens with an unbridled imperialism which, with Nazi Germany vanquished, would stop at nothing to extend its dominion to the outermost limits, it is not certain that the Administration in Washington would have won American public opinion over so easily. The memory of Woodrow Wilson was enough to show us that in the United States the government is not all-powerful: it has to *convince*. But things being what they are, one can say that in the postwar years Moscow played America's game, and at the same time that of free Europe.

The Americans often take a long time to make up their mind: sometimes the course of history has to force their hand, as with the Japanese at Pearl Harbor. But once they do, they 'go for broke'; they do not allow themselves to be swayed from their purpose by petty interests. That is what happened with the aid they gave to Europe after the war.

Consisting essentially of grants, it attained *amounts never known before or since*. Over the forty-five months from April 1, 1948 to December 30, 1951, when aid under the European Recovery Programme officially came to an end, the ECA allotted $12.4 billion to Europe. This figure represented 1.2% of US gross national product for the years 1948–51. On a year-to-year basis ERP aid amounted to nearly 2% of American GNP in 1948 declining to 0.5% in 1951[6]. Some idea of the magnitude of that aid effort may be gained by recalling that the seldom-achieved target set later by the industrialized countries for official aid to the Third World was 0.7% of GNP.

With war debts expunged, reparations forgotten and reconstruction financed in large part by non-repayable US government aid, and not by private capital as in the twenties, the extraordinary difference between the two postwar periods starts to become clear. But there was more to it than that.

The US army was occupying a large part of Germany (and all of Japan). Given that the Americans were also financing Germany's reconstruction, they had the most say in what economic, financial and monetary policies that country would have to follow. Their position was clear almost from the outset, witness the speech made by Dean Acheson in Cleveland on May 8; 1947 in which he said:

The . . . thing we must do in the present situation is to push ahead with the

231

reconstruction of those two great workshops of Europe and Asia – Germany and Japan – upon which the ultimate recovery of the two continents so largely depends[7].

In fact, the Americans directed Germany's reconstruction in the years immediately following 1945 (they did the same in Japan) and created the conditions needed for that reconstruction to continue after a German government had taken charge of affairs again. Among those conditions, I am thinking in particular of the 1948 monetary reform, which was a complete success. Not only did Germany rapidly regain her place as western Europe's leading industrial country, but the buoyancy of her economy played an essential role in the economic boom of the fifties and sixties in this part of the world. The impetus was even generated a little earlier, thanks to the rapidity of her reconstruction, for the US recession of 1949 did not affect western Europe very much, with the exception of Britain for the reasons I gave earlier.

If one remembers, in addition, that for western Europe as a whole the USA, in the late forties and early fifties, was the chief protagonist of the European Payments Union and of trade liberalization through the phasing-out of quantitative restrictions on intra-European trade, one will appreciate the full extent of the contrast between American withdrawal after 1919 and American leadership in the reconstruction of Europe after 1945.

In this the Americans were not thwarting the Europeans: the latter's prime concern too was to avoid the tragic errors of the years after World War One. But the Americans had an overall view that the Europeans lacked in many cases; they were in a position of strength; they wanted Europe, and in fact the whole of the free world, to organize itself, to the furthest possible extent, into a system where goods and services would circulate freely and currencies would be stable against one another. That is why in 1944 they contributed so decisively to the establishment of the International Monetary Fund and in 1947 to that of the GATT. But they were sufficiently realistic to understand that these worldwide institutions could not function effectively unless western Europe and Japan had first been reconstructed. This led them for several years to patronize purely European commercial and monetary institutions that practised a discriminatory policy towards the rest of the world. Yet the fact remains that, largely owing to the dual effort made by the Americans in Europe and in the free world as a whole, postwar Europe was essentially spared the monetary convulsions and outrageous protectionism that had marked the inter-war years.

The Americans also succeeded in conducting their own postwar economic policy in such a way as to avoid a repetition of the Great Depression. To explain how they did this I would need much more room than I can spare here. Suffice it to say that, except for a minor recession in 1948–9, the US economy showed remarkable stability during the years that followed the war. This stability enabled the Europeans to attend strictly to their own affairs, without having simultaneously to contend with the consequences of a major recession in the United States.

It might be inferred from the foregoing that the United States single-handedly prevented a recurrence of the fatal events that had marked the period from 1919 to 1939. It is true that for ten years or so after 1945 the American influence was predominant. But the European contribution was also crucial, if only in the forming of new relations between the ex-belligerents.

I and my team at OEEC, in close affinity with the representatives of national governments in Paris, were convinced that a new chapter of history had to begin. In fact, it had already begun with the war, the invasions, the foreign occupations, the destruction or exile of the governments of the West European countries. It was necessary now to draw the inferences from this gigantic historical change. I think I can say that, with the possible exception of a few minds behind the times, no one considered a war in western Europe any longer conceivable. The overwhelming military superiority of the Americans, on the one hand, and of the Russians, on the other, completely ruled out that danger. From an understanding of the impossibility of war to an actual reconciliation was, admittedly, a long road. But the different stages along that road were reached much sooner than anyone could have hoped in 1945.

The crux of the problem was the reconciliation of France and Germany, whose antagonism had rent Europe in the twenties. I shall be speaking later on of this reconciliation, in which men like Robert Schuman, Jean Monnet and General de Gaulle, each in his own way, played a decisive part. But the idea was already in people's minds when the war ended. It constitutes the dominant theme of European history between 1945 and 1960, although at first there was a great temp-tation, and many in France succumbed, to reenter the same blind alley that had been followed after 1918.

There was one last major difference between the two postwar

periods. As I have said earlier, there was no international cooperation, other than sporadic, from 1919 to 1939. Each country applied the policy that seemed best suited to its immediate interests, regardless both of the implications for other countries and of the latter's possible reactions. Under the aegis of the Americans and with the assent of the Europeans, a real system of international cooperation progressively established itself after the end of the war. The OEEC was its centre in Europe for a few years. We were not deluded into thinking that the different governments would henceforth shape their policies to the interest of Europe, which was often difficult to define. In fact, as I have said earlier, national self-interest then was as strong as ever. But stern trials had taught governments to take into account the probable or possible repercussions of their actions. We talked, we informed one another, we devised scenarios in which each would have his part to play. That was often enough to channel national initiatives into a direction conforming to the general interest, as we could see it at the time. In the last analysis, the Americans exerted the bare minimum of pressure necessary to ensure that things went off reasonably well. The state of affairs might still be far from ideal, but at least we were managing to avoid major crises.

In this chapter I have tried to explain the economic rebirth of Europe after 1945. But there is still one link to be added to the chain of reasoning. Economics, a science of man, remains incomprehensible if one does not start out from the source, man himself, the living being full of vitality, only too eager to express himself, to engage in the pursuit of money, power and fame. But this vitality, this urge to act, this desire for success, may be curbed, temporarily paralysed or even seem to vanish altogether if the circumstances are too adverse. That is what happened between the two wars. Inane foreign policies, economic policies often devoid of reason, constant international tension, the ever-present threat of external conflicts – in short, a feeling of total insecurity – had in most countries, and during the greater part of the period, crushed or deadened the will to achieve.

Suddenly, after 1945, all the conditions for a flowering of individual resolve were present. Exhausted, the states of western Europe had lost the taste for war; nothing now, neither territorial gain, nor superiority of power or prestige, seemed worth tearing each other apart for. Before France and Germany were formally reconciled one knew that it was over, that there would be no more war between the two countries; Hitler had been the last misfortune of a long and tragic history. The US presence on the Continent, the atomic bomb and America's

234

overpowering military strength in general convinced even the most sceptical. America provided the guarantee that there would be no more war between peoples who had lost all desire to fight anyway. Even more important, she was protecting them against any external threat, i.e. against the threat from Russia.

Piece by piece, under the aegis of America and with continuing action on her part, an international economic order was being built up which was the least unsatisfactory that could be hoped for in the circumstances, if there was any right to hope for it at all. Countries' economic policies, despite a few errors of detail, were avoiding the serious miscalculations of the interwar years. In this setting, where his security was completely assured and the broad lines of national policies had been durably laid down, the individual could venture and create. And, by and large, he knew what he wanted to create. America was, one might say, the exemplar, a free, democratic country that had succeeded in increasing labour productivity and, consequently, in raising living standards to a level never before known in the history of man. Europe's economic rebirth after the war was the doing of the Europeans who, profiting by experience and guided by the United States, with its aid and its protection, set out in pursuit of an American pattern adjusted to European circumstances.

7

THE LAST YEARS
OF THE MARSHALL PLAN

If the problems confronting me and my team during the years from 1945 to 1950 were simple and straightforward, as were the objectives we set in order to resolve them, equally the years that followed, from 1950 to 1953, have left an impression of confusion on my memory. The fact is that after June 25, 1950, when the Communist attack on South Korea was launched, the western world had swung back again into preparations for war. True, the needs imposed by European reconstruction, by the creation of a dynamic economy that could develop without any external assistance, had not been completely forgotten, but they no longer had pride of place.

Today, some thirty-five years later, Korea seems to us like a minor war, a local conflict, but at the time many wondered if it were not the first act of World War Three. Indeed it is possible that, had it not been for the vigorous American reaction, the world's equilibrium would have been seriously endangered. With their characteristic decisiveness, the Americans immediately drew conclusions that caused their whole policy stance to shift. The by now traditional American objectives of European recovery and economic cooperation were replaced in thought and in speech by the goal of 'mutual security'. The North Atlantic Treaty Organization was established in 1949; in September 1950 the NATO Council decided to set up an integrated defence system in Europe.

As far as I was concerned, there was no doubt about the necessity of the new defence drive. The prewar years were still too fresh in my mind, with all the instances of weakness, the waverings, the half measures that had characterized France's and Britain's attitude to the Nazi quest for domination, to say nothing of American isolationism, for me not to be convinced that the West had to show all the firmness needed towards Soviet Russia. But I was just as certain that the economic recovery effort had to go on and that, in the last analysis, it was the strength of the western capitalist regime that would determine the outcome of the titanic ideological conflict in which the world was engaged. The criterion of success would be the continuance of strong economic growth in conditions of internal and external monetary stability.

The Korean war and western rearmament did not, initially at any rate, have the negative impact that might have been feared. In fact, European recovery was even hastened. Production growth in 1950 was much the same as in 1949; intra-European trade expanded rapidly and European exports to the rest of the world showed a higher rate of increase; the dollar payments deficit narrowed to about $1 billion, from $5 billion in 1949. A number of European countries succeeded at the same time in increasing their gold and dollar reserves. The standard of living was nearly back to its prewar level in most countries[1].

But strong inflationary pressure had been building up. As early as September 1950 I felt bound to say officially that the danger of inflation was threatening European recovery. 1951 saw Europe's dollar gap reopen as a result of rearmament requirements that led to an increase in imports and a slowdown in exports. In the second half of 1951 Europe's trade deficit with the rest of the world reached its highest level since 1947, averaging some $650 million per month[2].

It was clear that substantial American aid was still needed in order to make it possible to increase the defence effort while maintaining the people's purchasing power at a politically tolerable level. Tensions began to develop between America and her European allies owing to the former's impatience at the slowness of Europe's rearmament and to the Europeans' fear of seeing the economic progress made since 1947 compromised. It was with the utmost difficulty that the ECA got Congress to agree that a proportion of aid should consist of goods for civilian use; it succeeded only by insisting that economic aid was necessary in order to sustain the arms production effort.

The aid total remained high, but most of it was military aid. In 1950–1 military aid, which went by the name of Mutual Defense

Assistance, amounted to nearly $5 billion, whereas the figure for economic aid and technical assistance, included in the Mutual Security Program, was $2.31 billion, declining in 1951–2 to about $1 billion against military aid of the order of $5 billion. Additional economic aid of about $500 million was, technically, released to Europe in the course of the year, but it was taken out of the military aid appropriation and had to be used for 'defense support'. Finally, the ECA itself was abolished and replaced by the Mutual Security Agency (MSA).

Relations between OEEC and NATO

If I have dwelt a little on the political and psychological changes entailed by the Korean war, it is because those changes caused a profound crisis in European cooperation, even though every effort was made to conceal the fact. As Secretary-General of the OEEC I found myself in a very difficult position, and the time soon came when I had to contend against certain Americans who wanted a purely military emphasis, and also against the British government, which on this occasion showed its true colours where European cooperation was concerned.

The rearmament effort was the central concern in 1951–2 and it had obvious economic implications. The two key problems were, first, the allocation of certain raw materials that defence requirements as well as stockpiling had caused to become scarce and, second, an apportionment of military expenditure among the different countries according to the economic capabilities of each. For more than two years the question was debated of what role the OEEC would play in the treatment of these problems. The question was an important one, for the economists of the OEEC had acquired since 1948 a high reputation for competence and it was almost impossible to assemble at short notice another group of experts equally skilled.

I shall spare the reader all the ups and downs of these discussions, which sometimes amounted to head-on clashes.

The moderates, of whom I was one, were prepared to ask the OEEC to act as a kind of economic branch of NATO or again to put a number of OEEC economists temporarily at NATO's disposal. One theoretical difficulty was that Switzerland and Sweden, officially neutrals, were members of OEEC, but their wish to be able to keep an eye on things got the better of their neutrality, ideologically speaking. In the event, their representatives were as conciliatory as could be. The extremists, who included the British – or, at any rate, those who were expressing the British government's point of view – would have been satisfied only if the OEEC had been virtually abolished and all its activities transferred to NATO.

Why did Britain take this stance when through the preceding years she had been a very staunch member of OEEC? It is hard to avoid the conclusion that, as far as London was concerned, the OEEC had been, if not solely, at least essentially, the channel for American aid. On that reasoning, European cooperation had no intrinsic value: it was a means to another end. When in 1950–1 US aid became for the most part military aid allocated on other criteria than the OEEC had used, the organization lost all its importance for the British and they showed that they were ready to sacrifice it. Other countries thought the same but did not show it so openly.

I can remember a very acrimonious discussion that took place at a dinner to which Maurice Petsche, the French finance minister, had invited a number of persons to talk about precisely this question of relations between OEEC and NATO. I was there, together with Britain's Chancellor of the Exchequer, Hugh Gaitskell, and Hall-Patch. Gaitskell took the extreme stance I have described above, and when I defended the OEEC and stressed that, despite the gravity of the circumstances, it was impossible to subordinate all European economic activity to the defence effort, he went so far as to accuse me of defending my own outfit and my own status. I in turn lost my temper and the dinner ended very badly. Next day, Hall-Patch presented his regrets and asked Gaitskell to apologize to me. I cannot recall exactly what happened afterwards, but my relations with Gaitskell were never the same again.

It was at the Ottawa meeting of the North Atlantic Council in September 1951 that a Temporary Committee of the Council was set up to analyse the economic capabilities of each country and the possibility of its stepping up its rearmament effort. The members of that committee were Averell Harriman, Jean Monnet and Edwin Plowden. I had provided a team of economists with myself at their head.

A close working association was formed between the experts of OEEC and NATO in 1951–2, the necessary economic studies being handled essentially by OEEC. Confronted by the resistance of certain Europeans and of the American officials who were deeply attached to the development of European cooperation, the British backed down.

The Financial and Economic Board of NATO, which had been set up to deal with eco-financial issues in the NATO context, was dissolved and the member countries of NATO and OEEC agreed that the OEEC should take charge of all economic questions. And so the OEEC came out of this crisis without any apparent damage.

In a public statement dated September 29, 1951, which I drafted, the OEEC Council declared that it was resolved to take the necessary steps to put an end to the inflation that was then developing. In the same statement it adopted the target of a 25% increase in aggregate production over the next few years. Those were the happy days when it seemed that a public statement would virtually suffice to have a wish fulfilled. The truth, of course, was different.

Pessimism and prosperity

Today, with hindsight, one can state unhesitatingly that by 1950, as I have said earlier – or, at any rate, by 1952–3, when the commotion caused by the Korean war had died down – Europe had definitely put behind it the great difficulties it had known in the thirties, during the war and in the immediate postwar years. In particular, the problem of the external deficit had been virtually resolved. Throughout the rest of the decade the position was consolidated. Admittedly, the OEEC countries continued to run a large trade deficit with the rest of the world. But earnings from US defence transactions and invisible exports increased greatly. The net result was that in 1959 Europe had a current payments surplus of over $3.5 billion.

Thus the world monetary situation changed radically in the space of a few years and almost without the knowledge of the interested parties, American and European. The dollar gap had imperceptibly vanished. A large deficit on the United States overall balance of payments was about to emerge, mainly as a result of massive exports of American capital to Europe. But that belongs to the history of the sixties. During the fifties America was delighted to see western Europe's situation improving. America's overall balance of payments was already in deficit, but no one cared. All attention was focussed on the way in which the international payments imbalance was disappearing and how Europe was beginning to rebuild her depleted reserves. When countries began to use dollars to buy gold from the United States, this too was welcomed, the result being a better distribution of inter-national gold reserves[3].

Europe, on the other hand, continued to feel despondent for quite some time. I too felt that way, for a while at any rate. In a note dated June 4, 1952 and entitled 'Programme for a durable solution to the dollar problem', I wrote:

After a continuous improvement from 1947 to 1950, Europe and the sterling area are once again heavily in deficit with the dollar area ... If the dollar gap were due solely to exceptional causes like the Korean war, ultra-rapid western rearmament, and so on, we could resign ourselves to it for a while and try to make the best of a bad job. But it is clear now that this is a durable imbalance that will persist indefinitely, unless fundamental adjustments are made on both sides of the Atlantic ... The prospect before us is therefore that of a Europe (and the countries monetarily associated with Europe) going from crisis to crisis and obliged, every two or three years, to ask for further American aid.

Then I emphasized the need to put an end to US aid to Europe:

Although American aid has been a necessary remedy over a period, and will continue to be for a time, one is bound to acknowledge that in the long run it has had dangerous psychological and political effects ... It is making more difficult the task of the governments of western Europe trying to bring about a thorough economic and financial rehabilitation. The idea that it is always possible to call on American aid, that here is the ever-present cure for external payments deficits, is a factor destructive of willpower. It is difficult to hope that, while this recourse continues to exist, the nations of western Europe will apply, for a sufficient length of time, the courageous economic and financial policy that will enable them to meet their needs from their own resources, without the contribution of external aid.

There followed a lengthy programme the details of which it would be tedious to enter into.

Looking through my papers of that time, I see that I soon relin-quished the idea that Europe's dollar gap would continue indefinitely. I realized by 1954 at the latest, possibly earlier, that we were out of the Marshall Plan era and confronted by new problems that would require different approaches. At the end of 1954 I gave an interview to the *Journal de Genève* which was something in the nature of a testament, since I was to leave OEEC three months later. Here are some extracts:

I consider that Europe's economic situation is better than at any time since

241

the end of the war and even than at any time in its history, for the level of production is higher than it has ever been. We have beaten the 1929 record by a very wide margin and per capita output is the highest that Europe has ever known ...

In addition, the balance of payments in most member countries is now in equilibrium and Europe is continuing to increase its gold and dollar reserves. Although this increase in gold and dollar reserves is due, of course, to non-recurrent defence spending by the United States in Europe and to the continuation of American aid on a reduced scale, it is nonetheless true that, even discounting those two factors, Europe's deficit with the dollar area on ordinary current transactions, visible and invisible, has narrowed very considerably and now stands at less than one billion dollars.

The situation is therefore good. One can even say that, without our realizing it, we have come out of the period of postwar reconstruction. The European countries, individually and as a whole, have regained their equilibrium or are on the point of regaining it. This applies both to internal and to external equilibrium. Inflation has been subdued and balances of payments are satisfactory ...

[But] if reconstruction is complete, this does not mean that our work is over, for we do not consider that the task of rebuilding the European economy is sufficient in itself. We have to go further; we have to build a new economic equilibrium with a level of productivity and living standards higher than those we have known until now and which will bring us closer to those existing in the United States.

Part Four

THE COMMON MARKET

1

INTERLUDE: I LEAVE THE OEEC

By 1952 Europe's reconstruction was virtually over; the European Payments Union, established in 1950, had greatly improved the payments situation in Europe; trade liberalization, through progressive dismantlement of quantitative import restrictions, had advanced – not to the same extent in all the countries concerned, but on the whole sufficiently to permit a very considerable expansion of intra-European trade. What more could the OEEC do? The idea of a European customs union was in many people's minds, but it was inflexibly opposed by the British. The number of times I went to London to try to convince them! All to no avail. The OEEC, they said, had no jurisdiction over customs duties, that was the business of the GATT. And they made no bones about the fact that, within the framework of the GATT, they did not intend to avail themselves of the clause which allowed the use of a preferential tariff policy as an interim arrangement to lead to the formation of a customs union or free-trade area within a reasonable length of time. They did not come around to the idea of a free-trade area until a few years later, when the creation of the Common Market forced their hand.

I cannot help thinking, all these years afterwards, that the British missed at that point a momentous opportunity which, had they grasped it, would probably have altered the course of their own history and spared Europe fifteen years of sterile polemics. With the prestige that was theirs at the end of the war, the memory in everyone's minds of the courage and strength of will they had shown in 1940–1, the vital part they had played in the liberation of Europe, the stoicism they had displayed in the face of adversity, with the feeling in Europe generally and in the United States that Britain was still a great power with great resources all over the world, they might have taken, to universal acclaim, the leadership of a movement towards the unification of Europe. France would have been happy in this postwar period, notably at the end of the forties, to be their partner in guiding that movement. The USA was urging them to take initiatives along these lines. Nothing could budge them. The movement towards European unification had come to a standstill and I could see nothing in the OEEC context that would be able to provide the necessary impetus.

That is why in 1952, or at any rate in 1953, I decided to leave OEEC. It was not easy, for since 1947 I had identified myself completely with the organization of which I was in charge. It took me about two years to shake myself free, during which time I went through a real moral upheaval, asking myself continuously what I was going to do. To leave would be to take a leap into the unknown; I did not know, I could not know, whether I would be given other opportunities to be useful. At that point I kept a diary in which, from time to time, I recorded my moods, my hesitancies, my resolutions. On June 3, 1953 I wrote:

The growing sense of boredom, the enervation, the loss of any real interest, these are due to the degeneration of the job that has been mine for more than five years. From a man I have turned into a function, and a not very interesting function at that. If today I were not in my post, I should certainly refuse it if it were offered to me. The reasonable thing to do would be to make preparations for my departure, to find another job, to write a book I would be ready to publish soon after regaining my freedom. But all my sense of initiative is paralyzed by the boredom, the intellectual 'idleness', the burden of unimportant responsibilities which have now become mine. My only chance of recovering my energy and a sense of direction is to take my decision and announce it.

Again, on December 16, 1953:

What does the future hold for me? In what activity shall I find peace and enjoyment? I am sure that I must leave the OEEC, which has outlived its time. But should I leave it before I have found another path? How shall I fare in the intervening period? Shall I find freedom or shall I become completely demoralized?

In January 1954, at Denyse Harari's invitation, Dottie and I spent a few weeks in Egypt. This provided an opportunity for some serious self-examination. In my diary I find the following passage under January 14:

The first conclusion I have come to is that I must leave the OEEC soon. That place and the cumbersome machinery of it are crushing me – or, rather, what is crushing me is my realization of the futility of this form of international action (at least in the present circumstances).

This shilly-shallying went on for a year – the whole of 1954, to be precise – until the day when I notified the OEEC Council of my decision to quit my post. In doing so, I jolted others and myself too. I left without any prospect of another activity. Dottie, who had sensed for many months that I was unhappy, encouraged me in my decision, regardless of the possible consequences for her and the children.

I left my office for the last time in April 1955.

Campaigning for a European customs union

In the spring of 1955 I asked to be reinstated in the university system. I could not apply for a teaching post in Paris as I had not done my stint in a provincial university. Eventually I ended up at Nancy, where I taught political economy from September 1955 to the beginning of 1957. I spent two days a week there; the rest of the time I was in Paris. I have the nicest memories of that period. My colleagues of the Nancy faculty of law welcomed me with open arms. I became friends with several of them.

But the real focus of my activity lay elsewhere. I had convinced myself that my primary task, in the interests of European unification, was to persuade the government and French public opinion that the country's salvation lay in the establishment of a European customs union. In that summer of 1955 the goal was a long way off.

During the month of July I published a series of articles (eleven in all) in the daily newspaper *Paris-Presse-l'Intransigeant* under the blanket title: *Les chances de la France dans l'Europe de demain* [The opportunities for France in the Europe of tomorrow]. The paper prefaced the first article with a capsule biography, along with my picture, in which the main outlines of my life were put before the reader with the title: *Il a choisi la vie* [He chose life]. In that series of articles I took stock of France's situation, analysed the economy's cyclical and structural weaknesses and tried to show the path that France had to follow in order to become a modern power able to deal on equal terms with the main western countries.

I began by noting that the chances of a full recovery and sustained expansion were good. The material disasters of the tragic prewar and war periods had quickly been repaired and a new generation was growing up, numerically larger than the preceding generations and one to which France should offer unlimited opportunities. But the underlying psychological note was not one of hope:

More pervasive is the idea that the present holds no prospects, the feeling that life will remain as hard as it is now or will become harder, that the new generations will have even more trouble than today's in finding the security and ease of living to which every human being aspires. The discontent may not be expressed in so many words, but it is present in most French people.

This nationwide gloom was admittedly justifiable on economic grounds, but for me there were other and probably more important reasons:

I do not believe that the reasons for this feeling of helplessness are solely economic. In fact, I am convinced that they are not primarily economic, and that just below the surface of today's complaints and demands lies the wish of the French people to be governed, to have stable political institutions which they can respect, which would protect them from external dangers, which would ensure the observance of reasonable and well-made laws, which would enable France to progress, without further disasters, from the era of colonial empires to that of federations of free peoples, which would give her a leading role in the inevitable integration of nation-states into broader entities.

But this series of articles was supposed to be concerned with the economic problem, so I had to get back to that. Today I find it hard to reconstruct the situation of France and of Europe in the mid-fifties. We know that the decade was marked by a prodigious economic expansion that was to continue during the sixties. But few people were aware of it at the time. The overriding impression was that in the ten years following the war we had just about made up the ground lost during the ten years preceding it and during the war itself. It seemed as if after this effort the course of history had suddenly stopped.

There is another reason for the demoralization of the French and their discontent besides the mediocrity of their present situation or the glaring inequalities they see around them. It is the absence of progress. It is the standstill in their living conditions, the immobility that seems to have over-taken so many things. Ultimately it is the lack of hope, for in most cases hope is no more than a projection of the improvements of the past.

And yet remarkable progress has been made since the Liberation and is still being made each day. The reason for this seeming contradiction is that it has taken us virtually all of the past ten years to regain the ground we lost during the fifteen preceding years, so that we are now roughly back to where we were in 1929. Only in the past year or two have we progressed slightly beyond that point.

France's industrial output did not regain its 1929 level until 1951 and was only about 18% above it by 1954. Meanwhile, industrial output doubled or more than doubled in Britain and Norway; it also doubled or nearly doubled in Germany and Holland. France was the only industrialized country of Western Europe to have marked time. I attributed the cause to France's degeneration during the prewar years, and specifically to the errors of all kinds committed by governments of all persuasions from 1930 to 1939. I shall not return to this subject, as I have already discussed it at length in an earlier chapter. However, I should say that since the memories of the prewar years were upper-most in all minds, including mine, this analogy between the two eras was not totally unjustified. A large share of our difficulties in 1955, as in 1931–6, stemmed from the refusal to accept a realistic currency parity and defend it. After the inflation surge of the postwar years, which gained further momentum at the time of the Korean war, France found herself once again burdened with an exchange rate that did not match the reality of international trading conditions:

Today stability has been restored, but the recent troubles have left deep scars: notably, an all-round disparity between French and foreign prices. French prices are too high to allow us to trade on equal terms with other countries. To offset these differences in price levels, the French government is granting export subsidies . . . and levying special import taxes. The rational solution to the problem would be to adjust the exchange rate; that is what any other West European government would do.

This took me back to the question of France's political institutions:

The deeper one probes, the more one becomes convinced that France's monetary problem is that of her political institutions. It is the lack of stability of her governments, their absence of authority due to their ephemerality, their consequent inability to define a consistent economic and financial policy of any kind, and to carry it through, which are responsible for the postwar monetary disorders. Another factor is the French elite's ignorance of these questions, but that is a matter of education.

As a result, France was the least industrialized country of north-west Europe. For me, there was no possible doubt that this was the origin of nearly all our difficulties.

In the 19th century France did not make the transition to an industrial economy that the other countries succeeded in doing; nor, unlike them, did she change her farming methods. She preferred to retain, by means of high protective barriers, her traditional agricultural structure. This was not necessarily a wrong choice. A country can legitimately prefer social stability and time-tested methods to modernization and a rapid rise in living standards. But things start to go wrong when one wants the best of both worlds. Since 1900 France has continued to protect her traditional structures more than any of her neighbours, and the result is a comparatively low standard of living not only for the urban dwellers, who are having to pay high prices for their food, but also for the rural people, whose average income is lower than that of almost all other population categories.

France's industrial weakness, I maintained, was essentially attributable to a traditional protectionism, which the mistakes of the thirties had aggravated by choking off the great industrial surge of 1920–9 which, had it been allowed to continue after the break caused by two years of crisis, would have transformed France completely.

These reflections brought me to my first conclusion:

The structure of the French economy is an archaic one. Through wonders of intelligence our productive system can be made to yield more than anyone would have believed possible, but if the system itself is not adjusted more rapidly than is at present the case, it is difficult to take an optimistic view of the future, not only as regards the French economy, but for French society in its entirety and for the French state.

Having arrived at this point, I ventured to describe the economic psychology of the French:

There is a strong tendency in France for each individual to claim as his until the end of his days the job (as opposed to *a* job, which is a genuine moral right) that he is practising at present; for each firm to consider that the government should protect it from all business setbacks, normal and abnormal, and keep it going even if it is utterly inefficient; for each industry to defend not only its existence, but its present size and place in the country's economy, even if the demand for its products is diminishing.

There followed an all-out attack on the conservatism which, by shielding the endangered activities and labour categories from domestic and foreign competition, had attempted to halt, or at the very least to slow down, the inevitable course of economic developments.

France is the most protectionist country in Western Europe ... We are surrounded, and our overseas territories too, by a high, thick wall that virtually isolates us from the rest of the world; all that can get through is a selection of goods carefully chosen by a watchful administration, itself closely watched by private interests that feel themselves threatened. Foreign competition, in the true sense of the term, is confined to a very few sectors.

This wall has been built up over the past seventy or eighty years by a long succession of governments of every hue; by contrast with the divisive spirit that reigns in the country today, protectionism is something on which nearly everyone is ready to agree.

Not only was France at this time, i.e. the mid-fifties, one of the high-tariff countries, but trade liberalization by way of quota dismantlement had been a virtual failure. After a genuine effort at liberalization in 1949–50, France had backslid at the beginning of 1952, following a grave balance-of-payments crisis, and reintroduced across-the-board quotas on all her imports from other European countries. France returned to the path of trade liberalization in 1954, but the results were modest. And even these she achieved only by subjecting a proportion of the newly derestricted products to an import surcharge of 7 to 15%, and this on top of customs duties that in many cases were very high.

Liberalization concerned only trade between European countries. There were no rules for imports from the dollar area. However, most of the European countries had phased out a large share of their quantitative restrictions on dollar imports. France, by contrast, had maintained a strict quota system for all these imports. In addition to the protectionism in metropolitan France, there was the protectionism in France's overseas territories; these had been made into a preserve for metropolitan industry, which was assured of being able to sell its products there at higher prices than those prevailing in other external markets.

As I went along, I developed the philosophy that a little later was to convince France to enter the Common Market. It was true that our economy included sectors of activity that were completely out of step,

251

whatever the exchange rate, with the world market and even with the European market. But they were few in number; and all the other countries had their high-cost sectors – which did not prevent them from generally practising more liberal import policies than our own. Moreover, there was no surer way than excessive protectionism to prevent the necessary adaptations. I therefore came out in favour of a currency adjustment, since the French general price level was too high. This was the result of the price and wage surge in 1951 and the reason why it had been necessary to introduce import surcharges and export subsidies, which were tantamount to an indirect devaluation. 'The remedy,' I concluded, 'lies in fixing the exchange rate at a realistic level.'

Having reached this point in my argument, I broached the problem of Europe. Our protectionist policy, I wrote, is interpreted throughout the world as a mark of weakness, as the sign of the French economy's inability to compete on equal terms with other countries; it is in flagrant contradiction with our will to be numbered among the great western powers; it is a constant disproof of our assertions that we want the unification of Europe or even the development of European cooperation. Only by accepting the risks inherent in free trading and in the international division of labour can France hope to see a rapid improvement in her conditions of existence.

The final article, published on July 30, 1955, was entitled *L'Union douanière, test de la volonté européenne* [The customs union, a test of European will]. In it I stated that if Western Europe did not unite, not only would it fail to regain the world role it had been accustomed to play, but its weight in international political and economic affairs would continually diminish, whilst that of the two continent states of West and East would correspondingly increase. The Europeans could not attain the living standards being enjoyed by the Americans then, let alone those they would be enjoying in the future, without the development of a large-scale European industry, which could be created, in the absence of customs barriers, on the basis of a market of at least 150–200 million consumers. Unification could therefore mean only one thing: forming a customs union, a single market, by abolishing the quotas and tariffs, as well as other barriers, that were separating the European states from one another and by unifying their trade policy towards the rest of the world.

The issue has to be put squarely: either a certain number of European states agree to set up a customs union, or all the discussions about European

252

integration are just so much talk that will not succeed for long in concealing the general infirmity of purpose. The only way of demonstrating beyond all possible doubt that things are really moving is to decide immediately to form such a trading entity. This is not a decision that can be taken in steps, even if its implementation is phased over a period that may be fairly long. For example, it is conceivable that the member states may give themselves five years in which to attain the ultimate goal, but the dates for the successive stages in the reduction of customs duties, the elimination of quotas, the unification of tariffs vis-à-vis the rest of the world, and other measures, have to be set now.

I was critical of a sectoral Europe as embodied in the European Coal and Steel Community. It would be with a mixture of regrets and misgivings, I wrote, that I would see the European countries create new specialized communities without first setting in place the framework of a customs union. For one thing, it would probably take many years to functionalize the institutions necessitated by each community, with the consequent risk of seeing the historic opportunity to 'make Europe' pass by; for another, the emergence of these communities in a market which otherwise – and probably for the most part – would remain compartmented would inevitably cause distortions in price and consumption patterns and hamper the development of our continent as much as if not more than it would facilitate it.

Turning finally to the vexed question of 'supranationality', a cause of keen dispute between 'Europeans' and Gaullists in particular, I tried to cut it down to size, for to me it seemed a minor issue. No progress could be made towards cooperation among states without some inroads into their sovereignty, but there were many ways in which this limitation of national sovereignty could be introduced. What was essential was that 'states should agree on the goal and the stages by which it would be reached, on the measures to be taken in order to smooth the way, on the establishment of permanent machinery for consultation in the event of unforeseen difficulties.'

Thus, halfway through that year of 1955, I already had in mind the principles that were to give rise some two years later to the Treaty of Rome and to the machinery which it set in motion. All that remained was to convince the French government. I helped to do so through a combination of patience and luck.

After leaving the OEEC, I renewed acquaintance with a man I held in the highest esteem, Christian Pineau. Following heroic service in the Resistance, he had held various ministerial posts since the Liberation.

253

In 1955 he had decided to devote his time to drawing up a programme which a new government might put into effect; for this purpose he had set up a working group which he called the *Comité d'études pour la République* and on which sat a large number of prominent socialists and radicals, together with personalities having no party affiliations. He offered me a place in his group and I accepted with pleasure. I was asked to write a draft report on the economic programme for France; I had already done a lot of work on the question and I had no trouble in building into the report both the result of my OEEC experience and the fruit of my reflections during the previous months which had led to the series of articles I have just mentioned.

I shall pass over the report's general considerations, since these were the same as those I had developed in the articles. The essential objective was to make France a modern state with a high standard of living, that is to say with high productivity. While recognizing that normative figures are bound to be somewhat arbitrary, one could say, to give a general idea, that France had to aim at 4–5% average annual growth in per capita national income. To achieve this, she would have to open her frontiers wide to world trade. With no other alternative than to waste away without any hope of revival, it was high time that the French economy communicated again with the outside, that it reintegrated itself into the European and world economy, that it put itself in a position to trade freely with other countries, with no more protection than that enjoyed by countries comparable to France. It was not a question of blindly submitting to all the shocks, to all the impulses from outside, but of becoming a member of a community of nations that would have the same objectives as ours and would follow the same general policy. Above all, it was a question of participating fully in the exchange of ideas, products and technologies that were changing today's world and of preparing for the advent of a new civilization as different from ours as ours was from the rural civilization of the 18th century. With the endorsement of Christian Pineau, I came out in favour of a European common market:

To put France on a par with the historic standards of the second half of the 20th century, it is necessary to integrate her economically into a larger entity in which all trade restrictions will be progressively abolished: not only quotas, but also customs duties, discriminatory rail freight rates, cartel practices, and so on. In this framework she will, under the spur of competition, regain the vigour of industrial development that she has shown at different times in her history. This consideration is made all the more cogent by the approach of the atomic and electronic revolution, which can produce its full impact only in an area larger than that bounded by national frontiers.

It is by making Europe that it will be least difficult to arrive at this enlargement of the economic framework in which we operate, because we shall be dealing with partners that have reached the same or approximately the same degree of economic development as ourselves; and also because it will be possible to arrange the transitions and set up the institutional machinery necessary to the management of the common market.

This European manifesto caused something of a stir; less, however, than did my call for an exchange-rate adjustment, which for me was the precondition of trade liberalization and creation of the Common Market. Not until General de Gaulle came to power in 1958 would this requisite be fulfilled. In 1955–6 when I, almost alone, was saying these things, I came in for fierce criticism from the economists and also from the upper echelons of the French civil service. A leading light in the Finance Ministry wrote a memorandum in which he claimed to show that a devaluation would in no way help to redress our balance of payments and that equilibrium would not be attained until the arrival of Saharan oil in the sixties; meanwhile, there was nothing for it but to ration meat. At a reception at the Elysée Palace the then President of France, René Coty, chided me, in a friendly manner, for stirring up a hornet's nest. When the Guy Mollet government was formed in January 1956 a rumour, which I never bothered to verify, went around that my monetary misdemeanour had cost me the finance portfolio. With the benefit of hindsight I can only be glad, if the rumour was true, that my imprudence had this result. What could I have done as Finance Minister in 1956?

Adviser to Foreign Minister Christian Pineau

When Guy Mollet formed his government, in late January-early February 1956, he asked Christian Pineau to take over Foreign Affairs. He in turn asked me to become his technical adviser with special competence for European questions. That was how the Common Market adventure began for me.

The European questions did not prevent me from concerning myself with other issues. The major event of 1956 was the Suez crisis and the Anglo-French intervention, the story of which I need not tell here. From the outset I was frankly against the move; for me it was a cardinal error, a backslide into a colonialism we were already having great difficulty in putting behind us. I spoke many times on the subject with Christian Pineau, who brought me into certain discussions, notably with the British. I still remember one conversation of Pineau with a British minister, probably the Foreign Secretary of the time, at which I was present. In the course of it the British minister observed wistfully: 'What we need is a *casus belli.*' Maurice Couve de Murville, then ambassador in Bonn, dropped in to see me, in my imposingly tapestried office on the ground floor of the ministry building on the Quai d'Orsay, whenever he came to Paris. Together we bemoaned this crazy venture which could only end badly. I did not know at the time exactly what Christian Pineau's feelings were. At certain moments it seemed to me that our points of view were much the same, as on that morning when, at a meeting of ministry heads of department, he said: 'Marjolin is the one here whose thinking is closest to my own.' Things ultimately took a different course. But the Suez affair, like other affairs of the time, did not hold a very important place in my thoughts. It was the matter of Europe that prepossessed me to the exclusion of almost any other – by this I mean the matter of France, her economy and her necessary rebirth in the framework of a unified Europe.

2

WHAT TYPE OF EUROPE?

It would be true to say that, in the matter of Europe the postwar period and more specifically the fifties and sixties, was dominated by two great currents of thinking, one embodied by Jean Monnet, the other by General de Gaulle. The former and his followers thought that one day, in the not too distant future, national sovereignties would merge into a European sovereignty and that for headway to be made in that direction, national sovereignties had to be progressively dismantled. The 'Europeans', as they were usually called, fell into several categories with different leanings: they ranged from the federalists, for whom none of the big problems facing France and Europe could be solved unless federal European institutions were rapidly set up, to the pragmatists, for whom the movement towards the ultimate goal was all that counted and who were ready to support any initiative, even of minor importance, as long as it tended in the desired direction. Jean Monnet himself was in this last category. As for the position of General de Gaulle and the Gaullists, as set out in the former's *Memoirs of Hope* and in Maurice Couve de Murville's book *Une politique étrangère 1958–69* [A foreign policy, 1958–69], it can be summed up thus: today and for a long time to come, as far as one can see ahead and perhaps for all time, the fundamental political reality is and will be the nation-state; the latter may, by treaty concluded with other nation-states, relinquish certain tokens of its sovereignty, but these can only

257

be individual and specific relinquishments, carefully defined and explicitly agreed to.

It was on the institutional issues – role and powers of the Strasbourg Assembly and of the Commission, possibility of majority voting in the Council of Ministers – that the 'Europeans' and the Gaullists were to clash most sharply. But the actual existence of the Common Market would never be brought into question. I personally was to find constant support in Paris for the completion of Europe's construction as defined in the Treaty of Rome.

One may understandably be tempted to ask the following question: if General de Gaulle had come to power two years earlier, in 1956, when the Rome Treaty negotiations were only beginning, would they have led to the outcome we know or would they have taken a different course? This is one of those hypothetical questions to which there can be no precise answer. Assuming the best, which is to say that France would have agreed with her five partners to create the European Economic Community, it is almost certain, in the light of the years which followed, that the treaty would have been different in a number of important respects. The principle of unanimity would have been asserted without any limitation of duration. The Commission's role would have been reduced; it would probably have become merely a secretariat of the Council of Ministers. It is unlikely that France would have been content with the few articles in the treaty that laid the foundations of a common agricultural policy; she would have wanted that policy spelled out in the treaty, at least as far as its essential rules were concerned. Would the other five countries have agreed to France's demands on these different points? No one can tell.

When he became head of the government in 1958, de Gaulle accepted the Treaty of Rome as signed a year earlier. He accepted its economic philosophy, which corresponded to his own. In his *Memoirs of Hope* he makes himself clear on this point:

Expansion, productivity, competition, concentration – such, clearly, were the rules which the French economy, traditionally cautious, conservative, protected and scattered, must henceforth adopt[1].

And further on, speaking of the Common Market itself, he says:

I was concerned with international competition, for this was the lever which could activate our business world, compel it to increase productivity, encourage it to merge, persuade it to do battle abroad; hence my determination to [practise] the Common Market, which as yet existed only on paper, to [work towards] the abolition of tariffs between the Six, to liberalize appreciably our overseas trade[2].

This resolve to put the Common Market into practice was one of the reasons that led de Gaulle to take the difficult monetary and financial decisions of 1958[3]; these put the French economy back on an even keel and enabled France on January 1, 1959 to make the same tariff cuts and the same advance towards alignment with the common external tariff as her EEC partners. 1958 was also notable for the adoption of France's new constitution, which put an end to the governmental instability from which the country had suffered so much under the Third and Fourth Republics. The end of the Algerian war in 1962 completed the decolonization process and enabled the French government to devote itself entirely to the task of strengthening France's economic position in a Europe where the Common Market was being built stone by stone.

Over the ten years that followed de Gaulle's coming to power France, often with the support of the Commission, played a decisive role in Brussels, where Maurice Couve de Murville, the Minister for Foreign Affairs, and Olivier Wormser, his principal collaborator, represented her in a continuous period of service unprecedented for length. As will be seen later, it was thanks to them and a few others that France, working closely with the Commission, succeeded in pulling the common agricultural policy out of the rut of generalities in which it was liable to stick and making it a practical reality.

De Gaulle and the United States

Having paid my tribute, a deserved one, to the nascent Fifth Republic, I feel easier about expressing the reservations I have concerning some aspects of Gaullist policy. I wish to speak in particular of certain instances of extreme language, as in the condemnation of the Fourth Republic, which was presented as being utterly without merit. To read General de Gaulle, one would think that the years from 1946 to 1958 were a period of total anarchy in France, during which the United States all but dictated French foreign policy. It is true that French diplomatic action at that time was usually in line with American views. But is it not equally true that those American views were, essentially at least, in line with French interests? Why stand apart and oppose when there is fundamental agreement on the goals to be achieved? I would not deny that the USA, given its economic and military power, had great weight in the decisions taken at that time, but I find it very difficult to accept the theory that, on important issues, US policy ran counter to the interests of France and of Europe.

I shall say nothing about the definition of Europe as extending 'from the Atlantic to the Urals'. I have never understood it. On the other hand, I cannot conceal the fact that I feel distinctly uncomfortable with the idea of 'the two blocs' from which Europe had to demarcate itself, this particular expression being employed, more often than not, without any indication of the essential difference that exists between the two. I am the first to want western, i.e. non-communist, Europe to find an identity that will distinguish it from the USA. Moreover, America was never opposed to the union of Europe, whatever form it might take; at different times she even vigorously promoted or encouraged it. What I cannot accept is the apparent equation of Soviet Russia, the most absolute totalitarian regime that the world has ever known, and America, which has a democratic regime comparable to ours. In our dealings with America we, France, are not in the same position as countries like Poland, Czechoslovakia and Hungary are vis-à-vis Soviet Russia. We can say no to the Americans, as de Gaulle did in 1966 when he pulled France's armed forces out of NATO, without our being threatened with invasion or even economic reprisals. For France's EEC partners, the movement towards European unification and the maintenance of a close and friendly alliance with the United States were not only compatible, but complementary. I think they were the ones who were right. The extremes of Gaullist language at times deeply disturbed France's relations with the other five countries. These extremes were all the more pointless in that France's foreign policy under de Gaulle was not essentially different from those of her European partners. At certain times even, such as in the Berlin and Cuban crises, de Gaulle showed himself to be the staunchest and most resolute ally of the United States.

Arguably, therefore, it was inordinate language more than acts or failures to act that brought France's membership of the Atlantic Alliance into question. The pity of it is that, since thought is expressed in language, the Americans and France's European partners themselves had cause to think, on certain occasions, that France's intentions were different from what they really were. The words through which the deed is expressed are often as important as the deed itself.

De Gaulle and Jean Monnet

There can be no question here of writing a Plutarchan account of two parallel lives: those of de Gaulle and Jean Monnet are comparable only in a few respects.

At once a thinker, a propagator of ideas and a statesman whose coming to power had a profound effect on France, de Gaulle realized at a very early point in the thirties what the nature of the coming war would be; if that war began with a disaster for France, it was because the prophet of mobile warfare with emphasis on large motorized and armoured units had not been heeded. During the war he embodied the resistance to the enemy, when the Liberation came he maintained peace at home. In 1958 he gave France the best constitution she has ever had. Finally, he completed the decolonization process by giving Algeria its independence, thus leaving France entirely free to concentrate on European matters.

Jean Monnet's sum of accomplishments was more modest, or different, if one prefers. The only political post he held in France was that of Commissioner General of the French Plan, to which de Gaulle had appointed him. Earlier, in Washington, he had played a big part in the Anglo-American war effort. At the beginning of the fifties he devised and created the European Coal and Steel Community, which represented an important stage in the construction of Europe.

The lives of the two men were thus very different. And yet, if one were to ask in France or abroad, especially abroad, which Frenchmen made the deepest imprint on the past half-century, almost certainly the two names that would be mentioned first would be those of General de Gaulle and Jean Monnet. Each was, in his own way, an illustrious Frenchman of whom France can be proud.

There is certainly nothing arbitrary or fallacious in drawing this analogy between the two men, even though the contrasts between their respective lives and philosophies are very marked. De Gaulle, apart from a sojourn in Lebanon and, of course, the London years, spent virtually the whole of his life in France in that most national of French institutions, the army. Jean Monnet, on the other hand, despite his peasant origins, to which he often referred, was a cosmopolitan who lived a large part of his life abroad, notably in America and China. Their passions were different. De Gaulle's sole aim, during and after the war, was to restore France to her rightful place in Europe and in the world. 'De Gaulle,' wrote Maurice Couve de Murville, 'was most certainly a man of unyielding passion, and his passion was

France'⁴. Jean Monnet, too, was passionately devoted to his country; he undoubtedly saw no contradiction between the relinquishments of sovereignty that he was proposing and the greatness of France. For him, that greatness lay by way of a united Europe, which would include Britain, and close ties with the United States, whose hegemony he did not perceive as a threat.

It was probably on this last issue that the differences between the two minds were most marked. Jean Monnet felt deep affinities with the United States, where he had lived for a long time. He was at home there. He had many friends there. The idea that America could threaten France's independence seemed absurd to him. De Gaulle, on the other hand, had an invincible distrust of the giant across the Atlantic. There is a rational explanation for the way he felt: one result of the war had been to relegate France, like Britain and Germany, to the status of a second class power carrying relatively little weight in world affairs, whereas the influence of the United States had grown prodigiously and asserted itself in all parts of the globe, with the exception of the communist countries. How could one not conceive that one day the United States might misuse that influence? In Europe, Britain was seen by many as an American outpost. Germany, feeling herself threatened by the Soviet Union, counted on the Americans to ensure her safety and was prone to follow them in all their economic and political moves. But de Gaulle's mistrust of, if not hostility towards, the United States had been aggravated by his treatment at the hands of Roosevelt during the war, who saw in him the leader of a French faction instead of the man who embodied the Resistance. Not until the war was over did the American attitude change. I shall not discuss the question of how this misunderstanding arose; it is unlikely that all the blame lay on one side. The fact remains that US policy with regard to de Gaulle was singularly lacking in percipience for a number of years.

This contrast between de Gaulle's and Jean Monnet's feelings towards America was duplicated in their respective reactions to Britain's applications to join the Common Market, first in 1961 and then in 1967. Jean Monnet, immediately and with deep conviction, supported Britain's candidacy, once it seemed to him that the British had accepted the Treaty of Rome and the decisions that had been taken to implement it. De Gaulle opposed it with equal determination, not only because in his view the British presence would complicate or even prevent the treaty's execution in full, but because Britain's entry would in effect be America's entry. The Common Market, he thought, would become a worldwide free trade area; that would be the end of Europe, which would cease to be European.

If one were to try to list all the divergences in the thinking and action of the two men, one would never finish. For example, de Gaulle sharply criticized the ECSC, of which Jean Monnet was the founding father, and vehemently opposed the European Defence Community, which Monnet tried so hard to promote. He was utterly against any form of 'supranationalism', the latter being in his view no less than tantamount to a plot to undo France, with Jean Monnet as one of the chief instigators, if not the chief.

At bottom, the nation-state for de Gaulle was something virtually immutable, fashioned by centuries of history. The idea that one day the European nation-states might be merged into a vast entity called 'Europe' or 'United States of Europe' seemed to him the manifestation of a dangerous delirium that could only lead to the disappearance of France, without anything real, anything genuinely European, being able to take her place. His thinking, moulded by a profound knowledge of history, centred on the balance of power between states, whereas Jean Monnet liked to ignore it, or to pretend to.

And yet, in spite of all these opposites, the two men were very close to each other in a number of fundamental respects. Both were modernists, they wanted a modern France in tune with the times. De Gaulle spoke of the need for the economy to grow, to expand investment, to increase productivity, to accept international competition, in terms that Jean Monnet would not have disowned. The two men came together after the war in the creation of France's Plan of Modernization and Equipment. De Gaulle accepted the Common Market without argument, when he could have brought the whole thing into question.

For de Gaulle, as for Jean Monnet, Europe, or perhaps it would be more accurate to say the cornerstone of Europe, was essentially Franco-German rapprochement. It was necessary to forget two centuries of intermittent war, to make sure not to compromise the future by trying to keep Germany in a state of subjection, to settle rapidly what might remain of the Franco-German dispute. Jean Monnet inaugurated this policy with the treaty establishing the ECSC; de Gaulle, when he returned to power, gave it added impetus by creating a relationship of close cooperation between himself and Adenauer. After the old Chancellor died in 1963, the special Franco-German relationship weakened somewhat but never disappeared completely.

Although firmly rejecting federalist ideas because he saw in them a threat to France's independence, de Gaulle constantly thought of a political Europe able to hold its own with the United States – a third force, so to speak. Hence the endeavour to establish political cooperation among the members of the Common Market in the early sixties. Jean Monnet, though following different paths and failing to share Gaullist ideas about the American peril, had goals that were not far removed from the General's. He too wanted a Europe that could treat on equal terms with the United States; he had nothing to say against the efforts to establish political cooperation among the Six.

The dialogue, more often than not indirect, between de Gaulle and Jean Monnet, with its overt points of disagreement and its generally covert points of agreement, lasted for twenty years, from 1950 until the General's death. Throughout that time I saw Jean Monnet very frequently. As of 1958, de Gaulle received me regularly, perhaps once or twice a year. Above all, during the whole time that he was Foreign Minister, I had many long conversations with Maurice Couve de Murville. As a rule, I saw him every Saturday afternoon. I did not approve of General de Gaulle's extreme language, but in all the periods of tension that the Common Market experienced during the sixties, in all the crises that shook it, my stance was often close to his and to that which Couve de Murville expressed in Brussels. My relations with Jean Monnet were friendly and trusting, even if our views differed on some important issues such as Britain's entry into the Common Market at a time when the latter's construction was not complete. I also thought that the nation-state was not on the way out and that one could not expect the emergence of a European state in the foreseeable future. I often conversed on this subject with Monnet.

One man we both knew well, and who has remained one of my best friends, was a witness to many of these conversations. This was George Ball, for many years Under-Secretary of State in Washington – an extraordinarily clearsighted and courageous man who, though a member of the US government, strongly opposed the Vietnam venture. This is how he described the stances of Jean Monnet and myself:

Monnet and Marjolin addressed [Europe's] problems from different angles of attack. Monnet invariably set goals that might be approached but never attained. Marjolin, whose task was to translate broad concepts into functioning institutions, was necessarily aware of the limits of the feasible and the need for compromise. I refrained from taking sides in the argument, since I was devoted to both men. But their disparate attitudes illuminated the basic question. Was Monnet really right in believing that a change in institutions would cause men and women to conform their thoughts and actions to a new set of principles? Could allegiance to a united Europe some day play the same activating role that national sovereignty had played in the past? Or did it really matter whether he was right or not? Would not the insistent pressure for the unattainable goal at least lead toward greater solidarity and common policies and actions that could never be achieved by more modest objectives?

Marjolin did not believe that the concept of nationality could be displaced [by the concept of 'Europe'] within a single generation, or even several generations, merely by creating new institutions. Patriotism had been the coalescing force animating Germany's neighbours to resist her ravaging armies in two world wars, and Britain, in Marjolin's view, was not ready for Europe. He did not think – as Monnet did – that deeply entrenched habits of thought could be quickly modified in the pressure chambers of new institutions[5].

George Ball himself did not think that Europe could, in the foreseeable future, set itself up as a United States of Europe, but he did believe in the power of ambitious ideas, in their ability to change reality, at least to some extent.

The inner logic of integration?

The difference in standpoints which George Ball noticed between Jean Monnet and me was even more pronounced, as far as I am concerned, when it came to certain theories representing the views of a number of fervent 'Europeans', who were quite a strong force during the fifties and early sixties.

For them, federal Europe was within reach, if the political will were there. Practically speaking, once the first step had been taken in this direction, events would necessarily follow on from one another and inevitably lead to the desired result. This is the gist of the so-called theory of *engrenage* [chain reaction] or the 'spill-over effect'. It is set out in the fullest detail in what maybe regarded as the political testament of Walter Hallstein, who, as a close collaborator of Konrad Adenauer, then as President of the EEC Commission from 1958 to 1967, played a large part in the construction of the Common Market[6].

The forces which the Europeans had let loose in deciding to create a common market, so Hallstein's thinking went, must inevitably take Europe to economic union, then to political union. If one started out with a customs union and a common agricultural policy, one would inevitably be drawn much further. Neither of them would be able to function, or at any rate to function satisfactorily, unless currency parities remained invariable, in short unless a European currency were created; which, in turn, would entail a merging of the economic policies of member states into a single economic policy; and this would necessitate the merging of national sovereignties into a European sovereignty.

One arrived at the same conclusion if one considered the European Community's relations with the rest of the world. Once the Common Market had been set up, there could no longer be national trade policies vis-à-vis third countries – only a common commercial policy, for which, moreover, the Rome Treaty would explicitly provide. But trade policy was an essential part of foreign policy, itself closely bound up with defence policy ... Thus, a process that began modestly with the establishment of a customs union and a common agricultural or commercial policy would reach its logical outcome: a European federation or, as others would name it, the United States of Europe. This is what Walter Hallstein called the 'material' or 'inner' logic of integration.

My own reaction to these 'federalist' ideas was one of extreme scepticism. I did not believe in the *engrenage* or 'spill-over' theory.

To begin with, I did not think it true that the customs union or the common agricultural policy would be unable to survive unless Europe formed itself into an economic union, in the strongest sense of the term. Nearly thirty years after the signing of the Rome Treaty and some eighteen years after the completion of the customs union, Europe has still not become an economic union. National economic policies differ greatly; European currency parities change frequently against one another, despite the introduction of the European Monetary System; unity of agricultural prices has been shattered by the refusal of national governments to adjust domestic farm prices to the movement of exchange rates. I am not trying to say that the customs union and the common agricultural policy have been untroubled by these developments, but essentially the Common Market has survived. Above all, it would be a fundamental error to think that a government having to contend with acute domestic problems, often threatening its very existence, could be constrained to take crucial decisions involving relinquishments of sovereignty, simply because an 'inner logic', the reality of which is moreover debatable, left it no other alternative.

However, with these reservations, I was not then, nor am I now, in profound disagreement with the 'federalists'. I would be one myself if events were to take a turn that allowed me to think that the goal of a

European federation could be achieved in the foreseeable future. At present I can do no more than ask myself sometimes whether the European peoples, or at any rate some of them, have a genuine aspiration, however confused, towards European unity? Is there such a thing as a European sensibility, intrinsically distinct from, say, the American sensibility? Are we French, for example, further removed in our feelings and reactions from the people of North America than we are from the Germans or the British? Was Walter Hallstein right in stating that Europeans are intuitively aware that, beyond their native countries, there is a greater homeland, Europe? No one would deny the cultural unity of the Continent; but are not the United States and other countries with inhabitants of European stock a part of that cultural unity? I leave it to each reader to answer these questions, for the matter is eminently subjective. Not that the reply would necessarily resolve the issue. It is possible that there is no specifically European sensibility and that, nevertheless, European union is vital for reasons of international policy, in order to enable Europe to go on playing a world role and to preserve her freedom.

The institutional quarrel has always seemed rather pointless to me. Between maintenance of national sovereignties *in toto* and dismantlement of the latter, there is a middle way. For me, this middle way represented the reality, the hypothetical extremes – full maintenance of sovereignties or their dismantlement – being mental constructs. The middle way was a treaty whereby the signatory states would pledge themselves to one another indefinitely and undertake to carry out certain acts by specified dates, such as the progressive abolition of customs duties and import quotas, the gradual derestriction of movements of labour and capital, the organization of agricultural markets, and so on. After a transition period, which might vary according to the circumstances, the result would be a Europe which, if perhaps not wholly unified economically, would nevertheless present a degree of unity unachieved hitherto.

Of course, a treaty is just a piece of paper. One or more signatory states can tear it up, admittedly, but that is equally true of any organizational formula: any legal construct is perishable. It is not by creating a pseudo-executive, to which sovereign powers would be given but which would have no means of enforcing them, that the problem will be resolved. The only answer is the existence of a will to live together, the realization by nation-states that, whatever the disadvantages of the Community, they are better off in it than out of it.

The fact that I felt so uncomfortable with extreme European views also explains why I never spoke of the 'United States of Europe', an expression used by many excellent minds fascinated by the power that unification had given the British colonies of North America in the late 18th century and thenceforward. This analogy between the two continents always seemed to me eminently superficial. What could there possibly be in common between the British establishments of the Atlantic coast in 1780 or thereabouts, which were less than a century and a half old, which shared the same language, the same law and, essentially, the same institutions, which had never fought one another, and the old states of Europe – France, Britain, Germany, Italy – some of which, admittedly, had unified in the 19th century, but which had national traditions going back to the Middle Ages? Because the term 'United States of Europe' creates illusions in minds that are ignorant of history, I have always refused to use it.

3

THE EUROPEAN COAL AND STEEL COMMUNITY: THE GREAT TURNING POINT IN FRENCH FOREIGN POLICY

A European customs union could have emerged directly from the effort to reconstruct Europe after the war and pave the way for future expansion. It did not. The Marshall Plan made it possible to create the Common Market but did not actually engender it. The direct ancestor of the Common Market was the European Coal and Steel Community, which brought together a group of countries (the Six) that had decided to go further in the construction of Europe than Britain and a few small countries, notably the Scandinavian countries, were prepared to at the time. The ECSC was devised in 1950 and brought into being in 1952. It stemmed both from the aspiration to a closer unity of Europe than that embodied in the OEEC and from the need to define a new French policy vis-à-vis Germany. Its two protagonists were Robert Schuman, then France's Minister for Foreign Affairs, and Jean Monnet.

I shall speak only briefly of the ECSC as I had no hand in its creation, being engaged at OEEC in less ambitious tasks, namely the forming of a European market through abolition of import quotas and multilateralization of payments. If I mention it here, it is because it constitutes an essential stage in the formation of the Europe we know today.

Robert Schuman and Jean Monnet had similar ideas on Europe, but their immediate concerns were different. True, Monnet was convinced that France's policy in regard to Germany was on the wrong track and that it was vital to come up with an idea that would initiate the reconciliation of the two countries and enable them to work in partnership. He was certain that, in order to avoid future wars, Germany had to be recognized as having equality of rights. On this issue he was far in advance of French public opinion of the day. 'Peace can be founded only on equality of rights,' he told Robert Schuman. 'We failed in 1919 because we introduced discrimination and a sense of superiority. Now we are beginning to make the same mistakes again[1].'

But the idea uppermost in Jean Monnet's mind at that time was a different one. He wanted to create a Europe endowed with efficient institutions resembling, even very remotely, the United States constitution, a Europe which could take its decisions by majority vote and which, in consequence, would go well beyond the Europe as represented by the OEEC where all decisions had to be unanimous. He made no attempt to hide his contempt for what he called 'intergovernmental cooperation'. True, he admits in his *Memoirs* that the latter, as embodied in the OEEC, if one accepted it for what it was, with its limitations, was a factor of progress for a European economy that was too compartmented. The abolition of quotas and the establishment of payments agreements would facilitate and stimulate trade; better knowledge of the other's resources and goals would enable each to direct his own efforts to better purpose. But that was where the effectiveness of this type of organization ended. To ask more of a system that entailed no delegation of sovereignty would have been unrealistic, and very soon, he said, the OEEC had become purely technical machinery. It had outlived the Marshall Plan because it had been able to serve as a source of useful information[2]. In a letter to the then Foreign Minister Georges Bidault, which must date from 1948, Jean Monnet wrote that the idea of sixteen sovereign nations cooperating actively was an illusion. 'I believe that only the establishment of a *federation* of the West, including Britain, will enable us to solve our problems quickly enough, and finally prevent war[3].' And in a letter to Robert Schuman he wrote:

Everything I have seen and reflected on here leads me to a conclusion which is now my profound conviction: that to tackle the present situation, to face the dangers that threaten us, and to match the American effort, the countries of Western Europe must turn their national efforts into a truly European effort. This will be possible only through a *federation* of the West[4].

At the same time Jean Monnet, dominated as he was by one idea, was aware that it was unrealistic to think of a federation in the near future. He had become persuaded of this in 1949, when he proposed to the French and the British a Franco-British union, a merging of the French and British economies, and a hark-back to Churchill's proposal of 1940. This would have been the first step towards a European federation. But the British would hear no talk of federation nor of delegation of sovereignty; it is not even certain that they understood what the latter expression meant. Edwin Plowden, a senior Whitehall official, was later to say to Jean Monnet: 'We'd won the war, [we had worldwide responsibilities] and we weren't ready to form special links with the continent[5].'

Jean Monnet found that his attempt to create a federal nucleus around which Europe might be formed had failed to interest the one great power in the Old World then in a position to take on a political responsibility of that magnitude. Even in France, national sentiment was still too strong for the idea of a federation to have any chance of winning acceptance. It was necessary to come up with a scheme of smaller compass, one that would go some way towards the final goal without offending public opinion, which was as yet unreceptive.

It was then that he devised the plan that was to lead to the creation of the European Coal and Steel Community (ECSC). Its whole underlying philosophy was summed up in a few lines: 'A start would have to be made by doing something both more practical and more ambitious. National sovereignty would have to be tackled more boldly and on a narrower front[6].' The word 'federation' was mentioned in the Schuman declaration that gave birth to the ECSC, not as something accessible in the short term but as the outcome of a long process of which the ECSC would be the starting point. The resulting new institutions defined what, for want of a better term, might be called 'supranational Europe'. The latter would be the result of more and more extensive delegations of national sovereignty to supranational bodies. These delegations of sovereignty would, according to the thinking of those who were promoting them, lead in the first instance to sectoral communities of clearly delimited scope, and later to a federation of Western Europe. The pooling of certain powers, hitherto national, would set off a process that would end in the emergence of a European state. Lastly, France's chief partner in this undertaking would not now be Britain, but Germany.

The project thus conceived would probably not have come off had it not matched the immediate concerns of Robert Schuman, then Foreign Affairs Minister. He could not but be aware that French policy towards Germany was deadlocked. Since 1945 successive French governments had tried in vain to prevent the reconstruction of Germany as a great industrial power, essentially by restricting German steel output and thus releasing large quantities of coking coal that could be exported, notably to France. These efforts had encountered not only German resistance, as after World War One, but also, and infinitely more seriously, the American will to rebuild the industrial power and, soon thereafter, the military power of Germany, in order to make her a bulwark against Soviet political and military expansion. France could only fight rearguard actions, from which she regularly emerged beaten.

When Jean Monnet came to Robert Schuman early in 1950 with his project for the ECSC, the latter quickly recognized that here was a way out of the difficulty and a means of shifting the stance of French policy towards Germany, without appearing to capitulate to American demands. His *directeur de cabinet* [chief private secretary] Bernard Clappier, later Governor of the Bank of France, played a major role as an intelligent and convinced intermediary between the two men.

The Germans for their part, in the person of the then Chancellor Konrad Adenauer, immediately perceived the prospects that the ECSC project held for their country. The controls that applied to their coal and steel production were discriminatory, and Bonn wanted them out of the way as soon as possible. On the other hand, the Germans accepted at once the idea of an authority that would oversee not only Germany's production, but also that of France, Belgium, Luxembourg, the Netherlands and Italy. The hope was even entertained for a while that Britain would join the Community. What the Germans wanted to avoid at any price, and they were ready to make heavy concessions to this end, was the differential treatment they had been receiving. Their objective was to regain sovereign power status as rapidly as possible. In accepting the principles of the Schuman Plan (as the ECSC project was christened), Adenauer publicly stated his satisfaction: 'The proposal that France has just made to us is a generous move. It is a decisive step forward in Franco-German relations. It is not a matter of vague generalizations, but of concrete suggestions based on equal rights.' With his habitual realism, the chancellor also recognized an immediate advantage: 'Since the production of the Saar will be pooled, one cause of tension between France and Germany will be removed[7].'

Finally, the Americans threw their weight behind the enterprise, which fitted in perfectly with their plans for Germany. Like Jean Monnet, they also saw in it the embryo of the European unity for which they had now been hoping for several years. Disappointed by the attitude of the British in the OEEC, they turned to the ECSC; the vigorous support they gave it helped to convince the Germans.

On May 9, 1950 Robert Schuman made his formal declaration initiating the project. In 1952 the deal was settled and the ECSC became a reality; the six member countries (France, Germany, Benelux and Italy) formed a common market for coal and steel within which those products would move freely. Institutional machinery, comprising notably a High Authority, a Council of Ministers, a Court of Justice and a Parliamentary Assembly, was set up to keep markets orderly and ensure that they functioned smoothly. This was an institutional system similar to the one that would be adopted a few years later when the European Economic Community was established, but with essential differences to which I shall come back later.

The ECSC is estimable on two counts. First, it represented a step forward, a new start on the road to a united Europe. Second, it represented a revolution in Franco-German relations. Nearly a century of wars, of attempts at domination, of an antagonism that had come absurdly to be called hereditary, had given way to a will to cooperate on completely equal terms. It would take a few more years for mentalities to change and adjust to the new situation, but the movement was under way and there would be no stopping it until the goal had been achieved.

Even without the ECSC, Germany would have regained her place in Europe. The Americans, who were working actively for her reconstruction as a great industrial power, would eventually have carried the day. But this reconstruction would have been effected against France; a great deal of bitterness would have persisted for a long time in the two countries. If only in this respect, the ECSC was an inspired idea.

De Gaulle was unjust when, in his memoirs, he accused Jean

Monnet and the French governments of the time of having undersold France's interests:

Thus, the re-establishment of a central German administration in the three western zones had been accepted, in spite of the absence of genuine guarantees. Then, the European Coal and Steel Community had been inaugurated, under an agreement which, without offering us the means of restoring our devastated mines, exempted the Germans from having to provide us with fuel deliveries and gave the Italians the wherewithal to equip themselves with a large-scale iron and steel industry[8].

The path that de Gaulle seems to be indicating as the one he would personally have followed would have been the surest way to preclude any Franco-German rapprochement; any form of European construction would have become impossible. But there was much that was intentionally polemical in what de Gaulle said. No one can tell how he would have behaved had he been in power at the time. When he did come back to power in 1958 his attitude would be quite different. He and Adenauer would join forces to make a Franco-German Europe. Even today, a certain complicity between France and Germany, a certain Franco-German political will, constitutes the hidden mainspring that enables the Franco-German mechanism to go on functioning.

But the contribution of Jean Monnet and Robert Schuman to Europe's construction does not end there. It was they who in 1950 brought the Six together under the leadership of France. The Luxembourg of the ECSC constituted a school in which the Six learned to work together. When the day of the Common Market dawned they were ready to continue their collaboration in a much wider area than that of coal and steel.

Admittedly, the ECSC did not fulfil all the hopes that its founders had placed in it, particularly with regard to its institutions. The 1951 Treaty of Paris had given the High Authority extensive powers in the coal and steel sectors; it had made the Authority a sovereign power whose decisions were, within certain limits, binding on national governments. By 1956, when plans for the EEC were taking shape, ideas had been scaled down concerning the prerogatives of the 'Commission' (the name was already less ambitious than that of High Authority). One of the reasons, in fact the most important one, was that the High Authority had found itself constrained, in the exercise of its powers, by the fact that any decision of consequence in regard to coal and steel inevitably had repercussions in other areas of the member countries' economies. As a result, close cooperation had become a practice between the High Authority and the Council of Ministers. Furthermore, the energy situation had changed radically during the fifties. With oil progressively replacing coal in many uses, the ECSC was no longer in the centre of the European economic scene, contrary to what might have been expected a few years earlier. Finally, the failure, in 1954, of the efforts to set up a European Defence Community had rebounded on the ECSC, the two ventures being linked in the public's mind by the fact, in particular, that both sought to reintegrate Germany into the concert of nations while preventing her from recovering her might of prewar years. But on the whole, the verdict on the ECSC has to be a positive one. It opened the way to more ambitious ventures.

4

NEGOTIATING THE TREATY OF ROME

The treaty establishing a European Defence Community (EDC) was rejected by the French National Assembly on August 30, 1954. For a while, the proponents of a united Europe felt that their whole world had collapsed around them, that Europeanism was finished for good, that the old national antagonisms would return as fierce as ever, that the fragmentation of the Continent would be perpetuated in all areas – political, military and economic. In France, moreover, the bitter disputes over the EDC had left deep wounds that looked as if they might never heal; national unity, restored at the time of the Liberation under the aegis of General de Gaulle, seemed shattered. It was almost like the Dreyfus affair. I remember dinners in town where the conversation having strayed by mischance on to the subject of the EDC, the good vibrations snapped and the table companions, after a violent argument, parted company without even saying good-bye to one another. A number of *idées-forces* which, in preceding years, had ruled the thinking of those who regarded themselves as 'Europeans', were totally discredited, even for many of their advocates. One could no longer mention the subject of European defence, nor that of supranationality, European constitution, relinquishment or delegation of sovereignty, or even European institutions, without in most cases eliciting from the listener a wry smile of disappointment, scepticism or irony, and sometimes even a sharp reaction, as though one had suggested an abdication on the part of France, a renunciation of national independence, a total submission to a foreign will.

Yet less than three years later, the treaties establishing the Common Market and Euratom were ratified by the Parliaments of the Six, including the French Parliament, without any major difficulty. They were accepted, especially the treaty setting up the European Economic Community, by the greater part of public opinion, if not with enthusiasm, at least with the feeling that this was something inevitable and possibly beneficial. In retrospect, this is all the more surprising in that the Common Market's creation was a step towards a much closer unity of Europe than anything that had gone before. It was more significant in this respect than the Marshall Plan, which had been above all an operation of collective rescue, and than the ECSC, which only concerned two industries. More significant, too, than the projected EDC, whose realization was at best very uncertain and from which Gaullist France would certainly have withdrawn.

In the circles pledged to the construction of Europe the mood was now turning to elation; the feeling that many things, if not everything, had become possible was replacing the sense of frustration caused by the failure of the EDC.

Origins of the change

What was the origin, or rather what were the origins, of this event which, at least on the face of it, was a near-miracle? A few men had, it is true, worked zealously and perseveringly for it to come about, but their efforts would probably have remained unavailing or would not have succeeded completely if the economic and political climate in Europe (including France) and in the world as a whole had not changed imperceptibly over the previous two or three years, to the point where this slow process of change had produced, in relation to the prewar and immediate postwar periods, a radical transformation.

The essential fact was that peace reigned in Western Europe. People knew instinctively that the nations situated in this part of the world would never war against one another again. Depending on how one looked at human nature, this state of affairs could be seen either as the triumph of wisdom over blind violence, or as evidence of utter exhaustion. Either way, the fact remains that none of the great nations that had made European history – notably, France, Britain and Germany – any longer had territorial claims on the others. Much more important, the conditions of warfare had changed so much with the advent of the atomic weapon that each of these erstwhile great powers suddenly found itself, militarily, almost completely powerless.

277

As to the ever present threat from the East, it did not constitute a real danger as long as the United States remained in a position of world supremacy. Of course, there were the occasional mishaps like the blockade of Berlin in 1948–9 and, later, the Berlin crisis of 1958, without forgetting the Korean War of 1950–3. But public opinion was disturbed only for brief periods by these events. As of the mid-fifties, the peoples of Europe felt safe in a way they had never known before in their history. The time had come when daring initiatives were possible.

For twenty years after the end of the war the western world lived through the period of the *Pax Americana*. Not only from the military standpoint, but also economically. During the years from 1945 to 1950 the United States had admirably succeeded in making the transition from a war economy to a peace economy that was prosperous and stable. The prodigious bound in US production during the war years had given way to moderate but sustained expansion during the years when Europe, for its part, was rebuilding itself. By 1950 it was a virtual certainty to everyone that the world in general, and America and Europe in particular, would not again experience a deep recession of the kind suffered after the First World War. This conviction induced immense relief among peoples who were fearing the worst; it helped to generate the optimism that prevailed during the sixties.

For Europe, as I have already said, and for the whole of the non-communist world, the United States had become the ideal. The aim was simple: to catch up with the United States, or at any rate to come as close as possible. The way to get there seemed quite clear: adopt American methods of production and organization, duplicate American economies of scale in Europe. Those who were more perceptive felt that the success of such an undertaking necessitated the formation of a vast European market, comparable to the American market. The idea of a customs union was brewing. The Americans were giving it all their support. As early as 1949 Paul Hoffman, in Paris, had introduced the notion of a European customs union in the context of the Marshall Plan. The Americans backed Jean Monnet strongly in his efforts to set up the ECSC. They supported the ill-fated endeavour to bring about a military union of Europe in a European defence community. In the second half of the fifties they showed that they were completely in favour of the idea of a European common market.

Their motives were essentially political: to consolidate Europe, after the terrible trials of the war, in such a way that democracies would be proof against totalitarian acts of aggression or subversion. With such an important political objective, America was ready to forget temporarily her own economic interests, or at least her apparent economic interests. The European customs union would inevitably mean discriminatory treatment for all US goods. But the Americans, or in any case the individuals and groups that determined American policy, were prepared to overlook this troublesome consequence, trusting that the future would iron out the situation.

It has to be said, in part explanation of this attitude, that the America of the fifties was seen throughout the world and saw herself as being at the peak of her power, even if that power, in relative terms at any rate, was beginning to decline. The dollar gap seemed forever unbridgeable, all efforts notwithstanding, whereas in fact it was already fast dwindling away. As for Europe, the fifties were years of rapid progress. The coming of the Common Market would give even more momentum to Europe's economic expansion, but the latter was already well under way beforehand. The reconstruction of the war-ravaged Continent during the Marshall Plan years had imparted an impetus that would continue through the years that followed, making the years from 1948 to 1973 one of the most dynamic eras Europe had ever known. This is true of France, but also, with slight variations, of the other countries that were to come together in the Common Market.

Peace in Europe, safety throughout the world, the presence of an intelligent protector ready to sacrifice his immediate interests to consolidate the western world and to give whatever help was needed to overcome temporary difficulties, and who moreover constituted a fascinating model to emulate, how could all these factors fail to bring about a gradual change of thinking in Europe? It should be added that a new generation was emerging, one that recognized the Malthusianism of prewar years for the absurdity it really was. The groundwork had been laid for a transformation of economic relations between European countries, but many obstacles remained. It was at that point that the action of a number of men became necessary, for without it the fruit that was already ripe could probably not have been plucked.

The Messina conference

The change in thinking of which I have just spoken did not take place with equal rapidity in the different countries that were to come together in the Common Market. This was clearly apparent in the talks and negotiations that marked the years from 1955 to 1957.

In June 1955 a conference of foreign ministers of the member states of the European Coal and Steel Community was held at Messina. The purpose of that conference was to see what could be salvaged of the European idea after the failure of the project for the European Defence Community. How could European integration be relaunched along new lines? Everyone realized that the political and military avenues were now closed. As for the ECSC, there was a growing awareness in many that it represented an auspicious beginning but that there was little hope of going much further along the same path, namely that of sectoral agreements. The customs union was the only path that remained open, and even then care had to be taken to avoid the pitfalls of all kinds that had arisen in the preceding years.

The Benelux countries did not have to be won over to the idea of a single European market. Notable trading countries with a high exposure to the world economy, exporting and importing about 50% of their national product, practising low tariffs and imposing no industrial import quotas, they were not bothered by any proposal for the complete dismantlement of tariffs and quantitative restrictions on imports of industrial goods. They had even made a move in that direction themselves: on May 20, 1955 they had put before their ECSC partners a plan that provided for the free movement of goods and services, capital and labour. The idea of institutions with supranational powers did not frighten them, although they were on their guard against a possible coalition of the big powers, notably of France and Germany, which might threaten their own trading interests. They sought to remove that danger, however, by means of a system whereby votes in the European institutions would be weighted in such a way as to give them a virtual right of veto.

The Italians took similar stances to those of the Benelux countries, although with many ulterior motives. The conditions of extreme poverty, even distress, in which much of the Italian population lived, especially in the Mezzogiorno [southern Italy], meant that their main concern would inevitably be to try to obtain, by various means, large amounts of financial aid from their partners.

The Germans, as far as economic philosophy went, were the natural allies of Benelux. The extensive reforms carried out by the US occupation authorities after the end of the war had made Germany a low-tariff country, with no quantitative restrictions on industrial imports and with a high foreign trade ratio. But the German delegates at

Messina were bound to extreme caution, and for two reasons. First, the Minister for the Economy Ludwig Erhard, liberalist though he was, was lukewarm, not to say negative, on the idea of a united Europe. He was a universalist, a fervent advocate of total freedom of trade on a world scale, who feared that a six-country Europe might become to some extent protectionist and thus constitute an obstacle to his grand design. The other factor that made the Germans wary of aligning themselves with the Benelux countries was the extreme importance they attached to their relations with France. Adenauer was in power, and in matters of foreign policy what counted most for him was the Franco-German rapprochement. I never saw the German delegations' negotiating instructions at that time, but I am sure that they were to the effect that at no time must the Germans get too far out of line with the French.

This meant that everything depended on us. With our agreement, anything could be done, including the creation of a European common market based on the principles of liberalism, open to the world economy and equipped with supranational institutions. Without us, all roads were barred. It is hardly surprising, then, that at Messina and during the negotiations that followed, right up to the signing of the Rome treaties, France was the country that largely set the tone of the proceedings. It also meant that, in the main, the issues raised by the creation of an economically united Europe had to be settled in Paris, in a series of clashes between the adherents of liberalism, of whom I was one, and those who, consciously or unconsciously, overtly or covertly, advocated a France closed to Europe and to the world. I was fortunate enough to have a certain amount of influence at that time, which I was able to bring to bear.

But I am getting too far ahead. What was the French stance at Messina? Antoine Pinay, who was France's representative, was well-disposed towards the European idea, but he was deeply bothered by what he knew of French feelings, those of the industrial and administrative elites, and those of the general public itself, on the issues under discussion. Let us be frank about it, in 1955–6 the vast majority of the French, that is the thinking French, were fundamentally opposed to any freedom of trade, even if geographically confined to Europe. I maintain now what I said in the articles and reports I wrote back in 1955: *France at that time was essentially protectionist*. Any move towards freedom of trade aroused a fear that was difficult to overcome. There had certainly been a slight shift in thinking: the French, like the other Europeans, were impressed by America. But this progress was taking place very slowly; three centuries of protection-ism weighed heavy in the balance. Had these circumstances not changed in 1956, the handful of men who believed in an economically united Europe would have had no chance of seeing their idea prevail.

Another factor which was very influential in France, and which dictated my attitude towards European institutions, was a skin-deep reaction on the part of most politicians and government officials to any form of supranationality. The origin of this reaction was the quarrel over the European Defence Community which had raged for nearly four years. The rejection of the EDC was, by extension, that of all supranational institutions.

As for the British, who were not at Messina and were observing things from the outside, their profound wish was that nothing should happen. They were not prepared to be part of a movement towards European unification, but wanted even less that the continental states agree on a formula that would lead to the formation of a bloc which would exclude them, as it were, from Europe. Macmillan, in 1958 or in 1959, denounced the Common Market as a new form of continental blockade.

The Americans, for their part, continued to support any form of European integration, even if their immediate trading interests were to suffer. Their diplomacy was active along these lines in all the European capitals.

French inhibitions and German reserve explain why, despite the drive and enthusiasm of the Benelux negotiators, the results of the Messina Conference were modest. The conference did not take any substantive decision. It entrusted to an independent committee of government representatives the task of studying a programme for the establishment of a European transport network, the development of exchanges of gas and electricity, a common organization to develop the peaceful use of atomic energy, and the progressive establishment of a common market free from customs duties and quantitative restric-tions. The same committee would also study the institutional arrange-ments, the idea of an extension of ECSC competence to other fields having been ruled out.

The future of six-country European unification thus remained uncertain. At the very most it can be said that the governments represented at Messina had gone on record as being favourably dis-posed towards the idea of extending European action to certain clearly defined sectors and of studying the possibility of a customs union, the French and the Germans emphasizing the sectoral aspect of future

European integration, the Beneluxers the customs union. However, the subsequent course of events was to show that Messina had been a decisive turning point in the process of Europe's creation, probably because the participants had decided implicitly to forgo overambitious ideas like those that had inspired the establishment of the ECSC and the project for the EDC.

The committee of independent government representatives, known as the Intergovernmental Committee, met in Brussels on July 9, 1955 at the Château de Val-Duchesse, which was actually a short way from the city. The chairman was Paul-Henri Spaak, the French representative was Félix Gaillard, former minister, deputy, a convinced 'European', who at one time in his life had been a collaborator of Jean Monnet. The members of the committee, who had been appointed by their respective governments, spoke only in their own names, however. That applied to everyone, but more especially to the Frenchman. This was to become apparent the following year, when the real negotiations began.

The fact remains that in the space of a few months, from July 1955 to April 1956, the committee did an excellent job. The report it produced was a treaty blueprint, both for the Common Market and for Euratom, many of its points being built into the two Rome treaties. Inevitably there were some gaps, notably as regards association of overseas territories, whilst certain chapters, such as that concerning agriculture, had to be heavily reworked. But it constituted an excellent basis for negotiation. Much of the credit is due to Pierre Uri, whose assistance Spaak had requested, particularly in the design of the future Common Market. A German high official, Hans von der Groeben, later to become a member of the EEC Commission, worked closely with Pierre Uri on this matter.

As for me, although I was not at Messina and did not participate in the work of the Intergovernmental Committee, I was thinking along exactly the same lines as the Committee, as was evidenced in the articles and reports I published at that time. I was therefore in perfect readiness to take an active part in the negotiations proper. When Christian Pineau asked me to do so in the spring of 1956, I accepted with alacrity. In the months that followed I was to work closely with Maurice Faure, *Secrétaire d'Etat* for foreign affairs, who led the French delegation. We both had the same ambition for France and for Europe, and our ideas were very similar. For one year we worked on the drafting of what was to become the Treaty of Rome in a climate of trust and friendship. The essential difficulty that had to be overcome was *the hostility of almost the whole of French public opinion* to the removal, even gradual, of the protection which French industry enjoyed – I should really say suffered from. As for French agriculture, arrangements had to be devised which would continue to protect it from the rest of the world but would still permit the expansion of intra-European trade.

In the pages that follow, I shall speak solely of the creation of the Common Market and say nothing about Euratom. The reason is that, from the outset of the negotiation process, I considered that the Common Market was the really important thing. I did not 'feel' Euratom, because in any case its importance seemed limited to me; the day when atomic energy would begin to be used on a significant scale was still far off (particularly in view of the very low price of oil at that time), and the problems of its civilian use were closely bound up with those of its military use, of which it was difficult even to speak.

The 'Battle of Paris'

The Spaak Committee handed in its report to governments on April 23, 1956. It was after that date that the real negotiating began. The ball was set rolling by the Foreign Ministers, who met in Venice on May 29 and 30, 1956. The negotiations continued for nearly a year, until the signing of the treaty on March 25, 1957.

It was in that spring of 1956 that France's reactions to the Spaak report made themselves known, that French officialdom and the leading representatives of industry and agriculture expressed their fears, their hostility towards the common market project. Up to that point no one had thought that a venture of this kind could even take shape on paper, let alone become fact. And suddenly here was a text which, of course, had not been formally accepted by anyone, but whose provisions to a large extent prefigured a possible European customs union. Above all, it became known that certain members of the government, and important ones at that – President of the Council Guy Mollet, Foreign Affairs Minister Christian Pineau – were favourably disposed. There was a small group of 'Europeans', namely Jean Monnet, myself and a few others, who were determined that Europe should get over the EDC failure. But the obstacles were enormous. Almost all of them were manifestations of the fear that had seized French business and especially government officialdom at the idea that the wall of protection, of all kinds, built up during the prewar, war and postwar years might one day come down and that French industry would then have to face foreign competition without customs duties, quotas or state subsidies. The very thought made the interested parties feel as helpless as Spartan babes on the mountainside.

As for me, I was delighted. Here at last was a task worth giving one's all to! A successful outcome would mean the start of an era of trading freedom from which France and Europe – the two were inseparable in my mind – would benefit. That it would be necessary to do battle on all fronts, in Brussels against our partners, who found it difficult to agree to certain of France's demands, in Paris against officialdom, which was almost unanimously opposed to the idea of the Common Market, and also against a number of industrial and agricultural lobbies that wanted special advantages, guarantees or additional protection, made the task even more stimulating. Never, since my entry into higher education twenty-five years earlier, did I work so hard. I felt as though I were in the centre of a web which would finally encompass the myriad subjects of negotiation and which, fortified by the trust placed in me by Guy Mollet and Christian Pineau, I was helping to weave strand by strand.

French officialdom was the first battlefront. Its stance was entirely negative. On April 24, 1956, the day after the Spaak report was handed in, a heads-of-department meeting chaired by Alexandre Verret, *chargé de mission* to the President of the Council, took place at which all the economic ministries were represented (Economic and Financial Affairs, Industry and Commerce, Agriculture, Transport, Social Affairs, Labour, Overseas Territories, etc.). It was at that meeting that I had my first opportunity, in a government service setting, to express my opinion on the project for a European economic community. It was positive, though guarded. I said that the Spaak report could serve as a basis for discussion, but that it would need amending here and there. My words met with an icy reception. Verret then asked all the officials present to state their views in turn. All were against, except Bernard Clappier, former *directeur de cabinet* of Robert Schuman and now director of External Economic Relations, who took the same position as myself.

The minutes of the meeting, which summarized its conclusions, admirably reflects the negative attitude of almost all the participants. The meeting, so the record states, produced the following findings: on the French side, none of the relevant ministries was involved in the phase of preparatory study[1]; the text circulated drew major criticisms from all the ministerial departments; further preliminary and, probably, lengthy studies would be desirable before any negotiations began.

It was decided at the meeting that a memorandum, defining new principles, would be drafted for the information of our partners. 'It is already considered,' the minutes read, 'that, on numerous points, these principles should be different from those that form the basis of the Spaak report, and even that they should be opposite.'

One important conclusion did emerge, however, from this long, apparently fruitless discussion: the offices of government were obliged to acknowledge that the ultimate goal of the government's policy was the creation of the Common Market, as Guy Mollet had stated a few months earlier in his inaugural declaration. It was suggested cautiously that the Spaak report might be used as a working document.

In May a 'Memorandum by the French Government' on the establishment of a Common Market was drafted and transmitted to our partners. The gist of this text was that France was not in a position to engage in competition on equal terms. Employers' social insurance contributions in French industry were much higher than in the other European countries. Before customs barriers were lowered, and possibly removed altogether, it was therefore necessary to equalize the conditions of competition. This, of course, would have to be done by levelling up; thus it was for France's partners to take measures that would have the effect of increasing their manufacturing costs. To which it should be added that, in the view of many government officials, equalization of social insurance costs was only a beginning, to be followed by equalization of wages and other production costs.

After extolling the benefits of competition, the French memorandum went on:

It is essential, however, that this competition should not be distorted by the series of disparities that are adversely affecting equality of the conditions of production. Thus, harmonization of national legislations should be pursued in conjunction with the reduction of tariff protection. In this regard ... the harmonization of social legislations is of particular importance. Indeed, not only have wage and social insurance costs a decisive effect on production costs, but the extension to all participating countries of the social improvements introduced by some of them will also make more apparent to the workers the link that must exist between the Common Market's establishment and higher standards of living.

Then the idea of planning on a European scale was introduced:

A policy of expansion ... implies investment which, in the basic industries, in the chemicals industry, in many of the processing industries, rests on a precise conception of the targets to be assigned to production over a period of several years. Convergence of the different national economic policies can therefore be ensured only by reconciling and harmonizing national production objectives.

The creation of a common market was inconceivable without the inclusion of agriculture; the special circumstances in which the latter operated would necessitate official intervention in this area.

The reduction of obstacles to trade in agricultural products should be accompanied by a progressive alignment of the regulations laid down in each of the countries, by the establishment of a common organization [of the market] that will be more efficient and less costly.

France's responsibilities in her overseas territories meant that she had special costs to bear.

Specific agreements should therefore be reached whereby the countries constituting the Common Market would participate in the financing of those costs, in consideration of an enlargement of overseas markets to their advantage, having regard to the nature of the political links that bind the overseas countries to metropolitan France.

In this memorandum France took a position in favour of a trial period of four years, after which it would be decided whether the game was worth the candle. During that period there would be a first round of tariff and quota cuts; at the same time a set of measures would be taken to harmonize conditions of production and social legislations in particular, and to initiate a common economic policy. At the end of the experimental phase, new intergovernmental agreements would determine the form and content of the subsequent stages.

The elimination of general price disparities through adjustment of exchange rates was rejected on the following grounds:

A lowering of the exchange rate means a lowering of the population's standard of living ... The reduction of disparities, whether they be general or specific, should, on the contrary, be sought in increasingly close harmonization of the individual costs that enter into the formation of production costs.

In the social field, France asked that during the first stage the following measures be taken: equalization of pay for men and women; standardization of the number of hours worked per week at basic pay rates and also of overtime rates; standardization of the length of paid holidays; application of a European standard of social security at the highest level. Since these arrangements would constitute only part of the measures necessary to eliminate the existing disparities, provision should be made for temporary compensation mechanisms to bridge the gap.

As regards the reduction of tariff differences, it would be necessary to take into account the cases of member countries which had not introduced import duties for certain products and to which goods from third countries had free access. In those cases the reductions of intra-community duties should be smaller. In the event of serious imbalances, the governments concerned should be able to make automatic use of appropriate safeguard clauses.

As of the first stage, close coordination of the economic policies followed by the different governments would have to be established. It would also be necessary to accelerate the process of harmonization of fiscal and social legislations and regulations. This harmonization should itself be designed in such a way as progressively to increase the share of national income allocated to wages.

Increasing freedom of movement for workers could not be obtained by means of rigid rules and automatic procedures. The measures taken to increase workers' freedom of movement should not go counter to the efforts made by each government to reduce or eliminate such structural unemployment as might remain.

As to movements of capital, it would be for each government to define measures which would make it possible gradually to increase freedom of movement for capital within the Common Market.

The list of French demands and reservations was endless. The negotiation of the Rome treaty would be concerned with getting the largest possible number dropped and retaining only those demands that were consistent with the spirit of the Common Market, such as the extension of the customs union to agricultural products and the association of overseas countries and territories. On the other hand, the equalization or harmonization (the latter a term which no one was ever able to define) of the conditions of competition, as a prerequisite for the removal of customs barriers, seemed to me, from the outset of the discussions, an absurd demand. Countries with welfare legislations, social insurance costs, and production costs in general that are different can very well enter into a customs union. If, overall, one of those countries has higher production costs than the others, the balance should be redressed by an exchange-rate adjustment backed up, for a time, by a policy of economic stringency. That is what General de Gaulle did in 1958 and what enabled France to enter the Common Market without problems.

But fallacies die hard, especially when they are presented under a veneer of good sense. For an example I need look no further than the speech made by Pierre Mendès France in the National Assembly on January 18, 1957 in the course of a preliminary debate on the Common Market when the drafting of the Treaty of Rome, in its essentials, was almost complete. This exceptionally intelligent man, who was so often right, but was often wrong too, was singularly misguided in the attitude he took that day with regard to the ongoing negotiations, one which he was to confirm six months later by voting *against* the Treaty's ratification.

Freedom of movement for manpower was the first to come under attack, Pierre Mendès France fearing that the Italians would export their unemployment. At that time, of course, Italy was suffering from large-scale unemployment and underemployment. In the event of an economic crisis, he maintained, emigration of Italian workers to France would be compounded by that of the German unemployed, who were traditionally more mobile than their French counterparts. On the other hand, in periods of buoyant economic activity, we would have to contend with formidable competition in the Common Market. Certain of our industries might be unable to adjust or would adjust badly. The result would be unemployment in various sectors of our underdeveloped regions. The populations of those regions might then be driven to emigrate, or else have to accept a very low standard of living *in situ*. Attracted by higher living standards, the Italians would flock into France and, in certain circumstances at any rate, the French into the Ruhr. An apocalyptic vision.

The conclusion which Pierre Mendès France reached on this issue was that the treaty should give us guarantees against risks of this kind. We had to retain the right to limit immigration into France, especially when economic conditions made this necessary, and obtain safeguards against the risk of imported unemployment. The underscoring of this eventuality was above all intended to influence the trade unions, whose first concern, naturally enough, was the maintenance of full employment.

Another set of arguments, to which I have already referred earlier, emphasized the state of economic inferiority in which France allegedly found herself. France was severely handicapped in international competition; she had to bear costs which the others did not have to, at least in the same proportion: defence costs, welfare costs, and outgoings due to France's presence in Algeria and in the overseas countries and territories.

As to the matter of welfare costs, the only guarantees we had obtained, said Pierre Mendès France, concerned equal pay for men and women, on the one hand, and the special rate for overtime, on the other. And even the second of these guarantees might prove insecure. But above all, no other general extension of social advantages was really being organized or had even been guaranteed. Yet a number of these social advantages had a far from negligible impact on productivity and production costs, two such being family allowances and wages for youth. The situation of the latter was probably much more satisfactory in France than in the other countries. Pierre Mendès France's conclusion on this issue was categorical: the French thesis to which we must hold fast, he stressed, was equalization of social insurance costs and rapid generalization of social advantages within all the countries of the Common Market. 'Standardization, equalization of costs must be effected, it must be general and it must in all cases be done by upward adjustment of the lower levels.'

Equalization not only of social insurance costs, which were payable in addition to wages, but also of wages themselves. Our experts had shown, said Pierre Mendès France, that wages proper in Holland, Italy and even in Germany were generally lower than ours. Moreover, in addition to the inequalities as regards social insurance costs and wages, there were inequalities of taxation: the rate of turnover tax was approximately twice as high in France as in the other European countries. The truth, Pierre Mendès France went on, was that our partners wanted to retain the trading advantage they held over us as a result of their 'backwardness' in social matters. Our policy must consist, no matter what, in ensuring that Europe would not be constructed in retrograde social conditions, to the detriment of the working class and, indirectly, to that of the other social classes whose livelihood depended on the purchasing power of the workers.

This assertion that production costs were considerably higher in France than in the other countries of the future Common Market, and that these costs should be harmonized before the single market was created, was to weigh very heavy in the discussions that took place during 1956. The trade unions and employers' associations were very much swayed by it; and it even became the official position of the

French government for a while. We, along with a few associates, had a great deal of difficulty in combating the argument, wholly specious though it was. Insofar as the figures put forward were correct – and in many cases they turned out to be wrong – comparison between the different countries demanded an exchange-rate weighting. And all the economists (except the few for whom their dogma, whatever it might be, mattered more than the truth) knew that the franc was overvalued. The existence, at the time, of special import taxes, additional to ordinary customs duties, and of export subsidies was proof enough.

Pierre Mendès France was too good an economist not to know this. He was aware of a French protocol of agreement which I had negotiated in Brussels, and which permitted France to retain its import surcharges and export subsidies. But, for him, this concession from our partners was not sufficient. In the first place, if we were to acquire in this way the right to retain special taxes and subsidies in specific circumstances, we would not be able to increase them subsequently. What would happen if the differential between French and foreign prices were to widen? In consideration of this eventuality, and of what he regarded as the precarious character of the French protocol, Mendès France suggested a situation in which a franc devaluation would be forced on us from outside. 'Then, devaluation would no longer be a sovereign national decision; it would be imposed on us from outside, as though to curb our social initiatives, judged to be too generous.' More generally, the most advanced countries, in matters of social welfare, would find themselves prohibited, at any rate temporarily, from making further progress.

It was strictly a clever speech, designed to influence all the socioeconomic categories by making them fear that the advantages they had gained would be brought into question. Furthermore, it played up the nationalist angle for all it was worth in order to mobilize the powerful emotions that surface, both on the right and on the left, whenever there is mention of a possible encroachment on national sovereignty:

Is not any increase in wages or any award of new social advantages consequently, and for a long time, precluded for French workers?

Dear colleagues, I have often had occasion to recommend more stringency in our economic management. But I am not resigned, I must own, to letting the judge of such things be a European areopagus in which reigns a spirit that is far removed from ours.

On this point, I caution the government: we cannot allow ourselves to be stripped of our freedom of decision in matters that so closely concern our conception of progress and social justice; the consequences may be too grave from both the social and the political standpoints.

The speech went on at length, setting out all the possible objections to the Common Market, mentioning all the risks, real and imagined, that it would entail for France. The speaker would have liked France to be able, after an initial period of six years, a trial period, to pull out completely and come back to square one. But the draft treaty did not provide for any such arrangement. 'Even if the experience of the first six years proves to have been damaging for us,' Pierre Mendès France stated, 'we shall be unable to withdraw.' I shall return to this point later, but the idea of a trial period, attractive to someone not in the know, represented a major difficulty that took a great deal of ingenuity to overcome.

The objections kept on piling up. As regards the Community's trade relations with the rest of the world, the common external tariff, being the arithmetic mean of the different countries' tariffs, would be lower than the French tariff, which, with the Italian tariff, was the highest among those of the Six. Furthermore, this external tariff, already very low, could be suspended entirely for certain products by a simple majority decision. Where quotas were concerned, Germany and Belgium were already admitting quota-free imports from dollar-area countries and from a number of other countries; there was a serious risk that, as a result of rapid quota enlargement among the Six, goods from third countries would flood our market.

As for the free movement of capital, this would lead, if conditions were not harmonized, to a mass outflow of French capital. The result would be a fall in business fixed investment, losses of French output potential, and higher unemployment. The risk would be all the greater for France in that among the countries of the future Common Market she was in the vanguard of social progress.

Capital has a tendency to leave the socializing countries and its leaving brings pressure to bear for the abandonment of an advanced social policy ... But it is not only French capital that is liable to escape ... Foreign capital, such as that of international institutions or that of the United States, is also liable to flow into Germany, Italy or Benelux ... The danger of seeing the French economy decline in relation to the economies of the neighbouring countries will therefore be very real.

The conditions in which merchandise and capital movements would develop were bound to have easily foreseeable consequences for our balance of payments, whose deficit was liable to become permanent.

True, the treaty had a safeguard clause, but its use was superintended by the community institutions.

It will be a law above French law that will be imposed on us. The majority will be able to force on us devaluations that will result in lower standards of living or in deflationary measures of which we shall not have been the judge ourselves.

Concerning the European investment fund proposed in the Spaak report, Pierre Mendès France revealed his fundamental thinking, which was essentially compounded of *dirigisme* and *planisme*. The notion of a free market was totally absent from it:

This is what I already proposed in 1945. I believe that all reconstruction of Europe, all postwar European development should have been conceived in terms of European investment coordinated according to plans of common interest, so as to avoid duplication, excessive or superfluous investment, ruinous competition and also common shortages.

The common market project as presented to us or, at any rate, such of it as is presented to us, is based on the classical liberalism of the 19th century, which holds that competition pure and simple resolves all problems.

In conclusion, Pierre Mendès France all but said that a successful outcome for the negotiations, in the conditions that could be foreseen as at the beginning of 1957, would be tantamount to a surrender of democracy:

The abdication of a democracy can take one of two forms, either the recourse to an internal dictatorship by handing over all powers to a man of the moment, or the delegation of those powers to an external authority which, in the name of technical efficiency, will in fact wield the political power.

This is how Pierre Mendès France expressed himself on January 18, 1957. In the ratification debate on July 6 of the same year he gave utterance to an idea that probably constituted the essence of his attitude: 'To decide to enter the Common Market shortly is to subscribe to German hegemony.'

I have analysed in some detail the position of Pierre Mendès France because it expressed, cumulatively, the objections to the Common Market that were to be found in the government service, in different political groups, and in certain sectors of economic and social life as represented by farmers, industrial employers and trade unionists. He gave those objections a systematic form that probably disserved his cause, recognizing politically no merit in the project of European integration, seeing in it only perils, which he magnified inordinately, moreover. Yet some of his arguments impinged on the relatively small segment of public opinion that was following the course of the negotiations.

I knew Pierre Mendès France well and had a great respect for him. His courageous conduct during the war, his clear-sightedness regarding French policy in Indochina, his role in 1954 in the provisional settlement of the war that had been going on there for eight years, his efforts to hasten the decolonization process, these have earned him an exceptional place in the history of France under the Fourth Republic. What perhaps prevented him from holding an even greater place was his systematism, his unyielding attachment to government economic intervention and planning, a conception of economic affairs that revolved around the domestic economy, at a time when national frontiers were bursting wide open and an international economy of unprecedented power was starting to form.

Admittedly, the French economy's integration into this international economy, where market forces reigned for the most part, was not without its dangers. Pierre Mendès France had perceived them, even if to the real dangers he had added many that were imagined. What he had failed to see was not only the advantages that France could derive from maximum participation in the new international economy, but above all the danger for France, greater than any other, of withdrawing into herself at a time when all the developed countries, including France's five European partners, were opening wide their economies to the rest of the world.

This is what many people felt instinctively. I noticed it in the numerous discussions I had at that time, notably with the representatives of industry and agriculture. For it was part of my job to establish close contacts with the different categories of management and labour, whose opinions were to be decisive in the public debate that took place from mid-1956 to mid-1957.

I undertook to answer the objections and dispel the doubts, while endeavouring at the same time to find solutions to the real problems. Thus, the trade unions (except for the CGT, whose position was as always tied to that of the Communist party) never took seriously the apocalyptic image of a mass invasion of France by Italian manpower and of equally large-scale emigration by the French to the Ruhr. On the other hand, they were sensitive to the argument that since France was in the vanguard of social progress (which was doubtful, even at that time), the French working class risked losing in the integration process some of the advantages it had gained in 1936 or since the end of the war. Something had to be done to reassure them. By and large the non-communist unions, which numbered many convinced 'Europeans' among their members, did not create any major difficulties for the negotiators.

As for the employers, accustomed to living in the hothouse atmosphere of an economy that was virtually sealed off, the great majority of them dreaded the thought of sudden exposure to the outside world. The idea of a German industrial hegemony haunted them. Overestimating the threat from Germany, Italy or Benelux, they were acutely aware of the weaknesses of French industry and unaware of its strengths. To convince them to support the project of European integration that was taking shape, I pointed out to them that probably the main reason for France's low standing in international trade was too high an exchange rate, which was hampering exports and stimulating imports. If a government ever had the courage to devalue and apply simultaneously a tight economic policy that would contain domestic demand, a great many of French industry's difficulties would vanish overnight. For the time being, however, something tangible was needed to reassure the French industrial class. This was a key factor in the Brussels negotiations.

The problem was different with the farmers. It was with their organizations – the cooperatives, the wheat and other commodity producers, the farmers' boards – that I had the lengthiest discussions and, for a while at least, the most difficult. At the outset, they insisted that European agriculture should have preference on the European market over the agricultures of other parts of the world. Now, the word 'preference' was anathema to the Beneluxers and, above all, to the Germans. That Europe needed special protection in this sector was something that everyone recognized; all the European countries had their own systems of protection. Essentially it was a matter of semantics. Even so, a solution had to be found. The search lasted several months. However, discussion was facilitated by the fact that the French agricultural organizations realized the absolute necessity of finding export markets. I recall with some feeling my long discussions with their representatives, most of them, unfortunately, now gone. I made a number of firm friendships here.

One issue that was raised from the outset of negotiation, but did not take on acute proportions until near the end, was the association of the overseas countries, which at the time were still French colonies. France, it was said, could not commit herself to a European common market if she alone continued to bear the costs of an empire. Our partners would certainly have preferred the issue not to be brought up, but once it had been they perceived the benefits, in the form of new trading outlets, which they might derive from an association of overseas France with the Common Market. A deal was possible, but its content had to be defined. The matter was settled finally at a meeting of the Six held in Paris at the beginning of 1957. Guy Mollet was in the chair and Adenauer was one of the participants. I was sitting next to Christian Pineau. The talk was getting nowhere and I began to inundate my neighbour with scribbled notes for suggested solutions. Finally, Pineau, a little out of patience, said to me: 'Marjolin, you're doing an awful lot of writing. Let's just let the discussion take its course, it'll work out.' He was right: the meeting was concluded in the evening after several hours of discussions. The two main speakers, Guy Mollet and Adenauer, wanted to wrap it up.

A more delicate issue, but one on which everyone finally reached agreement, once the ambiguities and hidden fears had been dispelled, was the matter of institutions. From the outset the Six wanted to avoid the pitfalls that had destroyed the projected EDC. It was essential to give the new treaty a purely economic character, ignoring the grand principles and political goals which in the years from 1950 to 1954 had fired the enthusiasm of the 'Europeans', but which in 1956 were arousing hostile reactions in large segments of public opinion. Consequently, there was no question of making the Common Market treaty an extension of the Treaty of Paris, which had established the ECSC. The term 'High Authority' was dropped without argument. The institutions would be the same as those of the ECSC, but the relative powers of each would be modified. As to the notion of 'supranationality', nowhere did it appear in the documents drafted during the negotiations; no one so much as mentioned the word. That did not mean that all the institutional questions had been settled. Some were kept open and resolved during the negotiations. Others remained in the background and were not settled until after the Common Market had been set up and at the time of the great crisis of 1965–6.

One major difficulty was not resolved until the negotiations were in their final phase. It had to do with the nature of the commitment the Six would undertake in setting up the Common Market. Would the stage-by-stage establishment of the latter represent an irreversible process, a movement which, once begun, would inevitably have to be carried through to its conclusion, or would it be possible to stop it *en route* if the results turned out to be different from those expected? Could one or more countries pull out, say, after a trial period of a few years? That was the type of arrangement towards which the French government leaned for several months, whereas our partners, especially Benelux and Germany, insisted on irreversibility.

The negotiations

The negotiation of what was to become the Treaty of Rome can be divided into two broad phases. The first of these was a period in which the partners were feeling their way and France's hesitations were preventing any decisive progress from being made; it lasted roughly until August–September 1956. The nationalization of the Suez Canal on July 26, 1956, followed by the ill-fated Anglo-French expedition in November of the same year, marked the end of that phase. From that moment on, things moved forward rapidly. Guy Mollet, who had long been wedded to the idea of European integration, but who had hesitated to defy the hostility of most of his ministers, virtually the whole of the central civil service and large segments of public opinion, felt that the only way to erase, or at least lessen, the humiliation that France had just suffered from the Suez affair was to conclude a European treaty quickly. He brought all his influence to bear and was able to tip the scales in the right direction.

I remember a series of interministerial committee meetings in Paris to settle certain difficult problems that had arisen in the course of negotiations. I had come back from Brussels especially in order to take part. We found ourselves, Christian Pineau, Maurice Faure and I, confronted with a majority of ministers opposed to a continuation of the talks. After hearing the views on both sides, Guy Mollet ruled in our favour, saying in substance: 'We are therefore agreed to ask our negotiators to continue the discussions and bring them to a successful outcome as rapidly as possible.' This conclusion was plainly at variance with the general sentiment of the ministers present, but no one ever dared contradict the President of the Council – though they might send him the next day a letter containing the objections he had not taken into account the day before, a letter which, incidentally, he would ignore completely.

One man played a very important role in the battle waged in that summer of 1956 between the proponents and opponents of the Common Market. This was Emile Noël, then the *chef de cabinet* of Guy Mollet and much heeded by him. A 'European' from the start, ardent in his convictions beneath an affable and tolerant exterior, clear-sighted and keen, he helped, often decisively, to get the President of the Council to take the decisions that enabled the Brussels negotiators to carry out their task effectively. After the Treaty of Rome had been signed, I succeeded in having him appointed executive secretary of the EEC Commission; he later became its Secretary General. For twenty-five years he has been the pillar on which the Brussels administration rests. Time and again, his personal influence, which grew rapidly with the years, enabled the Commission to avoid grave errors. We have been friends since the inception of the EEC; during the time I was in Brussels and afterwards, I sought his advice whenever I found myself up against a difficult problem, and not once have I had occasion to regret taking it.

When a major disagreement arose in Verret's committee between myself and the opponents of the Common Market, Verret would refer it to the President of the Council, requesting his arbitration. The request would come to Emile Noël, who would draft Guy Mollet's reply. It was invariably favourable to the arguments of the Brussels negotiators. After a while, the senior government officials who had expressed reservations and objections grew tired and, with heavy hearts, let events run their course.

For a time, the situation was complicated by divisions between 'Europeans'. Many of them were distinctly unenthusiastic about the Common Market. Jean Monnet and his Action Committee for the United States of Europe were passionately keen on the Euratom project, in which they saw the future of Europe. They feared that by working simultaneously towards the establishment of both Euratom and the Common Market one would be overloading the boat and that the whole lot would founder. Pascal Fontaine, who was a close collaborator of Jean Monnet in the last years of the latter's life, wrote of this untoward development in a book about the Action Committee for the United States of Europe published in 1974[1]. Noting that for a time, during the negotiation of the Rome Treaty and afterwards, the Action Committee hardly mentioned the Common Market, Fontaine wondered why:

What was the reason for this omission? Could it have been a miscalculation on the part of Jean Monnet and the members of the Committee? In fact, it was a deliberate choice and a gamble. To choose the domain of atomic energy, to propose a supranational community, this was inherently consistent with the principles and the method that had brought the ECSC into being: namely, the delegation of sovereignty in a circumscribed but decisive area. A new, specialized community would do more for European construction than the scheme, too vague and too general, for economic unification. Jean Monnet was not unaware that this economic Community was receiving as much attention from the experts and politicians as the atomic Community. The conclusion of the Spaak Committee's report was that two treaties were necessary. Did Jean Monnet think that only the Euratom treaty would be fortunate enough to see the light of day, being more realistic, more limited in its scope and in the sacrifices it would impose on the signatory states? Be that as it may, there is no doubt that he visualized the atomic Community the more clearly of the two, the economic union being only a hazy image in his mind.

Furthermore, it seemed to him more effective to concentrate the Committee's efforts on one goal, and here he had the members' agreement. The gamble was lost, as we know, for the future of Euratom would soon be compromised both by France's nuclear policy and by the massive exploitation of oil deposits.

At some point in 1956, Jean Monnet had managed to convince the French government that preference should be given to Euratom and that the Common Market negotiations should be postponed until better days. Approaches were made to Adenauer, but he, after some hesitation, came out against any separation in the timing of the two treaties. The Germans, on the contrary, set up a firm link, a *Junktim*, between the two sets of negotiations. The progress made in Brussels in the drafting of the Common Market treaty disposed of the matter. I should add that, after this initial vacillation, Jean Monnet and his Committee actively supported the development of the Common Market in the years that followed.

The negotiations in Brussels went ahead briskly. The French team I had chosen, which was composed of officials wholeheartedly in favour of the Common Market, worked from start to finish in perfect accord. Real ties of friendship, born of everyone's devotion to the common cause, were formed among the team's members. I owe a great debt of gratitude to a high official now no longer alive, Jacques Donnedieu de Vabres. His great intelligence, his extensive legal knowledge and his tireless energy contributed much to the success of the enterprise. The team also included Jean-François Deniau, who played an active part in the negotiations and later became, at a very young age for such a post, director, then director general in the services of the Commission, before going on to a brilliant political career in France. Finally, I cannot omit to mention Pierre Uri, who was not part of the French delegation but who, as Spaak's right-hand man, used his constructive imagination to great effect in the negotiations, on many occasions proposing solutions that enabled the difficulty of the moment to be overcome.

I said earlier that all the countries taking part in the negotiation were behind the Common Market project, *except France*. The problem was therefore to come up with answers to the sensitive issues that would reassure the French without unduly disquieting the other partners. As of a certain moment, a real complicity developed in Brussels between the French delegation and the others in the search for those answers. I can remember certain dinners at which we French, Belgians, Dutch and Germans would tell one another frankly what was acceptable to each of us. I think it was at one of those dinners that, during a conversation with Robert Rothschild and Etienne Davignon, who both held high posts in the Belgian government service, I suggested the drafting of a special text that would help to allay French fears. That was the origin of the 'Protocol relating to certain provisions of concern to France', which was annexed to the Treaty.

This protocol allowed France to retain, during such time as the French balance of payments remained in deficit, her special system of export aids and import surcharges. France was thus spared the need to devalue her currency, at least for a time. The financial and monetary reforms carried out by General de Gaulle in 1958 were to make this provision redundant. The same protocol contained provisions concerning overtime pay, while somewhere in the body of the treaty there was a provision for gradual equalization of pay for men and women. The French, who were convinced that their social legislation was much in advance of that of the other countries, found some satisfaction on these two points, which made them forget the rest of their demands in this area. If I remember rightly, investigations by the Commission during the years that followed showed that the French fears were unfounded, either because the social inequalities mentioned did not exist, or because, in those cases where they did, they were offset by other inequalities in France's favour.

The notion of the Common Market postulates free movement of factors of production, including capital. The treaty ought therefore to have provided for the derestriction of capital movements, as it did for that of manpower movements. But France was deeply attached, then as now, to the practice of exchange control. To introduce freedom of capital movements would, it was thought, be playing into the hands of the speculators, who would take advantage of it to attack the franc. The Minister of Economic and Financial Affairs, Paul Ramadier, sent memo after memo to Guy Mollet to put him on his guard against what he, Ramadier, regarded as a surrender to Mammon. A formula therefore had to be found that would take French fears into account. Finally it was decided to say in the treaty that member states would progressively eliminate, during the transition period and to the degree necesary to ensure the proper functioning of the Common Market, restrictions on capital movements among themselves. The matter of defining the degree of liberalization necessary to the proper functioning of the Common Market was put off until later, each being free to choose his own interpretation. Needless to say, France's interpretation would be more restrictive than that of Benelux and Germany.

Thanks to Adenauer, the problem of association of the overseas countries was settled quite easily. The solution adopted guaranteed that those countries' products would have free access to the Community. As regards exports from Europe, the member countries of the Common Market were placed on an equal footing, the overseas countries being able to go on protecting their nascent industries to a degree. Furthermore, the Common Market countries undertook to contribute to the investment necessary to the progressive development of the overseas countries. It was a simple solution, which continued to be applied when the overseas countries acceded to independence shortly afterwards. France, though she was progressively to lose the preference she enjoyed in her colonies, ultimately came out ahead. She was obliged to seek out other markets, where she would face international competition, and thus to become competitive.

The agricultural problem was more difficult to resolve. A lot of effort had to be expended for several years after the signing of the Treaty in order to frame the common agricultural policy, but the foundations of it had been laid in the Treaty. I have said that the French wanted community agriculture to enjoy a tariff preference, to which a number of our partners, notably the Germans, were opposed for doctrinal reasons. This opposition was all the less justified in that Germany's agriculture, like that of every other member country, was highly protected. All that was needed was to combine each country's protective measures into a community protection, while at the same time establishing free movement of farm goods within the Community, and the common agricultural policy could see the light of day.

But a way had to be found around the obstacle represented by the word 'preference'. I believed I had found it with the idea that in a common market where the industrial products of the various member countries circulated freely, and naturally at much the same prices, it was unthinkable that governments, or official agricultural bodies, should pay different prices to the producers of farm goods according to their nationality. I said as much in a note to French government department heads, dated December 21, 1956:

The objective to be achieved is a situation in which the national authorities have ceased to discriminate between their own producers and those of the other countries of the Community and in which they offer to pay the other countries' producers the same prices as they pay their own producers.

The notion of 'preference' would thus be replaced by that of 'non-discrimination'; in each country there would be only one system of prices, regardless of product origin. I put forward my proposal in Brussels at the end of 1956. In it I accordingly suggested that the idea of a European preference be dropped and that henceforth one should speak of non-discrimination. I no longer requested preferential treatment for French farm goods, on entry into Germany, for example, but I maintained that it was inherent in the logic of the Common Market that French products in Germany should receive the same treatment from the German authorities as German products, the same principle holding good for the other countries of the Community.

This proposal caused quite a stir. It was easy to reject the notion of 'preference', which was part of the language of protectionism. It was impossible not to accept that of 'non-discrimination', which had a free-market connotation. And yet, given the systems of agricultural protection in force in the different countries that were to form the Community, the end result was practically the same. But such is the power of words! It was decided, therefore, that the treaty would provide for a common organization of agricultural markets. Thus a path had been opened up that was to lead, during the sixties, to a series of community regulations establishing systems of market organization for the different products and stipulating the way in which the interventions would be financed. Before the final outcome was achieved, however, an enormous amount of effort had to be expended by the Commission and by the French government in order to find effective and equitable solutions. I shall have more to say about this later.

The Common Agricultural Policy got a bad press outside the Community and sometimes inside. It was accused of being protectionist, of shielding a farming system that was not as efficient as those of countries overseas. That is true. The Common Agricultural Policy is protectionist. But is there one European country that does not protect its agriculture? And do not the Americans protect theirs in other ways? Far be it from me to say that this policy is unchangeable; extensive reforms are undoubtedly needed, but some degree of protection will persist for an indefinite period. Another argument that seems decisive to me is the following: the only way to have avoided a common agricultural policy, providing for protection from the rest of the world, would have been not to include agriculture in the Common Market. But France would never have accepted a customs union that did not include agriculture and did not guarantee French producers protection comparable to that which they were receiving under French law. Without a common agricultural policy there would never have been a Common Market.

The special interest of the farmers weighed heavy in the balance. Moreover, the French government and its services were convinced that the Common Market would primarily benefit German industry, would add still further to its might, which already seemed awesome. The only way to redress the balance was to allow French farmers to export to Germany, where they would be on an equal footing with German farmers. The Germans were ready to accept the French demands. Their agriculture, although limited in scale, had a high protective wall around it. It was difficult for them to refuse, in the name of principles, comparable protection for European agriculture as a whole. Chancellor Adenauer's will to integrate Germany into a European community, thus erasing, as far as was humanly possible, the tragic memories of a war not long past, and in particular his determination to set the seal on Franco-German reconciliation, took care of the rest.

The question of the Community's institutions did not present the difficulties that had been feared, or rather the difficulties were put off until later. The negotiators were able to avoid notions like 'supranationality', or pretentious designations like 'High Authority'. Care had to be taken not to produce unfortunate reminders of the EDC. They had the wisdom to define concretely and simply the respective powers of the Commission and the Council of Ministers, in such a way as not to arouse the hostility of all those who in 1950–4 had opposed the first efforts to construct Europe.

The Council of Ministers is the decision-taking body. The Commission makes proposals; it has, as it were, the monopoly of proposal-making. Its proposals cannot be amended by the Council of Ministers other than by unanimous decision. These provisions, seemingly modest as regards the powers of the Commission, in fact give the latter great weight. In a way, it calls the tune; nothing can be done without it, insofar as the treaty's implementation is involved. The situation becomes different, of course, when it is a question of venturing into areas not covered by the treaty. But that eventuality did not materialize until much later, when the treaty had to all intents and purposes been implemented.

In fact, the Commission proved to be much more powerful or, if one prefers, much more effective in solving the problems that arose at the European level than the High Authority of the ECSC, at least during the first ten years of the European Economic Community's existence. There were two reasons for this. The first was that the EEC was much broader in its scope than the ECSC. Second, it was only logical that when formulating proposals concerning the customs union or the common agricultural policy, the Commission should add general economic policy recommendations that stood a good chance of being accepted because their implementation was necessary to that of the treaty. This situation would last for ten years or so. Things did not really begin to go wrong until the early seventies.

To conclude on the subject of the Commission's powers, I would simply add that, apart from its power of initiative, it is responsible for enforcing the decisions taken by the Council. It is also the treaty's custodian, responsible for seeing that the treaty itself and the decisions taken by the Council for its application are observed by the member states and by their citizens. In the event of an infringement, its duty is to try to redress the situation by seeking voluntary termination of the infringement and, if this fails, to refer the matter to the Court of Justice. Finally, in certain limited areas, it has the power to issue a formal decision itself.

I can say that I experienced no difficulty in Paris on the question of institutions. The provisions I have just described were consonant with the spirit of caution that prevailed there at the time. After the rejection of the EDC no one wanted a repetition of that unfortunate affair. Benelux did not insist on introducing into the treaty the elements of supranationality to which it said it was very attached; there, too, caution triumphed. The Germans supported the French whenever this was necessary; their greatest desire, as I have already said, was to find themselves, in so great an enterprise, on an equal footing with their ex-enemies.

The Parliamentary Assembly being without any powers, the sole element of supranationality introduced was the ability of the Council of Ministers to take decisions on a qualified [i.e. weighted] majority basis. Even so, majority decisions on important issues were not provided for until the third stage of the treaty's implementation, i.e. as of 1966. Curiously enough, few at that time, at any rate as far as I remember, were sufficiently worried about this eventuality to make a stand against clauses that would one day enable the majority to impose its law, with the risk that France might be in the minority. Not until eight years later did General de Gaulle bring pressure to bear so that the provisions for majority voting would become a dead letter.

There remained one last issue to be settled, that of the reversible or irreversible character of the Common Market. As I have already said, France wanted to be able to pull out after a trial period of some four years if results fell short of her expectations, notably in the event of failure to carry out the harmonization of social and fiscal regulations which she considered essential to the establishment of fair conditions of competition. On this basis, all that would be prescribed at the outset would be a programme of action for those four years, the rest to be negotiated subsequently. Such an eventuality was unacceptable to our partners, to the United States and other third countries, and of course to the GATT, which authorizes customs unions only when there is certainty that the process of dismantling tariffs and other barriers to trade will be carried to completion; otherwise, a customs union constitutes a preferential system, which is formally condemned.

In the autumn of 1956 I drafted a memorandum in which I stressed that if, at the end of the trial period, no agreement had been reached on how to continue the enterprise, the Community would find itself in a crisis. The Six would then be forced to choose between undoing all that had been done since the establishment of the Common Market and extending the tariff reductions already implemented to all the third countries to which they were bound by treaties containing the 'most favoured nation clause'. These two eventualities being equally unacceptable for various reasons, I said that our partners would probably refuse to agree to a trial period. They would insist that all the stages that were to lead to a complete customs union should be spelled out in the treaty. They might just possibly accept a clause permitting France, and France alone, to withdraw from the Community after a certain time, but they themselves would insist on entering into an irreversible process. When the time was up, if France decided not to go ahead, she would find herself completely isolated. But even now, as the treaty was being drawn up, she would be seen as a country unsure of herself, which refused obligations that the other countries were ready to accept, whereas up till now she had been the spearhead of the movement towards European unification.

An interministerial committee convened on September 4, 1956. As I suspected, the French government rejected the idea of an arrangement that would have given France a special status, distinct from that of the other countries. It accepted a compromise which I had drafted in the form of a treaty clause before the meeting, and which stated that the move to the second stage, at the beginning of 1962, would not take place unless the Council found that the obligations prescribed for the first stage had been fulfilled by all; it was not stated what those obligations might be. All this was virtually self-evident and I knew that such a clause would not create serious difficulties in Brussels. In the event, it was less imprecise than it looked at first sight. The first stage would comprise customs duty reductions, at specified dates and in very precisely defined proportions, and steps towards a common external tariff. But it also provided for an effort to construct a common agricultural policy, and here no one knew, in 1956, how much ground would have been covered by 1961.

With all the difficulties settled, the treaty establishing the European Economic Community was able to be signed in Rome on March 25, 1957, at the same time as the treaty establishing Euratom.

I do not believe it is an exaggeration to say that this date represents one of the great moments of Europe's history. Who would have thought during the thirties, and even during the ten years that followed the war, that European states which had been tearing one another apart for so many centuries and some of which, like France and Italy, still had very closed economies, would form a common market intended eventually to become an economic area that could be likened to one great domestic market?

As will be seen clearly later on, France, which of all the Common Market countries was the one that most feared this exposure to the outside world, was the one that ultimately derived the greatest benefit. The straitjacket of protectionism was suddenly removed. There may be some question of whether Germany and Benelux really needed the Common Market in order to expand their production capacity as they did; their development might not have been all that different without the Treaty of Rome, given their low tariff levels and the Americans' wish for a worldwide reduction of customs duties. But the evolution of the French economy would certainly have been very different and less favourable, without it being possible to say what course things would finally have taken.

5

THE HONEYMOON
(1958–1962)

The Treaty of Rome formally came into effect on January 1, 1958. In the weeks that followed, the Community administration began to be set up. Representatives of the governments of member states met in Paris on January 6 and 7, 1958 to designate the members of the EEC Commission; Walter Hallstein was appointed President, Sicco Mansholt, Piero Malvestiti and myself Vice-Presidents. During the next few weeks, the Commission organized itself and its members were assigned their areas of responsibility. As I had hoped, I was put in charge of economic and financial affairs, as well as energy problems and, in collaboration with Jean Rey, trade policy questions. We set up shop temporarily in a building rented from the Belgian government, in the Rue Belliard in Brussels, before moving to our permanent headquarters in the Avenue de la Joyeuse-Entrée.

Dottie and the children had moved with me to Brussels at the beginning of 1958. We were able to find very comfortable accommodation in a large duplex apartment in the Avenue Jules César, in what was called the 'Quartier de l'Europe'. Thus began for me a new existence that was to last ten years and to bring me all the satisfactions that one could want from a creative activity. I had the feeling that I was building something and helping to shift the course of Europe in the direction I had always hoped for, towards greater unity in a context of freedom. The changes that were taking place in Paris gave me particular pleasure; at last France was emerging from the era of protectionism in which, for more than fifty years, she had vainly sought a solution to her problems and had slowly languished.

The Treaty's execution

The Common Market was almost entirely built during those ten years from 1958 to 1967. This period can be divided into two parts. The first, from 1958 to 1962, was the honeymoon, a time of harmony between the governments of the member countries and between the institutions. Not that this phase was without its times of tension, as in 1961–2, when it was necessary to reach a first agreement on the principles and manner of implementation of the Common Agricultural Policy, but at no time did these tensions endanger the Community's existence. Admittedly, from time to time General de Gaulle spoke on a note which suggested that France might pull out of the Common Market if the commitments contained in the Treaty of Rome and ensuing texts (or which he considered to be contained therein) were not honoured, but since everyone was resolved to reach agreement, these were distant rumblings that did not give any real cause for alarm.

I shall discuss later the period from 1963 to 1967. Although the process of setting up the Common Market was never interrupted durably, the risks of breakdown were very much present in the crises that punctuated this period, notably in 1963, 1965 and, to a lesser degree, in 1967. The reason was that certain fundamental ambiguities present from the outset in the Treaty of Rome, and in the philosophy which many regarded as its justification, suddenly came into the spotlight.

As for me, I left Brussels in 1967, convinced that the creative phase was essentially over and about to give way to a period of pure administration that I was not tempted to experience personally. It was a repetition of what had happened when I gave up my post of Secretary-General of the OEEC in 1955, certain that others would do equally well or even better what remained to be done, which consisted mainly of administrative tasks. I had learned many things during those ten years, in particular the art of negotiation. As Maurice Couve de Murville said, 'Brussels really was, for all the partners, the school of negotiation[1].' Knowing how not to show one's hand, remaining silent about the concessions one knew that one would be making eventually, and giving away to one's partners only as much as was necessary to get them to make a move in the desired direction, this is one of the many principles of international diplomacy.

To understand properly what went on in those first ten years, during the idyllic opening phase and the time of violent clashes that followed, it is essential to distinguish between what is actually spelled out in the treaty and the much more ambitious and often confused aspirations that reigned in the minds of some of the treaty's authors.

What is clearly spelled out is the progressive dismantlement of barriers to trade in industrial products and the establishment of a common external tariff, as well as the gradual derestriction of movements of manpower. It can be considered, too, that the articles concerning the future common agricultural policy and the association of the overseas countries likewise constituted specific commitments which it was possible to cite in order to give the relevant chapters of the treaty a factual content. These are only a few examples; a much longer list of the obligations contained in the treaty could be compiled.

On the other hand, when there was mention of economic union, no one knew then, if they know now, what that meant. The words 'harmonization' and 'coordination' appear over and over again in the treaty or in the commentaries of the time, but not once were they defined with any degree of precision. There was an intellectual gulf between those for whom the precise stipulations were all that counted and those who cared little about the immediate economic objectives and for whom the essential thing was the ultimate political goal, which is no more than vaguely alluded to in the treaty. For these last, the customs union, with its appendages, was only a step along the way to economic union, which itself would be a stage in the movement towards a federation of the states of Western Europe.

This contrast in thinking emerged very clearly on the subject of institutions, notably the European Commission. To take the two extreme views, one was that the Commission was composed of high officials who had been appointed by national governments and whose role was to help the latter in negotiation and to enforce the resultant decisions; it did not and should not have any particular authority. This view was expressed mainly by the French government, but most if not all of the other governments shared it more or less tacitly. If they did not usually voice it, or at any rate as forcefully as the French did, it is because they had to reckon with parliamentary and public opinion that was attached to the idea of a federated Europe.

In that opposite view, which prevailed among most of the members of the European Assembly in Strasbourg, the community institutions prefigured the future European federation. The European Assembly would, of course, be its legislative body, the Commission its executive. As for the Council of Ministers, it was rather awkward trying to find it a role; it would, perhaps, be a second chamber, the Upper House. The Strasbourg parliamentarians were encouraged in their ambition by an article in the Treaty of Rome which is the exact replica of an article in the Treaty of Paris establishing the ECSC and making the European Commission responsible to the European Parliamentary Assembly.

Thus the issue seemed clear: the opposition between federal Europe and the Europe of States would be resolved, one day, by the defeat or victory of one or the other, or by a compromise. But things started to become complicated when the question arose of Britain's becoming an associate member of the Common Market, and then of her joining as a full member. Then ideas grew confused, especially for many federalists who wanted a supranational Europe and, at the same time, British entry. But Britain was as Gaullist as de Gaulle in that she would not hear of anything that hinted at a move towards a European federation. As for de Gaulle himself, he wanted neither a supranational Europe nor British entry, these two negative attitudes each having specific reasons which I shall discuss later.

During the years from 1958 to 1962 these divergences, sometimes expressed, more often than not implied, did not lead to any open conflict. For one thing, federalists and Gaullists alike were seeking then to implement the Rome Treaty's provisions as quickly as possible. But the main reason for this harmony was Chancellor Adenauer's determination to do nothing that might distance him from Paris. He was ready to accept French demands in every case where these did not encroach on fundamental German interests. This Franco-German entente, which was at its most effective during the time between General de Gaulle's coming to power in 1958 and Adenauer's departure from office in 1963, reflected the link that had been forged between the two men and the understanding which each had of the vital political interests of the two most important countries of the European Economic Community.

I recall an interview with Adenauer in 1960 or 1961 which had been arranged by Hallstein. Almost the only subject of conversation was de Gaulle. 'General de Gaulle is sometimes criticized for being nationalist,' Adenauer said in substance, 'I do not agree with that judgment. What de Gaulle thinks in his innermost being is that a country cannot be itself, cannot maintain its unity, cannot assert its presence in the world, unless it is moved by a powerful national feeling. I agree with him entirely. I hope that the German people, which has permanently abandoned all idea of conquest, will recover its identity and, with it, its self-respect.' It is possible that these are not the exact words used by the old chancellor. But the conversation impressed me sufficiently for me to be able even today to remember the essence of it and almost the very words that were spoken.

There can be no doubt that Germany's choice of a close association with France admirably served German interests. As Hallstein wrote, 'it was not long before Federal Germany's deliberate policy decision ... brought its first rich harvest: such seemingly intractable problems as the Ruhr, the rearming of Germany, and the future of the Saar were all rapidly resolved; above all, Franco-German relations were rebuilt on a positive, constructive basis, with immeasurable benefit to the future of Europe as a whole[2].' It is certain that one of the essential motivations of Adenauer and his disciple Hallstein was the restoration of full and entire sovereignty to Germany. They were patriots. But this was only one, albeit fundamental facet of their political philosophy. To quote again Maurice Couve de Murville, who saw a great deal of Adenauer, 'he was really European, I mean really conscious of the fact that our countries represented, through their individual traditions and character, in short through their civilization, something special and precious that had to be preserved at all costs. For this reason, and also because of evident tastes and affinities, he was especially attracted to France ... He did not see any future for his country without a permanent reconciliation with ours and the establishment of ties of friendship for which, in his mind, the European organization would provide the best soil in which to take firm root and flourish[3].'

This Franco-German attachment was constantly in evidence in the meetings and decisions of the Commission. The latter had a membership of nine, two Germans, two French, two Italians, one Netherlander, one Belgian and one Luxembourger. When the Commission was divided over an issue and a vote was taken, it was done on a simple majority basis, which meant that five votes carried the decision. During the first five years the question that dominated all others, by far, was the progressive construction of the Common Agricultural Policy. The Commission was often unanimous in approving the proposals to be submitted to the Council. When there was disagreement, the two Germans, the two French and the Netherlander constituted a stable majority.

The Netherlander, Sicco Mansholt, was the chief architect of this construction. Mansholt had been his country's Minister of Agriculture and knew perfectly the mechanics of the farm sector; he was convinced of the need to organize agricultural markets on the scale of the Europe of the Six. A Dutchman and a socialist, Mansholt felt little sympathy with General de Gaulle, whom he saw as the embodiment of everything he detested in politics. But he was also 'European', that is to say a fervent partisan of everything conducive to the unity of Europe. He did more than anyone to build a common agricultural policy, which for the French was a *sine qua non* for their staying in the Common Market. I gave him my strong backing in the Commission. I did so because I was convinced that if there were no agreement on a common agricultural policy, France would pull out of the Common Market. I also made my own contribution by finding solutions to the problems of financing the policy.

Hallstein and his German colleague von der Groeben also supported Mansholt's proposals. Since Hallstein was President of the Commission, his support was especially valuable. He rendered outstanding service to the Community during its first years. A fine lawyer, he had an exceptional talent for abstraction and felt perfectly at ease with the most complex legal constructs. Chosen by Adenauer to assist him in his European policy, he kept scrupulously, at least until 1965, to the lines that the former had laid down. Like Adenauer, he sought in the understanding with France a complete reintegration of Germany into the concert of European nations and the removal of any trace of discrimination. During the period from 1958 to 1964 he saw that no misunderstanding arose between the two countries. Under his guidance, and with my help, the efforts of the Commission converged with those of France to create the Common Market as foreseen in the Treaty of Rome. Relations between the French government and the Commission were excellent as long as the old chancellor ruled in Bonn. If they soured afterwards, it was largely because Adenauer's determination above all else to maintain good relations with Paris was not present to the same extent in his successor, Chancellor Erhard.

My relations with Hallstein were excellent until the crisis of 1965. I sometimes found him excessively dogmatic but was able to take it in my stride quite easily. I can remember a few good-natured exchanges in the Commission. I would often use the word 'reasonable' to describe a project or a proposal that seemed to me not only to be consistent with reason, but also to have qualities of moderation and good sense. 'I don't understand what you're trying to say,' Hallstein would object. 'What does reasonable mean? An idea is rational or it is absurd, there is no intermediate term.' He was a very secretive person.

In spite of the fact that I saw a great deal of him over a long period during which we conversed several times a week on business matters, I cannot say that I knew him much better when we parted company in 1967 than when I first met him ten years earlier. In particular, I never knew, and I do not think anyone else in the Commission had any more idea than I, whether he had a private life, or rather what that life might be. When Hallstein's term as President of the Commission expired in 1962, I took myself out of the running and interceded in Paris for his term to be renewed. This is because I was convinced that, in view of General de Gaulle's unpopularity in Benelux and in a large area of German public opinion, it was better that a German, as opposed to a Frenchman, should defend the common positions. I was heeded; Hallstein remained President of the Commission until 1967, when he left at the same time as I did.

I should not like it to be inferred that Hallstein was little more than a tool of Adenauer's; by the same token, I did not always agree with the French government. The truth of the matter is that, inevitably, the members of the Commission, however dedicated to the European idea, had to take the positions of national governments into account or else risk losing all effectiveness. An essential part of their action, as Maurice Couve de Murville kindly wrote concerning me[4], consisted in reconciling what they considered to be the common interest with what they knew of the concerns of the different governments, including the government of the country to which they belonged. In other words, the Commission's function was all the more productive in that the proposals it made and put before the Council of Ministers were certain to get a favourable reception, or in any case not to encounter an outright veto that would have left no room for negotiation. This is how things were during what I have called the Common Market's honeymoon; if a grave crisis erupted in 1965, it was because the majority of the Commission strayed from the golden rule I have just described.

Someone else who played an important role at this time was the Belgian commissioner Jean Rey. In charge of External Relations, that is to say the Commission's relations with nonmember countries, he had the often thankless task of putting across to the GATT, the Americans and others what sometimes, and in most cases mistakenly, was seen as community protectionism. Born in Liège, a convinced Francophone, an ardent friend of France, he often entertained towards the latter the fiercely critical sentiments of a disappointed lover. A 'European' from the very first, a federalist in the full sense of the word, he often found himself in profound disagreement with the views of General de Gaulle, notably in the crises of 1963 and 1965. But discussion was always possible with him. I can remember conversations which began quite badly but which, once the reasons for the difference in points of view were explained, ended on a note of sincere cordiality, even if the respective positions had not really drawn any closer together. I should add that Jean Rey succeeded admirably in his duties as negotiator with third countries, where he was held in general esteem.

When the Commission's proposals had been drafted, after consultation with national governments, they would be put before the Council of Ministers for their decision. There was considerable coming and going among the members of the Council, as a result of the changes of government that occurred in the member countries following ministerial crises or general elections. If I am not mistaken, Maurice Couve de Murville set the all-time record for longevity, having retained the Foreign Affairs portfolio for eleven years. At that time, it was the Council of Foreign Ministers that was the supreme body of the Community. After discussion by the ministers with special competence, the major issues, such as those concerning the common agricultural policy, came before the Council of Foreign Ministers. There Maurice Couve de Murville often played a decisive role, given his keen insight, his supremely analytical mind, his thorough knowledge of the issues, and the feeling among France's partners that he was there to stay. Added to which, he possessed great coolness under fire and an aptitude for argument that never let him down.

In the almost uninterrupted sequence of talks that went on in Brussels, Maurice Couve de Murville was able to rely on a senior French government official who was the centre of the negotiation process, Olivier Wormser. Economic and Financial Affairs Director at the Quai d'Orsay from 1954 to 1966, he possessed to an exceptional degree a set of qualities rarely found in one person. An excellent economist, at home in the arcana of the most complicated community texts, unruffled in what appeared to be the most critical of situations, a tough but fair negotiator, incapable of anything underhand, he was consequently admired and at the same time feared by those on the opposite side. Although he liked to be sceptical about 'European' lyricism, his contribution to the Common Market's construction was on many occasions decisive, for it was only too true that France's interest lay in the implementation of the Rome Treaty. Our friendship, which went back to prewar days and had been cemented by our experiences together in Morocco and London during the war, was often of invaluable help to me.

I have spoken of some of the people who played key roles in this great enterprise of the Common Market's creation. There were others, like Edgar Pisani who was France's Minister of Agriculture almost continuously from 1961 to 1966 and who contributed a great deal to the establishment of the agricultural regulations. In the countries other than France, in Germany, Benelux and Italy there were many, ministers and high officials, who worked with might and main to create what can without exaggeration be called the new Europe.

Much of the success achieved during this period from 1958 to 1962 was due to the fact that, in the heat of action, theological quarrels were temporarily forgotten. If I correctly remember my state of mind at the time, I refused flatly to be either for or against Federal Europe or the Europe of States; I inclined, almost instinctively, to the idea of a European federation, but no less instinctively I felt that it was not of the moment. Anyway, why take a stance, seeing that, for various reasons, all the protagonists were agreed for the time being that the most important thing was to execute the Treaty of Rome? In particular, as far as the Commission's role was concerned, I felt little affinity with those who wanted to inflate its importance and present it, by juggling with protocol, as a government in embryo. The reality, in the shape of the powers conferred on it by the treaty, was enough for me. Clear-cut objectives, creative imagination, unremitting effort, there were all the ingredients needed for it to be more than able to carry out its mission in the circumstances of that time.

So far I have spoken of the factors inside the Community that furthered the aims on which the six countries had agreed in 1956–7. I shall discuss later the problems posed by the uncertainties over Britain. To make the picture as near complete as possible, I should say a word or two about the attitude of the United States, which, whatever the issue of the moment, played a leading role in the world's affairs. Having backed all the European initiatives during the fifties, the Americans continued to support the efforts made by the Europeans between 1958 and 1962 to achieve a certain form of unity. Although they had certain misgivings about the way the common agricultural policy was shaping, they did not actually voice them while the policy was being framed and certainly did not try to put any obstacles in the way. George Ball, the US Undersecretary of State from 1961 to 1966, and the man in Washington who was keeping a very close eye on European affairs, was unstinting in his encouragement and support for those who, on this side of the Atlantic, were trying to put an end to the Continent's fragmentation. The prime reason for this attitude was that the Americans continued to hope that the states of Western Europe would one day form a federation which would be closely allied to the USA, and would enable the latter to scale down its efforts to ensure the safety of that part of the world. For the present, however, they wanted a cutback in the 'discrimination' applied to American products entering the Common Market, by comparison with the member countries' products. This was the origin of a series of tariff negotiations which I shall be speaking about later.

The free trade area

It is not my purpose to relate the history of the Common Market. Others have already done so, or will do, better than I could. I shall simply pick out the salient points and say how and to what extent I contributed to the most important decisions. The first years of the Community's existence, what I have dubbed the honeymoon, were notable for the removal of the British obstacle and the failure of the projects to create a vast free trade area that would have taken in the Common Market. At the same time, through the financial and monetary reforms of 1958, France put herself in a position to participate fully in the new enterprise. The customs union for industrial products was off to a flying start and the common agricultural policy was taking shape.

I had the feeling of having been right all along. The disasters which the Treaty's opponents in France had presented as inevitable were proving to be imaginary. France was at long last emerging from that long period of economic isolation, of unconscionable protection vis-à-vis the rest of the world, which, more than any other factor, was responsible for her economy's having lost so much ground in relation to Britain, Germany and many smaller European countries. I was at one in thought and sentiment with all those, of whatever political persuasion, who aspired to a modern France, whether they took General de Gaulle or Jean Monnet as their reference. Day after day in the Commission I was able to formulate or support proposals that made it possible to move forward swiftly.

I have to admit that times were relatively easy. Thanks to the

Marshall Plan and to its own efforts, Europe had rebuilt itself; output and living standards were rising fast. A general mood of optimism had taken hold; the prophets of doom now had the look of malcontents who had missed the main turning in the fifties, when the European and world economies had started to grow rapidly. The crises that were to rock the Community in the second half of the sixties were still some way off. The idea that this rapid growth, which was changing the face of Europe almost visibly, might one day cease or slow down drastically did not occur to anyone.

From the outset, though, the Community had had to face a great danger, that of being more or less sucked into a vast European free trade area in which it would have lost its individuality, and which might have prevented it from fully establishing itself according to the terms of the Treaty of Rome.

The British had initially been highly sceptical of the project for the Common Market of the Six; they did not think that the thing could be done. So after taking part in a number of the Spaak Group sessions in autumn 1955, they decided to back out. The picture changed in the course of 1956. When the success of the undertaking looked possible, and then probable, they were obliged to review their position.

The possibility of Britain's going into the Common Market was broached in London, only to be promptly rejected. A number of seemingly insurmountable obstacles stood in the way: first and foremost, the Commonwealth and the imperial preference. A customs union, like the Common Market, presupposes by definition a common tariff. If the British had joined, they would have been obliged to levy the same duties on Commonwealth products entering Britain as on products from third countries. Much more important, they would have had to tax Commonwealth products while equivalent products from the Six would have been admitted duty-free. It would have been a 'reverse preference'. Needless to say, in such an eventuality the overseas countries linked to Britain would have ceased to give preferential treatment to British products. It would have meant the end of the imperial preference, and the British were not yet ready to take the plunge. Nor could they accept the idea of the Common Market's extension to agricultural products. For one thing, they were attached to their own system of deficiency payments, a system of subsidies that guaranteed a fair price to the producer while holding down the price paid by the consumer. For another, as big importers of food, they wanted to be able to go on buying cheaply, in the Commonwealth and in third countries, the produce they needed.

318

The Common Market project was therefore totally unacceptable to Britain at this stage in her thinking on European issues. But the idea that there was going to be a six-country trading bloc at her doorstep which would charge dues before admitting British products, thus in effect discriminating against those products by comparison with goods produced in the Common Market, was likewise unacceptable. Hence the ingenious idea – too ingenious for its own good – of a free trade area encompassing Britain, the Common Market and the other OEEC countries that wished to join. Each country or group of countries would retain its own external tariff vis-à-vis the rest of the world, but customs duties and other barriers to trade in industrial goods would be abolished within the free trade area. Technical arrangements would make it possible to reconcile maintenance of differing external tariffs with free movement of goods within the area. Needless to say, agriculture would be completely excluded from the system.

It was in the autumn of 1956, while the negotiations to set up the Common Market were in full swing, that London put forward this proposal. The British idea at that time was that the two sets of negotiations, for the establishment of the Common Market and for the free trade area, would be conducted side by side. Later, when it became clear that the Six were soon going to reach agreement whereas the discussions on the free trade area had barely begun, the British asked that the two envisaged agreements should be implemented side by side.

From the outset, I was strongly opposed to the British proposals. This time I found myself in complete agreement with the whole of French government officialdom and, from the beginning of 1958, with my colleagues in the European Commission. The key objection was essentially this: the free trade area would have given the British, in respect of the products that interested them, i.e. industrial products, the same advantages as those which the Common Market partners granted to one another, without the British having to accept the various *quid pro quos* and obligations which the Six had considered necessary to write into their draft treaty in order to ensure a proper balance – namely, the establishment of a common external tariff, the progressive development of a common commercial policy and a common agricultural policy, and harmonization of social legislations on certain points.

The free trade area project was, in French eyes, an outright return to a simplistic, 19th century-type liberalism. Let it be added that it would have enabled the British to retain trading advantages that seemed exorbitant, such as the possibility of buying their food cheaply outside the area and importing without duty or at low rates of duty the raw materials processed by their industry. Furthermore, while British industrial goods would have been able to enter Europe freely, Britain would have continued to benefit from the imperial preference in her possessions and ex-possessions overseas; she would thus have been at the meeting point of two preferential systems, enjoying the advantages of both.

But French fears went further. We knew that Germany and Belgium, in particular, had been unenthusiastic about the idea of a common agricultural policy; they had accepted it because it was the condition that France had posed for her entry into the Common Market. But this common policy still had to be constructed. What would happen in the event of disagreement on this central issue? The Common Market might collapse, but the free trade area, into which it would have been incorporated, would remain. British and German industrial goods would be able to go on circulating freely in this vast area. Given this eventuality, would not the Germans, and some of France's other partners, be tempted to evade the common agricultural policy and other parts of the Rome Treaty that France cared a great deal about, such as the association of overseas countries, seeing that in the free trade area they would be able to obtain what they most cared about, without these onerous conditions? In that case, it would be very easy for them to see to it that those parts of the treaty became a dead letter.

The fact of the matter was that the Six had spent a year or a year and a half (if one includes the few months of preliminary discussions in the Spaak Group) negotiating, in difficult conditions, a complex treaty that gave the impression, especially to the French, of being balanced. Along came the British with their plan, and suddenly there was readiness to accept the free movement of industrial goods, without conditions and without *quid pro quos*. The switch was an implied criticism of the Rome Treaty: if it was really so easy to decide on free trade for industrial products, why have complicated things to such a degree in the Brussels negotiations?

The Commission performed a considerable feat in maintaining unity of the Six in the face of the full-scale offensive which the British led, with support from the small European countries outside the Community, from the second half of 1956 to the end of 1958. It was fundamentally opposed to the British scheme, not only for economic reasons, but for political reasons too. In taking this stance it was expressing the joint attitude of all the Europeans who saw the

320

Common Market as the first step towards an economic union and perhaps, eventually, a federation of Western Europe. Now it was common knowledge that the British were radically opposed to any ambitious idea of this kind; for them it was purely and simply a question of avoiding discriminatory treatment for their industrial products at the point of entry to the Common Market. Hallstein and I led the fight to prevent the Common Market from being diminished or even swallowed up by a vast free trade area.

In Paris, General de Gaulle's accession to power in the spring of 1958 lent greater strength to France in the last stage of the negotiations with Britain, in the second half of 1958. In Germany, Adenauer continued to follow the policy he had adopted many years earlier, which was not to get out of line with France on European issues; he had no trouble in imposing his will on his Minister of the Economy Ludwig Erhard, a convinced partisan of the big free trade area. Even the Benelux countries, which were drawn to the British proposal, behaved with moderation and thus ensured that the tension, which undeniably existed within the Six, did not lead to the kind of crisis the Community was to experience some years later. The fact was that, with the negotiation of the Rome Treaty already very far on if not concluded, a feeling of solidarity vis-à-vis the rest of the world had developed among the Six which the British were unable to weaken seriously. They had overestimated their strength; when the moment of decision came, the Six stayed together.

It was France that took the initiative to break off the talks at the end of 1958. For want of anything better, and as though to establish a first foothold for the future, Britain formed in 1959 an association with the Scandinavian countries, Switzerland, Austria and Portugal to set up a small free trade area, whose economic significance was to remain very limited.

In retrospect it may be asked whether it would not have better for the Community to become Britain's partner in a big free trade area in 1958 or 1959, rather than have to enlarge itself some fifteen years later with the entry not only of Britain, but of Ireland and Denmark, and later of Greece, Spain and Portugal. Like all hypothetical questions, this one is impossible to answer. It could be argued that the Community of the Six would have continued to show a greater degree of homogeneity than the enlarged Community has; its institutions arguably functioned better with a smaller Council and Commission. Yet, and this is probably the decisive argument, it is not certain that the Community of the Six would have established itself in the way it did in the sixties. Plunged into a vast free trade area, the centrifugal forces within the Community would have been very strong. The Germans, especially after Adenauer's death, would probably not have given in to the demands of the French on the common agricultural policy, knowing from experience that another trading system excluding agriculture, but giving them the same advantages as the Common Market did, was possible.

Construction of the customs union and the common agricultural policy

The year 1959 opened under the best possible auspices. The British problem was out of the way. Thanks to the financial and monetary reforms carried out under General de Gaulle's authority, France could take full part in the construction of the Common Market. All the governments concerned were resolved to make a success of the undertaking. Furthermore, the general economic climate had become very favourable and was to remain so during the greater part of the sixties, which saw high growth rates, stability of the international monetary system, and only a very slow rise in prices.

The first round of tariff cuts and quota dismantlements took effect on January 1, 1959. The Community served notice that it did not intend to practise a protectionist commercial policy by broadly extending these derestrictions to trade with third countries. Once under way, the movement rapidly gained pace. At France's suggestion, the timing of intra-Community tariff reductions laid down in the Rome Treaty was accelerated twice, in 1960 and in 1962. By the end of 1961, quantitative import restrictions had been completely removed; France, whose economy had been rigorously protected by measures of this kind up until 1958, made a remarkable effort in helping to see that this target was met. The common external tariff was gradually coming into being. By mid-1962 intra-Community customs duties had already been reduced by 50%.

This movement of trade liberalization would continue as scheduled, or faster, throughout the rest of the sixties, with the result that the customs union and the common agricultural policy were in place by July 1, 1968, a year and a half ahead of the time limit set by the treaty. Intra-European trade grew rapidly during those years. Although trade with the rest of the world grew more slowly, it too increased very considerably, showing that the Common Market was a factor in the world's prosperity as a whole.

Along with trade, productivity and output in the Community grew at unprecedented rates. I shall come back to this subject later on when I attempt to take stock of what the Common Market contributed to Europe. But here and now I wish to emphasize that France's initial misgivings proved to be unfounded. True, Germany is still the most powerful industrial country in Europe, but the gap between France and Germany, far from having widened, has to a great extent been bridged. The living standards of the French are almost equal to those of the Germans, while those of the two countries are now not very far short of American living standards. It can be said, without exaggeration, that of all the countries of the Community, it was France that derived most benefit from the trade liberalization which the Treaty of Rome prescribed or indirectly brought about.

An agreement on the common agricultural policy, giving effect to the relevant articles in the treaty, this was for France the real test of her partners' will to create a common market; for her, no Common Agricultural Policy meant no more Common Market.

At the time of the ratification debates, the vagueness and inadequacy, from the Gaullists' point of view, of the treaty articles on the CAP had been one of the reasons for their negative vote. I remember a face-to-face discussion I had on radio at that time with Michel Debré, in the course of which he accused me of having settled for too little and predicted that there would never be any common agricultural policy. I replied that it was not possible to spell out everything in detail in a treaty and that I had confidence in the French government's will to arrive at specific agreements in the first years of the Community's existence, and in the good faith of our partners. We became worked up to the point where we were literally wrenching the microphone away from each other. Since there was no moderator, the broadcast ended in an uproar. A few minutes later we found ourselves out in the street a little ashamed of ourselves; shortly afterwards we accepted a proposal from the radio authorities to do the broadcast again, but with a moderator who would call on us to speak in turn. This time, everything went off properly. In recalling this little story I have to admit that Michel Debré's misgivings were not entirely unfounded. As will be seen later, it took a great deal of firmness on the part of General de Gaulle's government, a lot of hard work and imagination on the Commission's part, and Adenauer's unfailing support over several years, to arrive at the result that had been no more than outlined in the Treaty of Rome.

In the Commission during that time, Hallstein, Mansholt and I joined forces as a real team to put through the proposals drawn up by Mansholt and his services. As early as July 1958, Mansholt organized at Stresa, in Italy, a European conference that laid the foundations of the common agricultural policy. In June 1960 the Commission transmitted to the Council of Ministers its proposals for the policy's implementation. In December of the same year, the Council approved the fundamental principles of this policy[5].

A year and a half of arduous negotiation was required before the Council adopted a set of regulations organizing the markets for cereals, products with a cereal input (pig meat, eggs and poultry), fruit and vegetables. The first financial regulation established a solidarity among the Six [in the form of a system of national contributions to finance agricultural expenditure] for the following three years (1962–4) and stipulated that by July 1, 1965 at the latest a new regulation would enter into force specifying the system that would apply until the end of the transition period, that is until January 1, 1970. As we shall see later, July 1, 1965 was to be a very important date in the Community's history, owing to the crisis which erupted at that time.

The end of 1961 and the beginning of 1962 were marked by a marathon session of the Council that lasted from December 15, 1961 to January 14, 1962, with many night sittings. The 'clock was stopped' on December 31 so that the session's decisions would theoretically have been taken before the end of 1961. France, principally represented by Maurice Couve de Murville, Edgar Pisani and Olivier Wormser, thoroughly supported the Commission's proposals, which were also backed firmly by Holland, whilst the Germans, although defending their country's own interests, as was their duty, took care not to stray too far from the French position. The climate was auspicious, therefore. Even so, the matter could not have been settled successfully without the imaginative and meticulous work done beforehand by the Commission and the efforts it made to reconcile differences during that interminable session of the Council. It is unfortunate that when speaking of these events in his *Memoirs of Hope*, General de Gaulle could not find one word of praise for the Commission. Thus even the greatest men nearly always have their petty side.

In addition to taking these essential decisions concerning the common agricultural policy, the Council found, on the Commission's proposal, that the main objectives set by the Treaty of Rome for the first stage had been achieved and that it was now possible, in

Community jargon, to proceed to the second stage, i.e. continue to construct the customs union and at the same time take the many decisions still necessary to complete the common agricultural policy.

I should like to make two more points in order to round off the story of the events that took place in Brussels at the end of 1961 and the beginning of 1962. The first is that there was a real danger of breakdown. Rightly or wrongly, the French government was convinced that without a European farm policy the Treaty of Rome would be heavily weighted against France and in favour of the industrial states in the north of the Community, especially Germany[6]. Had there not been an agreement on January 14, 1962, would France have pulled out of the Common Market? In his *Memoirs* de Gaulle says that she would have:

We French were determined to seize the opportunity to tear aside the veil and induce our partners to make formal commitments on what we regarded as essential. When they proved reluctant to give way, and indeed showed signs of some disquieting reservations, I judged that now or never was the moment to take the bull by the horns. Our ministers in Brussels, Couve de Murville, Baumgartner and Pisani, made it quite clear that we were prepared to withdraw from the Community if our requirements were not met.

If there had been a rupture, it would probably not have been permanent; the situation would have been repaired later. But the Community would have been paralyzed for some time.

My second point is intended to dispel an illusion: if the Six had not succeeded in agreeing on a common agricultural policy, would not everyone have benefited, the nonmember countries that would have been able to export more to Europe and the member countries themselves, which would have been able to import more cheaply? I say illusion, because at the outset, before the agreement on a common policy, it was not free trade that prevailed in Europe for farm goods, but protectionist national policies with very extensive state intervention, which had given rise to highly involved and complicated regulations. In the absence of a European farm policy, it is certain that national legislations and regulations would have continued to operate essentially. Would the upshot, all told, have been more restrictive or less restrictive policies? It is impossible to answer that question with certainty. The degree of protection ensured by the Common Agricultural Policy, as previously by national policies, is linked to the price level it is sought to maintain. Looked at from this angle, the CAP has often proved to be inordinately protectionist, but in most cases this was equally true of national policies.

6

THE TIMES OF CRISIS AND THE FAILURE OF TWO CONCEPTS (1963–1967)

As the day of January 14, 1962 dawned most of those who had taken part in the past weeks of negotiations justifiably felt that one of the chief obstacles in the way of European unity had been removed; although a lot of ground remained to be covered before one could speak of a common agricultural policy as such, its principles had been accepted by the six governments and the first commodity regulations had been adopted, along with a first financial regulation that established solidarity of the Six in the matter of agricultural expenditure. In a way, we were right, but we did not suspect that Europe was going to live through five years of various crises, which it would succeed in overcoming but which would leave it bruised and with a great many illusions shattered.

The title of this chapter mentions two failures of concept. The first was that of Gaullist Europe in 1962, when the Benelux countries refused to accept the political organization of Europe that General de Gaulle had proposed in mid-1960. His plan was for a Franco-German Europe which France would have led and from which Britain would have been excluded, at least while she continued to represent, to Gaullist thinking, a United States bridgehead in Europe that encouraged American hegemonic ventures.

326

The second was the failure, in 1965, of 'federalist' Europe with supranational institutions. It was then that the Commission majority tried and failed to obtain important budget decision powers for the Strasbourg Parliamentary Assembly and for itself. Another outcome of this unfortunate initiative was that it gave the French government the opportunity to abolish, in effect, the provisions of the Rome Treaty which allowed for the possibility, as of the third stage, i.e. from January 1, 1966, of the Council of Ministers taking a certain number of important decisions by majority vote.

During those same years, 1962–7, the problems which the European Economic Community had to contend with were infinitely complicated and made much more difficult to resolve by the question of Britain's entry into the Common Market. It was in mid-1961 that London had officially applied for membership and in January 1963 that France, in circumstances of which I shall speak later, vetoed the proposed enlargement of the Community, thereby violently shocking most of her partners. It can be said that the moral unity of the Community was broken then for a time, until the necessities of communal life reasserted themselves.

While the Six were engaged in trying to complete what they had undertaken and in negotiating with Britain, the Americans were unveiling their own ideas about the political and economic organization of the western world. In January 1962 President Kennedy announced his Grand Design, and in May 1964 the first talks opened in Geneva with a view to drastic across-the-board tariff cutting both on an Atlantic Community scale and worldwide.

Thus from 1961–2 there was a period of several years that saw simultaneous negotiations for the completion of the Community, the creation of a political Europe, British entry into the Common Market, and the general reduction of import duties. Inevitably these different negotiations reacted on one another, positively in some cases, negatively in others.

The sixties therefore presented us with a complex skein of interests, ambitions and national calculations that was often difficult to unravel. For my own part, I was in no way involved in the negotiations on Europe's political organization, which took place entirely outside Brussels. On the other hand, I was very active in the discussions on the Community's agricultural policy, on Britain's entry into the Common Market, on the general lowering of tariffs, and finally in the events that led to the crisis of 1965, when I found myself in the deepest disagreement with Hallstein, Mansholt and the majority of the Commission.

Without any attempt to be exhaustive, I shall now briefly recall the different negotiations that marked the sixties, the positions I was led to take and the thoughts occasioned in me then, or now, by the issues under discussion at the time. Then I shall try to define, in its essentials, the Europe which subsequently emerged in 1967–8 and which, all things considered, was not very different from the one we know today, nor from the one which the negotiators of the Rome Treaty had conceived in 1956–7.

The Fouchet Plan[1]

As Maurice Couve de Murville wrote, 'political union has always been, at least in France, the distant but paramount prospect ultimately justifying the efforts made in the now conventional name of European construction. It was, in a sense, written into the Rome treaties . . . if not as an idea, at least as a hope and doubtless an intention.' Admittedly, General de Gaulle, when he resolved in 1958 to go along with the Common Market, was primarily concerned with accelerating France's economic development, but he also saw the Market as 'the kind of scheme which could create among its members a solidarity that would lead them naturally, as it were, to try to extend their enterprise to the political domain[2].'

I spoke briefly of the French proposals for the creation of a political Europe when I tried, earlier in this chapter, to define General de Gaulle's ideas on the European issue. At the time of negotiation, these proposals went under the name of 'Union of States'. This was not a plan for a supranational Europe, nor for a federation, nor even for an extension of the so-called Community method, i.e. the system of institutions and their interrelationship established by the Treaty of Rome, to a new sphere of action. The Union of States was to consist entirely in intergovernmental cooperation.

The original scheme was simple: periodic and regular meetings of heads of state and government of the Six states to concert their action in the political, economic, cultural and defence spheres; meetings of the different ministers directly concerned for the purpose of preparing and implementing decisions; likewise, regular debates by an Assembly of delegations of national parliaments; finally, when the time came, a general and solemn referendum of the European peoples to sanction the organization of Europe and to give the latter the character of a 'decisive creation by the people'[3].

The Times Of Crisis And The Failure Of Two Concepts (1963–1967)

The first discussions took place between de Gaulle and Adenauer on July 29 and 30, 1960. Talks then went on until April 27, 1962, in other words over a period of nearly two years. At no time did Franco-German solidarity fail, the two countries generally having the support of Italy. The opposition came from Benelux, from the outset from the Netherlands and a little later from Belgium; it was those two countries that were responsible for the project's ultimate failure.

The Belgians and the Dutch wanted Britain to be party to the political discussions that the Six were embarking upon among themselves, even before she joined the European Economic Community. Secondarily, they took the stance that, in Britain's absence, the only conceivable political Europe was a supranational Europe. The truth of the matter is that these small northern European countries feared, above all, a Franco-German hegemony, which at that time would have meant a French hegemony; they were being true to their traditional policy of seeking in Britain a counterbalance to the power of their neighbours to the south and the east. Through Britain, it was America they were counting on, taking the view that, with Britain present, the Americans would bring their influence to bear on the matter of European political union.

The French, for their part, were not without ulterior motives. At least, that was the impression they gave during those two years. There was reason to think at one moment that their intention was to integrate the Common Market and its institutions into the political structure they were proposing, and thus to take away the special character which the former had been given by the Treaty of Rome. The community institutions would thus have become intergovernmental institutions. At a certain point in the negotiations the French asserted that these had never been their intentions.

On the other hand, our partners knew full well that General de Gaulle was fundamentally hostile to Britain's entry into the Common Market, although he had not yet had occasion to say so publicly. They knew, too, that at the first opportunity he would pull out of NATO. Now, not only for Benelux but also for Italy, and still more for Germany, participation in an integrated defence organization was a guarantee of security which those countries were on no account prepared to give up. What they saw as a kind of disloyalty to the Atlantic Alliance on France's part weighed heavily in the discussions at that time.

I have to say here that, personally, I found it very difficult to understand the French position; to me it seemed highly unrealistic.

329

What could General de Gaulle hope for from a Union of the Six States? As demonstrated by the difficulties of the negotiation and then by its ultimate failure, Benelux, Italy and even Germany had a different conception of international relations from that of France. True, de Gaulle shared their desire for security from the threat of the East; on several occasions he showed himself to be a staunch ally of the United States, notably at the time of the Berlin and Cuban crises; he was always loyal to the Atlantic Alliance. But he also had another concern which our European partners did not share: that of not allowing an American domination of Europe to establish itself, or of putting an end to that domination as quickly as possible. He saw NATO as the tangible expression of this danger. He refused to see the French army placed under foreign command and he took France out of NATO as soon as he could, in 1966. His refusal to accept Britain's entry into the Common Market was due less to British demands concerning relations with the Commonwealth or the system of agricultural price support than to the fact that he regarded Britain either as a satellite of the United States, or as being so closely linked to that nation that she would somehow represent an American presence in Europe.

What hope could there be of defining a common foreign policy and a common defence policy with partners who did not share this obsession at all? Nearly all the Gaullist initiatives in the field of international relations provoked sharp, if not violent reactions from the Benelux countries and from a very large segment of German public opinion. General de Gaulle's only strong card in this affair was the support he almost always received from Adenauer, over whom he exerted a kind of fascination. But the great majority of the German public found it difficult to go along: they were fundamentally Atlanticist and viewed with concern and resentment any expression of doubt over US intentions. It has to be said that the Soviet danger was closer and more obvious to Germany than the risk of seeing an American domination establish itself in the world, and more particularly in Europe. In fact, German foreign policy resolved itself into two concerns: security on the eastern front, non-discrimination on the western front. On these two points, and especially on the first, the Germans were prepared to put themselves in the hands of the Americans.

After the failure of the projected Union of States in April 1962, de Gaulle and Adenauer got together to conclude a treaty that established between France and Germany the same political cooperation that de Gaulle had tried to get accepted by all the members of the Common Market. The treaty was signed on January 23, 1963, although the political climate at that time was not very propitious, given that some ten days earlier General de Gaulle had unilaterally terminated the negotiations between the Six and the British. At the time of the treaty's ratification, however, the Bundestag added a preamble setting out a foreign policy very different from the one that General de Gaulle would have liked applied and even going directly counter to it on a number of essential points, such as the maintenance of close links with the United States, integration into NATO and British entry into the Common Market.

After the preamble was adopted, the Franco-German treaty appeared to have lost much of its effectiveness. Erhard's arrival in office in the autumn of 1963 aggravated the situation. A convinced Americanist, advocate of Common Market membership for Britain, fervent partisan of free trade on a world scale, lukewarm over the European Economic Community, his thinking was the opposite of de Gaulle's on many points.

Yet the deepgoing interests of states almost always prevail over the moods and even the ideologies of men; despite the differences of view I have just mentioned, and despite the great crisis of 1965, France and Germany remained very close in the debates of all kinds that took place in the Community during the years that followed the treaty's signing. Threatened eastward by a powerful neighbour, Germany needed to be able to count westward on a power that would sustain her in times of difficulty. Even today, more than twenty years after the events I have just recounted, the Community rests to a large extent on a Franco-German cooperation or complicity that is unspoken when not spoken. Europe, as we know it, is largely a Franco-German creation. One could say without exaggeration that the Franco-German rapprochement, the sympathy that over the years and in spite of the horrors of Hitlerism has developed between the two countries, between the two peoples, is the real milestone in the postwar history of Europe.

I should note in passing the very important role played at this time by small countries like Belgium and Holland. Had it not been for their opposition, a political union would have been created; France, Germany and Italy were in favour. How long that union would have lasted is another matter. France's veto of Britain's entry into the Common Market would probably have put it into abeyance. France's withdrawal from NATO when the Germans and the other members of the Community, except for France, were more Atlanticist than ever would have created another trial for the political union from which it might never really have recovered. The creation in the seventies of the European Council, and the discussions that take place there on the political issues of the moment, probably represent the utmost in political cooperation now possible in Western Europe.

The first negotiation between the Community and Britain

The Community of the Six was subjected to its first trial one year after the conclusion of the agreements that had brought the Common Agricultural Policy into being. In January 1963 General de Gaulle publicly announced that the negotiations for Britain's entry into the Common Market had broken down and that they should be terminated, to strong protests from the other five countries. A chill then settled on the Community that threatened for a while to interrupt its normal development.

These events, which were accorded a dramatic significance by contemporaries, were in fact no more than an episode in a long evolution that was to lead Britain gradually to realize that her role as a great world sea power, whose interests were utterly distinct from those of the neighbouring continent, was ended and that her future lay in joining the Six, economically at any rate. As I write these lines, it is not absolutely certain that this evolution has reached its conclusion.

The relationship, or rather the absence of relationship, between Britain and the Continent had been summed up in a few sentences by Keynes in 1919 in one of his first works and, of them all, the most prophetic:

For one who spent in Paris the greater part of the six months which succeeded the Armistice an occasional visit to London was a strange experience. England still stands outside Europe. Europe's voiceless tremors do not reach her. Europe is apart and England is not of her flesh and body. But Europe is solid with herself. France, Germany, Italy, Austria and Holland, Russia and Roumania and Poland, throb together, and their structure and civilisation are essentially one. They flourished together, they have rocked together in a war, which we, in spite of our enormous contributions and sacrifices (like though in a less degree than America), economically stood outside, and they may fall together[4].

I could not resist quoting this text which neither General de Gaulle nor the British of the immediate postwar years would have repudiated. True, in 1945 the objective circumstances were very different. The eastern part of Europe was cut off from the rest of the Continent. Britain's loss of economic and political stature had linked her fate with that of continental Western Europe which, in alliance with America, she had just liberated; but she did not yet see it that way. During the years from 1945 to 1960 she would try, on many occasions, to assert her identity as a nation outside or, rather, on the fringe of Europe. The Empire was dead, but the Commonwealth was still an emotionally powerful reality. The pound would go from crisis to crisis, but the sterling area was still regarded as giving Britain's currency worldwide acceptability and as having to be preserved. A special link with the United States, by way of language and culture, which the British liked to think of as stronger and more durable than it really was, completed the set of factors that convinced them that they were somehow different, apart from the rest of Europe, if not from Europe itself.

How can one be surprised, then, that in the late forties Britain spurned the European customs union proposed by the Americans; that she distanced herself from the OEEC when it ceased to be the essential channel for American aid; that in 1950 she rejected any idea of participation in the ECSC; that in June 1955 she refused to take part in the Messina conference, to which she had nevertheless been invited; that after a few meetings her representative left the Spaak Group, which was in the process of preparing the Common Market and Euratom treaties, so unbending and unrealistic were the instructions which he had received from London? How can one be surprised that in 1956 the British government should have sought, in proposing the creation of the European free trade area, to submerge the Common Market in a much larger scheme in which it would have lost its distinctive features?

I should not like it to be thought that this catalogue of lost opportunities constitutes an indictment of a country that I learned to admire while sharing its experience of the war. I could draw up a different but equally damning list of charges against any of the other European nations which the war had reduced from the status of a great world power to that of a middle-rate regional power. In every case the adjustment was painful and sometimes tinged with tragedy. The wars that France fought in Indochina and Algeria reflect the same refusal to accept reality as Britain's postwar endeavour to go on playing the role of arbiter in Europe without herself entering into European affairs.

After the failure of the European free trade area, government thinking in Britain began to take a different line and one that public opinion had some difficulty in going along with. The shift in attitude was due essentially to the fact that Britain's economic difficulties were steadily worsening and to her feeling that she could not cope on her own, even with the special relationship she maintained with the Commonwealth. Finally, on July 31, 1961 the then Prime Minister Harold Macmillan issued a statement to the effect that Britain was ready to negotiate her entry into the Common Market. This statement shows clearly that the change in thinking I mentioned earlier was not complete and that Britain was having difficulty in resigning herself to becoming 'European'. She was not purely and simply applying for membership: she was asking to negotiate with the states of the Community the terms of her membership.

The central issues that would be discussed during the next year and a half were clear from the outset. For Britain it was important to safeguard the interests of the Commonwealth, of British agriculture and, additionally, of the other members of the small free trade area. Essentially, the problems stemmed from the inclusion of agriculture in the Common Market, although at the time that Britain put forward her application the decisions that would give shape to the common agricultural policy had not yet been taken.

The big question on everyone's mind during the first year of negotiation was how to make room in Europe for the so-called 'temperate foodstuffs' which Canada, Australia and New Zealand were accustomed to sell to Britain. Although the issue was never put in such terms, what would have gratified the wishes of certain British political and administrative circles, still wielding very considerable influence in Whitehall, would have been a combination, for Britain, of free trade with Europe and preferential imports of farm produce from the Commonwealth – an ambition which, naturally, it was impossible even to mention in the official discussions, but which was definitely in the minds of many Britishers. So the British negotiators fell back on another proposition, asking the Six to give the Commonwealth countries the assurance that they would have outlets in Europe, for an indefinite period, comparable to those they had in Britain. This would have meant creating, in those countries' favour, a series of such consequential exceptions to the rules of the future common agricultural policy that there was reason to wonder what would remain of that policy if they were accepted.

In this area, as in others, one was led to think, for a while, that in the minds of Britain's negotiators it was not so much a question of

Britain's acceding to the Treaty of Rome and to the decisions that had issued from it or were about to be adopted (the British lodged their application on July 31, 1961, the first Community regulations on agriculture were adopted in January 1962) as of renegotiating, if not the treaty itself, at least the principles of the common agricultural policy, the aim being a compromise between the Community system and a British system composed of two essential elements: protection of British agriculture by methods different from those adopted by the Community, and maintenance of preferential trading relations with a certain number of Commonwealth countries.

The British government's task was made more difficult by the fact that British public opinion was in the main distrustful of, if not hostile to the Community; it could just about have brought itself to join, provided that ties with the Commonwealth would not have been broken or even weakened as a result – in other words, it refused to choose between Europe and the Commonwealth. Had it been obliged to choose between them, there was reason to think that it would have preferred the Commonwealth. Hence the need for the government's spokesmen to use ambiguous language, which did not make the task of the British negotiators in Brussels any easier. Thus, Edward Heath, the British minister in charge of negotiations, was obliged to say at the opening of the talks: 'I am sure that you will understand that Britain could not join the EEC in conditions under which this trade connection [between the Commonwealth and Britain] was cut with grave loss and even ruin for some of the Commonwealth countries.'

France, firmly backed by the other member countries and the Commission, opposed all Britain's efforts to obtain preference for the temperate-zone Commonwealth countries on the agricultural markets of the Community. At the same time she urged that the Six conclude the first agreements that would give content to the common agricultural policy and make it possible to move on to the Common Market's second stage.

Personally, while I perfectly understood the dramatic problem with which Britain was confronted and which, in the economic context, was nothing less than the need, if she wanted to 'enter' Europe, to cast off the last vestiges of her former imperial power, I could not go along with demands that might have had the result of dissolving the Community bond or that would have caused it to become something very different from what it was. One of the most able and probably the most clear-sighted of the British negotiators then, Eric Roll (now Lord Roll of Ipsden), recounts in his memoirs conversations we had during the summer holidays of 1961, when the talks were on the point of beginning:

He [Robert Marjolin] was fundamentally in favour of our accession, but having participated in the negotiations leading to the Treaty of Rome and being a Vice-President of the Commission, he was also strongly imbued with the *communautaire* spirit. As a result, I was left under no illusions about the limits to which concessions might be granted to ease our path, limits that were determined – in his mind and that of the Commission generally as it turned out – by what would or would not in their opinion seriously impair the foundations of the Community[5].

These, then, were the ideas which governed my thinking, and that of men like Hallstein and Mansholt, in that summer of 1961, but there were others, less precise but equally compelling, which I kept to myself at the time. Even assuming that agricultural Europe were set up, skeletally, and that one obtained all the assurances one wanted concerning observance of the *communautaire* spirit, what would happen later, after the British had joined the EEC, when it became necessary to come to grips with the big questions that could not possibly be settled before the end of the negotiations with Britain, such as the regulations applicable to dairy products and beef and veal, and the financial regulation for the end of the transition period? At that point, when those different questions were under discussion, might not Britain take a stance that would reflect her wish to maintain close links with the Commonwealth and to reduce as far as possible the cost, to her, of the common agricultural policy, say by refusing to agree to Community appropriation, after the transition period, of the proceeds from agricultural levies and customs duties? In other words, would it not be prudent to defer Britain's entry into the Common Market until such time as the common agricultural policy had been completed?

In this crucial matter of Britain's trade relations with the Commonwealth, the British fought a rearguard action until the beginning of the summer of 1962, when the Conference decided to adjourn for the holidays, after adopting a beautifully vague text which, as such, satisfied everyone. The Community declared its intention to pursue a 'reasonable price policy', which could mean that this policy would be designed in such a way as not to stimulate European farm output too much in order to leave plenty of room on the Community market for imports from overseas (including imports from the Commonwealth). In addition, the Community undertook to put the development of world trade on an equal footing with the protection of European agriculture. Finally, the Six stated that, during the transition period at least, it was their intention 'to ensure that the operation of the intra-Community preference would not lead to sudden and considerable alterations in trade patterns', and that if this were nevertheless to occur 'the Community would review the operation of the intra-Community preference in consultation with Commonwealth countries.'

When we reconvened in the autumn, the main item on the agenda was the matter of the arrangements to be made for British agriculture. The latter was protected by a system of subsidies to farmers so as to guarantee them a minimum income, whereas the Community used a system of levies on imports. The British had undertaken to adopt the Community's methods, but here again they took an extreme position at the outset, requesting a transition period of twelve to fifteen years during which they would maintain their system of subsidies, while adjusting it progressively. Only at the end of the twelve or fifteen years would they change over to the Community system. Additionally, they asked that a guide price considerably lower than the lowest prevailing Community price be set for British wheat. This position was unacceptable to the Six, who asked the British to begin to come into line with the common agricultural policy, and notably to change over to the system of levies, on entry into the Community. This started a long battle that was not over when de Gaulle put an end to the negotiations. It is possible that, on this point too, a compromise would have been reached. A committee had been formed under the chairmanship of Mansholt with this precise purpose in mind. Furthermore, the British government had resigned itself to accepting a much shorter transition period than the one it had requested initially.

At the end of 1962, apart from the problem of the adjustment of Britain's system of agricultural protection to the Community's system, a number of important questions had still not been settled, such as the level of duty on Community imports of certain raw materials from the Commonwealth, for which the British wanted duty-free entry, and relations with the other countries of the European Free Trade Association and with the English-speaking developing countries[6].

This was the situation on January 14, 1963 when General de Gaulle put an end to the negotiation by stating that Britain was not yet ready to accept the Common Market as it was:

It is possible that Britain may one day change herself enough to become part of the European Community without restrictions and without reservations,

337

and in preference to anything else, in which case the Six would open the door to her and France would place no obstacle in her path, although, of course, the mere fact of Britain's joining the Community would greatly change its nature and its worth. For this to happen, Britain would have to accept the common external tariff without reservations, relinquish all preference in her relations with the Commonwealth, cease to request privileges for her agriculture and regard as null and void the commitments she has contracted with the countries that form part of her free trade area.

This decision to terminate the negotiation between the Six and the British offended France's continental partners possibly more through its form than through its content. France was within her rights; it requires the unanimous decision of the countries already members to admit new countries to the Community. Furthermore, the French were not alone in feeling that the negotiation was bogging down and that the choice lay between failure and a compromise that was liable to affect the Community's construction in important respects. But from there to the announcement at a press conference that the negotiations were to be broken off, without prior diplomatic consultations, as though France were somehow the custodian of the Community's purity, was quite a step, albeit one which General de Gaulle did not hesitate to take.

In Brussels circles and in the European capitals, many wondered at the time whether the General had not taken his decision right at the outset and simply waited for a favourable opportunity to put it into execution. There were a lot of arguments for thinking that way. The Europe that was being constructed in these first years of the sixties was essentially a Franco-German Europe. It can be said without exaggeration that when France and Germany were agreed on a draft decision, and provided that they applied a little diplomacy, that decision went through. Britain's entry would alter the balance of power. By way of a symbol, it can be said that the use of French would be very considerably affected. In the Europe of the Six, French was the language generally used. In the Commission, Mansholt, Hallstein and my Italian colleagues all expressed themselves in French. The inclusion of Britain (and also Ireland, Denmark and perhaps Norway) would alter the situation completely. English would begin to assume in the European institutions the place it already held in the worldwide institutions. Franco-German cooperation was liable to be disturbed if not interrupted, especially as one could already foresee, in the not too distant future, Adenauer's departure from Bonn and the probable arrival of Erhard, who felt closer to the British than to the French and who, for example, had been an ardent advocate of the free trade area.

For de Gaulle, there was an even more cogent reason for fearing British entry, a reason that subsumed all the others. Britain's attraction to countries across the ocean was not just to the Commonwealth but, above all, to America. De Gaulle was convinced that Britain was not European, other than in a purely geographical sense. Long years of history had forged, then preserved, a special link between her and the United States. If one day she had to choose between America and Europe, there was no doubt in the General's mind that she would choose America. A recent event, only a few days old, had confirmed him in this conviction. The Nassau agreement of December 1962 between Macmillan and Kennedy was for the integration, at least in peacetime, of Britain's nuclear strength into the NATO framework, i.e. its placing under American control.

Does this mean that from the outset of the negotiation the die was cast, that the talks were bound to end in failure? I think one should beware of jumping to that conclusion. I have tried to state what I believe to have been the deep feelings of General de Gaulle on the subject, but these were only propensities. The General, as the whole of his history shows, was not a dogmatist; within a framework of deeply held convictions that nothing could shake, he was ready to adapt to circumstances. If the British in 1961 had, at the start of the negotiations, taken positions which showed that they were ready, subject to certain details, to join the Community as it was or was preparing to be, though once inside they might have tried to alter it, their chances of success would have been greatly enhanced. France's five partners in the Common Market and the Commission itself would have supported them much more enthusiastically than they did. Without trying to rewrite history, let us say that it would have been difficult in those circumstances for General de Gaulle to block their entry into the Common Market, knowing that the result of doing so would probably have been the breakup of the Community.

In the event, both on the question of Commonwealth food imports and on that of protection of British agriculture, as well as on other less crucial matters, the British took positions that were very far removed indeed from the Community's and retreated from them only step by step during the eighteen months of discussions, planting even in the minds of those most in their favour a serious doubt as to their will to reach agreements that would respect the essentials of the Community construction process.

Miriam Camps, an outside observer favourable to British entry into the Common Market and in most cases highly critical of General de Gaulle's attitudes, is nevertheless understanding about his decision to break off negotiations in January 1963:

The British had one concept of Europe and he had another ... Although the British might one day be prepared to look at the political, military and economic problems of Europe as he did, they were not yet ready to do so. Many people in all the Six countries shared General de Gaulle's scepticism about the readiness of the British fully to accept a 'European' point of view and agreed with him that the British had given fresh evidence at Nassau that they thought first of their Atlantic links and second of their European links. Many people on the Continent also shared General de Gaulle's desire for a Europe that would be a power group that could deal as an equal with the United States, and many agreed with him that the Nassau agreement did not respond to the need for a more effective European voice in decisions affecting the very existence of the peoples of Europe[7].

As far as I was concerned, I greeted the decision to break off negotiations in January 1963 with relief, not that I was against Britain's entry into the Community, but because I felt that the change in British thinking was not yet complete and also that the Six needed a few more years to finish what they had begun. But a new element had been injected into international economic discussion at the beginning of 1962 by President Kennedy, something which had affected the course of negotiations between the Community and the British and which would alter the world trade outlook for the years to come.

Kennedy's grand design

Ever since the end of the war, the United States had encouraged, I would even say urged, Europe to achieve the greatest degree of unity of which it was capable. This stance, which originated from the earliest days of the Marshall Plan, was maintained throughout the fifties. In favour of the Schuman Plan, the European Defence Community and the Common Market, the Americans saw those projects essentially as the means whereby their hopes for the political unity of Western Europe might be realized. They were aware that their trade might be adversely affected by a European customs union, but they felt strong enough to accept certain disadvantages if, politically, Europe put itself in a position to assume its responsibilities as a second great power. On the other hand, purely commercial projects, with no political end, did not interest them; in fact they were even very much against them. For example, they gave absolutely no support to the British project for the European free trade area in 1956–8 and probably opposed it through the diplomatic channels. Nor did the small free trade area which the British organized in 1959 find favour with them. When the Common Market was created, the Americans saw it as the embryo of the great power they wanted to emerge. At the same time, they wanted to anchor this new grouping firmly in the western camp. Secondarily, they tried to reduce as far as possible the discrimination applied to US products entering the Common Market, by comparison with the treatment given to European products.

This concern to see their exports hold firm or increase was made more pressing by the turnaround in the US balance of payments. The idea of a worldwide shortage of dollars, of a structural and therefore lasting dollar gap, was still being held by many eminent minds at the end of the fifties, but by then Europe and Japan had gradually rebuilt themselves. Although the US trade balance was still in the black, the overall balance of payments moved into the red as a result of the military aid given to a large number of countries in different parts of the world and the progressive expansion of American investment abroad. By comparison with today's magnitudes, the deficit was small, at least in the early sixties, but it jostled received opinion and worried the Americans. I remember a visit I paid President Kennedy in 1962 or 1963, accompanied by Hallstein and Jean Rey. It emerged very quickly that one of the essential concerns at that time was the balance-of-payments problem. Since I was the man in the Commission in charge of financial and monetary questions, it was I who sustained the conversation. I have kept no notes concerning this encounter, and I have no clear recollection of what the President and I said, but I do remember that for more than an hour the discussion dwelt exclusively on the monetary problem, my two colleagues from the Commission remaining silent.

Already under Eisenhower, in 1959, a first attempt had been made in the GATT to negotiate tariff cuts so as to reduce the discrimination that would be applied increasingly to American products as the Common Market was set up; in 1962 agreement was reached to cut existing import duties, including the common external tariff, by 20% on average. When John Kennedy entered the White House in January 1961, things took on a more imposing air. The term 'Grand Design' made its appearance. No one, to my knowledge, has ever defined precisely what that design was. Let us say that it aimed essentially to accelerate the movement towards unity in Europe, to enlarge the Common Market by bringing the United Kingdom into it, and to create an Atlantic free trade area for a large number of products, by means of drastic reduction or complete elimination of import duties on either side of the ocean. In John Kennedy's mind, the result was to be a partnership between Europe and the United States in which Europe, firmly secured to America, would assume all its responsibilities as a great power, including those in the defence sphere.

George Ball, who as Undersecretary of State was Kennedy's chief collaborator in this affair, and for the Europeans a constant friend, has commented in his memoirs on what he calls 'the mystique of a Grand Design'. Describing the political situation in Europe in the early sixties (a situation which has not changed much since), he makes the following very relevant points:

Though the peoples of Western Europe commanded aggregate resources approaching our own, that aggregate was, in political and military terms, a meaningless statistic. Lacking a common political structure through which they could mobilize and deploy resources in response to a common will, they could play only a marginal role beyond the boundaries of their own continent[8].

For Europe to be able to play a role as an effective ally of the United States, it therefore had to organize itself:

America would benefit by having a strong ally ... we Americans could afford to pay some economic price for a strong Europe that would sustain its share of world responsibilities[9].

I do not think I misrepresent the thinking of George Ball if I say that it was very close to that of Jean Monnet; he wanted to see a federal or confederal Europe, with common institutions that would be supranational in the sense that they would be able to impose a community will on national states, in majority voting conditions that would have to be determined. It was for the Europeans to fix the new rules; the Americans were ready to support them in their endeavour to achieve unity.

An integral and even essential part of the grand design was Britain's entry into the Common Market, a Britain that would have accepted the *political* goals of community Europe as expressed in the Rome Treaty of 1957 or, better still, the Paris Treaty of 1952 setting up the

ECSC. 'We could accept the added [trade] discrimination resulting from British entry,' wrote George Ball, 'only if it would reinforce the political character of the EEC[10].' Political Europe would then have assumed its true proportions. Although it was not said in so many words, Britain's presence in the European Community would have represented an additional guarantee of solidarity with the United States: the assurance that at no time would Europe break loose and drift away from America.

I saw George Ball frequently at that time and we exchanged our views on the British problem. I felt some scepticism regarding Britain's deep motives, but was cautious in expressing it; things had to be allowed to clarify themselves in future negotiations.

As for George Ball, with great clearsightedness he quickly perceived that the government in London was speaking with a double tongue. In connection with a visit to Washington by Macmillan at the beginning of April 1961, he says:

Though ostensibly agreeing that Britain should join the Common Market, Macmillan wanted the President to help him evade the political implications of full entry into the European Community. [...] no matter how much Macmillan privately asserted that entry into Europe was an act with wide-ranging political consequences, he presented it to the British people as an economic move dictated by commercial imperatives[11].

George Ball goes on to quote Macmillan's speech in the House of Commons on July 31, 1961:

I must remind the House that the EEC is an economic community, not a defence alliance or a foreign policy community, or a cultural community[12].

My object here is to stress the ambiguities in the positions of the parties involved in this first negotiation for Britain's entry into the Common Market in 1961–2. The British government which, echoing the British people's feeling on the matter, did not want a federal Europe, found itself pitted against a French government with an equally strong dislike of supranational institutions, while it was supported by an American government which, itself, advocated a *Europe communautaire* in the sense in which Jean Monnet used that term.

I come now to the last of the three constituents of the grand design, namely an across-the-board reduction of customs duties worldwide, or at any rate in the industrialized world. In its most ambitious form the plan aimed at no less than to create an Atlantic free trade area between North America and a Common Market that would include the United Kingdom, an Atlantic economic community as it were.

There can be no doubt that American ideas on this subject had developed as a result of the creation of the Common Market of the Six and its initial successes. Here was a way for the Americans to avoid the discriminatory treatment applied to their products entering Europe, by comparison with products originating from the Six. When I helped to negotiate the Rome Treaty in Brussels in 1956–7, I did not visualize with any precision the upheaval in world trading patterns that would result: first the membership applications by Britain and other European countries, then President Kennedy's request for negotiations. It was concrete, tangible proof that the creation of the European Economic Community was the most important achievement of the fifteen years that followed World War Two. Not only did it mark for France the end of the protectionism in which she had stagnated for so many decades, but it ushered in, for the world as a whole, a period of trading freedom the like of which had never been seen.

To come back to President Kennedy's proposals, in a message to Congress on January 25, 1962 he requested the necessary powers to negotiate what represented a real association with the Common Market. The resultant Trade Expansion Act empowered the Administration to reduce existing import duties by 50% on a reciprocal basis in relations with any other country. It also provided for the complete removal of import duties on those products in which Common Market and US trade together represented at least 80% of world trade. This second provision, in order to take effect, required that Britain and the European countries which had applied, at the same time as she, to join the Common Market should become members. The breakdown of the negotiations between the Community and Britain invalidated this segment of the Kennedy proposals. Congress passed the Trade Expansion Act on June 28, 1962. The Kennedy Round opened in Geneva on May 4, 1964 and ended with a general agreement on May 16, 1967. Jean Rey and I together represented the Commission in these negotiations for maybe two years, working on the basis of instructions issued by the Council of Ministers. In the latter stages of the talks Jean Rey took sole charge, all my time being then taken up in Brussels by other problems, notably the regulation on agricultural financing.

During those years I had some fairly sharp clashes with the main American spokesmen, Herter and Blumenthal, on different questions, especially that of 'tariff disparities'. The US tariff scale showed very high rates of duty on a certain number of products, of the order of 30, 40 or even 50%, whereas the Community's external tariff was much more homogeneous. This being so, a uniform reduction of the order of 50% in all customs duties would have left some US duties still very much higher than the European or American average; we were asking that, in view of this situation, the high US duties should first be brought down, before the across-the-board reduction could be applied. I can remember acrimonious discussions, many of them at night, in which tempers became frayed. Ultimately, an overall compromise was reached that was a great success for all parties. Import duties were reduced by a large margin and, once the cuts came into effect, ceased to represent a real barrier to trade. The active and positive role played by the Community in the Kennedy Round was proof that it was not protectionist-minded and inward-looking, as its opponents charged, and that it was perfectly conscious of its responsibilities on a world scale.

The accomplishments of the Grand Design, impressive though they were, fell far short of its authors' ambitions. George Ball, in his memoirs, looks back sadly on those years from 1961 to 1963 when America sought to create an Atlantic economic community.

If I look back with regret at events since the early 1960s, it is not because I spent so much time and effort trying to advance the building of Europe, but because the effort failed. Although, God knows, American governments have made plenty of mistakes, our encouragement of a unified Europe was not one of them. Failure came from no fault of ours, but because, when key decisions were made, the European leaders of the moment lacked adequate vision[13].

One might take issue with this conclusion, but it comes from a man of good will who, without any imperialist intentions, devoted a great part of his life to establishing and preserving close links between Europe and America.

The institutional crisis of 1965

After the turmoil created in Brussels and in the capitals of the Six by the breaking-off of negotiations for Britain's membership of the EEC in the circumstances I have described, work was resumed with a view to completing the Common Market, in a strained atmosphere to begin

345

with, then in quite normal conditions. The years 1963 and 1964 were among the most productive in the movement towards economic unity for Europe.

What I had been hoping happened. The Six were too deeply attached to the Community to let themselves be diverted from the common objective, even if many in the other five countries, and even in France, had been profoundly shocked by what they regarded as General de Gaulle's arbitrary decision. At the height of the crisis, the Germans did not exert any strong pressure on the French to get them to change their attitude; Adenauer himself had doubts about the wisdom of enlarging the Community at that precise moment. The Franco-German treaty, which I mentioned earlier, is an expression of the feelings and the wishes of the old chancellor. The Germans gave clear notice, however, that they would not agree to any further moves towards the establishment of the common agricultural policy unless parallel progress were made in the Geneva negotiations for an across-the-board worldwide reduction in tariffs on industrial and allied products. This linkage did not, incidentally, bother the French government, given its relative leaning towards a free-market stance.

1963 and 1964 saw the consolidation of the common agricultural policy, notably through its extension to new sectors – dairy products, beef and veal, rice – and the setting of common prices for cereals; this last decision opened the way to the adoption of common prices for the other agricultural products. On July 1, 1963, pursuant to a decision to accelerate the establishment of the customs union, intra-Community customs duties were further reduced and national external tariffs were adjusted again to bring them another step closer to the common external tariff.

It was in 1964, too, that the first attempt was made, if not to create an economic union, at least to coordinate national economic policies. I was personally responsible here, since economic, financial and monetary questions were my domain. That year inflationary pressures, which then seemed very strong, had emerged in the Community. Italy suddenly found herself in a difficult position that necessitated substantial foreign aid. This was the time to make use of the clauses in the Treaty of Rome that provided for Community aid in the event of balance-of-payments difficulties. I went to Rome, where the press hailed me as a saviour. During my stay there I was headline news in all the papers. Finally, the Italians preferred to apply to the Americans and the International Monetary Fund. *Sic transit* ... The Council adopted recommendations to governments which I had drawn up, inviting them, among other things, to tighten their fiscal policies. These recommendations were applied for a year or two, then laid aside. It was at that time that I started to have doubts about the possibility and perhaps even the utility, as a rule, of coordinating national economic policies. Either governments act spontaneously, guided by their own interest, or they are too weak to act, in both of which cases no amount of external pressure will be able to budge them.

Nevertheless, in that same year of 1964 the Council, on my proposal, established a Committee of Governors of Central Banks and a Committee on Budgetary Policy, while the functions of the Monetary Committee were augmented. At the same time the Council decided to draw up and implement a medium-term economic policy. The latter remained largely a dead letter. As for the new committees, although they did useful work and brought together for the discussion of Community business national government officials who, for the most part, had not known one another previously, they did not, at least at that time, do much to further the harmonization, not to mention the unification, of national economic policies. It has to be said that the need for this had not yet made itself felt acutely.

Thus 1956 seemed to have opened auspiciously, when in March there broke the most violent storm which the Community has had to traverse and in which I had to take stances that separated me from most of my colleagues in the Commission.

The history of the EEC between March 1965 and January 1966 appears to be full of confusion and contradictions. It was a period in which France and some of her partners (Holland and Italy notably) clashed violently, about the powers of the Strasbourg Assembly and also about the regulation on agricultural financing, which was a vital element, the keystone one might say, of the Common Agricultural Policy. When that period was over, the Community had assumed, if not its definitive form, at least the form it would retain for the next twenty years. Whatever the appearances, the Luxembourg 'compromise' of January 1966 consecrated, or probably just confirmed, the victory of Gaullist conceptions in the matter of European institutions. The Community was stripped of the few supranational elements that had been written into the Treaty of Rome. But even though federal Europe was cast aside, this does not mean that the Europe of States carried the day. France's partners were even less willing than in 1962 to accept Gaullist ideas about political Europe. Relations between

France and Germany cooled considerably, although there continued to be a special link between the two countries.

During those few months the majority of the Commission thought that the great day had come and that the members of the Community would solemnly pledge themselves to undying solidarity. I found myself in disagreement with most of my colleagues. Not that my basic instincts were any different from theirs, but their attempt not only to increase the budgetary powers of the Strasbourg Assembly, which would be realized later on a much more modest scale, but also and above all to become an arbiter between the Assembly and the Council of Ministers, thus greatly increasing the Commission's powers, struck me as premature and certain to end in a humiliating defeat.

Given the historical importance of the 1965 crisis, the effects of which we are still feeling twenty years later, and the positions I was led to take, I do not think it out of place here for me to recount briefly the origin, development and culmination of that crisis.

The point of departure was nothing out of the ordinary. In January 1962, at the marathon session on agriculture that was taking place then, the Council of Ministers adopted a financial regulation valid until July 1, 1965 that prescribed the method whereby expenditure in connection with the common agricultural policy would be financed up to that date; but at the same time it decided that a new financial regulation would be laid down by June 30, 1965, to operate throughout the rest of the transition period, i.e. until 1970. When, on December 15, 1964, the Council adopted a package of measures representing a big step forward in the construction of the CAP, it also invited the Commission to submit to it by April 1, 1965 proposals for the CAP's financing over the period from 1965 to 1970, together with proposals for the Community's appropriation of the levies charged on farm goods coming into the Common Market.

To clarify this last point, it is necessary to explain that up until the moment when the agricultural Common Market could be regarded as completed, that is until such time as common prices had been set for the different farm products, agricultural expenditure was to be financed by way of national contributions. But once the agricultural Common Market had been completely set up, the levies would be wholly paid over to the Community and used to finance common expenditure. A similar process might lead to the Community's appropriation of proceeds from import duties when the common external tariff became fully operative. Agricultural levies and import duties would then constitute the Community's 'own resources'.

348

This, then, was the background to the proposals which the Commission was to formulate in March 1965.

On March 24, 1965, in a speech before the Strasbourg Assembly, Hallstein revealed the gist of these proposals. His doing so was a highly unusual manner of procedure, the Community rule being that the Council of Ministers should be the first to hear the proposals of the Commission. This departure from custom shocked a lot of people, particularly in the French camp but elsewhere too.

Furthermore, the ideas put forward by the Commission on the subject of finance went well beyond what governments and informed circles were expecting. They were to the effect that the Common Market, both agricultural and industrial, would be completed on July 15, 1967 and that from this date the proceeds from agricultural levies would be payable in full to the Community. As to the proceeds from import duties, their appropriation by the Community would be phased in over a period of a few years. Everyone was immediately struck by the fact that the Community would thus have at its disposal resources far in excess of its requirements, a situation that might lead to wastage of the funds available. On this point, I would add that no government, and not only or even principally the French government, was in a particular hurry to forgo the proceeds from import duties. This was especially true of the big importers like Holland that re-exported to the other EEC countries much of the merchandise that entered the Community through their ports.

All this may have shown lack of judgment on the Commission's part, but it was not serious in itself. To put things back in their proper place, no more need have been done than to adjust the date set for the completion of the agricultural and industrial Common Market, or to specify that the date chosen would not mark the end of the transition period, which would continue until 1970 as provided for in the Rome Treaty. This, by the way, is what happened a little later.

But this was not the worst of it. The majority of the Commission had wanted to introduce a real institutional innovation and alter extensively, radically, the balance of power that had been written into the Treaty of Rome. Up to that point, in budget matters as on other questions, the Commission had made proposals, the Assembly had given its opinion, and the Council of Ministers had made the final decision. Henceforth, if the Commission's new suggestion were followed, the Assembly would be able to amend, by a simple majority vote, the draft budget adopted by the Council. The Commission would be able either to refuse or to accept these amendments; if it accepted them, the Council could only set them aside by a five-sixths majority with a non-weighted vote (one vote per country, whatever the size of its population). In the event of disagreement between the Commission and the Assembly, the Council could side with the Commission on the basis of a four-sixths majority. In all other cases, the Assembly's amendments would be adopted[14].

Beneath the complicated wording of these proposals lay a very simple reality that was not difficult to see. The Commission would become, in budget matters, a kind of government of the Community. For its proposals to go through, it would only need the agreement of the majority of the Assembly and, in the Council of Ministers, the support of two countries, say Holland and Luxembourg. Anything the majority of the Council might say, even if that majority included France, Germany and Italy, would be of no consequence.

With this strange legal construct the idea of a federal Europe made its last appearance. It was entirely the brainchild of Hallstein, who had won Mansholt over to it. The project had been drawn up in the utmost secrecy by a few of their collaborators, the other members of the Commission being carefully kept out of the picture. As soon as I had heard about it, I had stated my total opposition to what I regarded as an absurdity. I was not in any way impugning the intentions of my two colleagues; I knew that they wanted to use the opportunity presented by the new financial regulation to get Europe to take a decisive step towards unity. But I knew too, given the sentiments prevailing not only in Paris but also in government and civil service circles in the other capitals, that there was not the slightest chance of the project's being accepted, or even of its being considered seriously. I feared that, far from furthering the construction of Europe, it would prove to be a seriously retrograde step, notably by impairing the authority of the Commission, which up to then had been the dynamic factor in the Community.

In the ordinary way, the Council should have ignored these proposals and proceeded to adopt a financial regulation of the kind that had been in force since 1962, while gradually extending the Community's competence in agricultural matters. If the affair degenerated into a deep crisis which gave the impression for a time that it would cause the breakup of the Community, it was because most of the governments had ulterior motives and tried to use the situation to achieve their own ends.

To begin with, Benelux, Italy and, to a lesser extent, Germany were nothing loath to make General de Gaulle's France pay the price of the veto with which she had barred Britain's entry into the Common Market in 1963. In those countries, and especially in Holland and Germany, parliamentary opinion was violently anti-Gaullist and this the governments concerned were obliged to take into account, even when their own ideas and feelings were different, or partly so. Since it was known that France keenly wanted a financial regulation valid for a period of five years, in line with the commitments undertaken in 1963, those countries wanted her to make a move, even if it were not necessarily the one the Commission was proposing, but a move all the same, towards an arrangement that would give the Strasbourg Assembly certain budgetary powers.

Relations between Paris and Bonn were no longer what they had been in Adenauer's time. Erhard and his Foreign Minister Gerhard Schroeder were not moved by the same desire to strengthen the Franco-German alliance, though they did not want to see it weaken either. What they wanted to get from France was an assurance that she would not create unjustified difficulties in the Kennedy Round tariff negotiations that were going on in Geneva. Until they were assured of her good faith in this affair, they were not prepared to accept a financial regulation for a duration of more than one or two years.

Basically, none of the member governments was ready to part with the proceeds from import duties and agricultural levies, for as long as it could be avoided. Certainly none of them, whatever it might state publicly, was prepared to accept the Commission's institutional proposals, except possibly for the Netherlands government, and even that is doubtful. But it was convenient to hide behind France, knowing that she would oppose even a discussion of those proposals.

And it was in Paris that opposition to the Commission's ideas was the most violent. France considered that she was entitled to the five-year financial regulation that the Six had undertaken to adopt by June 30, 1965, and without that regulation's adoption being subjected to conditions which, as she saw it, had nothing to do with the affair. At that time still, as at the time of the Rome Treaty's negotiation, the common agricultural policy was regarded by the French as the necessary *quid pro quo* for the free movement of industrial products. They issued statement after statement to that effect. Thus, Alain Peyrefitte, then Minister of Information, made the following announcement on October 21, 1964 at the conclusion of a meeting of the Council of Ministers in Paris:

General de Gaulle, M. Pompidou and the government emphasized, once more, that France would cease to participate in the European Economic Community if the Common Market for agriculture were not organized as it had been specified that it would be organized. The resolution taken by the Council of Ministers was expressed in the most categorical fashion, so as to make the Common Market for agriculture the touchstone of any construction of Europe and the very precondition of that construction.

Georges Pompidou, the Prime Minister, had this to say on November 5, 1964:

The agricultural Common Market must be established, failing which the industrial Common Market will perish. The problem is not whether we shall come out of the European Economic Community or not. If France, at one moment or another, considers that the Common Market is stifled in its soul and in its deep potentialities, well then, it will die a natural death, whatever the texts and the arrangements which it is planned to apply and which, at that moment, could not be applied.

But there was more in the French position than an intention to 'break up the place' if the common agricultural policy did not see the light of day within the time limit set by the decisions of the Council of Ministers. There was also the resolve to render null and void at the first opportunity (and the Brussels Commission was providing just that opportunity) the Rome Treaty provisions that General de Gaulle did not like, particularly those that specified that from January 1, 1966 the Council of Ministers could take certain important decisions by majority vote. The government in Paris also considered that the Commission was getting ideas above its station, that it was tending to behave like a government and that it needed quickly to be put in its place.

All these more or less openly avowed intentions explain the fact that on June 30, or rather in the early hours of July 1, 1965, the crisis broke, with Maurice Couve de Murville stating that the problem was very simple: it was purely a matter of honouring the commitment entered into in January 1962 to the effect that, by June 30, 1965, a new financial regulation operative until the end of the transition period would have to be introduced. Since no one, he added, was insisting that 'own resources' should be created by the date envisaged by the Commission, the question of the Assembly's powers no longer arose. France recalled her permanent representative in Brussels; she was to practise the policy of the 'empty chair' until the beginning of 1966, being represented only at those meetings concerning the functioning of the common agricultural policy and the agreements of association with Greece and Turkey. During that time the Five continued to sit and procedures were invented for disposing of current business.

After the commotion of June 30, the Commission had pulled itself together. I found my colleagues more understanding. They realized that they had made a blunder and that it was now for the Commission to do what it could to see that the Community got back to normal. It began to think again, whereas from March to June it had been entrenched in the positions I mentioned earlier, stultified at once by the criticism to which it was being subjected and by the often embarrassing support it was receiving from certain frenzied anti-Gaullist quarters.

In a July memorandum, of which I did much of the drafting, it did what was in its power to prepare the way for a settlement of the crisis. The proposals it outlined then gave the French full satisfaction, to the extent that their demands were indeed the ones they had been defending publicly in the preceding months. These proposals included the adoption of a financial regulation operative for a period of five years and the postponement of any decision concerning the creation of 'own resources', and therefore also the possible powers of the Strasbourg Assembly.

But, as happens frequently in history, ideas that could have averted the crisis proved to be completely out of date once it struck. France was no longer content with the financial regulation she had requested, she also wanted any provision of a supranational character, such as the possibility of majority voting, if not written out of the Rome Treaty, at least invalidated for all practical purposes. The remarks of General de Gaulle at the time are perfectly clear. In a press conference on September 9, 1965 he said this among other things:

What happened in Brussels on June 30, in connection with the agricultural financing regulation, highlighted not only the persistent reluctance of the majority of our partners to bring agriculture within the scope of the Common Market, but also certain errors or ambiguities in the Treaties relating to the economic union of the Six. That is why the crisis was, sooner or later, inevitable . . . I should add that in the light of the event we have gauged more clearly the situation in which our country might find itself tomorrow if such and such provisions initially made in the Treaty of Rome were actually applied. Thus, by virtue of the Treaty's text, the decisions of the Council of Ministers of the Six would, from January 1 of next year, be taken by majority vote, in other words France would be exposed to the possibility of being

overruled in any economic and, consequently, any social and often even any
political matter, and, in particular, what would appear to have been achieved
in the domain of agriculture might, despite France, be brought into question
at any moment.

France was therefore asking explicitly that the Rome Treaty provisions to which she had nevertheless formally subscribed should not
be applied. She was calling into question the Treaty itself. What could
the other five countries do? Take decisions by majority vote after
January 1, 1966, establish that France was refusing to implement
them, bring her before the Court of Justice in Luxembourg for viola-
tion of the Treaty? It was conceivable, but absurd. The Community
would have fallen to pieces.

The affair ended in Luxembourg on January 29, 1965, with the
Commission absent. The questions concerning the Commission's behaviour were settled very easily: the French toned down their demands
and the Five agreed to ask the Commission to conduct itself with more
restraint and, in particular, to observe certain rules in its relations with
governments and with the Council. But the problem posed by majority
voting was well-nigh insoluble. The French did not want the majority
vote on any account, while the Five absolutely refused to abandon the
possibility of it, at least in writing and in a text having legal weight. In
the end the parties acknowledged that there was disagreement. This
meant, of course, that a great effort at reconciliation would have to be
made in any important discussion if unanimous agreement were to be
reached. But what would happen if it were not? As far as the Five were
concerned, it would then be necessary to vote. But the document
recording the positions of the different parties noted that France
'considers that, when very important interests are at stake, the discussion must be continued until unanimous agreement is reached.'

Given this difference of view on a point that many considered
fundamental, the Six had the choice either of going their separate ways
or of acting as if nothing had happened. Wisely they took the second
course. The governments agreed that this divergence '[would] not
prevent the Community from resuming its work according to a normal
procedure.' There lay the whole subtlety of what has been incorrectly
termed the 'Luxembourg compromise'. There was no compromise, at
least on the most serious question, that of the majority vote. It was
simply noted that there was disagreement, and the Six went on living
together. The result was that for the next fifteen or twenty years in the
Community no decisions were taken by majority vote on important

questions, and very few on comparatively minor issues, even when no member country's interests were seriously involved.

For my own part, I had tried throughout this long affair to prevent the Community from breaking up. The price that was paid in Luxembourg seemed to me in no way exorbitant. Among other things I did not believe that the Commission was already a federal or confederal government or had the makings of one. The title of 'Executive' with which it had dignified itself at the beginning of the sixties struck me as a little silly. I did not see how it could become a European government, since its members were entirely answerable to national governments by virtue of having been appointed commissioners. Each commissioner is appointed by the government of the country of which he is a citizen. The appointments' ratification by the Council of Ministers is, save in exceptional cases, purely a formality.

My idea of the Commission's independence was different. It rested entirely on the latter's role as a 'mediator'. First of all, as regards the proposals it was required to formulate and defend before the Council, these had to reflect to the greatest possible degree the interests and views of all the member states, while at the same time expressing the interests of the Community as a whole. Next, in the discussion of those proposals, it was the Commission's job to find the greatest common denominator and try to get it accepted. Often it could do so only by grouping a series of problems no more than remotely connected with one another and seeing to it that each government found, in the resulting set of proposals, satisfaction on one or more points, which allowed it to think, or at any rate to assert, that it had won. It was this method that came to be referred to by the name of 'package deals'. This role of mediator was the one I had tried to discharge at the OEEC and I remained attached to it in my activity within the EEC Commission.

I always found that the clause in the Rome Treaty which makes the Commission accountable to the European Parliamentary Assembly was difficult to understand. It is not the Commission that decides, even in matters covered by the Treaty, but the Council of Ministers. Why would the Strasbourg Assembly dismiss the Commission? Surely not for decisions that do not emanate from the Commission! The only eventuality that comes to mind is where the Commission would refuse to formulate proposals designed to implement this or that part of the Treaty. And that is highly unlikely. The truth of the matter is that in dismissing the Commission the Assembly would be trying to get at the Council of Ministers. In the event, even if it has on occasion been under threat of it, the Commission has never been subjected by the Strasbourg Assembly to a motion of censure, which, if passed, would have brought about its dissolution.

As to the 'majority vote', it was no hardship for me to see it shelved where very important issues were concerned. I had never thought the system could be used, at least in the European climate of that time. Was that surprising? How could one imagine that an issue affecting the fundamental interests of one or more member states could be settled in defiance of the opinion of those states? The Community did not have the means to enforce such a decision. If the people of an outvoted country were to react against a decision which had been taken, could that country's government be counted on to implement it, if by no other means than by force?

Moreover, my feeling was that most of the other governments, whatever certain of them might be led to say in order to gain the support of parliamentary opinion, did not want the majority vote any more than the French government did and that they sacrificed it to the French with no great pain, and some even with secret relief. Thirteen or fourteen years later when, as part of a task force to investigate a reform of the Community's institutions, I had to talk with the delegations of the member governments, which had increased from six to nine, I found that none of them (except one perhaps, and there I am not sure) wanted reestablishment of the majority vote for settling a question that was considered, even by just one government, to be of major importance. A few of them simply asked, and here I was and still am in complete agreement with them, that the unanimity rule should not be abused and that it should not be insisted upon when it was a case of questions that did not involve a very important interest in one of the member countries. In fact, even if France had not taken in 1965 the position I have described, it is unlikely that important questions would ever have been settled by the majority voting procedure. The newcomers to the Community, those that joined in 1973, notably Britain, would anyhow have taken care to see that this did not happen.

The truth is that between Europe, as we know it, and a European federation with a legislative power and an executive power, both set in place by the will of the people, it is difficult to imagine an intermediate position. What one regarded twenty or thirty years ago as steady progress towards a political reality of this kind – a High Authority invested with sovereign power or a Commission that would try to behave like a government, or again a Council of Ministers in which the major decisions would be taken by majority vote – has all proved illusory. The Common Market is not a federation and is not on the way to becoming one. It is an organization which, although having certain political connotations, is essentially concerned with the economic life of the member countries and which rests on the consensus, explicit or implicit, of all the states that compose it.

After the Luxembourg 'agreement', which was an agreement to disagree, things quickly settled down in Brussels and the Community resumed its advance, as though there were in the Rome Treaty, or in the ideas it expressed, a particular force that drove the Community forward, whatever the conflicts that might arise between member states. More prosaically, let us say that the different parties all felt that the EEC represented a framework they could no longer dispense with, in which their economic activity could expand and without which they would simply be reduced to their status of small or medium nation in a world dominated by the Great Powers.

In the first half of 1966 an agreement was concluded on a financial regulation that would see the Community through to the end of the transition period in 1970. By and large, it met French demands. The problem of the Community's own resources and the powers of the Strasbourg Assembly was put off until later. New agricultural decisions were taken making the common agricultural policy applicable to 90% of production by the six countries and setting prices for all the major foodstuffs.

The date of July 1, 1968 was adopted for the completion of the Common Market, both industrial and agricultural. Thus, a little over ten years after the Rome Treaty's entry into force, customs duties within the Community were entirely dismantled and the common external tariff set up. Common prices for the main agricultural products came into force. The Rome Treaty, in its essentials, was executed a year and a half before the date set for the end of the transition period, although much remained to be done in a large number of areas – harmonization of tariff legislations, right of establishment, liberalization of capital movements, abolition of fiscal and administrative frontiers, etc. – but in many cases it was now no more than a question of patience and perseverance. The main questions of principle had been settled, one way or another.

On May 16, 1967 the Kennedy Round produced a general agreement that everyone could accept with the feeling that the concessions made on the different sides were substantially equivalent. Thus the trade controversy between America and Europe was provisionally settled, until new problems arose.

To complete the story of this phase of continuous progress, the Community in 1970 was provided with its own resources, which, for a time at least, made it independent of national governments and parliaments. The proceeds from import duties and the agricultural levies would be made over to it on an incremental basis until such time as they became entirely its property, on January 2, 1975. They would be supplemented along the way by a proportion of the different countries' revenue from VAT. In 1970, too, an agreement on a common commercial policy entered into effect. Although still incomplete, that policy represented a decisive step towards unification of the conditions of access to the Common Market for the products of non member countries.

In May 1967 Britain had reapplied for membership of the Common Market. Again France stated her opposition and the discussions were wound up at the end of the year with an acknowledgment of disagreement. Not until 1970 would they be resumed, this time with a positive conclusion. My reservations about British entry into the Community had largely vanished. By 1970, unlike the situation in 1961–3, the Common Market had become a solid reality, the common agricultural policy had been established in all its essentials, all the important decisions necessary to the Rome Treaty's implementation had been taken. The Six had probably gone as far together as they could go in the foreseeable future. Britain's entry, along with that of Denmark and Ireland, would inevitably render the Community decision-making process more cumbersome, but it would not alter the latter's nature. Above all, it had become evident that France's five partners would not resign themselves indefinitely to keeping the door of the Community closed to the British. The risk of institutional paralysis in the EEC had become so great, at a time when Britain's entry no longer presented the same threats as it did ten years earlier, that France rightly decided to agree this time.

7

JOURNEY'S END OR POINT OF DEPARTURE?

The era of which I have been writing, in Parts Three and Four of this book, stretches from the end of the war to the late sixties or early seventies, an era during which Europe rebuilt itself, rapidly developed its productive forces and initiated a process of unification.

One could argue *ad infinitum* the point of whether Europe, as we know it in 1986, has moved forward or back from where it was in 1967, given all the decisions that were formally taken in the few years that followed but were already politically agreed by 1967. My personal feeling is that in the fifteen or so intervening years no major decision has been taken that has changed the essential nature of the Common Market. One could, in trying to define this period, speak of 'consolidation' or 'levelling off'. The truth is that there was neither progress nor regress to any significant degree.

Which were the momentous decisions of the seventies? For me there were five. The enlargement of the Community to include Britain, the establishment of the European Council, the election of the European Parliament by universal suffrage, the creation of the European Monetary System, and the use of a Community procedure to try to overcome the grave crisis in the European steel industry.

The entry of Britain, Ireland and Denmark into the Common Market did not change anything fundamental. It reinforced the ego-centricity of governments, their tendency to attach importance only to what might satisfy a national interest, at the expense of efforts to consolidate European unity; it weakened the Community's institutions to some extent, by the mere fact of having increased the number of members; it helped to make the Luxembourg 'compromise' a sacrosanct practice that would be used to deal with all questions, even those of only minor importance.

Direct election of the European Parliament by universal suffrage could have been a big step towards the creation of a political Europe, if at the same time new powers had been conferred on the Assembly, giving it, in the Community and for Community affairs, a position comparable to that of a parliament in a national state. As we know, this was not the case.

The establishment in 1975 of a European Council, comprising the heads of state or government of the member countries and meeting on average three times a year, facilitated summit-level discussion of the major economic and political issues confronting the Community and initiated intergovernmental cooperation in the foreign policy field. But in no way did it create a European executive. Decisions in the European Council are always taken unanimously or not at all. It may seriously be wondered whether the European Council is more effective than the Council of Foreign Ministers, which was the supreme body of the Community in the latter's heyday. I think it is less so. But that is probably due more to circumstances than to institutional arrangements.

The most important decision of the seventies was undoubtedly the creation of the European Monetary System in 1979. It represented progress towards the establishment of an area of exchange rate stability. Over the past six years [to 1986], although there have been several currency adjustments within the EMS, the parities of the European currencies have not fluctuated as widely against one another as they would have in the absence of the EMS. These parities have not shown the same volatility in their relationships to one another as in their relationships to certain currencies outside the system. It is also reasonable to say that, on certain occasions at least, the fact of belonging to the EMS has led a number of countries to adopt difficult economic, financial and monetary policy measures which brought them closer to other European countries or at any rate prevented them from drawing further away. This much granted, it would be absurd to speak of this practical and extremely useful arrangement as being a step towards a European monetary union.

The way in which the Community, and specifically the Commission, reacted at the time of the crisis that struck the European steel industry at the end of the seventies stands as an example of effective joint action to overcome difficulties that were present to varying degrees in most of the member states. It showed that with a little courage and determination it was possible to make use of certain articles in the ECSC treaty that had been somewhat overlooked since the fifties and obtain good results.

I could extend almost indefinitely the list of decisions taken by the Community which have significantly improved the functioning of the Common Market and brought Europe closer to the day when it can be regarded as constituting a single domestic market, like that of any national state. The fact remains that Europe is still a very long way from this goal, that member states pursue individual and often divergent economic policies and that there is as yet no sign of Europe's beginning to behave as a unit in world affairs.

From 1967 up to the present, I have been consulted from time to time by the Community on this or that aspect of European affairs, notably in 1974 concerning the project for an economic and monetary union, and in 1978 regarding the functioning of the Community's institutions and ways of improving it. I shall say a word about each of the reports that resulted from these two assignments.

The illusion of the Economic and Monetary Union

In 1974 the Commission asked me to head a group of experts to study the problems posed by the creation of the Economic and Monetary Union (EMU). We were called 'The Study Group, Economic and Monetary Union 1980'. To understand the significance of this strange title, it is necessary to look back at the circumstances of the time.

At the end of the sixties the member countries of the European Community, having realized that individually they carried little weight in the world economy, tried to strengthen their unity by extending the limits of the Common Market beyond what the latter's founding fathers had believed possible. That was the origin of the movement towards economic and monetary union which formally came into being at the Hague Summit of 1969. At the beginning of 1971 the Council decided to put into effect measures which in ten years should lead to the full realization of the Economic and Monetary Union, the latter being defined as the creation of a single European currency or the existence of irrevocably fixed parities between national currencies.

In the minds of the most fervent 'Europeans', this initiative would ultimately strengthen the links between the Community's members to such a degree that political union would then seem within reach. The EMU was a temporary substitute for political union and would inevitably lead to it. As the years went by without any noticeable progress towards the objective set in 1969, or with seeming progress followed by backsliding or worse, uneasiness set in, and this is why the aforementioned group was set up.

We worked for several months without getting very far and with a mounting sense of frustration. Finally we decided to prick the bubble and say aloud what everyone was secretly thinking.

Although some progress of a technical nature has been accomplished, notably as regards cooperation between central banks, the Study Group is of the opinion that, on balance, the enterprise undertaken in 1969 has failed ... Europe is no nearer to EMU than in 1969. In fact, if there has been any movement it has been backward. The Europe of the 60s represented a relatively harmonious economic and monetary entity, which was undone in the course of recent years: national economic and monetary policies have never in 25 years been more discordant, more divergent than they are today.

As a result, when one speaks of Europe, one is speaking essentially of a geographical entity situated between the USA and the USSR, composed of states which trade very actively with one another but which, in most cases, behave in national affairs and in world affairs each according to its individual leanings and affinities ... The fact that for a number of years no significant progress has been made towards the unification of Europe means that the authority of the European institutions has been weakened and that they are no longer regarded as the prefiguration of the institutions which would watch over the destiny of a united Europe.

In trying to establish the causes of the failure, we found three that predominated: adverse events, a failure of political will, and an insufficient understanding of what constituted an economic and monetary union and of the conditions that had to be met for it to come into existence and to be able to function.

The adverse events were the international monetary crisis that had been disrupting the western world since the end of the sixties and the economic and financial crisis caused by the sudden jump in oil prices in 1973.

As with any crisis, these events could have provided the opportunity for progress, by causing latent will to crystallize. The great achievements of the

362

past were nearly all born of crises. The recent crises could have been the occasion for a leap forward.

Why have they caused a retreat instead? It is because at no time have governments really tried to stand together in order to tackle these difficult circumstances. Theirs has not been a European will but a collection of national wills more or less unheeding of one another, with each government trying in its own way to extricate itself from the predicament.

But what seemed to my colleagues and me to be the chief reason for the failure of the venture to create an economic and monetary union was the absence of any real understanding of what was involved.

It was as if the governments had undertaken the enterprise in the naïve belief that it was sufficient to decree the formation of an EMU for this to come about at the end of a few years, without great effort nor difficult and painful economic and political transformations.

The general thinking seemed to be that EMU was just an extension or development of the customs union, without any appreciation of the fact that the two concepts were profoundly different. The customs union simply presupposes that 'governments give up, except in exceptional circumstances, the use, in the pursuit of their national interests, of the instruments of commercial policy, notably customs duties and quantitative restrictions', all the other tools of economic and monetary policy remaining at their disposal. In an EMU, by contrast, 'national governments put at the disposal of the common institutions the use of all the instruments of monetary policy and of economic policy whose action should be exercised in the Community as a whole. These institutions, moreover, must have a discretionary power similar to that which national governments possess now, in order to meet unexpected events.'

Truth to tell, the notion of an economic and monetary union was closer to that of a political union, federation or confederation, than to the notion of a customs union. Practically identical, in fact, to a political union, it would have to include a European political power, a Community budget, and an integrated system of central banks. All this would require profound changes for which the member countries were obviously not ready. We suggested, therefore, that it would be best for a while to stop building castles in Spain and talking about EMU and for governments to concentrate on the immediate problems: 'inflation', 'massive balance-of-payments deficits', 'unemployment'.

The only reasonable and possible course for member countries is to tackle these perils together, and in cooperation with North America and Japan, without asking too many questions about longer-term issues. If not even a modicum of cohesion and unity can be established in opposition to these grave threats, there is not much point in continuing the discussion on EMU or European union. If, on the other hand, a common will emerges in the next year or two, concerning concrete, specific and urgent problems, Europe will find itself at the end of this short period in a position such that the great projects that have been discussed at recent summits will once more be conceivable.

Basically what we were saying to governments was: 'Gentlemen, let us be serious! Let us not lose sight of the concrete, immediate problems amid a lot of empty talk about inaccessible objectives. Let us do what it is possible to do now and leave the rest until later, when there is definite proof of the existence of a political will that is not purely verbal.'

Not surprisingly, this report was very badly received by the Council, which regarded it as an indictment of the action, or rather lack of action, of governments. The Commission, for its part, did nothing to see that it was discussed. It was buried, as a lot of reports of this kind are. But it had its effect. There was no more talk of EMU. National policies, it is true, remained divergent, but Community discussions were now concerned with practical and concrete matters. It may not be making too much of a mistake to think that the report contributed indirectly and in modest measure to the creation of the European Monetary System.

The Report of the Three Wise Men

At the end of 1978 the European Council appointed a Committee of Three 'to consider adjustments to the machinery and procedures of the Community institutions'. It was understood that the group thus set up should not make proposals necessitating amendments to the Treaty of Rome and should confine itself to concrete proposals that could be acted on rapidly. My two colleagues in this group were Barend Biesheuvel, formerly Prime Minister of the Netherlands, and Edmund Dell, a former Chairman of the United Kingdom Board of Trade.

We were christened 'The Three Wise Men', as is customary in circumstances of this kind. Wise Men generally come in threes, as though a third person were always necessary to strike a balance between the divergent points of view of the other two. I hasten to add that the wisdom with which the said persons are credited vanishes the moment they hand in their conclusions.

We worked on our report for a year, in an atmosphere of trust and fellow feeling with no axes to grind. I had a high regard for the intelligence and integrity of my two colleagues, who became my friends. Recently, Jacques Delors, President of the Brussels Commission, stated: 'This report is still topical. All the problems that have to be settled in order to improve the functioning of the Community are clearly set out in it and the solutions offered are still valid.' Maybe M. Delors is right. I cannot help feeling a little sad that in the years that followed the submission of this report so little was done to implement the proposals we had put forward. It was not until recently that I thought I discerned in current Brussels discussions some progress in the right direction.

To be a little more specific, I shall now say briefly what the report contained[1].

In the introduction to our report, my two colleagues and I stressed for the benefit of governments that while we had agreed to consider what mechanical and procedural improvements could be made in order to facilitate the work of the European Communities, we were under no illusions about the nature of the difficulties: they were not essentially attributable to faulty machinery and procedures, but to substantive problems stemming from economic and political constraints. 'The role of the machinery and institutional procedures is a strictly secondary one.' We went on to list the successes of the Common Market to date and the problems that continued to exist, stating that we were 'struck in particular by the gravity of the difficulties likely to face the Community in the 1980s quite independently of its internal organization.'

We first presented the credit side, too often overlooked or undervalued.

The Community is a quite unprecedented creation. It may be less than a federation, or even less than a confederation, but it represents a great deal more than a traditional alliance or international organization. In establishing the Community member states have been ready to transfer important powers, although in a limited number of domains, to the Community institutions; they have done so not just once but repeatedly and across a wide range of what has become Community business. A new legal order has been created

and common laws have been extended over many fields of public administration. A major new entity – whose standing is often rated far higher by its
external partners than by its own members – has taken its place on the world
negotiating scene.

It is generally agreed that the greater part of the Treaties – which seemed so
ambitious when first drawn up – has now been implemented. The Common
Market with its remaining imperfections still comes closer than ever before
outside the confines of a single State to establishing a homogeneous economic
area with uniform conditions for competition.

In some cases the Nine member states had managed to cooperate
successfully in many ways not prescribed in detail in the treaties. But
what seemed to us to be the greatest success of the ten preceding years
was the preservation of the Community's core achievements in very
difficult economic circumstances.

In the 1970s the Community found itself plunged into a major economic
crisis, both external and internal. It was trying simultaneously to absorb three
new members and had no common economic or monetary system on which
to base a united front. Despite all this, it managed to survive with its central
policies and its political solidarity intact, thus sparing its peoples all the
consequences of a breakdown in European trading relations.

Having stressed the positive side of Community action during the
seventies, we were able to turn to the problems still unresolved and
express our misgivings without any risk of a misunderstanding. First
of all we pointed out that there were still many gaps in the implementation of the treaties, in such policy areas as transport, capital movements, financial services and so forth. Then we drew attention to the
difficulties that the Community would encounter in putting the
common agricultural policy into effect. As to incursions by the European institutions into new areas not covered by the treaties, the results
obtained had not lived up to expectations; the new objectives, notably
those spelled out in the summit declarations of 1972 and 1974, had
not been achieved; the new initiatives had not cohered into one or
more full-scale 'common policies'. This inability to sustain the integra-
tive momentum was seen by us as a sign of something fundamentally
wrong.

Regarding the economic crisis, the Community had survived it but
had been unable to combat it. There had been no real overall coordination of states' economic, financial and monetary policies. States had
'sought to protect their own industries by special measures which

[had] made the conditions more difficult not only for the harmonization of economic policies but for the functioning of the common
market itself.'

Ultimately, by way of these various detours, we arrived at the
problem that had been specifically put to us: 'the functioning of the
institutions.' We had, after some discussion, finally settled on a word
that would describe it: the French *'lourdeur'*: we could just as well
have spoken of 'bureaucratic paralysis', both at the level of individual
states and at that of the Community itself.

These problems are exposed most sharply in the Council, as the centre of
Community decision-taking. There are three or four times as many Council
meetings now as there were in 1958 and the lower levels of the Council
machinery have ramified even faster. Yet the significance of the business
concluded has not increased in proportion to the volume. Many would say it
has declined.

The creation of the European Council did not seem to us at that time
to have improved the situation decisively; it might even have added
some new problems to those already known. As for the Commission,
which at that time had thirteen members and would soon have
seventeen, it did not appear to us to have 'developed a coherent overall
vision of its own which could help to give proportion and direction to
the large number of its proposals.'

And so we came to formulate a certain number of precise, concrete
proposals regarding the structure and functioning of the institutions.
We did not delude ourselves with the belief that they would transform
the difficult situation we had described, but we did think that they
might improve it in some important respects.

To us it seemed essential that the Community establish at all times a
scale of priorities for the work it had to do and for the decisions it
wished to reach. In order to slim down the bureaucratic machinery,
which was becoming increasingly cumbersome and tending towards
paralysis, we suggested that a preeminent role should be given to the
Chairman of the Council of Ministers, that certain new powers should
be delegated to the Commission, and that the Committee of Permanent Representatives should have an increased decision-taking
function.

The part of our report which seems to me, in retrospect, to be one of
the most important is the section in which we dealt with the decision-
taking process in the Council of Ministers. The Community was
drifting more and more towards an intergovernmental system and

further and further away from the original conception of the Common Market.

The mood of the negotiation itself has become narrowly national, and hence more intergovernmental in character. These are symptoms of the general evolution in States' attitudes that has weakened the standing of the more 'supranational' institutions and increased the significance of the Council relative to the Commission within the Community machine.

The activity of the Council itself was being made very difficult by the fact that nearly all decisions, the only notable exception being budget decisions, had to be taken unanimously. On this point, our position was very clear.

We are trying to deal in our report with actual phenomena and practical solutions. We do not see it as our task either to propagate or to prejudice any particular philosophical view.

There can be no doubt that the 'Luxembourg Compromise' – in reality an agreement to disagree – has become a fact of life in the Community. In the reality of the Community today, voting cannot be used to override individual states on matters which they regard as involving very important interests.

An atmosphere has developed in which – even on minor issues and in quite humble forums – States can obstruct agreement for reasons which they know full well to be insufficient, but which are never brought into the open let alone seriously challenged by their colleagues.

We suggest the following working principle. In all cases where the Treaty does not impose unanimity, and very important interests are not involved for any State, voting should be the normal practice after an appropriate but limited effort for consensus has been made. This does not mean an actual vote will be taken each time. Often the mere prospect of resort to vote will encourage States to join in a compromise.

A little further on we defined our thinking on the subject in these terms:

Each State must remain the judge of where its very important interests lie. Otherwise it could be overruled on an issue which it seriously considered a 'major' one ... However, the manner of appeal to the 'Luxembourg Compromise' needs to be better defined. A State which wants to avert a vote because of very important interest should say so clearly and explicitly, and take responsibility for the consequences in the name of its whole Government.

We concluded on this point by saying that the solution of the problems posed by recourse to the majority vote should rest with the Chairman of the Council; his powers should therefore be increased.

Turning next to the Commission, we could not but note the decline in its authority. In the first place, its range of initiative had progressively shrunk as the specific prescriptions contained in the Treaty of Rome had been carried out. The Commission had had to move into new areas in which it did not have sole power of proposal and found itself in direct competition with member states that were trying, for the most part unsuccessfully, to define new Community policies themselves. It should be added that the acute economic difficulties of the seventies had led governments to take more nationalistic stances, and often to ignore the advice of a Commission that felt its responsibility to be a Community one and sought to administer policies in the European interest. Finally, the external constraints on the Commission's effectiveness 'were accompanied by a lack of coherence, and increasing bureaucracy, in its own internal operations.'

We felt almost completely at a loss to do anything about a trend of this kind. There was little more we could do than hope that the situation would not get any worse. We proposed that the number of commissioners be limited to one per country, regardless of its size, instead of two for the big countries, as is still the case today. Thus, after the accession of Greece, Spain and Portugal, the Commission would have had only twelve members, instead of seventeen. On this point we concurred with the conclusions of a committee appointed more specifically to study the functioning of the Commission and chaired by Dirk Spierenburg. Twelve is already a large number; seventeen is an assembly in which all productive work becomes difficult. We added that the powers of the Commission's President should be significantly increased.

To improve the functioning of the European Parliament and to extend its powers within reasonable limits, we thought that it should have a word to say in the appointment of the President of the Commission. We also felt that the President of the European Council should personally take part in certain sessions of the Assembly.

We were conscious of the difficulties the Community would have to face in the near future. We were convinced that it was about to enter a zone of high turbulence whose effects, as is often the case in public or private business, would be particularly apparent in the financial sphere. Because of the structure of its financial resources, the Community was approaching a point where clear-cut decisions had to be taken on 'the scale of and priorities for its spending in future'.

369

We concluded our report with a few general remarks on the outlook for 1980–5 and on progress towards European Union, which our mandate had requested us specifically to consider. On the first subject, we noted that all countries were 'agreed in recognizing inflation as the main threat to combat'. Given the constraints of all kinds weighing on member countries, we said, 'Europe will have a low economic growth rate in the coming years. Europe will have to come to terms with this situation. But there will be great difficulties on the employment front.'

On the subject of European Union, which had become a catchword in speeches and sometimes in official texts, we found it very difficult to conceal our scepticism. 'This last,' we said, 'is a term the meaning of which has been the subject of much empty talk during the last few years.' We would probably never have used it off our own bat, but since we were being asked to speak about it, we could only state that 'everything which strengthens the Community's internal unity, and its unity and that of the Nine in dealings with the rest of the world, constitutes progress towards European Union.' As to the situation at that time, we had this to say: 'In Europe today, the Community possesses only limited functions and powers in economic, financial and monetary matters ... Economic, financial and monetary decisions are and will most probably remain essentially national in the period we are examining.'

I have written about this 1980 report at some length, because in the six years since then things have not changed much. The same problems are present, calling for solutions similar to those that my two friends and I had suggested. Let us simply say, so as not to appear too pessimistic, that the Community has survived these six years as it survived the preceding ten. A limited amount of progress has even been made. The best example is the European Monetary System, which takes the form of cooperation between governments and central banks.

Could Europe have turned out differently?

Could the Europe we know, which is more than a customs union but less than a federal or confederal state, have unified itself economically, monetarily and politically during the thirty or so years that have elapsed since the Treaty of Rome was signed? In the abstract, the answer of course has to be yes. There was no obstacle of principle to the federation, if not of Western Europe, at least of the six countries that formed the initial nucleus. The Russians were not in a position to oppose it and the Americans were its fervent advocates. On the face of it, there was everything to induce the Europeans to unite, including the desire to play the role of a great power on the world stage. Why, then, didn't it happen, and why is it still unlikely to happen in the foreseeable future?

One could offer a lot of explanations, all of them plausible to a degree and all containing some element of truth. My own opinion is that the fragmentation of Europe, its inability to unify, other than incompletely in the field of trading relations, is the result of a tacit decision by the Europeans after the Second World War to leave their defence up to the Americans. The temptation was great: America had offered her services, a European defence would have cost two or three times more than Europe's defence spending total today, Germany had formally renounced the use of atomic weapons. Even so, if the Europeans had really wanted to be independent, they could, at the very least, have equipped themselves with conventional weapons sufficiently effective to enable them to resist any external attack of a conventional character. Instead they preferred butter to guns. Their standard of living on the whole is much higher than in Russia, their combined economic power (being the sum of the individual economies) is, on paper at any rate, very much greater than that of Russia. Yet Russia is a great world power, whereas Europe exists only sporadically as a political force.

Part Five

BUSINESS

1

ITINERARY
(1967–1984)

I hesitated a great deal over the choice of a title for this last part of my memoirs, covering the years from 1967 to 1985. For whereas my life up until 1967 was always dominated by one principal activity – the French Plan, the Marshall Plan, the Common Market – after that date, and for the next seventeen or eighteen years, my time was taken up with a great many different activities unconnected other than in my own mind. What finally decided me to choose the title 'Business' for this last period was that the activity, lasting from 1970 to 1982, which I consider to have been the most important of these, the one which was the most intellectually rewarding and around which nearly all the others tend to fall into place, was my membership of the board of Royal Dutch. It was also a point of departure: from that moment on my association with this prestigious corporation brought me many other opportunities, and those which I seized enabled me to familiarize myself, in the circumstances that I shall describe later, with the world of business.

But let us go back to 1967. I left the Common Market that year without having made any decision as to what I would do next. I was fifty-six. I was, as people say without knowing exactly what this means, in the prime of life, with at least fifteen years of potential activity ahead of me, health permitting. It was then that I began to think about what I could do. Three possibilities were open to me; teaching, which I could always go back to as an *agrégé* of the faculties of law and economics; an elective political activity; or business, of which I knew practically nothing. Politics and teaching are not incompatible, although I have always had many doubts about the teaching ability of a politician who returns periodically to the profession after his electoral setbacks, or who teaches when his mind and most of his time are taken up elsewhere. I have always thought that to be a good teacher, one has to devote oneself entirely to being a teacher and to a life's work that stems directly from this or is very closely linked to it. One can also combine politics and business, although nowadays there are fairly strict rules about multiple tenures. Anyway, it is a combination I don't like. So I had to make a straight choice.

Why I decided against politics

I began by ruling out politics, in the sense of parliamentary activity, or even simply party activity. I did so for three reasons essentially.

First, I felt that I was already too old to start down this path. I have never had any sympathy with amateurs in whatever sphere of activity. Politics is a profession; one has to begin relatively young, learn the trade, for it is one, familiarize oneself with the management of local and national affairs, climb rung by rung the ladder of office: municipal councillor, councillor-general, deputy, minister perhaps. I do not mean that this is a hard and fast rule, that there are not other channels, that certain personalities of exceptional stature cannot go straight into politics at a comparatively advanced age; history can provide us with a few examples of such exceptions. But I did not see myself as one of that group of nonpareils.

Second, I did not really know where to stand politically, which party to belong to, or which standard profession of faith to adopt. Even in my youth I had always found it difficult, if not impossible, to embrace any party's programme in its entirety, as the story of my experiences in the thirties clearly shows. True, over the years from 1945 to 1967 I had continued to have socialist leanings. I was a social democrat, or rather a liberal, in the European sense of the term, prepared to espouse a moderate socialist programme. But I was not really committed. It is one thing to say that one is a socialist, without being politically active, and quite another to be a militant. Although I say 'socialist' here, I could be speaking of any other party.

When I think about these questions today – now that all ambition has faded within me, now that the temporal dimension, in which far-ranging projects are necessarily situated, has in a sense been taken from my life and even from my thinking, and I am therefore totally disinterested – I find political activity, insofar as it is a partisan activity, difficult to understand. How can one totally embrace this or that party, whose programme inevitably reflects a certain ideology, generally debatable on certain essential points, as well as the self-seeking pressures exerted on it by the social groups whose votes it hopes to win? A man in love with truth may at best accept fifty per cent, or maybe a little more, of the positions defended by the party that has his preference. But he also has to swallow all the rest. And yet, in all the democratic countries, the party is an essential, indispensable element of all political life. The only way out of this dilemma is to acknowledge that action obeys certain rules that have no place in contemplative thought. To be effective in the things he considers essential, the politician is prepared to pay lip service to propositions he knows to be false, but which seem to him of secondary importance or which are not topical. Léon Blum was able, in a crisis, to defend the Republic, the while stating that he was a Marxist and proclaiming the need, at some undetermined point in the future, for a dictatorship of the proletariat. That is the case with the intelligent and scrupulous politican, but I fear that with most of the people who militate in a party the explanation is more simple, and that opportunism, coupled with a certain disdain for truth, and an irrational attachment to the party are the most powerful motivations.

Anyhow, in 1967 I was not prepared to side with any political grouping. This allergy, if you like, may be imputed to a certain scepticism of ideology. Having arrived at that point in life, I could no longer believe that anyone held the absolute truth, or even an approximate truth, concerning all the essential problems of a country or of a time.

For my third reason, I have to say that my thinking in 1967 was coloured by an unfortunate electoral experience I had had five years earlier and which is worth recounting briefly. It was a colourful, rather baroque, one might even say ridiculous incident in a life which has not been notable for extravagance and which I have always tried to lead with maximum rationality.

In 1962 I was a Vice-President of the Commission of the European Economic Community. I had done well there. The Community was establishing itself and my work was giving me full satisfaction. Suddenly, in the course of that year, General de Gaulle decided to amend the constitution. Henceforth the President of the Republic would be elected by universal suffrage instead of, as under the Fourth Republic, by an assembly of notables holding the elective mandates.

De Gaulle used the referendum in order to obtain this essential change in French political life. Many at the time considered this method to be unconstitutional. I had no opinion on that question, but I was firmly against the reform. It seemed to me that it would create a two-headed system in which the relations between the President of the Republic, elected by universal suffrage, and the Prime Minister, coming from an assembly likewise elected by universal suffrage, were liable to be complicated and even to pose insoluble problems the day that the President and his Prime Minister were not of the same political hue. The new constitution would be made of two juxtaposed elements that did not fit together. Far from rounding off the 1958 constitution, the constitutional amendment of 1962 could in certain circumstances, which I was convinced would arise sooner or later, make its application difficult. I should add that the idea *per se* of election by universal suffrage of a man holding very great powers made me uneasy for the future, in view of the emotional and impassioned character that French political life can take on at times.

I therefore voted 'no' in the referendum. General de Gaulle carried the day with a big majority and used the momentum this had generated to dissolve the Assembly, which had passed a vote of censure against the first Pompidou government, and call a general election. Without really thinking, without considering for an instant that, whether I was elected or not, I would in all likelihood be putting an end to a European career full of immediate satisfactions and promise for the future, swept away by an urge that made me forget all the rest, I decided to stand for parliament and started to look for a constituency. The socialists, in the person of Guy Mollet, offered me one and assured me that I had every chance of being elected. After all, the outgoing deputy was a socialist who was not seeking reelection. I accepted.

I found myself then in a rather curious position. I was on good terms with the ruling power. I had helped to steer the Brussels Commission in a direction that facilitated the action of France's representatives. I saw General de Gaulle from time to time, I had close ties with Maurice Couve de Murville, the Foreign Affairs Minister. On the other hand, I had not militated in the socialist party since 1936 or 1937 and knew virtually nothing about its internal affairs. I had no particular sympathy with the party's programme or what purported to be one. And yet, with no thought other than for the constitutional problem which in fact had been settled, I put myself forward as an opposition candidate, a decision that can only have displeased the government and the President of the Republic.

These, then, were the circumstances in which I turned up one day at Moulins. The constituency the socialists had given me was the first constituency of Moulins in the department of Allier in the Auvergne. The department had voted 'no' in the referendum that had just taken place, by 86,887 votes to 84,171. This was an element in my favour, but there were many negative elements which I discovered only little by little during the electoral campaign, by which time it was too late to back out. In any case, given my character, I do not think that I would have done so, even if I had convinced myself earlier on that my chances of being elected were, to say the least, uncertain.

These depended on a bare minimum of socialist organization in the department, active support from the militants in the constituency and the withdrawals of candidacy, especially in the event that the candidate of the *Mouvement Républicain Populaire* (MRP) stood down, that might help me in the second round. On each of these three counts, all my expectations were disappointed.

First of all, I discovered that there was now virtually no socialist party organization in the Moulins *arrondissement*. A few 'sections' still remained, but nearly all of them were now reduced to a single person. The federation had for many years been torn by such violent personal quarrels that finally peace was restored by the *de facto* disappearance of the federation itself. In short, by the time I came to stand as a candidate there were no premises, no newspaper, no active militants, and no money. The only real help I received was from two men, whose names I have forgotten, who were passionately wedded to the socialist cause in the department and who assisted me with all the means at their disposal, which were unfortunately very limited. They were sincere, honest and intelligent; it was largely because of them, in order not to leave them high and dry, that I did not take the next train back to Paris and thence to Brussels.

The situation quickly became complicated once my candidacy was announced. Certain militants, among the few that still remained, showed the customary reaction to a candidate from outside, 'parachuted' as the French say, imposed on them, it seemed, by the party machine in Paris. This reaction led to the emergence of a dissident socialist candidate, a man from those parts, the mayor of a village, president of an 'intercommunal syndicate for drinking water supply,' in short, a local personality. He had a notice posted up in which he denounced, in vague but forceful terms, the handful of pontificating socialists who had imposed their candidate. 'They went,' the notice read, 'to the Common Market for "Their" candidate. We found "Ours" right here.' I remember meeting my new opponent in the course of the electoral campaign. He was a decent, well-meaning man. In other circumstances we would have probably got along together, but now the die was cast. All I could do was see the thing through to the bitter end. Lastly, I noticed that the influence of the MRP, on whose votes I was counting for the second round, had dwindled to almost nothing in this part of the French provinces.

I put a brave face on things and took rooms in a hotel in Moulins. My EEC associates joined me there; Jean Flory and Robert Toulemon, who constituted my *cabinet* [private office] in Brussels, and Madame Lagarde, my faithful secretary, brought me their help and made up for the absence of any local assistance. Emile Noël, the Commission's Secretary General, whose judgment I have always valued, gave me advice. The profession of faith which I drafted with their help was an honest social democratic 'programme', a shade flat but intellectually sound. I declared myself to be in favour of General de Gaulle's Algerian policy and, of course, in favour of the construction of a united Europe. I said that I had voted 'no' in the recent referendum. The argument on which I was counting most to win over the voters in this rural constituency concerned the defence of agricultural interests. 'The Common Market,' I said, 'if it is used properly, will provide the livestock and crop farmers of the Allier with increased outlets and stable incomes.'

With the preparations thus completed, I waged a strenuous electoral campaign, visiting each of the eighty or so communes in the constituency, with differing degrees of success. The size of my audience varied. On several occasions, even, I was met by the *garde champêtre*, who had opened the doors of the meeting hall but who was the only person around. In that case, I had a drink with him and left. I have a rather touching recollection of a meeting in a *chef-lieu de canton* the mayor of which was a woman. After a difficult life, she had taken over a big farm that was doing very badly and had pulled it right round. The inhabitants of the little town had considered that she would be able to look after its interests better than anyone else, and had elected her mayor.

When I arrived at the town hall I found the council at full strength together with many of the commune's inhabitants. Before I started on my speech, the mayor, who was chairing the meeting, said something like this to me: 'Monsieur Marjolin, we here do not hold the same opinions as you, we are not socialists. But we shall vote for you because you are an excellent man and have done a lot of important and useful things. But don't put us off with talk about a programme. The less you say on that subject, the better your chances will be.' I took her at her word and confined myself to generalities of no relevance to the partisan positions of anyone present. The evening the results of the poll were announced I saw that I had obtained almost all the votes in that locality.

In spite of this local success, the results of the first ballot were hardly encouraging[1]. I came in fourth, behind the communist, the Gaullist candidate and an independent republican. Even on the assumption that my first-round score would be augmented by the votes obtained by the dissident socialist and the MRP candidate, who had done worse than I and were therefore out of the running, my chances of being elected in the second ballot were slim. I might have won, however, in a second ballot in which there were several candidates, as proved to be the case when the independent republican refused to stand down in favour of the Gaullist. The communists, although having won more votes than I, offered to withdraw their candidate and ask their electors to vote for me if I declared myself publicly to be in favour of a socialist-communist alliance, which naturally I refused to do. I purely and simply withdrew, asking those who had supported me in the first ballot to vote as their conscience dictated in the second. I reminded them, however, that I was a fervent partisan of the European Economic Community and of the Atlantic Alliance. I returned to Paris where I talked with Maurice Couve de Murville. He advised me to go back to Brussels, which I did. There I resumed my duties as a Vice-President of the Commission. After my return, I was told that my electoral escapade had caused much displeasure at the Elysée. But thanks to Maurice Couve de Murville and Olivier Wormser, things quietened down quickly and I went back to my Common Market activities.

This setback however, disagreable at the time, proved to be a blessing in disguise. I was able to devote the four and a half years that followed to the work I was really cut out for, given my experience and the few skills I possess: the execution of the Treaty of Rome, the construction of Europe. Had I been elected at Moulins, I should have spent the years of my mandate, and probably those that followed, in the National Assembly in the ranks of an opposition reduced to powerlessness, having more often than not to fight for causes I would not have believed in. The Moulins experience, despite the opportunities that were to present themselves later, did a great deal to dissuade me from seriously thinking of taking an active part in French political life.

A provisional decision

So it was with no hardship that I ruled out politics when I eventually returned to Paris in 1967. At that time I received different proposals from private business concerns, many of them big. My reactions were negative. I had the same prejudice that many intellectuals have about money-making, profit-oriented activities. For despite a long spell in national and international civil service, that is what I had remained essentially: an intellectual. One might say, if one wanted to be critical, that I had kept my blinkers on and that the only thing that really fired me was the conflict of ideas or, if one wanted to be indulgent, the search for truth. With the years, though, my life had taken on a possibly different dimension, that of action. But the forms which that action had assumed were very closely linked to what, in my conception, was truth, a universal and impersonal truth that could not be embodied in a person, or in a group of persons, or in an institution. My prejudices concerning essentially profit-oriented activities conflicted with my convictions as an economist. I have always thought that profit is the best or even the only possible criterion for ensuring an optimal allocation of productive resources. Let us say that I considered these activities to be normal and even necessary for others, but I preferred not to have any part in them myself. Provisionally, I decided to remain independent, to hold myself available to offer opinions and advice, but not to become part of any hierarchy or assume the responsibility of managing any kind of business. Since this was the way I saw things, a return to university teaching was the obvious solution. I would be free to do what I pleased, having a degree of financial independence, free, within the limits of the profession's ethics, to engage in any activity that attracted me. I had formed many friendships in those circles, some going back to my student days, others to the two years I had spent teaching in the Nancy faculty of law and economics in 1955–7, and still others to my years with the Common Market when I always derived great pleasure and intellectual benefit from the company of visiting French academics.

I therefore applied to join the Paris faculty of law and economics and was warmly welcomed in. I stayed there for two years, from 1967 to 1969, teaching the *licence* and doctorate courses. Those two years were rewarding for me. They enabled me to think, to renew a contact with economic theory which I had lost during my long years of administrative experience. In addition to preparing my lectures, I was able to take part in two working groups outside the university, both of which brought me a great deal. These were the Pearson Committee and the three-member Marjolin, Sadrin, Wormser Committee.

The first was formed in August 1968 by L.B. Pearson, a former Prime Minister of Canada, at the request of Robert McNamara, President of the World Bank. Pearson asked me and a number of others to join. Our assignment was to study the effects of twenty years of Third World aid, assess the results, identify the mistakes made and propose policies that might produce more rapid progress in the future. During the eleven months that followed we met in Canada, Rome, Copenhagen and Geneva in that order. We handed in our report at the annual assembly of the Bank's Board of Governors in October 1969. Our work and the recommendations we put forward were the point of departure for studies by numerous other groups and organizations which, during the seventies, examined the question of aid to the developing countries. Knowledgeable people tell me that, fifteen years later, the Pearson Report is still often mentioned in development studies. I shall say no more about it here since the problems of the Third World have never been, purely by one of life's hazards, in the forefront of my concerns.

The second committee was set up in December 1968 by Olivier Wormser at the request of the then Prime Minister, Maurice Couve de Murville, to study a 'reform of the money market and monetary policy conditions.' Olivier Wormser asked me and Jean Sadrin, a high official who in the course of his career had been the Finance Ministry's external finance director, to help him in this task. We spent a little over six months on our study and handed in our report to the government in June 1969. Wormser directed operations, devoting much of his time to the project and closely supervising the report's drafting, which was essentially the work of Joncour-Galignani, a young *inspecteur des finances* who was later to become managing director of the Banque Indosuez.

This, then, was how I spent my two university years from 1967 to 1969, the entirety of my time being taken up with the preparation of my lectures and the external activities of which I have just spoken. I had no other project during that period than to teach, while remaining available, within the time at my disposal, for other tasks of a public nature. The events of May 1968 and their aftermath disrupted this nice equilibrium. I did not live through the acute crisis that jolted the teaching profession then, as I was in a nursing home following surgery that kept me out of action for several weeks. But when I resumed my classes in the autumn of 1968 I could see the immense disorder that reigned in the university. I was not personally subjected to any baiting, but I found intolerable the continual restiveness of a minority of students that made life difficult for the teachers and for the other students. I had a fairly low opinion, moreover, of the reforms carried out at that time in the organization of teaching, which stemmed more from a signal weakness on the part of the government than from deliberate convictions. So I managed to get through the 1968–9 academic year, but I was ready for another change.

Shell

It was then that I was approached by a big private international corporation, Royal Dutch[2]. The man who spoke to me about it was André Charon. I had known him for many years and had the highest regard for him. For many years Chairman of Shell Française, the French subsidiary of the Royal Dutch-Shell group, he joined the board of directors of one of the parent companies, Royal Dutch, when he retired from Shell Française at the age of sixty. At that time he was approaching seventy, when, according to the company articles, he would also have to leave the board of Royal Dutch. He asked me to meet him. I remember his coming to see me in the small flat in the Avenue de la Motte-Picquet in which we were then living, Dottie, my son Robert and I; Elise had taken a room on her own.

André Charon offered me a consultancy with Royal Dutch to last until such time as I could succeed him on his retirement from the board of that company. Shortly after, I accepted the consultant's post offered to me but wrote to André Charon to say that this did not in any way preempt a subsequent decision on whether to join the board in due course. I also recall a dinner at Drouant with André Charon, Jan Brouwer, then Managing Director of Royal Dutch, and, I seem to think, Gerrit Wagner. Dottie was very ill just then and I spent half the time at the restaurant on the telephone. Perhaps that is when I reached my decision. I don't remember.

When I think back on that time and on my relations with those who were soon to become my colleagues, I realize that I must have seemed impossible to them. I had not yet rid myself of the idea that business was necessarily unclean and that there was something sordid about the pursuit of profit. With my background of the university and then national and international civil service, the idea of joining the board of a private enterprise repelled me deeply.

My friends at Royal Dutch showed infinite patience. Finally I made up my mind and took the plunge in autumn 1969. Why did I change my mind at that moment? What made me decide to take a step that hitherto I had regarded as an unwarrantable break with my past? I am not sure. One is almost never sure of one's motivations. Two factors seem to me, however, to have played a big part. First, I was struck by the personal worth, both moral and intellectual, of the men I was dealing with, and the idea of becoming their associate became increasingly agreeable to me. Second, my mind was not static; I was thinking about the role played in world affairs by a big concern like Shell, placed at a strategic point on the economic and political chessboard. I had already gained some experience of public affairs, why not supplement it by becoming part of a great private concern, one that had the size and the reputation of Shell? I shall say no more on this point, save that I never had occasion to regret the decision I took then.

I am told that in many companies the top management convenes the board only for form's sake and carefully avoids discussion of real problems on those occasions. That is certainly not the case with Royal Dutch-Shell. A few days before a meeting I would receive plentiful background material on each of the items on the agenda. I found myself as fully informed as a director not involved in the company's day-to-day running can be. These meetings lasted a whole day, from 9 or 10 a.m. to 5 or 6 p.m. Detailed reports were put before the members of the board, who were entirely at liberty to ask the questions or make the objections that they thought appropriate.

I have never sat on the boards of other oil companies[3] and so cannot venture to make comparisons. But what I can say is that from the very first day I was impressed by the abilities of the members of the top management. All having risen from the ranks, they had slowly climbed all the rungs of the ladder. Many had had several years' experience in running the Shell Group's activities outside Holland and Britain, in

385

Europe, Africa, Asia and America, and were thus completely know-ledgeable in their field. Furthermore, they were for the most part men of exceptional intelligence, as much at ease with general economic or political questions as with oil-related matters. To put in a nutshell what I think of these executives of one of the biggest world corpor-ations, I could compare them favourably with the most capable government officials or ministers I have ever met in Europe and the United States. The essential difference lay in the way in which their respective performances were rated, and rewarded or penalized accordingly. The national government official is accountable to his minister; in the event, given the rapidity with which at certain times ministers come and go in the same department, what is at stake in the official's performance is his reputation in civil service and political circles and, consequently, his chances of being promoted to more important duties than the one he is discharging at present. Often his is a diffuse responsibility, difficult to define with any precision and to place exactly. As for ministers, their responsibility is even more diffi-cult to determine. It is different in a private concern. Efficiency or inefficiency is measured by an objective gauge that does not exist in government service, namely the year-end profit and loss account and balance sheet. The bottom line shows the company's net profit or loss for that year.

It has been said that company directors and shareholders have no real authority. Since directors are chosen by the company's manage-ment, they are allegedly docile with the people who have appointed them, while the shareholders are too numerous and too much out of the picture to create any real difficulties. All that is true, to a certain extent, when business is good. The directors are often personal friends of the company executives and would not normally think of embar-rassing them with awkward questions or unduly critical remarks. But things change when the company is going through difficult times. Then the directors remember that they have a responsibility to the shareholders. The latter stop behaving like sheep when their dividends are threatened, and the management has to take or propose the exceptional measures that appear to be necessary. These are discussed by the board of directors. A change in the company's management may result. In point of fact, I never saw that happen while I was a director of the Shell Group. As we shall discover later, Shell managed to weather the storms of the seventies and early eighties without too much damage. But I did see it happen in other companies with which I was associated in various capacities.

I have been speaking of the executives in charge of the day-to-day running of the company. As to the board, appointment is by co-optation. In my time, and things have not changed since, it was partly composed of former senior executives who, in accordance with the company articles, had retired at the age of sixty, but could sit on the board until they were seventy. The other members were from outside, being either industrialists who had been very successful in areas other than oil, or eminent persons whose experience in public affairs management had been thought desirable. This combination produced a group of a very high intellectual standard. I made many friends, both among the management and on the board. The twelve years I spent on the board formed one of the most rewarding periods of my life.

One important feature which differentiated the Shell Group from other big oil companies, especially the American corporations, was the international viewpoint it took spontaneously when considering the problems with which the oil industry had to contend; unlike the others, it had no nationalistic stance to shed. This was due essentially to the circumstances in which it had been formed, namely through a merging of British and Dutch interests. Furthermore, unlike the American corporations, the Shell Group did not have an extensive national base like the US market, which meant that it had to protect its existence and ensure its expansion by developing its activities in a large number of countries and trying to get itself recognized there as a friendly force, a defender of national interests.

I should beware of taking this argument too far, however. The group is, first and foremost, Anglo-Dutch and it furthers its activities in those two countries especially. The discovery and development of the natural gas deposits in Groningen in Holland and of oil and gas deposits in the North Sea have reinforced this national trait; obviously, too, at certain times, especially in periods of crisis, relations with the British and Netherlands governments have taken on particular importance. But I have never noted a situation where, as a result, the essential interests of the other European countries have in any way been neglected.

I thus spent many years in this exceptional environment. All my initial prejudices were quickly dispelled. After only a short while I felt completely at ease with these businessmen who had welcomed me with such kindness into their midst. I learned an enormous amount. Without professing to have become an oil and energy expert, I can pride myself on having acquired a reasonable knowledge of the problems involved, enabling me both to understand what was going on and to express opinions which, sometimes, made a positive contribution to the discussion.

A new life

During the seventies and early eighties I also found myself associated, in very different circumstances, with another multinational company that leads the field in its own sphere of operations and whose prestige is worldwide: IBM.

Back in 1970 or 1971 Jacques Maisonrouge, then Chairman of the Board of IBM-World Trade, that is to say in charge of all IBM activity outside the USA, asked me whether I would be prepared to give my advice to IBM, not of course on technical matters, of which I am utterly ignorant, but on the general economic problems confronting the company. I accepted and served in that capacity until 1984.

I was not on the board of directors and met the company management only episodically. But I took part in the work and in the regular meetings of the IBM economists, those who were at the centre, at Armonk in the United States, and those who operated in the different national subsidiaries that IBM had hived off throughout the world. Three times a year we would meet in different locations. This group of economists was headed, as from a certain time and during the greater part of my association with IBM, by Al Karchere. The company's chief economist, outstanding in his own field, leaning rather to the left but completely objective, he wielded economic, statistical and econometric techniques like the best university economists, and, what is more, was gifted with a practical sense that enabled him to establish a link between theory and its concrete applications. We quickly became excellent friends and for many years I saw him regularly, not only at the meetings I mentioned earlier, but each time I had occasion to visit the United States for whatever reason. I stayed several times at his home in Westport, Connecticut.

I got to know other economists in the different companies with which I was associated, but the case of IBM is special. By and large, company economists work on the fringe of the industrial or commercial activities of the firms that employ them; their influence on the running of the business is seldom perceptible. At IBM, on the other hand, there is an operational link, so to speak, between the forecasts made by the economists, as to output, prices or exchange rates, and the decisions taken in the company's different sectors of activity.

My role, which at first was ill defined, became more precise as time went on. At the meetings of which I have spoken each national economist presented the situation in his own country, by reference to a certain number of assumptions drawn up at Armonk, and put forward short- or medium-range forecasts. My job, on the last day, was to assemble the different conclusions arrived at and produce an overall picture.

I did this for more than ten years and personally derived enormous intellectual benefit from it. Obviously, the forecasts I made at a given moment were supposed to link up, in one way or another, with those I had made a few months earlier. In cases where there was a big difference between successive diagnoses, I had, if only for my own sake, to admit that I had made a mistake or to identify, in some event that was unforeseeable at the time of the first diagnosis, the source of the discrepancy. Without undue exaggeration, I think I can say that these mental gymnastics taught me as much about economics as anything I learned during my years in the French government service or at the head of international organizations.

Shell and IBM, coming after my experience at the OEEC and with the Common Market, opened many doors. I made it a rule to accept only those offers coming from long-standing companies, well established in their particular sector and of unimpeachable integrity.

Even before these new experiences I had joined the board of advisers of the Chase Manhattan Bank in 1967. In 1970 I joined the board of directors of the ROBECO group companies. At the suggestion of an old friend, Eugene Black, a former president of the World Bank, American Express asked me in 1972 to act as adviser to the company on economic and financial affairs. At about the same time General Motors set up an advisory board for its European business; I served on it until I reached the age limit of seventy. More recently I served in the same capacity, for a limited period, with another American corporation, Air Products. Today, still, I am a member of the board of directors of a British investment company, Foreign and Colonial Reserve Asset Fund Limited, and of an advisory board set up by a big American regional bank located in Florida, the Southeast Bank. I am also an adviser to a British subsidiary of American Express, Amex Bank Ltd.

In addition to my work in the private sector I accepted various assignments offered to me either by the French government or by international organizations. I have already spoken of the reports I helped to draft for the European Community on Monetary Union and the Community's institutions, together with the Pearson Committee report and the study on the French money market. From May 1970 to June 1971 I worked on a report for the French government, the subject of which was 'France's cooperation with the developing countries.' The report's conclusions were considered in high places to be too critical of French policy and the document was buried.

In 1971–2 I took part in the activities of a group set up at the OECD and styled 'High Level Group on Trade and Related Problems.' Its chairman was my friend Jean Rey, now dead. Our job was to lay the groundwork for negotiations to begin shortly afterwards in the GATT for a further reduction in import duties and other trade barriers. The discussions were notable for a sharp clash between the US representative and myself on the Common Agricultural Policy, which the Americans already wanted out of the way or at least to be less protectionist. As usual, I objected to the American delegate that his country was far from being above reproach in this area and said that while two wrongs did not make a right, they did at least enable the parties to understand each other's motives. I made Jean Rey unhappy for a time by practising, if not the policy of the 'empty chair', at any rate that of maintaining a stubborn silence, from which I emerged only when the US delegate showed that he was prepared to make a slight move in my direction and the majority of the group agreed that the CAP was an essential part of the Rome Treaty and that there was no question of diminishing it.

1975 and early 1976 saw the planners at work drawing up the Seventh French Plan, for 1976–80. These were difficult times. The recession in the wake of the first oil-price shock had reminded France and the rest of the world that it was not necessarily economic growth all the way and that declines were possible. The efforts to boost activity in France, while in the rest of the world it remained depressed, had ended in failure, and in 1976 Raymond Barre was called in to try and pick up the pieces. The Seventh Plan was therefore of particular significance: it was a corrective plan. I chaired one of the Plan's key committees, ' External economic and financial relations.' I served in the same capacity in 1978 when the Seventh Plan underwent a revision. These two assignments provided me with the opportunity to meet and become friends with Robert Raymond, who was the committee's general rapporteur and who showed, both in the discussions and in the drafting of the report, the good sense and clear-sightedness that had already helped him to a brilliant career in the Banque de

France and would take him, a few years later, to the post of the Bank's general director of studies.

In July 1975 the OECD asked a group of economists 'to identify and consider the main policy issues involved in the pursuit, by member countries, of non-inflationary economic growth ... in the light of the structural changes which have taken place in the recent past.' The chairman was Paul McCracken, an American economist of worldwide repute. We spent nearly two years searching for an answer to the question put to us and handed in our report in June 1977. This document, like others I have mentioned earlier, clearly showed the degree to which the specialists and enlightened public opinion in general were baffled by the unprecedented character of the problems with which the world economy was confronted following the great inflation surge in the late sixties and early seventies and the 1973 oil shock. I shall have more to say about this situation later on. In 1977 I was part of a Banque de France working group on inflation. In 1979 the report to the European Council on the EEC's institutions was the last joint exercise in which I took part.

In addition to my work on boards of directors and advisers, and the counsels requested of me by the French government, various international organizations and a number of private companies, I gave a great number of lectures for various study and research bodies. I should also mention, for the record, several visits I made to countries with which I was unacquainted and which I thought presented an interest for my work as a whole. These included an East European tour that took me in 1973 to Yugoslavia, Hungary and Romania, and in 1974 to Poland, Czechoslovakia and East Germany. I thus completed an exploration of this part of the world which I had begun in 1967 with a trip to the USSR during which Dottie and I stayed at the French Embassy in Moscow at the invitation of Olivier Wormser and his wife Simone, who at the time were representing our country over there. I saw for myself the bleak and cheerless quality of life in the Soviet satellite countries, the wide gap in living standards between that part of the world and Western Europe. It made me more certain than ever that the prevailing economic and political regimes would not survive a withdrawal of the Soviet army. At about the same time I went to Israel, where I was able to acquire at least a superficial knowledge of the problems in the Middle East.

My activity in the seventies and early eighties thus necessitated a great deal of travel. Hardly a week went by when I did not have to pack my suitcase. I had, in fact, become very good at this: a list of necessaries that I had meticulously compiled ensured that I left nothing out. Over the years I had acquired a collection of suitcases, each appropriate to a particular kind of trip or series of trips, very short, short or long. These trips were organized intelligently, efficiently and with immense kindness by my secretary at French Shell, Mme Danièle Testaert.

To round out the catalogue of my activities, I should like to say a word about three lectures I gave in New York during the summer of 1980 at the invitation of the Council on Foreign Relations, and which were published under the title 'Europe in Search of Its Identity.' The lectures were a sort of a blueprint for these memoirs, or at least for such parts of them as cover the same period and the same problems. The initiative came from my friend Bill Diebold, who for many years kept urging me to leave something behind.

This last phase of my working life, from 1967 to 1984, was thus very different from the preceding ones: French Plan, Marshall Plan and European Economic Community. I no longer had any direct responsibilities, any operations to direct. I gave advice that was taken or not taken. Curiously, I found in this new way of life satisfactions comparable to those I had experienced in earlier times. I was able to reflect unhurriedly and to build myself an intellectual universe that was as coherent as possible, without having the thread of my reasoning suddenly broken by the need to decide. I should say, however, that the satisfaction would not have lasted very long if I had not had the feeling that my opinions and counsels were often appreciated and sometimes acted upon.

Now that this activity, or restlessness, whichever one prefers to call it, has almost ceased, since the end of 1984, I am beginning to have some difficulty in remembering how I was able to cope with it all. In any event, for as long as it lasted, it did not get me down and I nearly always set out on my assignments with a feeling of pleasure at the idea of the friends I was going to meet, the discussions in which I was going to take part, and the contribution I might be able to make to the pursuit of an elusive truth. These manifold professional activities helped me to forget, to some extent, the emotional void in my life created by Dottie's sudden death in October 1971. The constant travel and the intellectually stimulating occupations enabled me to escape from the loneliness I felt more often than not when I was in Paris.

Came retirement age, seventy in the case of most of the boards of directors and advisers of which I was a member, as well as for the individual consultancies I held in several companies, and I gave up one by one the many posts I had filled during the seventies. I saw these activities go each time with a certain regret, but also with a feeling of relief. I had given everything I had; no one any longer had the right to ask anything of me. I was like a machine that has completely earned back its cost. Anything it can still produce is net profit for the employer, in this instance myself.

So my itinerary ends. When I sat down at my desk to describe it, I had only confused impressions in my mind. Things got progressively clearer as I wrote. I hope the reader will feel the same way.

It now remains for me to speak of the conclusions I have reached over the past fifteen years or so in the areas of activity I chose. This obliges me to make a journey back in time which I shall try to keep as brief as possible.

2

OIL

I have already explained why my activity from 1969 to 1986 was primarily oriented towards oil. As a member of the supervisory board of Royal Dutch from 1969 to 1982 and of the board of directors of Shell Française from 1969 to 1986, I watched from a ringside seat the extraordinary spectacle which oil production and commerce put before the world in those years. Whereas in the sixties the oil industry was still essentially in the hands of a few big international companies, between 1970 and 1973 it gradually came under the control of a cartel of producing countries, until such time as, circumstances having changed, the oil cartel underwent the fate that almost always befalls cartels which try to fix the price of a raw material. Excessive price increases cause a fall in demand and an increase in supply; the quantities put on the market cannot be absorbed; prices collapse. In the case that concerns us here, neither the big oil companies, nor the producing or consuming countries were in the least degree able to maintain any kind of order on the market. But I am getting too far ahead.

In point of fact, my interest in energy problems predates my joining the board of Royal Dutch. Already at the time of the Marshall Plan and European reconstruction, Europe's energy supplies and the cost of imported oil were among my major concerns.

Before the war, the big oil companies were organized as a veritable cartel and could set prices higher than what the market prices would have been. After the war the cartel disappeared, but pricing still presented big anomalies. As Secretary-General of the OEEC, I remember stating on many occasions my conviction that Europe was paying too much for its oil. It took intervention by the governments concerned, and more particularly by the American government in the person of Paul Hoffmann of the Economic Cooperation Administration, to reduce the impact of a price system that treated all oil, regardless of origin, as coming from the Gulf of Mexico. Oil from the Middle East, where production costs were very low, was sold at the American oil price, which was much higher. The most serious anomalies were rectified then, but it was not until the late fifties that, thanks this time to a change in the state of the market, oil prices reflected production costs. The extremely keen competition between crudes of different origins caused a slow but steady erosion of prices that was to induce the producing countries to get together to form OPEC.

My second experience of energy matters dates from the time of the Common Market's creation when I was serving as a Vice-President of the Commission. When my colleagues and I shared out our areas of responsibility, I asked for, in addition to economic, financial and monetary matters, questions relating to energy. No one quarrelled with this assignment since things seemed so quiet in that domain. The ECSC High Authority took care of coal, the Euratom Commission of nuclear energy. That left me oil and natural gas, i.e. the forms of energy that were developing most rapidly. I and my colleagues from the other two institutions got into the habit of meeting periodically to take stock of the situation and try to define a possible European energy policy. I did not envy the ECSC's task of organizing the progressive changeover from coal in many areas of use, nor Euratom's, for the time of nuclear power had not yet come. The low price of oil made it both the cheapest and the most convenient form of energy.

During the fifties and sixties the coal era, which had lasted a century and a half, came to an end and the oil era began. Use of the latter developed with extraordinary rapidity. Over the twenty or so years that followed the war the demand for all forms of energy skyrocketed in the non-communist world and nearly 90% of the additional requirements were met by oil and natural gas. Oil consumption in the non-communist world increased from 10 million barrels per day in 1950 to nearly 40 million in 1970[1]. In Western Europe, consumption rose from 1.2 million b/d in 1950 to 12 million b/d in 1970. Whereas in 1950 oil and natural gas together accounted for only 14% of Europe's energy consumption as against 75% for coal, by the end of the sixties they had outstripped coal. And that was only the beginning. The big oil companies managed, by dint of great technological effort, to take this demand increase in their stride, boosting their output during these two decades by about 10% a year on average, and selling it at prices which, from 1955 at any rate, declined from year to year[2].

Something that tends to be forgotten is that the European economy's stupendous development, from the end of the war to 1973, was possible only because energy, mainly in the form of oil, was available in virtually unlimited quantities and at prices which now seem extremely low in the light of experience since 1973. Even so, as the one in charge of Common Market energy matters, I still considered those prices to be too high and I used such influence as I had to bring them down, or at any rate to prevent them from rising. But my chief concern was what is generally termed 'security', i.e. of supplies. Europe was becoming increasingly energy-dependent on the Middle East. What would happen if trouble broke out in that part of the world? The events of 1956–7, which had led to a temporary closure of the Suez Canal, were still in many people's minds and particularly in mine. A crisis of the same kind that would cut off part of Europe's energy supply could happen again. Could America, whose oil output at that time still exceeded domestic consumption, make up the shortfall?

I remember, without being able to place them exactly in time, a series of visits I paid to the top executives of the big American and European oil companies to ask them what arrangements they envisaged for such an eventuality. Then I invited the representatives of those companies to come to Brussels to discuss the same problem. This initiative caused some fuss in an industry which was shrouded in mystery and whose American members lived in constant fear of stringent antitrust legislation. But such was the prestige of the European Economic Community at the time that the people I had invited agreed without demur to come to Brussels. I seem to think that nothing specific came out of that meeting, since there was no serious problem then and no one seemed to have any presentiment of all the trouble to come a few years later.

The oil scene in 1970

When I joined the board of Royal Dutch the world oil scene was outwardly calm. Only someone completely knowledgeable, with a historical vision of things and endowed with exceptional powers of judgment, could have suspected that big events were brewing that would threaten not only the existence of the company of which I had just become a director, but the economic and political equilibrium of the whole world. As for me, I had no inkling that I was witnessing the twilight of an era and that I would soon become part of a drama full of vicissitudes that would last for twelve years. I did not sense that the seventies were going to be the oil decade, during which the jump in that commodity's prices would combine with monetary disturbances of various origins to remove, for a time at least, every trace of an orderly international economy.

And yet there were already many omens of the storm that was about to break in a few months' time. Not all of them had escaped me. I felt vaguely that changes were coming, but I had no idea that the hurricane would be so violent and that it would turn upside down, almost in the twinkling of an eye, the scene to which the energy people had long become accustomed. Even so, as early as 1971 the Shell Group sent to the governments with which it was in contact a report describing in detail the supply and demand outlook and the consequent potential threat to consuming countries. At the same time it suggested to the Brussels Commission the broad lines of a common oil policy.

In late 1969 and early 1970 the world oil scene was still the same as usual. Production, excluding the USA and the communist countries, lay essentially in the hands of a few big companies, often referred to as The Seven Sisters: five American companies, one British and one Anglo-Dutch, Royal Dutch-Shell. Another company, the Compagnie Française des Pétroles, was sometimes called the eighth sister.

The system was one of long-term concessions granted by the producing countries to the companies. The latter decided sovereignly how much oil they would produce in each of their concessions, although sometimes the producing countries – notably Iran, Iraq and Saudi Arabia – exerted more or less discreet pressure to have production increased. A producer price (posted price) was set as a basis for the calculations of companies' production-stage profits. Of these the companies paid half over to the producing countries. In addition to this tax there was a fixed royalty payable on each barrel produced, constituting the income which the producing countries derived from the oil extracted from their ground.

In point of fact this system had been slowly eroded during the sixties. The producing countries had begun to grant less advantageous concessions than those of the 'majors' to certain 'independents' (oil companies of smaller size than the majors, whose output was not as diversified and whose activity, unlike theirs, was not integrated from production through to the distribution stage) and to the state companies set up in a few consuming countries. Furthermore, the share of profits paid over by the oil companies to the producing countries in 1966 was significantly more than 50%, the latter having refused to lower the posted price, which constituted the tax base, at a time when oil prices were falling in the world market.

Even so, the Seven Sisters were still controlling about 75% of world oil production outside the United States and the communist countries. Their power had an aura of permanence and stability. Did they not own a very large proportion of the tankers, refineries and distribution networks that kept the free world supplied with oil products? Far from resting on their laurels, they had made, in the postwar period, and were still making great efforts to discover new sources of oil; the technology they had developed was making it possible to extract oil from the seabed at ever increasing depths.

As an economist observing the course of events, I think I can say without exaggeration that western (and Japanese) consumers, and especially European consumers, were the ones who derived most benefit from the system. At the same time, both in Europe and in America, the power of the oil companies caused the latter to be feared, and public opinion was always ready to blame them for every untoward event that occurred in the energy domain. This reputation dated back essentially to the epic and turbulent times of the oil industry's formation with its occasional scandals, the times of Rockefeller and Deterding. Another factor was a marked lack of regard on the part of certain American companies for producing and consuming countries alike.

At the time when my membership of the board of Royal Dutch became my most important occupation, the opinion was still widely held that there was a cartelistic arrangement among the big oil companies which worked against the consumers and produced huge profits for the companies. That this notion might derive more from myth than from hard fact did not seem unduly to bother most commentators, whether politicians, economists or journalists. As for me, I had formed another opinion on the matter, and my convictions were confirmed when I was able to examine things at closer range.

It did not take me long to discover that if the big oil companies did form a cartel, then it was a strange one indeed. A cartel in the true sense cannot be said to exist unless it has gained sufficient control over the industry in which it is operating to keep that industry's prices significantly above the level they would find in a free market; which means, in particular, that it must succeed in keeping out newcomers lured by the prospect of monopolistic pricing. Admittedly, at the production stage there were agreements between oil companies in a large number of countries. These reflected long-standing relations and sometimes also a preference for risk-sharing. Consortia of this kind existed in Iraq, Iran, Kuwait, Saudi Arabia, Nigeria, etc. The majors, sometimes joined by a few independents, set the level of production and shared it out among themselves. It is certain that in some cases this level was below potential, hence conflicts of interests between companies, between producing countries and also between producing countries and companies. The problem was particularly acute for the oil-producing countries with virtually no other source of revenue. In such a situation the companies knew how to maintain a united front against the states concerned, a glutted oil market being helpful to them here.

But that was the limit of the cartel element. At no time in the sixties, at least to my knowledge, was there any attempt by the big companies to fix an aggregate production level, which for example would have had the effect of driving up prices or even simply of holding them up. In fact, the majors, not to speak of the independents, competed very strenuously with one another in nearly every area of activity. Those who at the time accused them of using their power to try to make oil an organized market closed to all competition did not know what they were talking about. The big companies were, outside oil agreements of a local compass, the most determined of rivals. Each one made intense efforts to discover new deposits, obtain concessions to develop them, and expand its refining and transport capacities, even when the market was or appeared to be saturated and prices were falling. Every single year about half the industry's investment went into exploration. In many cases very large sums were lost outright in this way, as drilling revealed more often than not that whatever oil there might once have been had vanished long ago. Only one well in ten disclosed traces of petroleum and only one in thirty-seven revealed the existence of a deposit that could be commercially developed[3].

This kind of frenzy with which the oil companies searched for new reserves may seem odd today, but it is easily explainable in terms of those times. One of their main concerns was to find sources of crude as close as possible to the big markets, notably Europe, and especially sources west of Suez. Furthermore, they could not remain insensitive to the varying degrees of pressure being exerted by consuming country governments anxious to ensure security of supplies. Memories of the great postwar crises, Mossadegh's abortive attempt to nationalize Iranian oil in 1951, the closure of the Suez Canal, the Six Days War of 1967 with the embargo on oil shipments to Britain and America, were still fresh in people's minds. Exploration activity became particularly intense after the Suez crisis, one of the chief results being the discovery of extensive deposits in Libya and Nigeria.

But it was in northern Europe that the most important developments occurred. In 1959 Shell and Exxon, equal partners in this part of the world, had discovered big natural gas reserves in Groningen in Holland. In the event, natural gas proved to be much more important for the destiny of the Netherlands and its population's standard of living than Indonesia had been for centuries prior to World War Two. The presence of natural gas in Holland spurred the majors and many independents to undertake extensive exploration in the North Sea, which resulted in the discovery of very large deposits of natural gas from 1965, then of oil from 1969. For the Royal Dutch-Shell group this was a real stroke of luck. I had noticed, as soon as I stated to work with the group, that it was chronically short of crude oil resources of its own. In other words, to supply its distribution network, one of the most extensive and best organized in the world, it had to buy from other oil companies with crude to spare. For example, in 1966, with a crude oil requirement of 3.8 million b/d, its own resources did not exceed 3 million b/d. Another of the group's weaknesses, which was to prove serious at one point during the seventies, was that it did not have access to the reserves of Saudi Arabia, whose oil production was entirely in the hands of four big American companies.

These few examples, and there are many others I could give, show that far from forming a Malthusian cartel, at least at the time of which I am speaking, the big oil companies were engaged in an all-out race to discover oil and obtain the most productive concessions. In addition, they were competing keenly with one another to sell crude to certain national companies without or with insufficient supplies of their own, as well as on the market for oil products in the consuming countries, where they spared no effort to build the most efficient possible distribution networks and then to consolidate them by reaching out to an ever growing number of consumers. This is hardly the picture of a worldwide conspiracy to exploit the oil importing countries.

What is true is that it was not in the interests of any of the big companies, which had already won their place in the sun, to upset the equilibrium of the market and disrupt traditional flows by, say, a sudden steep cut in prices. Each company preferred to increase its share of the market by finding new reserves of crude oil and strengthening its distribution network. If they did not have an overall arrangement, the big oil companies observed one another closely, each being ready to profit from the mistakes of the others and to imitate as quickly as possible what it considered to be promising innovations.

During the years when I was able to watch things, before the big crisis of 1973, in the days when the majors could still set producer prices more or less freely, if there was, short of a cartel, at least a tacit understanding among them, it was to keep those prices relatively low, i.e. competitive, rather than to exploit the consumer. If they erred at times it was more in holding producer prices down too tightly than in overpricing refined products.

With the breakthrough of the independents in the fifties and sixties, moreover, any semblance of a cartel vanished. This development gathered great momentum following the discovery of Libyan oil very close to the European market. Led by highly individual, colourful personalities like J. Paul Getty, H. L. Hunt and Armand Hammer, the independents did not destroy the power of the majors, but gave the producing countries the possibility of playing off one company against another. With no Middle East interests to protect, the independents were not particularly concerned about preserving the existing price structure, either in their relations with the producing countries or in their dealings with the consumers of Europe, where they marketed most of their output. For the sake of completeness, one should mention, besides the American independents, the European national companies like Pétrofina in Belgium, Gelsenberg in Germany, Hispanoil in Spain, Elf-Aquitaine in France and, especially, ENI in Italy, which likewise tried to acquire crude oil resources.

Another thing I used to wonder about then was the size of the big oil companies' profits. Were they as enormous as the public often imagined them to be? Did the companies dodge taxes as many thought they did? How did they use those profits? In short, was society at large getting a square deal?

Let it be said right away that throughout the postwar years profits, without being exorbitant, were ample. How could it have been otherwise in a rapidly expanding industry where demand was rising every year by 10% or more? For example, Christopher Tugendhat writes that Exxon's return on its capital investment worldwide was 12.4% in

1966 and that the average for the seven biggest international companies was 11.4%. During the fifties the average return was 14%, declining subsequently to about 10%. These figures compare with those of any well-run industry operating in a favourable environment. I would add that these profits were made at a time when the pretax prices of oil products were falling steadily. The price fall was particularly steep in Europe where, because of the import quota system set up by the Americans to protect their own oil industry, the companies with production operations elsewhere in the world were obliged to sell their surplus output, often in difficult conditions.

One of the questions frequently discussed at The Hague or in London was that of profit origin: upstream, i.e. at the production stage, or downstream, at the transportation, refining and distribution stages. Almost invariably upstream profits were high, while downstream profits were low or even often negative. This was very largely due to the fact that, during the sixties at least, the producing countries refused any reduction in posted prices, even though these no longer reflected the state of the market. It was this high notional price that produced high upstream profits. By contrast, the subsidiaries that took care of transportation, refining and distribution, having had to buy their crude at an unrealistic price were not always able to break even and often sustained losses, as I have said, especially on the European market.

As to the tax question, it is true that the oil companies often paid very low taxes, or even none at all, in the western countries where they had their head offices. This was because they had managed to get the governments of those countries to allow them to set off against the taxes they had to pay in the West those they had paid to the producing countries. It always seemed to me that this was a normal practice, identical to what happens in all cases where there might be double taxation of the same income.

That leaves possibly the most important point, namely the use to which the oil companies were putting their profits and still do. At least half, and often more, was ploughed back. Without this injection of fresh money each year the companies in question would have had great difficulty in financing the expansion of an industry that had to meet constantly a growing demand. The enormous sums invested in research and development in the North Sea, Alaska, Nigeria, and a great number of other places, helped to ensure a certain security of supplies for the consuming countries. To wind up on this point, I shall quote what Walter Levy wrote concerning oil company profits in 1971, just before the great upheavals:

Since then [1965] ... the margins of profit of oil companies in the Eastern Hemisphere have continued to narrow, and rates of return are now barely in line with competitive rates in other industries or with the capital requirements to meet rapidly expanding oil consumption[4].

Having looked into these different questions, I came to the conclusion that, while pursuing their essential objective, which was that of any capitalistic enterprise, namely to make itself continually stronger by increasing its share of the market and making the maximum profit, the big oil companies, or at least those of which I had a fair knowledge, were at the same time performing their social function satisfactorily for the community at large. They were supplying, at a reasonable price, the energy needed for continuous economic growth. This does not mean that, in particular instances and over shorter or longer periods, errors and malpractices were not committed. But the importance of these was insignificant, I thought, when set against a spectacular success in the accomplishment of the oil industry's essential function.

The great upheavals

Whatever the merits of the big oil companies during the years that followed the war, it was obvious to any observer with a certain sense of history that the situation at the end of the sixties was highly unstable and that the relative calm prevailing on the oil markets was precarious.

The troubles of the seventies can be attributed to all sorts of economic causes or to various political accidents, to the fact that prices were too low, or to the Arab-Israeli wars. The simple truth is that the continual rise of nationalism in the countries that formerly were colonies, especially in the Arab countries, was bound to lead one day to a massive shift of power to the governments of the Near East and of the other oil countries. It is even surprising that the situation that existed after the war lasted as long as it did. What would we have done, we Europeans and Americans, if our main source of economic wealth, in many cases the only one of any importance, had been placed under the control of foreign companies and, indirectly, of foreign governments? The answer is not in any doubt. Even people with little nationalistic feeling would have found this dependence intolerable. The movement towards an entirely new situation, where the producing countries would themselves make the decisions concerning oil production and prices, was ineluctable. The only question was how the change would come about. In the event, the answer depended on the attitude of the different partners in this complicated game, and also on historical events that had little or nothing to do with oil. It can be said, however, that the rapid growth of world demand for oil accelerated the transition.

It became clear to me very early on that my friends at Shell were more sensitive to this aspect of things than the people who were running other oil companies, notably in America. But there was practically nothing they could do. The law of the market had to be obeyed. Yet when it seemed to them that the equilibrium of supply and demand was liable, a few years hence, to entail supply shortages and steep price increases, they informed governments and international organizations accordingly, at the risk of being suspected of trying to increase still further the profits that public opinion already considered to be as near as not scandalous. The issue was basically a political one that only the western governments could try to resolve. But governments, in that area, did not govern. They were even unaware of the need to govern, until confronted with a situation that to them was catastrophic.

The desire for change on the part of the producing countries slowly grew stronger, like river water piling up behind a dam. The pressure mounted ceaselessly, but the dam would hold until the day when the producing countries, acting individually or by joint agreement, succeeded in breaching it. What held them back for a time was the memory of 1951, in particular, when Iran had tried to nationalize its oil production. The common front presented by the oil companies with the support of their governments, the disunity of the producing countries, the fact that oil was not yet the vital commodity it was to become twenty years later and that it was in overplentiful supply with a multiplicity of production sources already, the ability of the United States and Venezuela to export large quantities, all these factors combined to cause the failure of the Iranian attempt and the fall of Mossadegh. But the circumstances had changed a great deal since. The producing countries had created OPEC (Organization of Petroleum Exporting Countries) in 1960, in a movement towards unity that was to gather strength in the ten years that followed. The Six Days War in 1967 revealed that this unity was not yet solid enough, nor the market situation propitious enough, to permit the Arab countries to use their oil as leverage. But by the end of the sixties, with the enormous expansion of western consumption, everyone, and especially the oil countries and companies, felt that the day was probably not far off when demand would exceed output at the then prevailing prices. The market was turning around and the power of the buyers was continuously decreasing, while that of the sellers, or rather of the oil countries, was increasing. A shortage which, though not yet real, was sensed or thought to be imminent emboldened the oil countries to try their luck.

If one wants to trace the course of events that led to the great crisis of 1973, one finds that 1970 is really the starting point. Subsequently, over a period of three years, the producing countries, led by Libya, tried to see how far they could go and, probably to the great surprise of many, found that there were no more obstacles in the way and that they could go as far as they wanted. The only force that could stop them one day was the invisible force of the market. But in the early seventies the market was on their side.

The crisis began in Libya after King Idris was deposed in 1969 and Qaddafi came to power. This little country found itself in a position of strength, the companies established there supplying one-fourth of Western Europe's oil. Furthermore, a large share of production there was in the hands of the independents, and they did not have the staying power of the big integrated international companies. They soon found that they were not in a position to oppose an increase, albeit modest at the outset, in prices and tax rates. Meanwhile the movement had begun to snowball, spreading rapidly to the whole of the Middle East and North Africa.

Between 1970 and 1973 oil countries and oil companies clashed at many stormy meetings in Caracas, Tehran and Tripoli, with pressure from the producing countries constantly increasing and the companies being continually obliged to make new concessions in regard to prices, tax rates and participation. It was clear that matters were being taken out of their hands. The governments of the consuming countries, helpless, watched the course of events with amazement and consternation. Episodic intervention, of no lasting consequence, in most cases merely aggravated the situation.

Something that was particularly noticeable at that time was the weakness of the American government, whose power in the Middle East, as in almost every other part of the world, had been immense during the postwar years, only to decline imperceptibly but continuously over the quarter-century that followed. This decline had been especially marked in the oil sector where, from having been a country with a positive oil balance and an exportable surplus, the United States had become a deficit country, with domestic consumption increasingly outstripping flat or sometimes even falling output. It was at that time, too, that one of the fundamental difficulties inherent in US foreign policy became clearly apparent. How could the United States be the defender, the accredited protector of Israel in the latter's conflicts with the Arab countries, and at the same time get those countries to respect the interests of the USA and its western allies where oil was concerned? America succeeded for a while in reconciling these two hardly compatible positions, but in the sixties her influence in the Arab world and especially in Saudi Arabia, though it did not entirely vanish, declined steeply. As for America's European and Japanese allies, their main concern, when the crisis broke, was to try to make the best of a bad job by negotiating bilateral agreements with this or that oil producing country.

From 1970 to 1973 the producing countries were able with impunity to force successive price and royalty increases on the oil companies, as well as a higher rate of tax on profits. They also obliged them to make over an increasing interest in the concessions they had granted them earlier and, to top it all, set a high price on the proportion of oil which they were prepared to sell outright to the companies. The roles were reversed. The power was now in the hands of the producing countries, which imposed their decisions unilaterally, then brought into question, six months or a year after they had been concluded, agreements supposed to last for fifty years.

This was the situation until 1973, when a new war broke out between Israel and the Arab countries. What would have happened if this event had not occurred? The question may seem otiose, like all hypothetical questions; but it is not without interest if one tries to determine what would have been a normal trend in the oil market during the seventies. Here I am about to venture an opinion that will certainly not be shared by everyone.

The price of Arabian light oil was $1.80 per barrel at the beginning of 1973 and $3 at the end of that year. Given the ambitions of the producing countries and mounting demand in the consuming countries, it is probable that the price rise would not have stopped there. It is not unreasonable to think that the price might have climbed to $5 a barrel in 1974–5, and that it would have subsequently continued to rise at the same rate as inflation in the purchasing countries without causing any crisis in the West; but if the oil price rise had been less steep, western inflation would itself have been lower. I shall spare the reader the details of my calculations. My conclusion is simply that now a price of $15–20 in today's money would be close to a medium- or long-term equilibrium price.

As to the nationalization of crude oil production by the producing countries, or by most of them, it seemed to me absolutely inescapable for the reasons I have given above. Experience has shown how the oil companies were able to adjust to it. In the event they showed an adaptability that over the years has always amazed me. True, they gradually lost ownership of much of the crude they were extracting in the Middle East, North Africa and elsewhere, but they remained the obligatory purchaser of that oil, which they alone, thanks to their fleet and to their powerful refining and distribution networks, were able to market throughout the world, to say nothing of the chemical indus- tries they set up, now absorbing a considerable share of the oil and natural gas that comes on to the market.

But on the price front, things were to be different. With the Arab- Israeli war of 1973 the realm of the irrational was entered. In October 1973 Egypt and Syria attacked Israel in order to win back the territor- ies lost by the Arabs in 1967 and to destroy the military power of Israel. The causes of this event were not economic, yet it was to trigger a sudden jump in oil prices, which was not the aim of all the producing countries. The latter began by demanding that the barrel price be raised to $3. The companies refused to take the responsibility for an increase which they thought would have serious economic conse- quences for the West. They wanted to consult the political authorities, which were not ready to respond. The negotiations were suspended and, in fact, never resumed.

The politico-military situation worsened. To save Israel, the United States airlifted large quantities of arms and munitions over the Atlan- tic and the Mediterranean. The members of OPEC decided unilater- ally to raise the barrel price to $5.12. The Arab members began to cut back their production rapidly and decreed an embargo on oil exports to the United States and Holland. Iran followed suit, seeing this affair as an opportunity to increase her oil revenues greatly.

It was then that a curious episode took place in the history of the big oil companies. Their power in the producing countries, in Asia and Africa, seemed to have vanished completely. Yet at the same time the seemingly impossible task fell to them of continuing to share out the available oil fairly among the consuming countries, while obeying the injunctions of the Arab producing countries. For that purpose, they organized a vast operation of worldwide distribution of oil, channel- ling to the embargo-hit consuming countries oil from the producing

407

countries not participating in the embargo. In Holland's case, for example, the Royal Dutch-Shell group arranged a massive reallocation of the oil at its disposal, tripling shipments from Nigeria and doubling those from Iran. The result was that Holland did not have her oil supplies reduced by more than the average for the consuming countries[5]. In the pandemonium the latter could no longer make their voices heard. The oil companies had to turn themselves into a sort of world government for a few months. They discharged that function efficiently and fairly. It is unlikely that this state of affairs could have gone on indefinitely, but the producing countries needed to sell their oil just as much as the consuming countries needed to buy it. At the end of 1973 the Arab countries eased their restrictions in regard to Europe; in March 1974 the embargo on shipments to the United States was lifted.

But during those fateful months, even though the purpose of the production cutbacks and the embargo was not, essentially at least, to drive prices up, they had taken off, partly because of the decisions taken by the producing countries and partly, too, because of a feeling of panic that had taken hold of purchasers ready then and there to pay almost any price to get their oil. In December 1973 oil was auctioned in Iran at $17 a barrel. In the same month, the Persian Gulf members of OPEC set the price at $11.65, four times the price prior to the crisis.

The board of Royal Dutch-Shell met, as usual, once a month. We followed events very closely, aware that stupendous changes were taking place in the oil world. The group's executives carried out perfectly and very collectedly the new task – new both in its nature and in its magnitude – which circumstances had imposed on them. When the storm had subsided and it became possible to take a provisional reckoning, some of the consequences were immediately apparent. The oil companies, and indirectly the consuming countries, had lost control of prices and production, which were now for a while completely in the hands of the producing countries. The movement towards oil nationalization had received a fresh impetus, and the day was not far off when, in many countries at any rate, production would be totally nationalized. The future of the oil companies looked gloomy. It would take some time for their relations with producing countries to get on to a new footing.

What nobody knew with any degree of precision was the effect that the quadrupling of oil prices would have on economic activity in the developed countries, on the balances of payments of the developing countries, on world oil production and on many other economic variables. No one had any inkling that this unprecedented price rise would act as a fantastic spur to oil exploration and production outside the OPEC area. No one was in a position to gauge the extent of the energy savings in general, and oil savings in particular, that would come about as a result of the oil price rise, or the magnitude of the substitution effects produced by the consequent replacement of oil by other forms of energy.

The years from 1974 to 1978 have not left me with any very precise recollections. However, for the Royal Dutch-Shell group they were crucial years during which it saw some of its traditional positions weaken, while at the same time it went to work to lay the foundations for future developments and made extensive efforts in new geographical areas, efforts which did not yield results, in terms of profit, until some years later.

The rapid nationalization of oil production in most of the OPEC countries, the growth of the national companies in producing and consuming countries, the increasing role being played by the independents, these were a violent trauma for the big oil companies in the seventies. They were losing an increasing share of the market. If one adds to this the fact that from 1974 worldwide consumption of oil products ceased to grow at the rapid pace of the preceding twenty-five years, and sometimes even declined, one has the measure of the changes that disrupted an industry hitherto accustomed to better days.

As regards the Royal Dutch-Shell group more particularly, the figures of the time show that their world sales of oil products fell by 37% between 1973 and 1980. Net income from these sales, after a very steep rise in 1973 due in part to an increase in the value of the group's oil stocks, remained almost flat for five years. The dividend distributed by Royal Dutch increased by 48% in guilder terms, whereas over the same period consumer prices in the Netherlands rose by 45% and hourly wages by 86%. Reflecting stock market sentiment on these results, Royal Dutch share prices on the Amsterdam stock exchange showed hardly any variation from 1972 to 1978.

It might therefore have seemed to the uninformed observer that the private oil industry had gone as far as it could and from now on was bound to decline. In fact, those years were marked by intense activity to redress a situation compromised by the events of the preceding period.

That was when the North sea, with its abundant reserves of oil and gas, close to the enormous centre of consumption represented by

Europe and therefore located in a zone politically controlled by the western states, became the happy hunting ground for Shell, which played a big role there as operator for account of the Shell-Exxon partnership. After the discoveries of natural gas in the years 1965–7, the largest oil deposit was found at Brent in 1971, then came Cormorant, in 1972 and Dunlin in 1973, followed a little later by Auk and Fulmar. Shell, Exxon and other companies interested in the development of the North Sea invested enormous sums during the seventies, amounting to several billion dollars. The production effort was augmented by spectacular technological innovations, like the construction of gigantic oil rigs or the laying of submarine oil and gas pipelines to collect the petroleum and natural gas from different sources. The result lived up to or exceeded expectations. At the time of the 1973 oil shock the North Sea, as a whole, was producing less than two million tonnes of oil a year. By 1984, 133 million tonnes was being extracted from the British sector and 33 million tonnes from the Norwegian sector, without counting the natural gas that places the North Sea in third position among the world's producers, after the USA and the USSR.

Shell thus reaped the reward of enormous efforts over several years that yielded no profit from the shareholders' standpoint. The lean years it had traversed after 1973 were to be followed by a period in which profits have risen steeply. As an indication, the Royal Dutch share price in Amsterdam climbed from about 60 florins at the end of 1978 to 180 florins at the end of 1985.

By comparison with Middle East oil, North Sea oil is expensive, since the conditions of exploitation for the latter are much more difficult. Had it not been for the fourfold price increase in 1973, North Sea production would probably not have become as extensive as it has. But in the conditions that were established in 1973 exploitation was profitable. One may wonder, however, what would happen if prices were to fall steeply and lastingly.

The 1973 price rise had been excessive, but an adjustment took place in the years that followed. Although this was a period of galloping inflation throughout the world, oil prices did not change in nominal terms, i.e. they fell in real terms. Moreover, the fall was steeper than the oil figures of that time indicate, as oil is priced in dollars and during the greater part of the seventies the dollar weakened steadily against the currencies of Europe and Japan. An equilibrium would very probably have been reached, with reasonable profits for the producers and tolerable costs for consumers, if a second price explosion had not occurred in 1979. This time it was not, like in 1973, a deliberate action by certain producing countries that used their oil leverage to make things difficult for the United States and other western countries that were supporting Israel, but the result of events that had nothing to do with oil.

A revolution broke out in Iran in the second half of 1978. Iranian oil production was shut down in October of the same year, and in January 1979 the Shah left the country precipitately. The oil market was suddenly thrown into disequilibrium; purchasers, oil companies and individual users panicked. Each tried to build up the security stocks that would protect them against the worldwide shortage that most experts were blithely predicting. The governments of consuming countries tried, in most cases vainly, to negotiate bilateral agreements with one or other producing country.

Prices took off. On the spot market they rose to $40 per barrel in 1979. In defiance of futures they had contracted, certain producing countries added special premiums to their prices. The official price set by the producing countries for Arabian light rose from an average of $12.70 in 1978 to $22 in 1979 and $31.33 in 1980. The war that broke out between Iraq and Iran in September 1980, with a very steep cutback in the two countries' oil production in consequence, strengthened the feeling that an oil shortage was imminent. In 1981 and 1982 the average barrel price was $34. By comparison with 1978, prices had all but trebled; by comparison with the period prior to 1973, they had increased twelvefold.

The oil price rise of 1973 was understandable; it corresponded, in part at any rate, to an objective need. That of 1979–80 can be likened to an act of collective madness. There was no real shortage; in fact, OPEC oil production reached an all-time high in 1979 with 31.7 million b/d, over 1 million b/d more than in 1978. Likewise, aggregate production in the non-communist world amounted in the same year to a record 53 million b/d. Afterwards, OPEC output would decline sharply.

I left the board of Royal Dutch at the end of June 1982. Over the preceding three and a half years the oil world had gone through a period of total uncertainty. No one seemed able to foresee where the price rise would stop. Those who did no more than project the movement that started at the end of 1978 arrived at absurd conclusions soon to be disproved by events. During these critical years the executives of Royal Dutch-Shell showed very great caution. They concentrated on expanding production in regions where they could still control it, first and foremost in the North Sea. From the figures published in the press it is very clear that they had no cause for regret.

A landscape transformed

Over the fifteen years from 1970 to 1985 in which I was able to examine things at fairly close range, the oil landscape, in fact the whole energy scene, changed completely. And the whole world economic situation changed radically in consequence. I do not mean that the oil price rise was the sole cause, but it certainly contributed greatly.

The oil price spiral between the years of 1973 and 1982 has resulted, as should have been expected, in a steep fall in demand, owing to the energy conservation it spurred, to the substitution of coal, natural gas and nuclear energy for oil wherever this could be profitably effected, and to the slowdown in world economic growth of which the rise in energy prices was one of the principal causes. Then, to complete the picture, there has been a progressive shift in economic structures away from industry, with its heavy consumption of energy, towards service activities, which for the most part are light consumers of energy.

I can personally testify that in 1973, and even in the years that followed, no one had any idea that energy demand in general, and oil demand in particular, would fall so steeply. And only gradually did it become apparent that this would be a two-stage fall. During the first stage, which immediately followed the oil price rise, enterprises and households curbed their consumption. Then users, rapidly becoming accustomed to the new prices, reverted to their old habits, and energy demand climbed back almost if not quite to its initial level. The second stage, which was spread over several years – five, ten, or even more – saw the almost invisible changeover from a cheap- to a dear-energy economy. By way of example, energy consumption has become a very important variable which has to be taken into account in the manufacture of new machines and the construction of new buildings and plants. It was during this second stage that the biggest and most durable energy savings were achieved.

The combination of all the factors I have mentioned above led to spectacular results. Whereas over the period from 1960 to 1973 total energy consumption had grown on average by 5.3% a year and oil consumption by 7.5%, for the period from 1973 to 1982 energy consumption growth averaged only 0.6% annually, while oil consumption decreased by 0.7% a year.

World oil output fell from an all-time high of 53 million b/d in 1979 to under 44 million b/d in 1984. Yet although the overall trend was downward, some regions showed steeper falls than others, while many increased their output. With the development of production in Alaska, the North Sea and Mexico, but also, though to a lesser extent, in West Africa, Egypt, India, South-East Asia and South America, it was the OPEC countries that took the full force of the blow. Their production collapsed from 31.7 million b/d in 1979 to a figure that today varies between 15 and 17 million b/d. Whereas in 1979 it represented nearly 60% of world production, in 1985 it accounted for no more than about one-third.

The posted price of crude declined by fits and starts to around $25 or $26 in 1985, before plummeting to $10 in 1986. OPEC oil revenues fell from $279 billion in 1980 to $159 billion in 1984. The OPEC balance of payments on current account swung into deficit.

One could see, within the OPEC group, the weakening of a discipline that had never been very strong in the first place. Such is the usual fate of cartels that try to control the prices and production of a core commodity. They are imperious, and seem powerful and fearsome, as long as the market is under strain. But the excesses in which they indulge or let themselves be tempted to indulge result more often than not in a fall in demand and an increase in supply. Then they disintegrate and either disappear or become utterly ineffective.

In addition to the market turnabout, the eighties have seen changes in the pattern of demand, which moreover have simply been extensions of trends that were already apparent. Demand for heavy products (notably fuel oil) has become much more sensitive to rising prices than demand for lighter products (gasoline, for example), given the possibility of substituting for the former coal, electricity (including, of course, nuclear power) and natural gas. At the refining stage, the oil companies have had to invest heavily in order to increase their capacity for converting heavy products into light products.

The producing countries were badly affected, after a time, by the absurd rise in oil prices. So were the oil companies, owing to the emergence of very considerable surplus capacity in transportation (by pipeline and tanker), refining and storage. They had to make great efforts to reduce that surplus capacity progressively, and these have accounted for most of their activity in recent years. At the same time, their investment requirements, and thus their financing needs, continue to be enormous. In 1980, for example, the total revenue of the majors, i.e. net income plus depreciation allowances and the proceeds from the sale of certain assets, amounted to $51.5 billion. Of this sum, $37.5 billion was invested or reinvested, while $7.9 billion was paid out to the shareholders. This internal financing was supplemented by large-scale borrowing from the banks and on the capital market. In 1982 the Royal Dutch-Shell group, if one includes the figures for its American subsidiary Shell Oil, was the oil group that invested most.

Where does the oil industry stand today? The OPEC cartel has proved to be short-lived; it lost its price-fixing power at the end of 1985, and nobody can be sure whether it will regain it one day. The big oil companies no longer call the tune, but despite all their trials and tribulations they are still there; it is not even certain that they have been seriously weakened. They have concluded with the producing countries an infinite variety of agreements among which it is sometimes difficult to find one's way. What is clear, however, is that their relations with those countries have changed radically as a result of all the developments between 1970 and the early eighties. Everywhere, national governments now tightly control the oil companies' activity. The days when it was possible to blame the big companies for all the world's energy problems, because of alleged overpricing or underpricing, are gone for good.

With extraordinary flexibility they have adjusted, month after month, year after year, to a constantly shifting situation. Financially they seem to have come through without any major damage. Admittedly, in many countries they have lost the ownership of production and reserves. But is the notion of 'ownership' in this context as important as one might think? Of two companies, one possessing this right of ownership but whose activity is bound by a system of complex, fussy and often arbitrary regulations, the other acting as an 'operator' with an adequate return on invested capital, which is the better placed from the shareholder's standpoint? The answer to that question is not always evident.

A final word about the French subsidiary of the Royal Dutch-Shell group, where, as I write these lines, I still have a few months left as a member of the board. It found itself in a difficult situation during the greater part of the seventies, and still does today, owing to the fact that it owns no large deposits of oil or natural gas and suffered, during the period under consideration, from a government system of price regulations that frequently sacrificed the interests of the French refining industry to other considerations of a political or even electoral nature. The result was that between 1974 and 1985 the company had a period of seven consecutive years in which it recorded losses, sometimes large one. Even though the company sold off a large share of its oil stocks, its indebtedness grew beyond tolerable limits and stern measures of reorganization had to be taken. In the case of an ailing enterprise, 'reorganization' nearly always spells 'retrenchment.' The enterprise has to cut back its costs, notably its overheads and staff expenditure; it has to give up its loss-making or low-profit activities. It is a painful operation that inevitably entails staff cuts and a reduction on market shares. The company has embarked on this exercise and is conducting it with courage and compassion.

3

1945–1985: EXPANSION AND STAGNATION – A COMMENTARY

A great part of my life has been spent in observing economic events and endeavouring to explain them. What caused the crisis of the thirties? What caused the spectacular revival during the twenty-five or thirty years that followed the war? What caused the virtual standstill, in Europe at any rate, over the period from 1973 to 1985?

This continuous reflection on the course of economic developments, from which it was not possible to dissociate the political events that were often their cause or effect, had become an essential part of me. First before the war, at the *Institut de Recherches Economiques et Sociales* under the benevolent guidance of Charles Rist, then in London and Washington during the war, on the staff of the French Plan of Modernization and Equipent from 1946 to 1948, in the Organisation for European Economic Cooperation from 1948 to 1955, and in the Common Market from 1958 to 1967.

My leaving the European Economic Community did not cause any break where this aspect of my life was concerned. Banks and industrial firms then asked me to give them regularly my views about ongoing or foreseeable economic developments. They attached, naturally enough, much more importance to the forecasts I was able to make than to my analysis of current events. Thus for about fifteen years I played the soothsayer at meetings held by Chase, IBM, American Express etc. On average I was asked to comment on the world economic situation eight or ten times a year. I often received as much as or more than I gave, as a result of the discussions that would follow my statements.

At these meetings of economists and businessmen I found myself in an unusual situation. When I was asked my occupation, at airports and elsewhere, I would answer 'economist.' In fact I had never truly deserved this style. Admittedly, in the prewar years I had striven to become one and did not do too badly then, but it would have taken me many more years of work to master the necessary techniques, notably mathematical, which have become indispensable to the practice of the economist's profession. The war had interrupted the course of my life, and I was never able subsequently to pick up from where I had left off in 1939. A few books read from time to time and great familiarity with the English-speaking economic press enabled me to hold on to what I had learned, and to follow and understand what was going on.

What gave me, in spite of these deficiencies, a certain force and authority was the long experience of the economic and political world I had gained over the years. I could never have aspired to compete with the economists who had spent their lives in teaching and research, but I had become very practised in analyzing situations. After I left the European Economic Community, my years with Royal Dutch, when energy problems were the foremost concern of governments and private enterprise, had added further to this stock-in-trade.

For this reason I did not cut too sorry a figure in my new activities during the seventies. In a period of great material and intellectual upheavals, when the most solidly established theories appeared quite inadequate to account for what was happening, an experience stretching back over some forty years, resting on common sense and a certain knowledge of the economic authors, enabled me to unravel, without too many errors, the causes and effects of developments that had no precedent. I did make the occasional mistake, but no more than my colleagues.

Throughout this endeavour at explanation that has lasted for several decades my thinking has, it is true, changed on a number of essential points, but the change has been not so much a rejection of convictions formed earlier as a shift of emphasis. Relationships that had hitherto seemed secondary to me suddenly took on great importance, while others were relegated to a lesser place. I think, moreover, that this particular process of change is specific to economic science. The latter is a system of interdependent variables whose movement is sometimes disrupted by shifts of attitude on the part of economic agents or by the sudden intrusion of exogenous factors. At a given time there are a certain number of relationships between variables which appear essential and on which the attention is focussed. At other times, when the situation has altered, the significant variables change and another theoretical construct becomes necessary in order to account for the phenomena observed. I shall stop at this point, as I have neither the intention nor the space to insert a lecture on economic philosophy here.

In my view of the place that economic reflection has held in my life, I shall try now to state or restate the conclusions I have reached concerning the golden period from 1945 to 1971 or 1973, when all uncertainties about the future seemed to have been dispelled, and also my conclusions concerning the years that followed, from 1971 or 1973 to the present, a period in which, by contrast, the fine postwar convictions appear to have vanished into thin air and all seems to have become dark, present and future alike.

1948–1973

For twenty-five years after the war the industrialized countries enjoyed an extraordinary prosperity, the like of which they had never known before, even in the halcyon days of the Industrial Revolution. Fantastic growth rates were recorded, an average of 8% a year in Germany between 1950 and 1960 and 8.8% in Japan. Admittedly these two countries, after the physical destruction and the disorganization of the economy caused by the war, started very low down the ladder; but growth remained buoyant and sometimes even accelerated during the sixties and early seventies, averaging 4.5% annually in Germany and 9.8% in Japan. France turned in a very respectable performance with average annual growth of 4.6% between 1950 and 1960 and 5.6% between 1960 and 1973. In the United States expansion was not so rapid, averaging 3.3% a year during the fifties and 4% from 1960 to 1973, but the starting point was much higher. Only Britain, among the big countries, did not share fully in the general advance, with average growth rates of 2.8% and 3.1% respectively in 1950–60 and 1960–73[1].

The increase in production was due essentially to rapidly rising labour productivity in many countries, while employment remained at a high level. This improvement in labour productivity was especially marked in continental Western Europe. One of the possible explanations is that Europe had set out in pursuit of the United States and was making great efforts to match the high productivity performance there. At the outset, in 1950 for example, hourly productivity in Western Europe was between one-third and one-half of what it was in the United States; by 1977 it was 79% of the US figure in France and 84% in Germany. Since productivity continued to rise more rapidly in Europe than in the United States during the years that followed, it can be said that by the early eighties the gap had become small. What were the mechanics of this rapid improvement in European productivity?

The twenty-five years that followed the war saw an investment boom in Europe. During the war the real capital stock had been greatly reduced, by destruction and by attrition. Capital had become relatively scarce and the economy labour-intensive. Since the new investment offered a very high return, it is not surprising that enterprises strove to invest to the utmost. The boom reached its peak during the sixties. It then gradually lost momentum as returns began to fall.

Augmenting the European effort, US direct investment in Europe grew strongly, especially during the sixties, the motive of investors being at first to profit from European prosperity, then to gain footholds in a market which the creation of the European Economic Community was beginning to unify. The contribution of American private capital to the increase in Europe's capital stock proved then to be bigger than that of the Marshall Plan. In 1950 US private capital invested in Europe – in buildings, plant and equipment – amounted to less than $1.7 billion; by 1970 it stood at $24.5 billion.

After the war American industry opened its doors wide to the Europeans who sent over many task forces to discover the secrets of US productivity. The revelations they brought back with them were incorporated into the new investment projects which the Europeans proceeded to put in hand. Needless to say, the American companies that invested in Europe used the most modern technologies. The overall result was a vast technology transfer from the United States to Europe.

Another factor that helped increasingly to make European industry capital-intensive, at least in a great many sectors, was the cheapness of energy. If oil prices had risen significantly during the years from 1950 to 1970, the task the Europeans had set themselves, namely to emulate American efficiency, would have been much harder.

Parallel with the rapid growth of investment, and to some extent because of it, there was a shift of European manpower from low- to high-productivity sectors. In the countries where the agricultural

419

labour force represented a high percentage of the total labour force, there was a massive drift from the land to factories and offices. In France, for example, whereas the agricultural share of the total labour force amounted to 30% at the end of the war, it declined rapidly thereafter to less than 10%.

The ratio of government expenditure to aggregate demand rose progressively, helping to support the economy, though no one clearly realized the potential danger this represented for the profit-earning capacity of firms. The population was convinced that growth and full employment were assured forever and that the secret of eternal prosperity had been discovered. If demand one day showed signs of flagging, all that would be required would be to step up government spending and the situation would right itself immediately. Although the dangers of inflation were not completely disregarded (they were particularly feared in Germany where the hyperinflation of the two postwar periods had not been forgotten), a slow rise in prices was not enough to cause inflation to be regarded as a present or imminent threat.

All that I have just said is true, I think. But the same phenomena – low level of the capital stock, high return on new investment, unsatisfactory distribution of labour among the different sectors of the economy, much higher labour productivity in America than in Europe – were present after the First World War and Europe had not experienced the prodigious economic expansion it did after the Second. Why? What was it that turned mere potentialities into such a dazzling reality?

Many different factors contributed to the result that is now part of history, and I shall make no attempt to list them all. But there is one that seems decisive to me, and here I must stress again the role played by the United States in the construction of a new world order. Whereas in 1919 the Americans turned in upon themselves, convinced that Europe was a hornet's nest in which they would never set foot again, resolved never again to let themselves be drawn into a European war, after 1945 they assumed in full the responsibilities of the great victorious nation that they were, with power immeasurably greater than that of their allies in the war which had just ended. The new world order they undertook to create, with the active participation of Britain and France at the outset, then a little later of Germany and Japan, was founded essentially on the reconstruction of Europe and Japan, monetary stability, liberalization of trade and, most important of all, political and military security.

How can one understand the course of economic life in a European country or in the whole of the West for that matter, if one does not acknowledge the presence, if not in every individual, at least in a large minority, of a will for power that expresses itself, on the economic plane, in the pursuit of gain, of financial success, of money, whatever name one likes to give this fundamental tendency? When it is not thwarted, this quest for fortune results more often than not in the creation of enterprises or the development of existing enterprises, that is to say in the consolidation of society as a whole. It can, of course, take the pathological forms profusely described in literature, where the desire for wealth leads to negative results for society, but the phenomena which fall into that category constitute the exception. This inner vitality, which has to be thought of as present in a great many individuals in order to account for observed facts, can be neutralized, wholly or partly, by a feeling of insecurity, by an adverse economic climate or untoward political events. That is what happened in many countries during the interwar years. To create enterprises or products, man also needs a relatively stable currency to enable him to make calculations that will prove valid in the months or years ahead; lastly, he needs as extensive a market as possible, in which goods, services, labour and capital move freely.

These were the conditions that the Americans, with the cooperation of the other big industrial countries, strove to fulfil after the war ended in 1945. They played a decisive role in the reconstruction of Western Europe and Japan, the creation of the International Monetary Fund and the World Bank and, a little later, the establishment of the GATT. Above all, with their immense military strength they ensured complete external security for their partners in Europe and Asia. Within the framework thus defined by American power, young people with the will to make something of their lives and with the necessary intellectual equipment were able to spread their wings and improve not only their own conditions of life, but also those of the whole society in which they were operating.

For this situation to last, the strength and stability of the system's linchpin, the United States, had to be maintained. This is what happened during the fifties and much of the sixties. US prices rose only very slowly, economic growth, outside of short-run fluctuations, was steady. Under American pressure, international trade was gradually freed of the impediments which the thirties and then the war had left behind. The Europeans, after letting themselves be guided initially by the Americans, had for their part taken a series of initiatives which the most ambitious minds saw as leading to the creation of a single European market, where goods, services, capital and human beings would circulate as freely as they were able to do in the United States.

When one tries to determine what part the Common Market played in Europe's postwar prosperity, two things seem evident. The first, as I have already said earlier on, is that the dynamism shown by Europe at that time existed before the creation of the European Economic Community; the process started at the end of the forties as a result of the Marshall Plan and currency stabilization, and Europe's expansion was in full swing during the early fifties. But this momentum might have given out if the Common Market had not taken up the running at the beginning of the sixties. Let us simply say that the Treaty of Rome imparted a fresh impetus to European growth. It constituted a tangible expression of the confidence the Europeans had in themselves, and at the same time it fortified that confidence through the immense opportunities it opened up. More extensively, it strengthened the movement towards trade liberalization on a world scale. Without the Common Market, there would probably have been no Kennedy Round and no sweeping reduction of customs duties among industrialized countries[2].

1973–1985

It is comparatively easy to explain the course of economic events between the end of the war and the beginning of the seventies. If one tries to take stock of those twenty-five or thirty years, one figure sums it all up. Over the period from 1950, when reconstruction was just about complete, in France and in many other European countries, to the beginning of the seventies real per capita income (generally referred to as the standard of living) *increased threefold*. Here was a fantastic transformation of the conditions of life; everything now was simple, outwardly at least, and moving in the right direction. It is much more difficult to account for what happened in the period that followed, the one that is still not over in 1986.

Growth continued to be strong until 1973. The steep rise in oil prices at the end of that year triggered the deepest recession the western world has known since the war. It lasted most of 1974–5. Growth began again in 1975. The upturn was modest by comparison with the postwar period, but substantial nonetheless. The second oil price shock choked it off in 1978–9. The new recession lasted in the United States and much of the world until 1982. Then a deliberately expansionary fiscal policy in the USA fuelled a brisk rise in output there, whilst Japan managed to sustain growth that was low by comparison with the extraordinarily high rates achieved during the sixties, but still comfortable in absolute terms. Europe emerged slowly and with difficulty from this new crisis.

Unemployment, which had been virtually nonexistent prior to 1974, averaged nearly 10% of the labour force in the OECD countries over the ten years that followed. At different times during the period under consideration inflation rates in many industrialized countries reached 10, 15 and even 20% a year. This conjunction of low growth, high unemployment and rapid inflation presented the western world, and the world at large, with a problem it had never known before. During the Great Depression the number of jobless reached a figure much higher than that of the seventies, *but prices were falling then*.

But this is not the whole picture. If one adds great monetary instability, with the dollar falling continuously and excessively during the seventies before rebounding to absurd levels in the first half of the eighties, plus the emergence of a new problem of international indebtedness, this time between developing countries and their industrialized-country creditors, a problem whose solution is not in sight, one can understand the disarray of the economic policy-makers. For many years the economic policies followed by the governments of the industrialized countries have been not only different, but often contradictory to one another; all international economic and monetary order seems to have vanished.

The same confusion reigns among the economists, whose job it is to explain and interpret events and propose solutions for mending the equilibria that have been disrupted. A simplistic reading of Keynes suggested that where a large proportion of existing productive capacity was lying idle, in the event of large-scale unemployment it was sufficient to increase government expenditure and lower interest rates for order to be restored. But what is to be done when at the same time there is high inflation and central governments are already heavily indebted? It is not possible to reduce interest rates when prices are rising steeply and continuously and real interest rates are already negative.

Along came the 'monetarists' with a simple and appealing solution. All that was needed was to hold money supply growth down and inflation would subside and the economy return to its natural rate of advance. The theory was simple only in appearance. How was the money supply to be defined? Should it include all the assets that are easily cashable or only those that are completely liquid? What was one to do about changes in the behaviour of economic agents, such as an increase in the liquidity preference; about external shocks, like the jump in oil prices in 1973 and 1978–9? The new theory, which generated great enthusiasm in certain economists during the seventies, gradually lost its influence and all that has survived is certain pragmatic rules such as that concerning the effect on inflation of a progressive reduction in the growth rate of the money supply, the latter variously defined according to country.

A third theory (and there are countless others I could mention), which negated the argument of certain Keynesians that it was sufficient to maintain or boost demand without bothering about the conditions of supply, put the emphasis instead on the situation of businesses. According to this theory, which has ancient roots that go back to the classical economists, the important thing is to maintain or rebuild corporate profit margins; sufficient demand will then arise spontaneously and take up the slack.

As I write these lines, the supply-siders seem to have carried the day in America and to a lesser extent in Europe. The European governments, in particular, are all (the socialist governments included) pursuing policies of tight management if not austerity, with the aim of shifting income from the household to the business sector; budget deficits are being progressively reduced; inflation is slowing everywhere. But this victory is a dubious one. In Europe, where the new policy is being resolutely applied, without any concessions to Keynesian ideas but without any appreciable reduction in tax pressure either, the situation of businesses is gradually improving, but demand is insufficient to cause a significant fall in the unemployment rate or even to prevent it from rising. In America, where demand has risen steeply and the unemployment rate has fallen significantly, with inflation declining to a comparatively low figure, economic policy seems to be partly inspired by the same principles as in Europe, but it also reflects another influence which, to the open-minded observer, seems to stem from Keynesian economics. Demand is being sustained by a huge budget deficit and there is good reason to wonder what will happen when the political authorities finally succeed in sharply reducing and then eliminating this deficit, or what would happen if they failed.

An analogous question arises in the case of Europe. The efforts in recent years to reduce budget deficits and inflation have yielded relatively satisfactory results (although unemployment has gone on rising), largely because world demand has been buoyant. And it has been so only thanks to the American budget deficit. If one wanted to sum up this situation simply, if not simplistically, one might say that the world is enjoying relative stability today because opposite principles are being applied in fiscal policy on either side of the Atlantic.

I shall go no further in this analysis of the present situation and of the economic policies adopted in the different countries. I shall not venture to propound a new theory to account for all the phenomena observed, first because I would be incapable of doing so, but above all because I do not believe that such a theory exists, even potentially. This may be due to the way in which I view the historical event in itself, and consequently the whole set of economic and political events that have marked the past fifteen years.

I cannot, indeed, view the crisis of the seventies and the first half of the eighties other than as the result of the fortuitous conjunction of several causal series that were in no way interrelated, although on many occasions they did influence one another. The slowdown in productivity growth, the American inflation of the late sixties and the collapse in 1971–3 of the monetary system established at Bretton Woods twenty-five years earlier, the two oil shocks of 1973 and 1978–9, the continuous rise of real wages and of direct taxes and social security contributions during the seventies, the changes that have disrupted the whole pattern of the western economy over the past ten or fifteen years – all these phenomena cannot be fitted into a single sequence of cause and effect; their near coincidence in time has been largely accidental, the outcome of a hazard that no philosophy of history could render intelligible.

The slowdown in European productivity increases during the seventies is easy to understand. The annual growth rates of 4.5 to 5.5%, and sometimes even more, recorded in continental Europe between 1950 and 1970 could not go on indefinitely. Labour productivity had increased as a result of investment and technological progress. After the war Europe had a great deal of leeway to make up in relation to the United States. As Europe drew nearer to the American model, it was inevitable that productivity growth would ease off before ultimately settling at something very close to the US rate, which, historically, is of the order of 2.5% a year.

But the fact of the slowdown in labour productivity growth does not get us very far in the explanation of the various phenomena observed; it accounts for a parallel slowdown in the rise of living standards, but not for the emergence of large-scale unemployment. The record shows that everywhere in Europe (but not in the United States) the rate of growth of gross domestic product between 1973 and 1982 was lower than the rate of productivity growth, when it ought to have been slightly higher for the increase in the labour force to be absorbed by the economy. Hence the existence of unemployment that would rise from year to year.

Part of the reason for this lies in the fact that, during the same years, real wages continued to rise, at least in Europe, at the same pace as before, or occasionally faster, while direct taxes and social insurance contributions went on mounting. The net result was a reduction of firms' profit margins, a fall in investment and a slowdown in hiring, often accompanied by redundancies.

The excessive rise in wage costs was a first source of upward price momentum that helps to explain the inflation recorded during the period under review. This rise in the general price level was, of course, augmented by the sudden jump in oil prices on two occasions. This last was a development which, in relation to economic activity, was purely fortuitous, having essentially political causes, as we saw in the previous chapter. Nevertheless, it would do a great deal to set the tone of the past fifteen years as we have known them, with unemployment and rising prices at the same time.

The start of the seventies saw the disintegration of the international monetary system set up just after the war by the Bretton Woods agreements. The dollar's convertibility into gold ceased in 1971, and in 1973 the dollar became a floating currency without fixed exchange parities.

With the disappearance of the old system, whatever its imperfections, and the introduction of freely floating exchange rates, inflation had a clear run for a time, until came the day when governments understood that the international discipline that had vanished had to be replaced by national discipline and put inflation control in the forefront of their concerns. They then adopted, in Europe at any rate, restrictive fiscal and monetary policies that slowed down economic activity even more. The creation of the European Monetary System in 1979 constitutes the first really effective effort to reinforce national discipline with a European discipline.

For the sake of completeness, it should be added that during these years very important structural economic changes took place or began

426

to take place which increased the incidence of frictional unemployment, meaning that large numbers of workers had to learn new skills.

A western world without a pilot

The contrast between the postward period and the years from 1973 to 1985 could not have been more striking. The western world of the seventies and early eighties puts one in mind of the thirties, although the two situations are very different. The depth of the slump in the two cases is not comparable; the worst excesses of protectionism have been avoided in the recent period; even when minds were plunged into what appeared to be total disarray, the lessons of the thirties had not been completely forgotten. But in both cases the impression is one of a ship without a pilot. The question that inevitably comes to mind is this: could we have averted or at least alleviated the crisis from which we are barely emerging at present?

A substantial rise in oil prices around 1973 was necessary, even if it went too far. We saw those prices fall back in real terms between 1974 and 1978 as a result of inflation in the oil-consuming countries and of the dollar's decline, without any serious problems for anyone. The 1978–9 oil price rise, on the other hand, did not correspond to any need. It was caused by panic on the part of purchasers whom a few producing countries had rashly exploited, without realizing that they were defeating their own ends. With a smaller rise in oil prices the producing countries would not have accumulated, over a few years, the huge payments surpluses we know, whilst for their part the oil-importing developing countries would not have contracted the intolerable debts they have been trying to lighten for a number of years now. The frenetic escalation of oil prices during the seventies was bound to end in a collapse that, once again, was inordinate.

A slowdown in the rise of living standards was also unavoidable. On the other hand, what we could have avoided in large part was inflation and unemployment. Leaving aside the structural changes in industrialized-country economies, which were bound to take place anyway and which inevitably created a certain amount of unemployment, most of the joblessness of the period was indirectly due to inflation, which itself was attributable to a combination of factors; an unduly rapid rise in real wages, the increasing weight of direct taxes and social insurance contributions, the disappearance of all international monetary discipline, the looseness of national fiscal and monetary policies for a time and then ultimately the tightening of those same policies in many countries, with the screws being applied in direct proportion to the excesses of the previous period. Of all the factors that were responsible for the inflation of the seventies, the oil price rise was admittedly an important one, but it would be wrong to credit it with the essential role. That was filled by government policies which, almost everywhere, lacked simple and clear objectives and the most elementary firmness, until the day that the need for corrective measures became imperative. It would seem that this need has not yet been perceived clearly in the most important of the developed countries, the United States.

To tell the truth, when one tries to identify the essential difference between the period comprising the late forties and the fifties and the period from the mid-sixties until now, one arrives at the conclusion that for the past fifteen or twenty years the western world has lacked a guide. Whereas in the postwar years the Americans had set the tone, from the end of the sixties they were swamped by their domestic problems and ceased to have the forceful international policy expected of them. They concerned themselves then almost exclusively with their own problems, seeming to forget that they had an international role to perform as leader of the free world. This, perhaps temporary, withdrawal of the United States from the world scene has coincided, moreover, with a weakening, in relative terms, of that nation's economic and military power.

Europe, for its part, showed itself to be incapable of uniting politically and economically and filling, at least partially, the void created by the trend of American policy. It remained for the national states to do what they could to maintain or restore a certain equilibrium in a world which, for a while, seemed to be adrift. Of the big countries, Germany and Japan were the first to succeed. As for France, she staged a remarkable recovery in 1976, which was temporarily halted by the second oil shock and later by the change of course in economic policy in 1981.

Notes

PART ONE

Chapter 1

1 *Livret de famille*: booklet a couple receive from the mayor at their wedding for the purpose of recording births, marriages and deaths in the family. (Translator's note)
2 *Salon des Indépendants*: annual art show in which the exhibits have been selected by a jury composed of members of the *Société des Artistes Indépendants*, mostly artists themselves. (T.N.)
3 Marcelle Marjolin died in 1986, one month before her brother. (Publisher's note)
4 Originating in a miscarriage of justice – a Jewish officer wrongly convicted of high treason – the Dreyfus affair was the cause of a major political crisis, from 1896 to 1905, opposing left and right, republicans and nationalists. The victory of the supporters of Dreyfus marks the definitive establishment of the republic as the French system of government and, beyond that, as the dominant political ideology of 20th century France. (T.N.)

Chapter 2

1 *Action Française*: extreme right-wing political movement, with daily newspaper of the same name, founded in 1908 and banned several times, the last being after the Liberation. (T.N.)
2 SFIO = *Section Française de l'Internationale Ouvrière*, also known as the *Parti Socialiste Français*. Founded in 1905 and replaced in 1969 by the present *Parti Socialiste*. (T.N.)
3 *Camelots du Roi*: groups of royalist combatants, founded in 1908 and originally responsible for selling the newspaper *Action Française*; dissolved in 1936. *Jeunesses Patriotes*: youth element of the *Ligue Patriotique des Intérêts Français* founded in 1895 and later to become part of the anti-Dreyfusard movement. *Jeunesses Socialistes*: young socialist movement. (T.N.)

429

4 *Quinzième Section*: primary geographical unit of the socialist organization, corresponding to the 15th arrondissement of Paris. (T.N.)

5 *Bac = Baccalauréat*: national examination taken at the end of secondary education and the basic requirement for university entrance. (T.N.)

6 *Universités populaires*: associations providing adult education for poorer people. (T.N.)

Chapter 3

1 *Association Philotechnique*: philanthropic association to promote the arts and sciences. (T.N.)

2 Hôpital Sainte-Anne: Paris hospital for mental diseases. (T.N.)

3 *Ecole Normale Supérieure*: the highest-ranking establishment, with entrance by competitive examination, for training prospective arts and science teachers in secondary schools. (T.N.)

4 *Agrégation*: competitive examination that entitles successful candidates to teaching posts in *lycées* and certain faculties. The title of *agrégé* used to carry great prestige, and still does to some extent. (T.N.)

Chapter 4

1 Georges Lefranc, *Histoire d'un groupe du parti socialiste SFIO Révolution constructive (1930–1938)* in *Mélanges et Histoires économiques et sociales en hommage au professeur Antony Babel*, Geneva, 1963.

2 *Ibid.*, p. 406.

3 *Ibid.*, p. 409.

Chapter 5

1 *Le Mecure de France*, 1932.

2 André Siegfried, *Les Etats-Unis d'aujourd'hui*, Armand Colin, Paris, 1927.

3 Robert Marjolin, *Les Expériences Roosevelt*, in *Les Cahiers du Socialiste*, No 5, Paris, 1934, p. 1.

Chapter 6

1 Charles Rist, *Une saison gâtée*, Paris, Fayard, 1983, p. 130.

2 Wicksell, Hayek, Myrdal, Hicks particular.

3 The content of this course was assembled and written up, under the supervision of Célestin Bouglé, by a group of friends and students of Elie Halévy: Raymond Aron, Jean-Marcel Jeanneney, Pierre Laroque, Etienne Mantouk and myself. Entitled *Histoire du socialisme européen*, it was republished in a revised and amended edition in 1974, in the collection *Idées*, by Gallimard.

4 *Chargé de mission*: civil service grade in which incumbents receive their assignments on an ad hoc basis. (T.N.)

5 *Le Populaire*: official newspaper of the French socialist party (S.F.I.O.) from 1921. (T.N.)

6 *Croix de Feu*: right-wing association of war veterans founded in 1921. *Jeune République*: left-wing Christian youth movement. (T.N.)

7 *Président du Conseil*: official title of the head of the government under the Third and Fourth Republics. (T.N.)

8 Alain Bergougnioux, *Le Socialisme français face à la crise des années 1930*, in *Commentaire*, summer 1985, p. 591. In this chapter I have followed the chronology of events indicated by M. Bergougnioux. His article has helped me to recall situations I have lived through but remembered only dimly.

9 CGT = *Confédération Générale du Travail*: France's largest trade union, which is communist-dominated. (T.N.)

Chapter 7

1 Mont Valérien: hill west of Paris on which the meteorological station for the Paris area is located; since 1960 a memorial to the French Resistance, several notable members of whom were executed and interred there. (T.N.)

2 Hôtel Matignon: official headquarters and residence of the head of the French government (since the institution of the Fifth Republic, the Prime Minister). (T.N.)

3 Later I found in the writings of Alfred Sauvy – *Histoire économique de l'entre-deux guerres* – and Jean-Marcel Jeanneney arguments identical with those I was developing then. In a paper on *La Politique Economique de Léon Blum* [The economic policy of Léon Blum] presented at a symposium held in 1965 by the *Fondation Nationale des Sciences Politiques* Jean-Marcel Jeanneney wrote: 'France could not live decently, that is give her inhabitants a standard of living at least equal to what they had known in 1929 and 1930, develop her means of production and ensure her defence in a threatening world, if she did not raise her output beyond what had been its highest point, i.e. in 1919 ... This meant that industrial output would have to increase by more than 40 per cent on 1935 ... The number of unemployed amounted to almost 500,000, but this represented only 3 per cent of the labour force and less than 10 per cent of male and female workers in industry.'

4 *L'Echo de Paris*; right-wing newspaper of the time. (T.N.)

5 The occupation of Austria by the Germans was imminent. The *Anschluss* would be proclaimed on March 15, 1938, a few days after the article concerned was published.

6 *L'Europe Nouvelle*, March 8, 1938.

7 *L'Europe Nouvelle*, August 23, 1938.

8 *L'Europe Nouvelle*, April 30, 1938.

9 *L'Europe Nouvelle*, May 7, 1938.

10 Journal of the *Institut de Recherche Economique et Sociale* directed by Charles Rist. Under the latter's supervision I contributed to this journal at the time, notably the sections concerning France.

11 *La Dépêche de Toulouse*: important provincial newspaper, official mouthpiece of the Radical party. (T.N.)
12 *L'Europe Nouvelle*, May 14, 1938.
13 *L'Europe Nouvelle*, May 28, 1938.
14 *L'Europe Nouvelle*, July 2, 1938.
15 *L'Europe Nouvelle*, August 27, 1938.

Chapter 8

1 *L'Europe Nouvelle*, October 8, 1938. *Gleichshaltung*: reduction to conformity.
2 *L'Europe Nouvelle*, June 25, 1938.
3 Rue de Rivoli: the offices of the Finance Ministry were located here. (T.N.)
4 Maurice Thorez: French political figure, leader of the Communist party from 1930 to 1964, a former miner. (T.N.)
5 Léon Jouhaux: trade unionist, secretary of the CGT from 1909 to 1947. (T.N.)
6 *L'Europe Nouvelle*, April 29, 1939.

Part Two

Chapter 1

1 See Jean Monnet's letter in Appendix I, p. 441.
2 See Appendix II, p. 442.
3 See Appendix III, p. 445.
4 Project adopted by the British government on June 16 at Jean Monnet's instigation and providing for a merging of the two states and the creation of a 'Franco-British Union' with joint citizenship. This plan was not seriously considered by the French government, in which the proponents of an armistice with the Germans were about to carry the day.
5 *Pour Mémoire*, private printing, Paris 1970, pp. 61–2.
6 *Memoirs*, Collins, 1978, p. 30.

Chapter 2

1 *Inspecteur des Finances*: the highest function in French finance administration and one of the highest ranks in the French civil service. (T.N.)
2 *Op. cit.*, p. 68.
3 *Op. cit.*, p. 71.
4 *Op. cit.*, p. 81.
5 *Ibid.*, p. 83.
6 See Emmanuel Monick, *op. cit.*, p. 101.

Chapter 3

1 Julliard, 1981, p. 87.
2 Jean Monnet, *Memoirs*, p. 209. There was no question at that time of any overall plan for aid to Europe. The Marshall Plan did not come into being until 1947.
3 Jean Monnet, *op. cit.*, p. 209.
4 Jean Monnet, *op. cit.*, p. 216.
5 Jean Monnet, *op. cit.*, p. 224.
6 *La science économique nouvelle, les industriels et l'Etat* in *La France Libre*, July 1943.
7 *La France Libre, op. cit.*
8 Passage underlined in the original text.
9 Project to create a Franco-British union.

Chapter 5

1 See, in particular, Chester Wilmot, *The Struggle for Europe*, Collins, London, 1952. I have also usefully consulted the more recent book by Jean Lesquiller, *Le Japon*, Paris, Editions Sirey, 1966.

Part Three

Chapter 1

1 J. M. Keynes, *The Economic Consequence of the Peace*, Macmillan, 1919, pp. 22–3.
2 *Op. cit.*, p. 125.
3 H. W. Arndt, *The Economic Lessons of the Nineteen-Thirties*, Oxford University Press, 1944, p. 13.
4 J. M. Keynes, *op. cit.*, p. 35.
5 *Ibid.*, p. 135.
6 *Ibid.*, p. 51.
7 *Ibid.*, p. 134.
8 H. W. Arndt, *op. cit.*, p. 9.
9 David S. Landes, *The Prometheus Unbound*, Cambridge University Press, 1969, p. 369.
10 *Op. cit.*, p. 372.
11 *Ibid.*, p. 365.
12 *The General Theory of Employment, Interest and Money*, first published in 1936.
13 H. W. Arndt, *op. cit.*, p. 61.

Chapter 2

1 Jean Monnet, *Memoirs*, p. 228.
2 *Op. cit.*, p. 228.

3 *Ibid.*, p. 238.
4 *Ibid.*, p. 254.

Chapter 3

1 CEEC, General Report, Paris, 1947.
2 Under pressure from Congress, the Administration had to make concessions on some points of particular interest to powerful pressure groups. Thus the Foreign Assistance Act of 1948 contained certain articles providing for the use of American ships to transport goods to Europe, and for the disposal of US agricultural surpluses through shipments to Europe. But the overall importance of these provisions was very small.

Chapter 4

1 Prince Colonna di Paliano.
2 For the chronology of events during the period 1948–52, see Ernst H. Van der Beugel's book, *From Marshall Aid to Atlantic Partnership*, Elsevier Publishing Company, 1966.
3 Eric Roll, *Crowded Hours*, Faber and Faber, London, 1985, p. 62.
4 Van der Beugel, *op. cit.*, pp. 166 to 172.

Chapter 5

1 Miriam Camps, *Britain and the European Community*, Princeton University Press, 1964, p. 3.
2 William Diebold Jr. *Trade and Payments in Western Europe*, New York, Harper and Brothers, 1952.
3 Imanuel Wexler, *The Marshall Plan Revisited*, Greenwood Press, Westport, Connecticut, 1983, pp. 197–8.

Chapter 6

1 I have taken these figures from Imanuel Wexler's recent book, *The Marshall Plan Revisited*, mentioned earlier.
2 *Ibid.*, p. 87.
3 Harry Bayard Price, *The Marshall Plan and its Meaning*, Cornell University Press, 1955, pp. 137–8.
4 Figures taken from Price's book mentioned above.
5 Dean Acheson, *Present at the Creation. My Years in the State Department*, New York, Norton, 1969, p. 231.
6 Imanuel Wexler, *op. cit.*, p. 249.
7 Dean Acheson, *op. cit.*, p. 260.

Chapter 7

1 Price, *op. cit.*, pp. 136–41.
2 *Ibid.*, p. 156.
3 Robert Salomon, *The International Monetary System 1945–1976*, New York, 1977, p. 19.

Part Four

Chapter 2

1 Charles de Gaulle, *Memoirs of Hope*, Simon and Schuster, New York, 1971, p. 134, first published in English-language translation by George Weidenfeld & Nicolson Limited, London, 1971.
2 *Ibid.*, p. 135.
3 These measures included a 17½% devaluation of the French franc.
4 Maurice Couve de Murville, *Une politique étrangère 1958–1969, p. 10.*
5 George W. Ball, *The Past Has Another Pattern*, W. W. Norton & Co., New York, 1982, p. 81.
6 See Walter Hallstein, *Europe in the Making*, W. W. Norton & Co., New York, 1972.

Chapter 3

1 Jean Monnet, *Memoirs*, p. 284.
2 *Ibid.*, p. 273.
3 *Ibid.*, p. 272.
4 *Ibid.*, pp. 272–3.
5 *Ibid.*, p. 280.
6 *Ibid.*, p. 274.
7 *Ibid.*, p. 304.
8 Charles de Gaulle, *Memoirs of Hope, op. cit.*, p. 10.

Chapter 4

1 Which culminated in the Spaak report.
2 *Le Comité d'action pour les Etats-Unis d'Europe de Jean Monnet*, Lausanne, 1974.

Chapter 5

1 Couve de Murville, *op. cit.*, p. 303.
2 Walter Hallstein, *op. cit.*, p. 21.
3 Couve de Murville, *op. cit.*, p. 36.
4 Couve de Murville, *ibid.*, p. 307.
5 See Maurice Couve de Murville's tribute to Sicco Mansholt in the former's book, *op. cit.*, p. 315.

6 The Commission thought the same at that time; see the Fifth General Report of the Commission, which covers the period from May, 1, 1961 to April 30, 1962, p. 10.

Chapter 6

1 Fouchet Plan: so named because the plan was produced by a European committee under the chairmanship of French minister Christian Fouchet. (T.N.)
2 Couve de Murville, *op. cit* p. 347.
3 *Ibid.*, pp. 359–60.
4 J. M. Keynes, *op. cit.*, p. 3.
5 Eric Roll, *op. cit.*, p. 111.
6 For a detailed history of the negotiation, the reader is referred to the excellent book by Miriam Camps. *Britain and the European Community 1955–1963*, Princeton University Press, Oxford University Press, 1964.
7 Miriam Camps, *op. cit.* p. 502.
8 George Ball, *op. cit.*, p. 208.
9 *Ibid.* p. 209.
10 *Ibid.*, p. 212.
11 *Ibid.*, pp. 215–17.
12 *Ibid.*, p. 217.
13 *Ibid.*, p. 222.
14 Regarding the 1965 crisis, an excellent book on the subject is that of John Newhouse, *30 juin 1965, Crise à Bruxelles*, Fondation nationale des Sciences politiques, 1968.

Chapter 7

1 *Report on European Institutions*, Council of the European Communities, 1980, pp. 2 *et seq.*

Part Five

Chapter 1

1 France has a two-ballot system (*scrutin majoritaire à deux tours*). The first ballot is unrestricted. If one candidate wins more than 50% of the total votes cast, he is elected. Where this is not the case, there has to be a second ballot, from which those candidates who have failed in the first ballot to achieve the statutory minimum of votes required are obliged to retire. For the second ballot, alliances are important. In most cases it becomes a straight fight between right and left, the weaker in either camp having agreed to stand down in favour of the stronger (*désistement*). But they are not required by law to do so, and sometimes will maintain their candidacy, thereby splitting the vote. (T.N.)
2 In this section I speak interchangeably of Royal Dutch, Shell and the Royal Dutch-Shell group. For my purpose here, these terms are synonymous. Royal Dutch, a Netherlands company, and Shell Transport, a British company, together form a single group and virtually constitute a single company whose profits are shared

between Royal Dutch (60%) and Shell Transport (40%). At the head of the group is a Committee of Managing Directors comprising persons from the two companies. The companies' boards of directors hold joint meetings once a month, alternately at The Hague and in London, to discuss all the problems confronting the group.

3 Except for the board of Shell Française, which is a subsidiary of the Royal Dutch-Shell group.

Chapter 2

1 The barrel is the unit of measure most currently used in the oil industry. An output of one barrel per day (b/d) represents approximately 50 tonnes per year.

2 For figures and in some cases for events, I have referred, in order to refresh my memory, to a certain number of works, including: Christopher Tugendhat, *The Biggest Business*, London, 1968; Anthony Sampson, *The Seven Sisters*, London, 1975; Walter J. Levy, *Oil Strategy and Politics, 1941–1981*, New York, 1982. This last work, which is a collection of articles, is the testimony of one of the world's foremost oil experts, a man of exceptional intelligence and judgment.

3 Christopher Tugendhat, *op. cit.*, p. 175.

4 Walter J. Levy, *op. cit.*, p. 185.

5 Anthony Sampson, *op. cit.*, p. 275.

Chapter 3

1 These figures, and most of the others quoted in this chapter, have been taken from an article by Angus Maddison, *Economic Stagnation since 1973, its Nature and Causes: A Six Country Survey*. The Economist, 131, NR 4, 1983.

2 The reader is referred to the text of the lectures I gave in New York in 1980, *Europe in Search of Its Identity*, Council on Foreign Relations, New York, 1981, p. 54.

APPENDIXES

Appendix I

Anglo-French Coordinating Committee
3 Richmond Terrace
Whitehall, S. W. 1.

By order of the President of the Council, M. MARJOLIN is instructed to proceed to Dunkirk. He will contact the civilian and military authorities who will provide him with all the means to carry out his mission. He will hand over the orders enclosed to the person designated by those authorities in agreement with him.

M. MARJOLIN will report on his mission to the President of the Council through M. Jean MONNET, Chairman of the Anglo-French Coordinating Committee.

LONDON May 25, 1940

(Signed: Jean Monnet)

441

Appendix II

May 30, 1940

*Report by Sous-lieutenant Marjolin
on the execution of the mission in northern France
assigned to him by M. Jean Monnet,
Chairman of the Anglo-French Coordinating Committee,
on behalf of the President of the Council.*

Thanks to the arrangements made by the Anglo-French Coordinating Committee and, in particular, to the letter handed to me by General Beaumont Nesbitt, head of the intelligence branch of the British army's general staff, on behalf of the Imperial General Staff, I was able to embark at Dover on the night of May 25–6 on board the drifter *Rob Roy*.

I arrived at Dunkirk on the 26th at 0600 hours. I contacted Admiral Abrial under whose authority the military forces in the Dunkirk area are placed. I handed him my orders together with a letter of introduction singed by Général de Division Lelong, military attaché and head of the French military mission in London. All the assistance necessary to the accomplishment of my mission was supplied to me by Admiral Abrial and his staff officers, in particular by Commandants Sticca and Iescanne. I reported to the civilian authorities in the person of M. René Le Gentil, subprefect of Dunkirk.

During my stay in Dunkirk events moved so swiftly that the details and even the essentials of the organization to be set up were called into question hourly. The military authorities' decision, at the time of my arrival, to turn back the Belgian refugees to their country of origin would have reduced the magnitude of the problem very appreciably. But other factors made that problem insoluble:

1. The German advance increasingly restricted the areas it might have been hoped to supply via Dunkirk. It was no longer possible to send convoys to Lille and its surrounding area.

2. The heavy bombing raids to which Dunkirk was subjected during my stay, particularly that of May 27 which almost completely destroyed the town, caused a dispersal of the civilian population that made distribution of supplies among the latter very difficult.

3. As a result of the aerial bombardments I have just mentioned Dunkirk harbour had become practically unusable. In any case, the intensity of the bombing and strafing during my stay was such that unloading of cargoes was brought to a complete standstill. Most of the boats that were alongside sank. It was for these reasons that already on Sunday May 26 the British Admiralty decided not to send the supply ships *Sapphire* and *Diamond* to Dunkirk and rerouted them to Ostend.

On my arrival, in collaboration with the civilian and military authorities, I set up a first scheme for dealing with the refugees. The person appointed to head this organization, as Refugees Commissioner for the Nord and Pas-de-Calais departments, was military intendant Lobel, previously in charge of maritime transit in the port of Dunkirk. In his former duties Intendant Lobel had shown that he possessed the drive and organizational ability to carry out this assignment. Intendant Lobel's collaborators were to have been M. Le Gentil, subprefect of Dunkirk, the *Ingénieur Principal des Ponts et Chaussées* [senior government civil engineer] Etienne, head of the Port of Dunkirk Commission, and Colonel Menuel, chief of transport of the 1st Army. That scheme was overtaken by events before it could be put into operation.

I then set about devising a new scheme to meet the needs of the situation. Its essential features were the following:

– the pooling of all available supplies, with no differentiation of supplies by category of recipients, i.e. the armed forces, the resident civilian population and the refugees:

– distribution of those supplies, by the military authorities, among the different categories of consumers, in a manner consistent with the best interests of defence;

– distribution among the civilian population (resident and refugee) by Intendant Lobel of the supplies placed at his disposal by the military authorities.

Once again, the course of events prevented this new scheme from entering into operation.

443

I reembarked on the evening of Tuesday May 28, at about 22.00 hours, on the *Chasseur 3* which brought me to Dover on Wednesday May 19 at 00.06 hours. I wish to state that I received from the civilian and military authorities, both British and French, all the assistance I needed in the course of my mission.

Appendix III

PRESIDENCY OF THE COUNCIL

The Vice-President   Paris, June 1, 1940

TB.YA.

Dear Mr Chairman,

Thank you for the information you have been kind enough to give me concerning the efforts that have been made, in the most difficult conditions, to endeavour to ensure the provisioning of the civilian population of northern France.

Would you please convey to your delegate, Sous-lieutenant Marjolin, and to the officers who assisted him in the accomplishment of his mission, the congratulations and thanks of the government.

Accept, Mr Chairman, the assurance of my highest consideration.

(Signed: Camille CHAUTEMPS)

Mr Jean MONNET
Chairman of the Anglo-French
Coordinating Committee

OFFICES OF THE WAR CABINET,
Richmond Terrace,
Whitehall, S.W.1.

June 3rd, 1940

Dear Marjolin,

Lord Hankey has asked me to thank you for sending him a translation of your report on your mission to Dunkirk. He wishes me to express to you his appreciation for the way in which you carried out your mission and also to say how glad he is that you yourself have returned safely.

Yours sincerely,

(Signed: HOPKINSON)

Sous-lieutenant R. MARJOLIN,
4, Richmond Terrace,
S.W.1

Epilogue

Robert Marjolin died suddenly on April 15, 1986. His manuscript went no further. He had revised only part of it, and, had he lived, he might have somewhat altered the structure and balance of the book. In particular, he was planning a conclusion which was to have been a personal and intellectual reflection on his life's experience. He had jotted down a few preparatory notes, which must suffice as a representation of the unwritten chapter:

I have worked a great deal.
I started very low; I climbed very high (or fairly high) by an effort of will.
At first I did not understand what was happening to me.
Then for a time I felt very proud of my achievement.
Now I don't know.

Index

Index

Index